WALKING IN THE SHADE

VOLUME TWO OF
MY AUTOBIOGRAPHY

1949–1962

ALSO BY DORIS LESSING

NOVELS

The Grass Is Singing
The Golden Notebook
Briefing for a Descent into Hell
The Summer Before the Dark
The Memoirs of a Survivor
The Diaries of Jane Somers:
The Diary of a Good Neighbor
If the Old Could . . .
The Good Terrorist
The Fifth Child
Love, Again

"Canopus in Argos: Archives" series
Re: Colonized Planet 5-Shikasta
The Marriages Between Zones Three, Four, and Five
The Sirian Experiments
The Making of the Representative for Planet 8
Documents Relating to the Sentimental Agents in the Volyen Empire

"Children of Violence" series
Martha Quest
A Proper Marriage
A Ripple from the Storm
Landlocked
The Four-Gated City

SHORT STORIES

African Stories
Volume I   This Was the Old Chief's Country
Volume II   The Sun Between Their Feet

Stories
Volume I   To Room Nineteen
Volume II   The Temptation of Jack Orkney and Other Stories
The Real Thing: Stories and Sketches (U.S.), London Observed (U.K.)

OPERA

The Making of the Representative for Planet 8 (Music by Philip Glass)
The Marriages Between Zones Three, Four, and Five (Music by Philip Glass)

POETRY

Fourteen Poems

NONFICTION

In Pursuit of the English
Particularly Cats
Going Home
A Small Personal Voice
Prisons We Choose to Live Inside
The Wind Blows Away Our Words
Particularly Cats . . . and Rufus
African Laughter
Under My Skin
The Doris Lessing Reader

DORIS LESSING

WALKING IN THE SHADE

VOLUME TWO OF
MY AUTOBIOGRAPHY

1949–1962

HarperCollins*Publishers*

HarperCollins books may be purchased for educational, business, or sales promotional use. For information please write: Special Markets Department, HarperCollins Publishers, Inc., 10 East 53rd Street, New York, NY 10022.

FIRST EDITION

Designed by Alma Hochhauser Orenstein

Library of Congress Cataloging-in-Publication Data

Lessing, Doris May, 1919–
    Walking in the shade / by Doris Lessing.
       p.   cm.
    "Volume 2 of my autobiography". Volume 1: Under my skin.
    ISBN 0-06-018295-4
    1. Lessing, Doris May, 1919–   —Biography.   2. London (England)—Intellectual life—20th century.   3. Women authors, English—20th century—Biography.
    4. Women communists—England—London—Biography.   I. Title.
    PR6023.E833Z478   1997
    823'.914—dc21   97-9959

97 98 99 00 01 ❖/RRD 10 9 8 7 6 5 4 3 2 1

The individual, and groupings of people, have to learn that they cannot reform society in reality, nor deal with others as reasonable people, unless the individual has learned to locate and allow for the various patterns of coercive institutions, formal and also informal, which rule him. No matter what his reason says, he will always relapse into obedience to the coercive agency while its pattern is with him.

IDRIES SHAH, CARAVAN OF DREAMS

Acknowledgments

My especial thanks to Jonathan Clowes for his good advice and his support, and, with this book, helping out my memories with his, for though we did not know each other then, we shared an experience of certain public events.

And to Stuart Proffitt, my editor at HarperCollins, for his excellent and sensitive editing.

My gratitude, too, to Dorothy Thompson, who generously wrote asking me if I would like to have copies of my letters to Edward Thompson. I had forgotten I had written them.

And to Joan Rodker, Tom Maschler, and Mervyn Jones, for useful corrections and suggestions.

Denbigh Road
W11

—◦◦◦—

HIGH ON THE SIDE OF THE TALL SHIP, I HELD UP MY LITTLE BOY and said, 'Look, there's London.' Dockland: muddy creeks and channels, greyish rotting wooden walls and beams, cranes, tugs, big and little ships. The child was probably thinking, But ships and cranes and water was Cape Town, and now it's called London. As for me, real London was still ahead, like the beginning of my real life, which would have happened years before if the war hadn't stopped me coming to London. A clean slate, a new page—everything still to come.

I was full of confidence and optimism, though my assets were minimal: rather less than £150; the manuscript of my first novel, *The Grass Is Singing,* already bought by a Johannesburg publisher who had not concealed the fact he would take a long time publishing it, because it was so subversive; and a few short stories. I had a couple of trunkfuls of books, for I would not be parted from them, some clothes, some negligible jewellery. I had refused the pitiful sums of money my mother had offered, because she had so little herself, and besides, the whole sum and essence of this journey was that it was away from her, from the family, and from that dreadful provincial country Southern Rhodesia, where, if there was a serious conversation, then it was—always—about The Colour Bar and the inadequacies of the blacks. I was free. I could at last be wholly myself. I felt myself to be self-created, self-sufficient. Is this an adolescent I am describing? No, I was nearly thirty. I had two marriages behind me, but I did not feel I had been *really* married.

I was also exhausted, because the child, two and a half, had for the month of the voyage woken at five, with shouts of delight for the new day, and had slept reluctantly at ten every night. In between he had never been still, unless I was telling him tales and singing him nursery rhymes, which I had been doing for four or five hours every day. He had had a wonderful time.

I was also having those thoughts—perhaps better say feelings—that disturb every arrival from Southern Africa who has not before seen white men unloading a ship, doing heavy manual labour, for this had been what black people did. A lot of white people, seeing whites work like blacks, had felt uneasy and threatened; for me, it was not so simple. Here they were, the workers, the working class, and at that time I believed that the logic of history would make it inevitable they should inherit the earth. They—those tough, muscled labouring men down there—and, of course, people like me, were the vanguard of the working class. I am not writing this down to ridicule it. That would be dishonest. Millions, if not billions, of people were thinking like that, using this language.

I have far too much material for this second volume. Nothing can be more tedious than a book of memoirs millions of words long. A little book called *In Pursuit of the English,* written when I was still close to that time, will add depth and detail to those first months in London. At once, problems—literary problems. What I say in it is true enough. A couple of characters were changed for libel reasons and would have to be now. But there is no doubt that while 'true', the book is not as true as what I would write now. It is a question of tone, and that is no simple matter. That little book is more like a novel; it has the shape and the pace of one. It is too well shaped for life. In one thing at least it is accurate: when I was newly in London I was returned to a child's way of seeing and feeling, every person, building, bus, street, striking my senses with the shocking immediacy of a child's life, everything oversized, very bright, very dark, smelly, noisy. I do not experience London like that now. That was a city of Dickensian exaggeration. I am not saying I saw London through a veil of Dickens, but rather that I was sharing the grotesque vision of Dickens, on the verge of the surreal.

That London of the late 1940s, the early 1950s, has vanished, and now it is hard to believe it existed. It was unpainted, buildings were stained and cracked and dull and grey; it was war-damaged, some areas all ruins, and under them holes full of dirty water, once cellars, and it was subject to sudden dark fogs—that was before the Clean Air Act. No one who has known only today's London of self-respecting clean buildings, crowded cafés and restaurants, good food and coffee, streets full until after midnight with mostly young people having a good time, can believe what London was like then. No cafés. No good restaurants. Clothes were still 'austerity' from the war, dismal and ugly. Everyone was indoors by ten, and the streets were empty. The Dining Rooms, subsidised during the war, were often the only places to eat in a whole area of streets. They served good meat, terrible vegetables, nursery puddings. Lyons restaurants were the high point of eating for ordinary people—I remember fish and chips and poached eggs on toast. There were fine restaurants for the well-off, and they tended to hide themselves away out of embarrassment, because in them, during the war, the rigours of rationing had been so ameliorated. You could not get a decent cup of coffee anywhere in the British Isles. The sole civilised amenity was the pubs, but they closed at eleven, and you have to have the right temperament for pubs. Or, I should say, had to have, for they have changed so much, no longer give the impression to an outsider of being like clubs, each with its members, or 'regulars', where outsiders go on sufferance. Rationing was still on. The war still lingered, not only in the bombed places but in people's minds and behaviour. Any conversation tended to drift towards the war, like an animal licking a sore place. There was a wariness, a weariness.

On New Year's Eve, 1950, I was telephoned by an American from the publishing scene to ask if I would share the revels with him. I met him in my best dress at six o'clock in Leicester Square. We expected cheerful crowds, but there was no one on the streets. For an hour or so we were in a pub but felt out of place. Then we looked for a restaurant. There were the expensive restaurants, which we could not afford, but nothing of what we now take for granted—the Chinese, Indian, Italian restaurants, and dozens of other nationalities. The big hotels were all booked up. We walked up and down and back and forth through Soho and around Piccadilly. Everything was dark and blank. Then he said, To hell with it, let's live it up. A taxi driver took us to a club in Mayfair, and there we watched the successors of the Bright Young Things getting drunk and throwing bread at each other.

But by the end of the decade, there were coffee bars and good ice cream, by courtesy of the Italians, and good cheap Indian restaurants. Clothes were bright and cheap and irreverent. London was painted again and was cheerful. Most of the bomb damage was gone. Above all, there was a new generation who had not been made tired by the war. They did not talk about the war, or think about it.

The first place where I lived was in Bayswater, which was then rather seedy and hard to associate with the grandeur of its earlier days. Prostitutes lined the streets every evening. I was supposed to be sharing a flat with a South African woman and her child: I wrote about this somewhat unsatisfactory experience in *In Pursuit of the English*. The flat we were in was large and well furnished. Two rooms were let to prostitutes. When I discovered this—I did not realise at once who these smartly dressed girls were who tripped up and down the stairs with men—and tackled the South African woman, because I did not think this was good for the two small children, she burst into tears and said I was unkind.

I spent six weeks looking for a place that would take a small child. There was a heat wave, and I couldn't understand why people complained about the English weather. My feet gave in on the hot pavements, and my morale almost did, but then a household of Italians welcomed the child and me, and my main problem was solved. This was Denbigh Road. Peter had been accepted by a council nursery. Circumstances had taught him from his very first days to be sociable, and he loved going there. When he came back from the nursery he disappeared at once into the basement, where there was a little girl his age. The house, dispiriting to me, because it was so grim and dirty and war-damaged, was a happy place for him.

We were at the beginning—but literally—in a garret, which was too small for me even to unpack a typewriter. I sent some short stories to the agent Curtis Brown, chosen at random from the *Writers' & Artists' Yearbook,* and Juliet O'Hea wrote back what I later knew was a form letter: Yes, but did I have a novel or was I thinking of writing one? I said there was a novel, but it had been bought by a Johannesburg publisher. She asked to see the contract, was shocked and angry when she saw it—they were going to take fifty percent of everything I earned, as a reward for risking themselves over this dangerous book. She sent them a telegram saying that if they didn't at once release me from the contract she would expose them as crooks. She then sold the book over the weekend to Michael Joseph.

Pamela Hansford Johnson was Michael Joseph's reader. She wrote an enthusiastic report but said that these and those changes should be made. Since I had spent years writing and rewriting the book, I did not feel inclined to make changes, particularly as I had broken my shoulder. How? It cannot be regarded as anything less than a psychologically significant event. I was in Leicester Square, seeing *Les Enfants du Paradis* with a young man. We had been most romantically in love when he was in the RAF in Rhodesia. Our lives had already taken dramatically different routes: he was about to join the Federation of British Industry, and I was still, if uneasily, a Red—though not a member of the Party. I came out of the cinema and walked straight into slippery tar painted on the street by workmen who said I should have looked where I was going. Gottfried had arrived in London, where he proposed to live, and was staying with Dorothy Schwartz from Salisbury in a large flat near the Belsize Park underground station. He took Peter for six weeks, while my shoulder mended.

Hindsight has given a jaunty tone to my memories of that time, for if it was difficult, I was coping with it all. This little scene paints a different picture: I am standing on the platform at Queensway underground station. My left arm is in a sling, and my yellow wool jacket is buttoned over it. A button flies off, a draught lifts the jacket off my left shoulder, I stand revealed in my bra. In London you could walk down Oxford Street nude and earn hardly a glance, and my embarrassment is unnecessary. I try futilely to get myself covered. A woman emerges from the crowd, turns me to her, takes a large safety pin from her pocket, pins my jacket onto the sling. She stands examining my face. 'Broken it, 'ave you? Well, a break takes forty-two days or six weeks, whichever is the shortest.' I can't speak. 'Cheer up. The worst may never happen.'

7

'This is the worst,' I manage. She laughs, that anarchic, gruff, well-what-can-you-expect laugh still heard from people who lived through the Blitz.

'Is that so? If that's the worst you can manage, then. . . .' She gives me encouraging little pats, then shoves me gently towards the train and helps me onto it. 'You just go and get yourself a nice cup of tea and cheer up,' I hear, as the doors grind shut.

I sent *The Grass Is Singing* back to Michael Joseph in the same parcel it arrived in. I got a letter from them, congratulating me on the valuable changes I had made. I never enlightened them.

Soon Alfred Knopf in New York said they would take the book, if I would change it so that there was an explicit rape, 'in accordance with the mores of the country'. This was Blanche Knopf, Alfred's wife, and the Knopfs were the stars of the publishing firmament then. I was furious. What did she know about the 'mores' of Southern Africa? Besides, it was crass. The whole point of *The Grass Is Singing* was the unspoken, devious codes of behaviour of the whites, nothing ever said, everything understood, and the relationship between Mary Turner, the white woman, and Moses, the black man, was described so that nothing was explicit. This was only partly out of literary instinct. The fact is, I have never decided whether Mary had sex with Moses or not. Sometimes I think one thing, sometimes another. While it was a commonplace that white men had sex with black women, and the continually enlarging Coloured community was there to prove it, I had only once heard of a white woman having sex with her black servant. The penalty—for the man—was hanging. Besides, the taboos were so strong. If Mary Turner had had sex with Moses, this poor woman so precariously holding on to her idea of herself as a white madam would have cracked into pieces. Yes, but she *was* cracked, she was crazy—yes, but she would have been crazy in a different way: as soon as I say it, the phrases and words appear that would describe that different lunacy. No, on the whole I think she didn't. When I wrote the book I was sure she didn't. The episode from which the story grew was this: I overheard contemptuous and uneasy talk on the verandahs about a farmer's wife on a near farm who 'allowed her cook to button up her dress at the back and

8

brush her hair'. This was—correctly, I think—described by my father as the ultimate in contempt for the man: like aristocrats permitting themselves every kind of intimate and filthy behaviour in front of servants, because they weren't really human beings.

I decided that the Knopf demand was hypocrisy: an explicit rape would have the shock of novelty—this was true then. I said I would not change the book. I was supported all the way by Juliet O'Hea, who said of course I should never change a word I didn't want to, but it was always worthwhile thinking about what they said. 'After all, my dear, they are sometimes right.' She thought that this time they were wrong. 'Don't worry. If they don't take it I'll get you another publisher.' They took it anyway.*

I had very little money left. The £150 advance from Michael Joseph was at once swallowed up by rent and fees for the nursery school. I took a secretary's job for a few weeks, where I did practically no work at all, for it was a new engineering firm, with young, inexperienced partners. I had taken the child out of the council nursery and put him in a rather expensive private nursery. How was I going to pay for this? But my attitude always was: decide to do something and then find out the way to pay for it. Soon I knew I was being stupid. I was supposed to be a writer: publishers enquired tenderly about what I was writing. But I had no energy for writing. I woke at five, with the child, as always—he went on waking at five for years, and I with him. I read to him, told him stories, gave him breakfast, took him by bus down to the nursery school, went to work. There I sat about, doing nothing much, or perhaps covertly writing a short story. At lunchtime I shopped. At five I fetched the child from the nursery, went back by bus, and then the usual rumbustious rowdy evening for him, downstairs, while I cleaned the place up. He did not sleep until ten or so. But then I was too tired to work.

*I was soon to have a sharp little lesson in the realities of publishing. The first paperback edition of *The Grass Is Singing* had on its front a lurid picture of a blonde cowering terrified while a big buck nigger (the only way to describe him) stood over her, threatening her with a panga. My protests, on the lines of 'But Moses the black man was not a great stupid murderous thug,' were ignored with: 'You don't understand anything about selling books.'

I gave up the job. Meanwhile the publishers rang—twice—to say they were reprinting, and that was before publication. I said, 'Oh good.' I thought this happened to every writer. My ignorance was absolute. They thought I was taking my success for granted.

Michael Joseph invited me to the Caprice for lunch, then the smartest show business restaurant. I had moved downstairs from my garret and was in a large room that had been once—would be again—beautiful but was now dirty and draughty, heated by an inadequate fireplace. The whole house was cracked and leaking because of the bombing. There was a tiny room, where Peter slept. The Caprice was adazzle with pink tablecloths, silver, glass, and well-dressed people. Michael Joseph was a handsome man, worldly, at home there, and he talked of Larry and Viv, and said it was a pity they weren't lunching that day. Michael Joseph, for some reason unfit for fighting, had started the firm during the war, against the advice of everybody, for he did not have much capital. The firm was at once successful, chiefly because he had been an agent with Curtis Brown, and Juliet O'Hea, his good friend, saw that he got sent new books. He enjoyed his success, ran a racehorse or two, frequented London's smart places. He kept greeting the people at other tables: 'Let me introduce you to our new writer—she's from Africa.'

The purpose of this lunch was not only because writers were supposed to feel flattered but because he was concerned that this author should not expect him to advertise. He told me exemplary tales, such as that a certain little book, *The Snow Goose,* by Paul Gallico, published during the war, was reprinted several times before publication on word of mouth alone. 'Advertising has no effect at all on the fate of a book.' All publishers talk like this.

In certain military academies is set this exercise: The examinee is to imagine that he is a general in command of a battlefront. In one area his troops are only holding their own, in another are being routed, in a third are driving back the enemy. With limited resources, where is he to send support? The correct answer is: to the successful sector; the rest must be left to their fate. It seems few people give the right answer; they mislead themselves with compassionate thoughts for the less successful soldiers. This is how publishers think. An already successful or known author gets advertisements, but struggling or unknown ones are expected to sink or swim. When the public sees advertisements for a novel on the underground, they are seeing reserves being sent to a successful sector of the battlefront. They are seeing a best-seller being created from a novel that is already a success.

Inspired by the atmosphere of the Caprice, I told Michael Joseph that if there was one thing I adored above all else, it was chocolate éclairs, and no sooner had I got back to my slum than a long black car purred to a stop outside it and a pretty pink box was delivered by the chauffeur. It contained a dozen chocolate éclairs. These were added to the already bounteous family supper downstairs.

Nothing I experienced in that household matched what I had expected to find, which was rationing, a dour self-sufficiency, even semi-starvation. I had sent food parcels to Britain. The woman of the house, Italian, was one of the world's great cooks. I don't think she had ever seen a recipe book. She took six ration books to a shop in Westbourne Grove, then a slummy road. But she always got three or four times the rationed amounts of butter, eggs, bacon, cooking fat, cheese. How did she manage it? She was scornful when I asked. It's time you knew your way around, she said. There were a couple of bent policemen, always dropping in and out, who were given butter and eggs from her spoils, in return for turning a blind eye. Did I share in this lawlessness? Yes, I did: our two ration books were given to her to manage. To make little shows of morality in that atmosphere would have seemed not only absurd but would have been incomprehensible to these amiable crooks. Besides, the newspapers were already clamouring for the end of rationing. There was no longer any need for it, they said. Never have I eaten so well. The rent did not include food, but like most fine cooks, our landlady could not bear not to feed anyone around who would sit down at her table. I ate downstairs two or three times a week, Peter most evenings. She asked for money for shopping when she ran out. Hers was an economy that absorbed not only me but other people in the house in complicated borrowings, lendings, cigarettes, a dress or shoes she fancied.

When I told middle-class acquaintances about the bent policemen and the butter and eggs and cheese, they were cold, and they were angry. 'Our policemen are not corrupt,' they said. They saw my sojourn on that foreign shore—the working class—as a whimsical foray for the sake of my art, for Experience. They waited for little anecdotes about the comic working classes, in the spirit of the snobbish *Punch* cartoons about servants.

From then until decades later, when it was admitted by Authority that all was not well with our policemen, I was treated by nearly everyone with the hostile impatience I was already earning when I said that South Africa was a hellhole for the blacks and the Coloureds—for this was still not acknowledged, in spite of Alan Paton's *Cry, the Beloved Country,* which had just come out, a little before *The Grass Is Singing*—and even more when I insisted that Southern Rhodesia was as bad and, some blacks thought, even worse than South Africa. Only Reds and malcontents said this kind of thing.

In the household in Denbigh Road, Southern Africa was not of interest. Nothing was, outside this little area of streets. They talked of going up to the West End, a mile or so away, as a serious excursion.

The exuberance, the physical well-being of that household was certainly not general then. They were a tired people, the British. Stoical. The national low vitality, that aftermath of war, as if the horrors or endurances of war are eating away silently out of sight, swallowing energy like a black hole, was balanced by something very different. That is what strikes me most about that time—the contrast. On the one hand, the low spirits, a patient sticking it out, but on the other, an optimism for the future so far from how we are thinking now it seems almost like the symptom of a general foolishness. A New Age was dawning, no less. Socialism was the key. The troops returning from all over the world had been promised everything, the Atlantic Charter (seen sardonically at the time) was merely the summing-up of those Utopian hopes, and now they had returned a Labour government to make sure they would get it. The National Health Service was their proudest achievement. In the thirties, before the war, an illness or an accident could drag a whole family down to disaster. The poverty had been terrible and had not been forgotten. All that was finished. No longer was there a need to dread illness and the Dole and old age. And this was just a beginning: things were going to get steadily better. Everyone seemed to share this mood. You kept meeting doctors who were setting up practices that would embody this new socialist medicine, who saw themselves as builders of a new era. They could be Communists, they could be Labour, they could be Liberals. They were all idealists.

The Zeitgeist, or How We Thought Then

Above all, a new world was dawning.

Britain was still best: that was so deeply part of how citizens thought, it was taken for granted. Education, food, health, anything at all—best. The British Empire, then on its last legs—the best.

The newspapers were full of warnings about rebuilding the area around St. Paul's, bombed into ruins. If this rebuilding was not planned, a nasty chaos would result. It was not planned, and nasty chaos did result.

Our prisons were a disgusting and shameful disgrace. Over forty years on, news from them is the same. There is something about prisons: we cannot get them right. Is it because deep in the British heart they believe, with the Old Testament, that there should be an eye for an eye, a tooth for a tooth? Retribution, that is what most citizens believe in. As I am writing this, the news is that women with small children are in prison for not paying their television licence. Their children are in care. When most citizens hear this for the first time they exclaim, No, it isn't possible that this is happening! But Dickens would not have been surprised.

Charity was for ever abolished by the welfare state. Never again would poor people be demeaned by gifts from others. Now we would dismantle all the apparatus of charity, the trusts, the associations, the committees. No more handouts.

In Oxford Street underground, I watched a little bully of an official hectoring and insulting a recently arrived West Indian who could not get the hang of the ticket mechanism. He was exactly like the whites I had watched all my life in Southern Rhodesia shouting at blacks. He was compensating for his own feelings of inferiority.

Everyone from abroad, particularly America, said how gentle, polite— civilised—Britain was.

And now . . . what was I going to write next? What the publishers wanted was a novel. What I was writing was short stories. All of them were set in The District—Banket, Lomagundi—and they were about the white community and how they saw themselves, preserved themselves, saw the blacks around them. I would call it *This Was the Old Chief's Country*. Juliet O'Hea said if that is what I wanted to do, then of course, but no publisher would be delighted at the news of short stories, which did not sell. In fact, I proved them wrong, for they did sell, and very well—for short stories— and have gone on selling ever since. But it was a novel I should be thinking about. And so I did think hard and long about the book that would be *Martha Quest*.

The Grass Is Singing had come about because people thought of me as a writer, I knew I would be one . . . and had been, so I know now, from an early age. I had forgotten this, believing that the decision to write came later, but when *Under My Skin* came out, a woman who had known me at the convent—Daphne Anderson, who wrote an admirable account of her childhood, *Toe-Rags*—told me she remembered us sitting on my bed in the dormitory, discussing what we would be, and I said I was going to be a writer. I must have been ten or eleven. But this figure—the writer—is a siren figure that comforts and sustains innumerable young people who are at sea, know it, and cannot direct their future in a conformable way. I left my job in the law firm in Salisbury, saying I was going to write a novel, since at some point I must stop talking about it and do it. Besides, it had occurred to me that those ideal conditions—solitude, time, freedom from care— would never happen. What was I to write? I had many ideas for a book. Now I am interested in how I then sat around, walked around and around the room, *wool-gathering*—an essential process—

taking my time, and all this by instinct. From the many ideas one emerged ... grew stronger. ... I remembered the talk on the verandahs, matrix for a thousand possible tales, I remembered the little newspaper cutting I had kept all those years. And so I wrote *The Grass Is Singing*. First novels are usually autobiographical. *The Grass Is Singing* was not. Dick Turner, the failing farmer, was a figure I had seen all my life. Only a minority of the white farmers were successful; most failed. Some struggled on, failing, for years. Some hated the country. Some loved it, like Dick Turner. Some were idealistic—like my father, who, if he were farming now, would be disdaining fertilisers, pesticides, crops that rob the soil, would be cherishing animals and birds. Mary Turner I took from a woman I had known for years, one of the Sports Club girls. When we went out into the bush for picnics, or simply to be in the bush, sit in it, absorbing it—for many town whites did this, as if the town were merely an unfortunate necessity and the bush was where they belonged—then this woman, who remained a girl until she was well into her forties, a good sort, every man's kind sister, used to sit on a bit of rock, with her feet drawn up away from the soil, sit with her arms tight around her knees, peering over them to watch if an ant or a chameleon or beetle crawled up on her trousers. If she was so afraid of the bush, why then did she go off on these picnics? It was because she was a good sort and always did what others did and wanted her to do. She was a woman essentially of the town, of streets, of nice tamed gardens. ... I watched her and wondered what on earth she would do if fate deposited her somewhere on a farm, not one of the new big rich farms but a struggling farm, like farms I had seen, and I ran through the names of the poor farmers in my head, and saw the shallow brick verandahs, the corrugated-iron roofs, which expanded and contracted and cracked in the heat and the cold, the dust, the yelling of the cicadas ... and then I had it, I had her, I had Mary Turner, the woman who loathed the bush and the natives and hated all natural processes, hated sex, liked to be neat and clean, her dress ironed afresh every time she put it on, her little girl's hair tied with a ribbon at parties.

And now, again, in London: What should I write?

There was a point when it occurred to me that my early life had been extraordinary and would make a novel. I had not understood how extraordinary until I had left Southern Africa and come to England. *Martha Quest,* my third book, was more or less autobiographical, though it didn't start until Martha was fourteen, when her childhood was over. First novels, particularly by women, are often attempts at self-definition, whatever their literary merits. While I was seeing my early life more clearly with every new person I met, for a casual remark could question things I had taken for granted for years, I was nevertheless confused. While I certainly 'knew who I was' (to use the American formula), I did not know how to define myself as a social being. In parenthesis—and it has to be that, for we touch on whole landscapes of query—this business of 'finding out who I am' (and it really was then American) has always left me wondering. What do they mean? Surely they can't be without a sense of self. A sense of: Here I am, inside here. What can it be like, to live without that feeling of me, in here; of what I am?

What I did not know was how to define myself, see myself in a social context. Oh yes, easy enough to say I was a child of the end of the Raj—but that phrase had not yet come into use. The end of the British Empire, then. Yes, I was one of a generation brought up on World War I and then as much formed by World War II. But there was a hiatus, a lack, a blur—and it was to do with my parents and particularly my mother. I had fought her steadily, relentlessly, and I had had to—but what was it all about? Why? And I was not able to answer that, entirely, until I was in my seventies, and even then perhaps not finally.

I started to write *Martha Quest* while still in Denbigh Road, and it was going along at a good rate, but I had to interrupt myself, I had to get out of that house, that street—which for a long time now has been a fashionable area. Sometimes I drive or walk through it and see those discreetly desirable residences, and I think, I wonder what you people would say if you could see how these houses were and how carelessly they were 'done up' by War Damage.

The trouble was, the little boy, Peter, was happy there, and I knew I would not easily find anything as good. For *him,* that is.

By chance I went to an evening party, in the flat of the brother of a farmer in Southern Rhodesia, who was the essence of white conformity. But this brother was left-wing and pro-Soviet, as was then common. He had an elderly girlfriend, who had once been beautiful, as the photographs that stood about everywhere averred, and whom he called Baby. Baby, with her great dark eyes in her painted pretty old face, her little ruffles and bows, dominated the scene, but there was another focus of attention, a vibrant, dark-eyed, dark-haired stocky young woman, who at first I thought was French. She wore a tight black skirt, a white shirt, and a cheeky black beret. We talked; she heard how I was living; she at once responded with practical sympathy. She had herself been a young woman with a small child in one bed-sit room in New York. She had been rescued by a woman friend, with the offer of a flat in her house. 'You can't live like this,' she had said. And now Joan Rod-ker said to me that she was getting rid of an unsatisfactory tenant, and she had been thinking for some time how to help some young woman with a child. There was a small flat at the top of her house, and I could live there, provided she liked Peter. So on the next Sunday I took Peter to see her, and they liked each other at once. So you could say that it was Peter who solved my housing problem for me.

And so I moved into Church Street, Kensington, an attractive little flat at the top of the house, where I lived for four years. It was summer 1950. But before I left Denbigh Road I saw the end of an era, the death of a culture: television arrived. Before, when the men came back from work, the tea was already on the table, a fire was roaring, the radio emitted words or music softly in a corner, they washed and sat down at their places, with the woman, the child, and whoever else in the house could be inveigled downstairs. Food began emerging from the oven, dish after dish, tea was brewed, beer appeared, off went the jerseys or jackets, the men sat in their shirtsleeves, glistening with well-being. They all talked, they sang, they told what had happened in their day, they talked dirty—a ritual; they quarrelled, they shouted, they kissed and made up and went to bed at twelve or one, after six or so hours of ener-getic conviviality. I suppose that this level of emotional intensity was not usual in the households of Britain: I was witnessing an extreme. And then, from one day to the next—but literally from one evening to the next—came the end of good times, for television had arrived and sat like a toad in the corner of the kitchen. Soon the big kitchen table had been pushed along the wall, chairs were installed in a semi-circle and, on the chair arms, the swivelling supper trays. It was the end of an exuberant verbal culture.

Church Street, Kensington W8

THE HOUSE NEAR THE PORTOBELLO ROAD WAS WAR-DAMAGED and surrounded by areas of bombed buildings. The house in Church Street had been war-damaged, and near it were war ruins. Bonfires often burned on the bomb sites, to get rid of the corpses of houses. Otherwise the two houses had nothing in common. In the house I had left, politics had meant food and rationing and the general stupidities of government, but in Church Street I was returned abruptly to international politics, communists, the comrades, passionate polemic, and the rebuilding of Britain to some kind of invisible blueprint, which everyone shared. Joan Rodker worked for the Polish Institute, was a communist, if not a Party member, and knew everyone in 'the Party'—which is how it was referred to—and knew, too, most people in the arts. Her story is extraordinary and deserves a book or two. She was the daughter of two remarkable people, from the poor but vibrant East End, when it was still supplying the arts, and intellectual life generally, with talent. Her father was John Rodker, a writer and a friend of the well-known writers and intellectuals of that time, who mysteriously did not fulfil the expectations everyone had for him and became a publisher. Her mother was a beauty who sat for the artists, notably Isaac Rosenberg. They dumped Joan as a tiny child in an institution that existed to care for the children of people whose lives could not include children. It was a cruel place, though in outward appearance genteel. Her parents intermittently visited but never knew what the little girl was enduring. Surviving all this, and much else, she was acting in a theatre company in the Ukraine, having easily learned German and Russian, being endowed with that kind of talent, when she had a child by a German actor in the company.

Since bourgeois marriage had been written out of history for ever, they did not marry. She was instrumental in getting him out of Czechoslovakia and into England before the war began. I used his appearance in *Children of Violence,* in the place of Gottfried Lessing, because I thought, This is Peter's father. One man was middle class, the other rich, very rich, from Germany's decadent time. My substitution of one man for another did not have the effect intended. Gottfried said I had put him in the book, yet all the two characters had in common was being German and communist. That could only mean Gottfried thought that what identified him was his politics. Hinze, a well-known actor, was around while Ernest—Joan's child—was growing up, helping with money and with time. He, too, was a remarkable man, and his story deserves to be recorded. Hard times do produce extraordinary people. I don't know what the practical application of that thought could be.

Joan returned to London after the war, from America, with the child—and found she had nowhere to live. She saw this house, in Church Street, open to the sky, and thought, That's my house. She brought in buckets of water and began scrubbing down the rooms, night after night, when she had done with work. War Damage sent in workmen to repair the house and found Joan on her knees, with a scrubbing brush.

'What you doing?'

'Cleaning my house,' she said.

'But it isn't your house.'

'Yes it is.'

'You'd better have documents to prove it, then.'

She had no money. She went to her father and demanded that he guarantee a bank loan. He was disconcerted; people who have had to drag themselves up from an extreme of poverty may take a long time to see themselves as advantaged. With a guaranteed bank loan, and her determination, she got her house, where she is living to this day.

All these vicissitudes had given her an instinct for the distress of others which was the swiftest and surest I have known. She knew how to help people. Her kindness, her generosity, was not sentimental but practical and imaginative. I had plenty of people to compare her with, because I was meeting people who had survived war, prison camps, every kind of disaster; my life was full of survivors, but not all of them had been improved by what had happened to them.

Peter had been happy in the other house, and he enjoyed this one as much. Joan's son, Ernest, then adolescent, was as wonderfully kind as Joan herself. He was like an elder brother. People who have brought up small children without another parent to share the load will know I have said the most important thing about my life then.

If living in the other house was as strange to me as if I'd been immersed in a Victorian novel, life in Church Street, Kensington, was only a continuation of that flat in Salisbury where people dropped in day and night for cups of tea, food, argument, and often noisy debate. Going up or down the stairs, I passed the open door into the little kitchen, often crammed with comrades, having a snack, talking, shouting, or imparting news in confidential tones, for a great deal was going on in the communist world which was discussed in lowered voices and never admitted publicly. I was again in an atmosphere that made every encounter, every conversation, important, because if you were a communist, then the future of the world depended on you—you and your friends and people like you all over the world. The vanguard of the working class, in short. I was in conflict. Having lived with Gottfried Lessing, a 'one hundred and fifty percenter'—a phrase used at that time in communist circles—I was weary of dogmatism and self-importance. When I was with Gottfried, who was now at the nadir of his life and, because of his low spirits, even more violently rude about people and opinions not communist, I was seeing a mirror of myself—a caricature, yes, but true. A line from Gerald Manley Hopkins haunted me.

> This, by Despair, bred Hangdog dull; by Rage,
> Manwolf, worse; and their packs infest the age.

I would wake out of a dream, muttering, '"and their packs infest the age"'. Me: Hopkins was talking about me.

I lived in a pack, was one of a pack. But when the comrades came up the stairs to the top of the house—and they often did, for up there lived a lively young woman and her delightful little boy, an exotic too, coming from Africa, which seemed always to be in the news these days—I found people interested in what I said about South Africa and Southern Rhodesia. Anywhere outside communist circles, my information that Southern Rhodesia was not a paradise of happy darkies was greeted with impatience. You are so wrong-headed, those looks said. How patronised I have been by people who *don't want to know*. But the comrades did want to know. An attraction of Communist Party circles was that if you happened to remark, 'I have been in Peru, and . . . ,' people wanted to know. The world was their responsibility. I was finding this increasingly ridiculous, but the thing wasn't so easy. I looked back to Salisbury, where we had assumed, for years, that what we did and thought was of world-shattering (literally) significance, but from the perspectives of London our little group there seemed embarrassing, absurd—yet I knew that these absurd people were the few, in all of white Southern Rhodesia, who understood the truth about the white regime: that it was doomed, could not last long. It was not our views but our effectiveness that was in question. And here I was again, being part of a minority, and a very small one, who knew they were in the right. This was the height of the Cold War. The Korean War had started. The communists were with every day more isolated. The atmosphere was poisonous. If, for instance, you doubted that America was dropping wads of material infected with germs—germ warfare—then you were a traitor. I was undermined with doubts. I hated this religious language, and I was not the only one. 'Comrade So-and-so is getting doubts,' a communist might say, with that sardonic intonation that was already—and would increasingly become—the tone of many conversations. But again, this was not simple, for it was certainly not only the comrades who identified with an idealised Soviet Union.

Although I was not a member of the Communist Party, I was accepted by the comrades as one of them: I spoke the language. When I protested that I had been a member of a communist party invented by us in Southern Rhodesia, which any real Communist Party would have dismissed with contempt, they did not care—or perhaps they did not hear. It has been my fate all my life often to be with people who assume I think as they do, because a passionate belief, or set of assumptions, is so persuasive to the holders of them that they really cannot believe anyone could be so wrong-headed as not to share them. I could not discuss any 'doubts' I might have with Joan or anyone who came to that house—not yet, but, if I found the Party Line hard to swallow, there was something else, much stronger. Colonials, the children or grandchildren of the far-flung Empire, arrived in England with expectations created by literature. 'We will find the England of Shelley and Keats and Hopkins, of Dickens and Hardy and the Brontës and Jane Austen, we will breathe the generous airs of literature. We have been sustained in exile by the magnificence of the Word, and soon we will walk into our promised land.' All the communists I met had been fed and sustained by literature, and very few of the other people I met had. In short, my experience in Southern Rhodesia continued, if modified, not least because again I was having to defend my right to write, to spend my time writing, and not to run around distributing pamphlets or the *Daily Worker*. But a woman who had stood up to Gottfried Lessing—'Why are you wasting your time? Writing is just bourgeois self-indulgence'—was more than equipped to deal with the English comrades. The pressure on writers—and artists—to do something other than write, paint, make music, because those are nothing but bourgeois indulgences, continued strong, and continues now, though the ideologies are different, and will continue, because it has roots in envy, and the envious ones do not know they suffer from a disease, know only that they are in the right.

It did help that I was now one of the recognised new writers. *The Grass Is Singing* had got very good reviews, and was selling well, and was bought in other countries. The short stories, *This Was the Old Chief's Country,* did well. Needless to say, I was attacked by the comrades for all kinds of ideological shortcomings. For instance, *The Grass Is Singing* was poisoned by Freud. At that stage I had not read much Freud. The short stories did not put the point of view of the organised black working class. True. For one thing, there wasn't one. There is no way one can exaggerate the stupidity of communist literary criticism; any quote immediately seems like mockery or caricature—like so much of Political Correctness now.

It was not only pressures from my own side that I had to resist.

For instance, the editor of a popular newspaper, the *Daily Graphic*—it was not unlike the *Sun*—long since defunct, invited me to his office and offered me a lot of money to write articles supporting hanging, the flogging of delinquent children, harsher treatment for criminals, a woman's place in the home, down with socialism, internment for communists. When I said I disagreed with all these, the editor, a nasty little man, said it didn't matter what my personal opinions were. If I wanted, I could be a journalist—he would train me—and journalists should know how to write persuasively on any subject. I kept refusing large sums of money, which got larger as he became more exasperated. I fled to a telephone in the street, where I rang up Juliet O'Hea. I needed money badly. She said on no account should I ever write one word I did not believe in, never write a word that wasn't the best I could do; if I started writing for money, the next thing would be I'd start believing it was good, and neither of us wanted that, did we? She did not believe in asking for advances before they were due, but if I was desperate she would. And she would tell the editor of the *Daily Graphic* to leave me alone.

There were other offers on the same lines, temptations of the Devil. Not that I was really tempted. But I did linger sometimes in an editor's office out of curiosity: I could not believe that this was happening, that people could be so low, so unscrupulous. But *surely* they can't really believe writers should write against their own beliefs, their consciences? Write less than their best, *for money?*

The most bizarre result of *The Grass Is Singing,* which was being execrated in South Africa and Southern Rhodesia, was an invitation to be 'one of the girls' at an evening with visiting members of the still new Nationalist government. I was too intrigued to refuse, fascinated that Southern African customs could hold good here: 'The English cricket team is coming—just round up some of the girls for them.' There were ten or so Afrikaners, ministers or

26

slightly lesser officials, living it up on a trip to London. I knew them all by name, and only too well as a type. Large, overfed, jovial, they joked their way through a restaurant dinner, about all the ways they used to keep the kaffirs down, for it was then a characteristic of these ruling circles to be proud of being 'slim'—full of cunning tricks. After dinner we repaired to a hotel bedroom, where I was in danger of being fondled by one or more. Another of 'the girls' told the men that I was an enemy and they should be careful of what they said. Why was I an enemy? was demanded, with the implicit suggestion that it was not possible to disagree with their evidently correct views. 'She's written a book,' said this woman, or girl, a South African temporarily in London. 'Then we're going to ban it,' was the jocular reply. One man, whose knee I was trying to refuse, said, 'Ach, man, we don't care what liberals read, what do they matter? The kaffirs aren't going to read your little book. They can't read, and that's how we like it.' The word 'liberal' in South Africa has always been interchangeable with 'communist'.

All the places where I had lived with Gottfried, in Salisbury, people had dropped in and out, and the talk was not only of politics, and of changing the world, but of war; in Church Street it was the same, except that here war was not all rumour and propaganda but men who had returned from battlefronts, so that we could match what really had happened with what we had been told was happening. Similarly, I was in a familiar situation with Gottfried, who disapproved of me more with every meeting. He was having a very bad time. He had believed he would easily get a job in London. He knew himself to be clever and competent: had he not created a large and successful legal firm, virtually out of nothing, in Salisbury? There were relatives in London, to whom he applied for work. They turned him down. He was a communist, and they were—or felt themselves to be—on sufferance in Britain, as foreigners. Or perhaps they didn't like him. He was applying for jobs on the level which he knew he deserved. No one would even give him an interview. The joke was, ten years later it would be chic to be German and a communist. Meanwhile he was working for the Society for Cultural Relations with the Soviet Union. This organisation owned a house in Kensington Square, where there were lectures on the happy state of the arts in the USSR. At every meeting the two back rows of chairs were filled with people who had actually lived under communism: they were trying to tell us how horrible communism was. We patronised them: they were middle-aged or old, they didn't know the score, they were *reactionary*. A well-chosen epithet, flattering to the user, is the surest way of ending all serious thought. Gottfried earned very little money. He was being sheltered by Dorothy Schwartz, who had a large flat near Belsize Park Underground. The height—or depth—of the Cold War made him even more bitterly, angrily, coldly contemptuous of any opinion even slightly deviating from the Party Line. I was finding it almost impossible to be with him. I did not say to myself, But how did I stick him for so long? For we had had no alternative. About the child there were no disagreements. Peter spent most weekends with Gottfried and Dorothy. I would take him over there, sit down, have a cup of this or that, and listen to terrible, cold denunciations, then leave for two days of freedom. I went to the theatre a lot. In those days you queued in the mornings for a stool in the queue for the evening and saw the play from pit or gallery for the equivalent in today's money of three or four pounds. I saw most of the plays on in London, in this way, sometimes standing. I continued madly in love with the theatre.

I also went off to Paris. There is no way now of telling how powerful a dream France was then. The British—that is, people who were not in the forces—had been locked into their island for the war and for some years afterwards. People would say how they had suffered from claustrophobia, dreamed of abroad—and particularly of Paris. France was a magnet because of de Gaulle, and the Free French, and the Resistance, by far the most glamorous of the partisan armies. Now that our cooking and our coffee and our clothes are good, it is hard to remember how people yearned for France as for civilisation itself. And there was another emotion too, among women. French men loved women and showed it, but in Britain the most women could hope for was to be whistled at by workmen in the street, not always a friendly thing. Joan adored France. She had spent happy times there and spoke French well.

Her father's current girlfriend was French. Joan saw her as infinitely beautiful, while she was a mere nothing in comparison. This was far from the truth, but there was no arguing with her. (This was certainly not the only time in my life I have known a woman who wore rose-tinted spectacles for every woman in the world but herself.) Isn't she gorgeous, she would moan over some woman less attractive than she was. She had had a very smart black suit made, with a tight skirt and a waistcoat like a man's, which she wore with white shirts ruffled at throat and wrists. She actually went over to Paris to get it judged. There, men would compliment you on your toilette. She came back restored. Quite a few women I knew said that for the sake of one's self-respect one had to visit Paris from time to time. This was not a situation without its little ironies. There was a newspaper cartoon then of a Frenchman, dressed in semi–battle gear, old jacket, beret, a Gauloise hanging from a lip, accompanying a Frenchwoman dressed like a model—a short stocky scruffy man, a tall slim elegant woman.

When I went to Paris my toilette was hardly of the level to attract French compliments, but it was true every man gave you a quick, expert once-over—hair, face, what you were wearing—allotting you marks. This was a dispassionate, disinterested summing-up, not necessarily leading to invitations.

A scene: I took myself to the opera, and in the foyer, at the interval, saw enter a very young woman, eighteen, perhaps, in what was perhaps her first evening dress, a column of white satin. She was exquisite, and so was the dress. She stood poised just in the entrance, while the crowd looked . . . assessed . . . judged. Not a word, but they might as well have been clapping. She was at first ready to shrink away with shyness but slowly filled with confidence, stood smiling, tears in her eyes, lifted on invisible waves of expert appreciation, approval, love. Adorable France, which loves its women, gives them confidence in their femininity—and that from the time when they are tiny girls.

On this first trip I was in a cheap hotel on the Left Bank, so cheap I could hardly believe it. Gottfried had said I should look up his sister's husband's mother. I did and found an elderly lady in old-fashioned clothes living in a tiny room high up under the roof of one of those tall ancient cold houses. Through her I was admitted into a network of middle-aged and old women, without men, all poor, shabby, living from hand to mouth in maids' rooms or in any corner that would let them fit themselves in. There they were, every one a victim of war, and some of them had lived in their little refuges through the war and, clearly, often did not know how they had managed it. They were witty and they were wise, and the best of company. As with the refugees in London then, it was hard to know what they lived on. I was served precious coffee in beautiful cups, by a stove that had to be fed with wood and coal—and whatever was burnable that could be picked up in the street, brought toiling up hundreds of cold stairs. Madame Gise had not heard from her son since the beginning of the war and said that he had chosen to despise her, because she was not a communist. She despised communists and communism. I said I was a kind of communist, and she said, Nonsense, you don't know anything about it. These women, whose husbands or lovers or sons had been killed or had forgotten them: they were so brave, supporting each other in their poverty and when they were ill. Again, as in London, I was hearing tales of impossible survivals, endurances. Our talk in London of politics, all ideas and principles, of what went on in other countries, dissolved here into: 'My cousin . . . Ravensbrook'; 'My son was shot by the Germans for harbouring a member of the Resistance'; 'I escaped from Germany . . . from Poland . . . from Russia . . . from Spain . . .'

In Paris I bought a hat. This needs explanation. I had to: it was a need of the times. A Paris hat proved you had captured elegance itself. Madame Gise stood by me. Saying, No, not that one, Yes, that one, she was representing Paris itself, that shabby woman with a carefully counted out store of francs in her handbag. I never wore the hat. But I owned a Paris hat. Joan said, But what are you going to do with it?

Another trip, and in another shabby hotel, I suddenly thought, But surely this was where Oscar Wilde died? Down I went to the desk, and the proprietress said, Yes, indeed that was so, he died here, and it was in the room you are in. People sometimes came to ask her about it, but she couldn't say much; after all, she hadn't been here. When I wanted to pay the bill, there was no one at the desk. I knocked at a door, and was told, *Entrez*. It was a dark, cluttered room, with mirrors gleaming from corners, shawls over chairs, a cat. There was Madame, in an armchair, flesh bulging over her pink corset, her fat feet in a basin of water. The maid, a young girl, was brushing her rusty old hair, while Madame tossed it back as if it were a treasure, in her imagination young tresses. This was a scene from Balzac? Zola? Certainly not a twentieth-century novel. Or Degas: *The Concierge,* perhaps? I lingered at the door, entranced. 'Leave your money at the desk,' she said. 'The bill is there. And let us see you again, Madame.' But I didn't go back: one shouldn't spoil perfection. And I didn't see Madame Gise again either, and about that I feel bad.

On one of these trips there was one of the oddest encounters of my life. The plane back from Paris was delayed, by hours. At Orly we sat around, bored, tired, fractious. At last we were on. Next to me was a South African man, who, hearing from my voice that I was from Rhodesia, began talking. He was, I thought, drunk, then thought, No, that's not drink. I hardly listened: We would land after midnight; I was years away from being able to afford taxis; Peter still woke at five. Slowly, what the man was saying began to penetrate. He was telling me that he had made a trip to Palestine to aid Irgun in its fight against the British occupying forces, and he had just helped to blow up the King David Hotel. Now, his duty as a Jew done, he was returning with a good conscience to South Africa. Women are used to hearing confessions, particularly if they are young—well, by then youngish—and reasonably attractive. Women don't really count, as people, to a man who is drunk, or not himself for one reason or another—or to many men sober, if it comes to that. Suddenly it occurred to me that this was an enemy of my country and I should be thinking of how to alert the authorities. We landed. The airport was almost deserted. I was imagining what would happen if I said to the air hostess, I want to speak to the police. 'What for?' I could hear—and the voice would be tart, for she would be longing for bed, just like me. The police—a man, or two men—would arrive, after a delay, while I watched other people going off to find a bus. 'I have been sitting on the plane from Paris next to a man who says he has been blowing up the King David Hotel. Among other things.' The policeman hesitates. He glances at his partner. They examine me. My appearance, tired and cross, does not impress.

'So this man told you he'd been blowing up this hotel?'

'Yes.'

'Do you know him?'

'No.'

'So he was telling a perfect stranger that he had been committing murder and treason and God knows what in Jerusalem?'

'Oh, forget it.'

But of course that would not be the end, and I'd have to hang around while sceptical officials questioned. If they didn't decide I was simply daft.

'There, there, just you run along home, dear, and forget all about it.'

The thing was—and is—I am sure he was telling the truth. Or—perhaps even more interesting—he had imagined it all so strongly, the blowing up of the hotel, the murder of policemen, that for him it was all true and had to be shared, even if only with a stranger in the next seat on an aeroplane.

I went to Dublin too, invited by writers, I am sure, for there was a convivial evening. But that is not what I remember most, what I cannot forget. I was just over a year out of all that sunlight, that dry heat, and I thought I had experienced everything in the way of dismalness and greyness in London, but suddenly I was in this city of old, unkempt buildings, and dignified, a city proud of itself, but everywhere ran about ragged children, with bare feet, legs red with cold, hungry faces. Never has there been such a poor place as Dublin then, and it was a sharp, biting poverty, which afflicted the writers too, for one of them pressed into my hands a book called *Leaves for the Burning,* unjustly forgotten, by Mervin Wall, the account of a drunken weekend, but this was the drinking of desperation. That city of rags and hunger had disappeared when I went again less than ten years later.

I reviewed *Leaves for the Burning* somewhere, probably *John O'London's Weekly.* Now, that was an interesting periodical. It was the product of a now defunct culture, or sub-culture. All over Britain then, in towns, in villages, were groups of mostly young people, drawn together by love of literature. They read books, they discussed books, they met in pubs and in each other's houses. Some of them aspired to write, but that was long before the time when anyone who had read a novel aspired to write one. *John O'London* was not highbrow, it was nowhere near the level of, let's say, *The London Review of Books* now. But it had standards and was jealous of them, printed verses, had literary competitions—a pity there is nothing like it now. Another periodical served the short story: *The Argosy.* It was serious enough, within limits. It would not, for instance, print a story by Camus or a piece by Virginia Woolf, but I remember enjoyable tales. This, too, had a readership far beyond London; its real strength was provincial literary culture. Another lost and gone magazine was *Lilliput,* a lively compendium of tales, odd pieces, pictures. It was edited for a while by Patrick Campbell, who will be remembered now as the man who in spite of—you'd think—an incapacitating stammer was on television, in panel games. A story of mine went into *Lilliput.* On the strength of it we had several lunches in L'Escargot, long and alcoholic lunches, as were then a perk for both writer and editor. L'Escargot has gone through several transmutations, even an unfortunate one as nou-velle cuisine, but it was a mystery then that often we were the only people eating there at lunchtime. In the evenings it was crammed.

A visiting American said, did I read science fiction? I offered Olaf Stapledon, H. G. Wells, Jules Verne, and he said it was a good beginning. Then he gave me an armful of science fiction novels. What I felt then I have felt ever since. I was excited by their scope, the wideness of their horizons, the ideas, and the possibilities for social criticism—particularly in this time of McCarthy, when the atmosphere was so thick and hostile to new ideas in the United States—and disappointed by the level of characterisation and the lack of subtlety. My mentor said, But of course you can't have sub-tlety of character, which depends on a cultural matrix, if the hero is pioneering engineer Dick Tantrix No. 65092 on the artificial planet Andromeda, Sector 25,000. Very well, but I have always felt that a sci-fi novel is yet to be written using density of characterisation, like Henry James. It would be great comedy, for a start. But if what we do get is so wonderfully inventive and astonishing and mind-boggling, then why repine? In science fiction are some of the best stories of our time. To open a sci-fi novel, or to be with science fiction writers, if you've just come from a sojourn in the conventional literary world, is like opening windows into a stuffy and old-fashioned little room.

My new tutor said he would take me to a pub where science fiction writers went. He did. It must have been the White Horse in Fetter Lane, off Fleet Street. There was a room full of bespectacled lean men who turned as one to look warily at me—a *masculine* atmosphere. No, the word suggests a sexual lordliness. 'Blokeish', then? No, too homespun and ordinary. This was a clan, a group, a family, but without women. I felt I should not be there, though chaperoned by my American, whom they knew and welcomed. What they were was defensive: this was because they had been so thoroughly rejected by the literary world. They had the facetiousness, the jokiness, of their defensiveness. I babbled absurdly about Nietzsche's Superman, and the Revelations, and they were embarrassed. I like to think the great Arthur C. Clarke was there, but he had probably left for the States by then.

My disappointment with what I thought of as a dull group of people, suburban, provincial, was my fault. In that prosaic room, in that very ordinary pub, was going on the most advanced thinking in this country. (The Astronomer Royal had said it would be ridiculous to think that we could send people to the moon.) What these men were talking about, thinking about, were satellite communications, rocketry, spacecraft and space travel, the social uses of television. They were linked with people like themselves across the world: 'The Earth is the cradle of Mankind, but you cannot live in a cradle for ever.'—Konstantin Tsiolkovsky. 'We are living,' said Arthur C. Clarke, 'in a moment unique in all history—the last days of Man's existence as a citizen of a single planet.' My trouble was that I didn't have mathematics, physics—couldn't speak their language. Because of my ignorance, I know I have been cut off from the developments going on in science—and science is where our frontiers are, in this time. It is not to the latest literary novel that people now look for news about humanity, as they did in the nineteenth century.

When lists are made of the best British writers since the war, they do not include Arthur C. Clarke, nor Brian Aldiss, nor any of the good science fiction writers. It is conventional literature that has turned out to be provincial.

And so I had made a life for me and for Peter. That was an achievement, and I was proud of myself. The most important part was Peter, who was enjoying this life, particularly the nursery school, in Kensington, and then the family atmosphere with Joan and Ernest. Never has there been a child so ready to make friends. Our days still began at five. Again I was reading to him and telling him stories for a couple of hours after he woke, because Joan's bedroom was immediately below, and the floors were thin, and she did not wake till later. Or he listened to the radio. We have forgotten the role radio played before television. Peter loved the radio. He listened to everything. He listened to two radio plays based on novels by Ivy Compton-Burnett, each an hour long, standing by the machine, absolutely riveted. What was he hearing? Understanding? I have no idea. It is my belief that children are full of understanding and know as much as and more than adults, until they are about seven, when they suddenly become stupid, like adults. At three or four, Peter understood everything, and at eight or nine read only comics. And I've seen this again and again with small children. A child of three sits entranced through the film *2001: A Space Odyssey,* but four years later can tolerate only Rupert Bear.

I was writing *Martha Quest,* a conventional novel, though the demand then was for experimental novels. I played in my mind with a hundred ways of doing *Martha Quest,* pulling shapes about, playing with time, but at the end of all this, the novel was straightforward. I was dealing with my painful adolescence, my mother, all that anguish, the struggle for survival.

And now there arrived a letter from my mother, saying she was coming to London, she was going to live with me and help me with

Peter, and—here was the inevitable, surreal, heartbreaking ingredient—she had taught herself typing and would be my secretary.

I collapsed. I simply went to bed and pulled the covers over my head. When I had taken Peter to nursery school, I crept away into the dark of my bed and stayed there until I had to bring him home.

And now—again—there is the question of time, tricksy time, and until I came to write this and was forced to do my work with calendars and obdurate dates, I had thought, vaguely, that I was in Denbigh Road for . . . well, it was probably three years or so. But that was because, having been returned to child seeing, everything new and immediate, I had been returned—well, partly—to child time. No matter how I wriggled and protested, No, it *can't* have been only a year, it *was* a year before I went to Joan's, and I had been there only six months or so when the letter came from my mother. Yet those months seem now like years. Time is different at different times in one's life. A year in your thirties is much shorter than a child's year—which is almost endless—but long compared with a year in your forties; whereas a year in your seventies is a mere blink.

Of course she was bound to come after me. How could I have been so naive as to think she wouldn't, as soon as she could? She had been in exile in Southern Rhodesia, dreaming of London, and now . . . She and her daughter did not 'get on,' or, to put it truthfully, had always fought? Oh, never mind, the girl was wrongheaded; she would learn to listen to her mother. She was a communist? She always had disreputable friends? That was all right; her mother would introduce her to really nice people. She had written *The Grass Is Singing,* which had caused her mother anguish and shame, because it was so hated by the whites? And those extremely unfair short stories about The District? Well, she—the girl's mother—would explain to everyone that no one outside the country could really understand the whites' problems and . . . But the author had been brought up in the country? Her views were *wrong,* and in time she would come to see that. . . . She proposed to live with a daughter who had broken up her first marriage, leaving two children, had married a German refugee at the height of the war, who was a kaffir-lover and scornful of religion?

Well, how *did* she see it? Now I believe she did not think about it much. She could not afford to. She longed to live in London again, but it was the London she had left in 1919. She had no friends left, except for Daisy Lane, with whom she had been exchanging letters, but Daisy Lane was now an old lady, living in Richmond with her sister, an ex-missionary from Japan. There was her brother's family, and she was coming home in time for the daughter's wedding. Her brother's sister-in-law had already said, 'I hope Jane doesn't imagine she is going to take first place at the wedding.' (Jane: Plain Jane, the loving family nickname, making sure that Maude didn't imagine she possessed any attractions.) And had written to my mother saying she must take a back seat.

Over twenty-five years: 1924 to 1950. That was then the term of my mother's exile in Africa. Now I have reached the age to understand that twenty-five years—or thirty—can seem nothing much, I know that for her time had contracted and that unfortunate experience, Africa, had become an irrelevance. But for me, just over thirty, it was the length of my conscious life, and my mother lived in, belonged to, Africa. Her yearnings after London pea-soupers and jolly tennis parties were mere whimsies.

How could she come after me like this? Yet of course she had been bound to. How could she imagine that . . . But she did. Soon she would toil up those impossible narrow stairs, smiling bravely, walk into my room, move the furniture about, look through my clothes and pronounce their unsuitability, look at the little safe on the wall—no fridge—and say the child was not getting enough to eat.

It was at this point Moidi Jokl entered into my life, an intervention so providential that even now I marvel at it.

Moidi was one of the first refugees from communism in London, then still full of refugees from the war, all surviving as they could. She had been Viennese, a communist, a friend of the men who after the war came back from the Soviet Union or wherever else they had been existing, biding their time, to become the government of East Germany. She went to East Germany because she had been their close friend. Then she had been thrown out, because she was Jewish, a victim of Stalin's rage against the Jews, referred to then as the 'Black Years'. I have never understood why those victims have never been honoured and remembered by Jews. Everything has been swallowed up by the Holocaust—but all over the Soviet Union, and in all the communist countries of East Europe, Jews were murdered, tortured, persecuted, imprisoned; it was a deliberate genocide. But for some reason Stalin's deliberate mass murders are never condemned as Hitler's are, although Stalin's crimes are much more, both in number and in variety. Bad luck about those poor Jews of the years 1948, 1949, 1950, 1951, 1952. No one thinks of them—many thousands, perhaps millions?

Moidi was escorted to that East German frontier by a young policeman in tears: he did not like what he was doing.

Gottfried had by this time visited East Berlin, had found his sister and her husband (the eternal student) working in the Kulturbund, and decided to go back to Germany. He had formally applied to the Party for permission to return home but could get no reply to his letters. Moidi Jokl told him he did not understand the first thing about communism. It all worked on whom you knew—this was later called *blat*. He should get himself over there, pull strings, and he had a chance of being allowed to stay. Not more than a chance. Anyone from the West was considered a criminal and an enemy, and might easily disappear for ever. Never have I heard such vituperation: Gottfried loathed Moidi. But he did take her advice, went back, pulled strings, and survived.

And then there was Peter. Moidi took a good look at my situation with Peter, shut up with me far too often, for long hours in that tiny flat. She had friends, the Eichners, also Austrians, refugees, who lived near East Grinstead. They had several children and were very poor. They lived in an old house on a couple of acres of rough rocky land and took in children at holiday times, up to twenty sometimes, and they all had a very good time. So Peter began to spend days, or a weekend, or—later—a couple of weeks, with the Eichners. I would put him on a coach at Victoria, and at the other end he became one of a gang of country children. This arrangement could not have been better for him, or for me.

And then, Moidi saw the state I was in because of my mother's imminent arrival and told me I should go to a friend of hers, Mrs.

Sussman (Mother Sugar in *The Golden Notebook*), because if I didn't get some help, I would not survive. She was right. These days, everyone goes to a therapist, or is a therapist, but then no one did. Not in England, only in America, and even there the phenomenon was in its infancy. And particularly communists did not go 'into analysis', for it was 'reactionary' by definition, or rather without the need for definition. I was so desperate I went. I went two or three times a week, for about three years. I think it saved me. The process was full of the wildest anomalies or ironies—the communist word 'contradictions' seems too mild. First, Mrs. Sussman was a Roman Catholic, and Jungian, and while I liked Jung, as all artists do, I had no reason to love Roman Catholics. She was Jewish, and her husband, a dear old man, like a Rembrandt portrait, was a Jewish scholar. But she had converted to Roman Catholicism. This fascinated me, the improbability of it, but she said my wanting to discuss it was merely a sign of my evading real issues. Enough, she said, that Roman Catholicism had deeper and higher levels of understanding, infinitely removed from the crudities of the convent. (And Judaism did not have such higher reaches or peaks? 'We were talking about your father, I think, my dear. Shall we go on?') Mrs. Sussman specialised in unblocking artists who were blocked, could not write or paint or compose. This is what she saw as her mission in life. But I did not suffer from a 'block'. She wanted to discuss my work. I did not want to. I did not see the need for it. So she was perpetually frustrated, bringing up the subject, while I deflected her. Mrs. Sussman was a cultivated, civilised, wise old woman, who gave me what I needed, which was support. Mostly support against my mother. When the pressures came on, all of them intolerable, because my mother was so pathetic, so lonely, so full of emotional blackmail—quite unconscious, for it was her situation that undermined me—Mrs. Sussman simply said, 'If you don't stand firm now, it will be the end of you. And the end of Peter too.'

My mother was . . . but I have forgotten which archetype my mother was. She was one, I know. Mrs. Sussman would often bring some exchange to a close: She, he, is such and such an archetype . . . or is one at this time. I, for example, at various times was Electra, Antigone, Medea. The trouble was, while I was instinctively happy with the idea of archetypes, those majestic eternal figures, rising from literature and myth like stone shapes created by Nature out of rock and mountain, I hated the labels. Unhappy with communism, I was unhappiest with its language, with the labelling of everything, and the vindictive or automatic stereotypes, and here were more of them, whether described romantically as 'archetypes' or not. I did not see why she minded my criticisms, for she liked the dreams I 'brought' her. Psychotherapists are like doctors and nurses who treat patients like children: 'Just a little spoonful *for me.*' 'Put out your tongue *for me.*' When we have a dream, it is 'for' the therapist. Often it is: I swear I dreamed dreams to please her, after we had been going along for a while. But at my very first session she had asked for dreams, preferably serial dreams, and she was pleased with my ancient-lizard dream and the dreams I was having about my father, who, too shallowly buried in a forest, would emerge from his grave, or attract wolves who came down from the hills to dig him up. 'These are typically Jungian dreams,' she would say gently, flushed with pleasure. 'Sometimes it can take years to get someone to dream a dream on that level.' Whereas 'Jungian' dreams had been my night landscape for as long as I could remember, I had not had 'Freudian' dreams. She said she used Freud when it was appropriate, and that was, I gathered, when the patient was still at a very low level of individuation. She made it clear that she thought I was.★

'Jungian dreams'—wonderful, those layers of ancient common experience, but what was the use of that if I had to go to bed with the covers over my head at the news my mother was about to arrive? Here I was. Here I am, Mrs. Sussman. Do what you will with me, but for God's sake, cure me.

I needed support for other reasons.

One of them was my lover. Moidi Jokl suggested that I should go with her one evening to a party, and there I met a man I was destined—so I felt then—to live with, and to have and to hold and be happy with.

Yes, he had a name. But as always, there is the question of chil-

★'Freudian' dreams are altogether more personal and petty.

dren and grandchildren. Since *Under My Skin* came out, I have met not a few grandchildren, children, of my old mates from those far-off times and learned that the views of contemporaries about each other need not share much with the views of their children. Whole areas of a parent's, let alone a grandparent's, life can be unknown to them. And why not? Children do not own their parents' lives, though they—and I too—jealously pore over them as if they hold the key to their own.

I say to a charming young man who has come to lunch to discuss his father, 'When James was working on the mines on the Rand—'

'Oh, I'm sure he never did that,' comes the confident reply.

To another: 'You didn't know your father was a great lover of women?' A faintly derisive smile, meaning: What, that old stick? So then of course you shut up; after all, it has nothing to do with him.

I will call this man Jack. He was a Czech. He had worked as a doctor with our armies throughout the war. He was—what else?—a communist.

He fell in love with me, jealously, hungrily, even angrily—with that particular degree of anger that means a man is in conflict. I did not at once fall in love with him. At the start, what I loved was his loving me so much: a nice change after Gottfried. The way I saw this—*felt* this—was that now I was ready for the right man: my 'mistakes' were over, and I was settled in London, where I intended to stay. All my experiences had programmed me for domesticity. I might now tell myself—and quite rightly—that I had never been 'really' married to Frank Wisdom, but for four years we had a conventional marriage. Gottfried and I had hardly been well matched, but we had lived conventionally enough. The law and society saw me as a woman who had had two marriages and two divorces. I *felt* that these marriages did not count. I had been too young, too immature. The fact that the bouncy, affectionate, almost casual relationship I had had with Frank was hardly unusual—particularly in those war years, when people married far too easily—did not mean I did not aspire to better. With Gottfried it had been a political marriage. I would not have married Gottfried if the internment camp was not still a threat. Then, people were always marrying to give someone a name, a passport, a place; in London there were organisations for precisely this—to rescue threatened people from Europe. But now, in these luckier times, people have forgotten that such marriages were hardly uncommon. No, my *real* emotional life was all before me. And I had all the talents needed for intimacy. I was born to live companionably—and passionately—with the right man, and here he was.

Jack had been one of thirteen children, the youngest, of a very poor family in Czechoslovakia. He had had to walk miles to school and back—just like Africans now in many parts of Africa. They scarcely had enough to eat or to cover themselves with. This was a common enough story, then, in Europe—and in some parts of Britain too: people don't want to remember the frightful poverty in Britain in the twenties and thirties. Jack had become a communist in his early teens, like all his schoolfellows. He was a real communist, for whom the Party was a home, a family, the future, his deepest and sanest self. He wasn't at all like me—who had had choices. When I met him, his closest friends in Czechoslovakia, the friends of his youth, the top leadership of the Czech Communist Party, had just been made to stand in the eyes of the world as traitors to communism, and then eleven of them were hanged, Stalin the invisible stage manager. For Jack it had been as if the foundations of the world had collapsed. It was impossible for these old friends to have been traitors, and he did not believe it. On the other hand, it was impossible for the Party to have made a mistake. He had nightmares, he wept in his sleep. Like Gottfried Lessing. Again I shared a bed with a man who woke from nightmares.

That was the second cataclysmic event of his life. His entire family—mother, father, and all his siblings, except one sister who had escaped to America—had died in the gas chambers.

This story is a terrible one. It was terrible then, but taken in the context of that time, not worse than many others. In 1950 in London, everybody I met had come out of the army from battlefields in Burma, Europe, Italy, Yugoslavia, had been present when the concentration camps were opened, had fought in the Spanish war or was a refugee and had survived horrors. With my background, the Trenches and the nastiness of the First World War dinned into me day and night through my childhood, Jack's story was felt by me as a continuation: *Well, what can you expect?*

We understood each other well. We had everything in common. Now I assess the situation in a way I would then have found 'cold'. I look at a couple and I think, Are they suited emotionally . . . physically . . . mentally? Jack and I were suited in all three ways, but perhaps most emotionally, sharing a natural disposition towards the grimmest understanding of life and events that in its less severe manifestations is called irony. It was our situations, not our natures, that were incompatible. I was ready to settle down for ever with this man. He had just come back from the war, to find his wife, whom he had married long years before, a stranger, and children whom he hardly knew.

It is a commonplace among psychiatrists that a young woman who has been close to death, has cut her wrists too often, or has been threatened by parents, must buy clothes, be obsessed with clothes and with the ordering of her appearance, puzzling observers with what seems like a senseless profligacy. It is life she is keeping in order.

And a man who has been running a step ahead of death for years—if Jack had stayed in Czechoslovakia it is likely he would have been hanged as a traitor, together with his good friends, if he hadn't already perished in the gas chambers—such a man will be forced by a hundred powerful needs to sleep with women, have women, assert life, make life, move on.

In no way can I—or could I then—accuse Jack of letting me down, for he never promised anything. On the contrary, short of actually saying, 'I am sleeping with other women; I have no intention of marrying you,' he said it all. Often joking. But I wasn't listening. What I *felt* was: When we get on so wonderfully in every possible way, then it isn't sensible for him to go away from me. I wasn't able to think at all; the emotional realities were too powerful. I think this is quite common with women. 'Really, this man is talking nonsense, he doesn't know what is right for him. And besides, he says himself his marriage is no marriage at all. And obviously it can't be, when he is here most nights.' How easy to be intelligent now, how impossible then.

If I needed support against my mother, soon I needed it because of Jack too. He was a psychiatrist at the Maudsley Hospital. He had wanted to be a neurologist, but when he started being a doctor in Britain, neurology was fashionable and 'a member of a distant country of which we know nothing' could not compete with so many British doctors, crowding to get in. So he went into psychiatry, then unfashionable. But soon it became chic, even more so than neurology. He was a far from uncritical practitioner. He was no fan of Freud, and this was not only because as a communist—or even an ex-communist—he was bound to despise Freud. He said Freud was unscientific, and this at a time when to attack Freud was like attacking Stalin—or God. One of my liveliest memories is of how he took me to Oxford to listen to Hans Eysenck lecture to an audience composed almost entirely of doctors from the Maudsley, all of them Freudians, about the unscientific nature of psychoanalysis. There he was, this large, bouncing young man, with his thick German accent, telling a roomful of the angriest people I remember that their idol had faults. (He has not lost his capacity to annoy: when I told a couple of young psychiatrists this tale, thinking it might amuse them—in 1994—their cold response was: 'He always was unsound.') Jack admired him. He knew psychoanalysis had feet of clay. This scepticism included Mrs. Sussman: And if Freud was unscientific, what could be said of Jung? But I didn't go to Mrs. Sussman for ideology, I said. And anyway, she used a pragmatic mix of Freud, Jung, Klein, and anything else that might come in appropriately. He did not find this persuasive; he said that all artists like Jung, but this had nothing to do with science: why not just go off and listen to lectures on Greek mythology? It would do just as well. He was unimpressed by my 'Jungian' dreams. And even less when I began dreaming 'Freudian' dreams. And I was uneasy myself. I was dreaming dreams to order. No one need persuade me of the influence a therapist has on a confused, frightened suppliant for enlightenment. One needs to please that mentor, half mother, half father, the possessor of all knowledge, sitting so powerfully there in that chair. 'And now, my dear, what do you have to tell me today?'

Some things I wouldn't dare tell Jack. For instance, about that day when she remarked, after nothing had been said for a few minutes, 'I am sure you do know that we are communicating even when we are not saying anything.' This remark, at that time, was simply preposterous. As far as she was concerned, I was a communist and therefore bound to dismiss any thoughts of that kind as 'mystical nonsense'. She was not talking about body language (that phrase, and the skills of interpreting people's postures, gestures, and so forth, came much later). She was talking about an interchange between minds. As soon as she said it, I thought, Well, yes . . . accepting this heretical idea as if it was my birthright. But to say this to Jack . . . For though he might have been, now, painfully—and for him it had to be painful—critical of communism, he was a Marxist, and 'mystical' ideas were simply inadmissible.

Jack attacked me for going to Mrs. Sussman at all. He said I was a big girl now and I should simply tell my mother to go off and live her own life. She was healthy, wasn't she? She was strong? She had enough money to live on?

My mother's situation was causing me anguish. She was living pitifully in a nasty little suburb with George Laws, a distant cousin of my father's. He was old, he was an invalid, and they could have nothing in common. She kept up a steady pressure to live with me. There was nowhere else for her. She found her brother's family—he had died—as unlikeable as she always had. She actually had very little money. Common sense, as she kept saying, would have us sharing a flat and expenses, and besides, I needed help with Peter. Her sole reason for existence, she said, was to help me with Peter. And she took Peter for weekends, sometimes, and on trips. From one, to the Isle of Wight, he returned baptised. She informed me that this had been her duty. I did not even argue. There was never any point. And of course it was very good, for me, when I could go off with Jack for three days. At these times she moved into the Church Street flat, where the stairs were almost beyond her. Joan did not mind my mother; she simply said, But she's a typical middle-class matron, that's all. Just as I didn't mind her mother, with whom she found it difficult to get on. I could listen to her self-pitying, wailing tales of her life dispassionately—this was social history, hard times brought off the page into a tale of a beautiful

Jewish girl from the poor East End of London surviving among artists and writers.

Jack said I should simply put my foot down with my mother, once and for all.

Joan was also involved—a good noncommittal word—with psychotherapy. Various unsuccessful attempts had ended in her returning from a session to say that no man who had such appalling taste in art and whose house smelled of overcooked cabbage could possibly know anything about the human soul. That was good for a laugh or two, as so many painful things are.

Joan saw her main problem as the inability to focus her talents. She had many. She drew well—like Käthe Kollwitz, as people told her: this was before Kollwitz had been accepted by the artistic establishment. She danced well. She had acted professionally. She wrote well. Perhaps she had too many talents. But whatever the reason, she could not narrow herself into any one channel of accomplishment. And here I was, in her house, getting good reviews, with three books out. She was critical of Jack, and of me because of how I brought up Peter. I was too lax and laissez-faire, and treated him like a grown-up. It was not enough to read to him and tell him stories; he needed . . . well, what? I thought she criticised me because of dissatisfaction over her son, for no woman can bring up a son without a full-time father around and not feel at a disadvantage. And then I was such a colonial, and graceless, and perhaps she found that hardest of all. Small things are the most abrasive. An incident: I have invited people to Sunday lunch, and among the foods I prepare are Scotch eggs, this being a staple of buffet food in Southern Africa. Joan stands looking at them, dismayed. 'But *why,*' she demands, 'when there's a perfectly good delicatessen down the street?' She criticised me—or so it felt—for everything. Yet this criticism of others was the obverse of her wonderful kindness and charity, the two things in harness. And it was nothing beside her criticism of herself, for she continued to denigrate herself in everything.

To withstand the pressure of this continual disapproval, I got more defensive and more cool. Yes, this was a repetition of my situation with my mother, and of course it came up in talk with Mrs.

Sussman, who was hearing accounts of the same incidents from both of us, Box and Cox, and supported us both. Not an easy thing. One afternoon Joan came rushing up the stairs to accuse me of having pushed her over the cliff.

'What?'

'I was dreaming you pushed me over the cliff.'

When I told Mrs. Sussman, she said, 'Then you did push her over the cliff.'

Joan was unable to see that I found her overpowering because I admired her. She was everything in the way of chic, self-confidence, and general worldly experience that I was not. And years later, when I told her that this was how I had seen her, she was incredulous.

Jack saw her as a rival—or so it seemed to me—for if she criticised him, then he criticised her. 'Why don't you get your own place? Why do you need a mother figure?' He did not see that being in Joan's house protected me from my mother, or that it was perfect for Peter.

Jack thought I was too protective of Peter. He found it difficult to get on with his son and said frankly that he was not going to be a father to Peter.

This was perhaps the worst thing about this time. I knew how Peter yearned for a father, and I watched this little boy, so open and affectionate with everyone, run to Jack and put up his arms—but he was rebuffed, his arms gently replaced by his sides, while Jack asked him grown-up questions, so that he had to return sober, careful replies, while he searched Jack's face with wide, strained, anxious eyes. He had never experienced anything like this, from anyone.

The difficulties between Joan and me were no more than were inevitable, with two females, both used to their independence, living in the same house. We got on pretty well. We sat often over her kitchen table, gossiping: people, men, the world, the comrades—this last increasingly critical. In fact, gossiping with Joan over the kitchen table is one of my pleasantest memories. We both cooked well; gentle competition went on over the meals we prepared. The talk was of the kind I later used in *The Golden Notebook*.

A scene: Joan said she wanted me to see something. 'I'm not going to tell you; just come.' In a little house in a little street two minutes' walk away, we found ourselves in a little room crammed with valuable furniture and pictures and, too, people. Four people filled it, and Joan stood at the doorway, me just behind, and waved to a languorous woman lying on a chaise longue, dressed in a frothy peignoir. A man bent over her, offering champagne: he was a former husband. Another, a current lover, fondled her feet. A very young man, flushed, excited, adoring, was waiting his chance. No room for us, so we said goodbye, and she called, 'Do come again, darlings, any time. I get so down all by myself here.' She was afflicted by a mysterious fatigue that kept her supine. It appeared that she was kept by two former husbands and the current lover. 'Now, you tell me,' says Joan, laughing, as we walk home. 'What are we doing wrong? And she isn't even all that pretty.' We returned, worrying, to our overburdened lives.

There we were, two or three times a week, discussing our own behaviour, and each other's, with Mrs. Sussman, but now all that rummaging about among the roots of our motives, then so painful and difficult, seems less important than, 'I've just bought some croissants. Want to join me?' Or, 'Have you heard the news—it's awful. Want a chat?' What I liked best was hearing her talk about the artists and writers she knew because of her father and of working in the Party. I used to be impressed by her worldly wisdom. For instance, about David Bomberg, who had painted her father; he was then ignored by the artistic establishment: 'Oh, don't worry, they're always like this, but they'll see the error of their ways when he's dead.' Quite calm, she was, whereas I went in for indignation. And David Bomberg lived in poverty all his life, unrecognised, and then he died and it happened as she said. Or she would come from a party and say that Augustus John was there, and she'd told the young girls, 'Better watch out, and don't let him talk you into sitting for him,' for by then Augustus John had become a figure of fun. Or she had been in the pub used by Louis MacNeice and George Barker, near the BBC, and she had been in the BBC persuading Reggie Smith, always generous to young writers, to take a look at this or that manuscript. She was one of the organisers of the Soho Square Fair in 1954, and they must have had a good time of it. I'd hear her loud jolly laugh and her voice up the stairs: 'You'd never believe what's happened. I'll tell you tomorrow.'

It was Joan who persuaded me to perform my 'revolutionary duty' in various ways. I organised a petition for the Rosenbergs, condemned to die in the electric chair for spying. As usual I was in a thoroughly false position. Everyone in the Communist Party believed, or said they did, that the Rosenbergs were innocent. I thought they were guilty, though I had no idea they were as important as spies as it turned out. Someone had told me this story: A woman living in New York, a communist, had got herself a job on *Time* magazine, then an object of vituperative hatred by communists everywhere because it 'told lies' about the Soviet Union. A Party official, met casually, said she should keep her ears and eyes open and report to the Party about the goings-on inside *Time*. She agreed, quite casually. Then, suddenly, there was spy fever. It occurred to her that she could be described as a spy. At first she told herself, Nonsense, surely it can't be spying to tell a legal political party, in a democratic country, what is going on inside a newspaper. But the papers instructed her otherwise, and in a panic she left her job. In that paranoid atmosphere there could be no innocent communists. I thought the Rosenbergs had probably said, Oh yes, of course, we'll tell you if there's anything interesting going on.

Not only did I think they were guilty, but that the letters they were writing out of prison were mawkish, and obviously written as propaganda to appear in newspapers. Yet the comrades thought they were deeply moving, and these were people who, in any other context but a political one, would have had the discrimination to know they were false and hypocritical.

An important, not to say basic, point is illustrated here. Here we were, committed to every kind of murder and mayhem by definition: you can't make an omelette without breaking eggs. Yet at any suggestion that dirty work was going on, most communists reacted with indignation. *Of course* So-and-so wasn't really a spy; *of course* the Party did not take gold from Moscow; *of course* this or that wasn't a cover-up. The Party represented the purest of humankind's hopes for the future—*our* hopes—and could not be anything other than pure.

My attitude to the Rosenbergs was simple. They had small children and should not be executed, even if guilty. The letters I got back from writers and intellectuals mostly said that they did not see why they should sign a petition for the Rosenbergs when the Party refused to criticise the Soviet Union for its crimes.

I did not see the relevance: it was morally wrong to execute Ethel and Julius Rosenberg. I was again in the position of public and embattled communist; I was getting hate letters and anonymous telephone calls. In times of violent political emotion, issues like the Rosenbergs attract so much anger and hate that soon it is hard to remember that under all this noise and propaganda is a simple choice of right and wrong. And after all these years, there is still something inexplicable about this case. Soon there would be many spies exposed in Britain and America, some of them betraying their country for money, some sending dozens of fellow citizens to their deaths, yet not one of them was hanged or sent to the chair. The Rosenbergs' crime was much less, and they were parents with young children. Some people think it was because they were Jewish. Others—I among them—wonder if their condemners got secret pleasure from the idea of a young, plump woman being 'fried'. There are issues that are very much more than the sum of their parts, and this was one.

Another 'duty' I undertook at Joan's behest was the Sheffield Peace Conference. My job was to go around to houses and hand out leaflets, extolling this festival. I was met at every door with a sullen, cold rejection. The newspapers were saying that the festival was Soviet inspired and financed—and of course it was, but we indignantly denied it and believed our denials. It was a truly nasty experience, perhaps the worst of my revolutionary duties. It was cold, it was grey, no one could describe Sheffield as beautiful, and I had not yet experienced the full blast of British citizens' hostility to anything communist.*

*The Sheffield Conference, November 1950, never took place, because the incoming delegates were refused visas; it was transferred to Warsaw.

With Jack I went on two trips to Paris. The little story 'Wine' sums up one. We sat in a café on the Boulevard St.-Germain and watched mobs of students surge shouting past, overturning cars. What was their grievance? Overturning cars is a peculiarly French means of self-expression: Jack had seen the same thing before the war, and I saw it again on a much later visit.

Another incident, the same trip, another café: We are sitting on the pavement, drinking coffee. Towards us comes, or sweeps, a wonderfully dressed woman, with her little dog. She is a *poule,* luxurious, perfect, and no, you don't see prostitutes looking like that in Paris now. Jack is watching her, full of regret and admiration. He says to me in a low voice, 'God, just look, only the French . . .' Coming level with us, she pauses long enough to stare with contempt at Jack and say, '*Vous êtes très mal élevé, monsieur.*' You are very ill-bred, sir. Or, You are a boor. And she sweeps past.

'But why present yourself like that if you don't want to be noticed?' says Jack. (This is surely a question of much wider relevance.) 'But if one did have the money for a woman like that, would one dare to touch her? I might upset her hairdo.'

On the second visit, we were in a dark cellar-like room, where a reverent audience, all French, watched a pale woman in a long black dress with a high collar, unmade up except for tragic black-rimmed eyes, sing 'Je ne regrette rien' and other songs that now seem the essence of that time. (This style would shortly become the fashion.) What it sounded like was a defiant lament for the war, for the Occupation. On the streets of Paris then you kept coming on a pile of wreaths, or bunches of flowers on a pavement, under bullet holes, and a notice: Such and such young men were shot here by the Germans. And you stopped, too, in an anguish of fellow feeling, not unpoisoned by a pleasurable relish in the drama of it.

And we went to the theatre, to see Brecht's company, the Berliner Ensemble, put on *Mother Courage.* No German company had yet dared to put a play on in Paris. Jack said he thought there would be a riot: Germans so soon; surely that was too much of a risk; but we should go. It would be a historical occasion. After all, it was Brecht. The first night: the theatre was packed, people standing, and outside there were too many policemen. Things did not go smoothly. There had been time only for an inadequate rehearsal. That story of war, so apt for the time and place, unfolded in silence. No one stirred. There was a hitch with the props, and still no one moved. No interval, because everything was dragging on so late. Soon the silence became unbearable: Did it mean they hated it? that the audience would go rioting onto the stage for some sort of reprisal or revenge? When the play ended, with the words 'Take me with you, take me with you,' and the disreputable old woman, stripped of everything, again tried to follow the army, there was something like a groan from the French. Silence, silence, no one moved, it went on—and then the audience were on their feet, roaring, shouting, applauding, weeping, embracing, and the actors stood on the stage and wept. It all went on for a good twenty minutes. About halfway through, that demonstration stopped being spontaneous and became Europe conscious of itself, defeated and disgraced Germany crying out to Europe, Take me with you, take me with you.

I've never had an experience like that in the theatre, and it taught me once and for all that a play can have its perfect occasion, as if it had been written for that performance alone. I've seen other productions of *Mother Courage* since.

Later the Canadian writer Ted Allan told me that when Brecht was a refugee in California, he was baby-sitting for the Allans. He asked Ted to read the just completed *Mother Courage,* and Ted did, and told Brecht it was promising but needed this and that. Helene Weigel was indignant. 'It's a masterpiece,' she said. Ted used to tell this story against himself, polishing it, as befits a real storyteller. His criticisms of Brecht became more crass, a parody of Hollywood film-makers. 'Get rid of that old bitch. You've got to sex it up. You need a babe there. I've got it—how about a nun. No, a novice, real young. Let's see . . . Lana Turner . . . Vivien Leigh . . .'

One trip with Jack was to Spain for a month. This was our longest yet. My mother stayed with Peter for part of it, Joan had him for a week, he was with the Eichners for the rest. We had very little money. Jack was not a senior doctor, and he had a family to keep. Could we each manage twenty-five pounds? The trip, with expenses for the car, travel, cost us fifty pounds. We ate bread and sausage and green peppers and tomatoes and grapes. I can't smell green peppers that still have the heat of the sun in them without being encompassed by memories of that trip. As you crossed the frontier from France, it was to go back into the nineteenth century. This was before tourism started. As we drove into the towns, like Salamanca, Avila, Burgos, crowds pressed forward to see the foreigners. Ragged boys competed to guard the car: sixpence for a day or a night. When we did actually eat in a cheap restaurant, hungry children pressed their faces against the glass. For Jack, we were driving through ghostly memories of the Spanish Civil War: he had lived, in his imagination, through every stage of every battle. He had suffered because of the betrayal of the elected Spanish government by Britain and France: for him and people like him, that was when World War II had begun. Now he was suffering over the hungry children, remembering his own childhood. He was angry to see the streets full of black-robed fat priests and the police in their black uniforms, with their guns. Spain was so poor then it broke your heart, just like Ireland.

And yet . . . We slept wrapped in blankets out in a field, in the open because of the stars. One morning, already hot, though the sun was just rising, we sat up in our blankets to see two tall dark men on tall black horses, each wearing a red blanket like a serape, riding past us and away across the fields, the hot blue sky behind them. They lifted their hands in greeting, unsmiling.

We ate our bread and olives and drank dark-red wine under olive trees or waited out the extreme heat of midday in some little church, where I had to be sure my arms were covered, and my head too.

We went to a bullfight, where Jack wept because of the six sacrificed bulls. He was muttering, Kill him, kill him, to the bulls.

In Madrid beggar women sat on the pavements with their feet in the gutters, and we gave them our cakes and ordered more for them.

We felt in the Alhambra that this was our place—the Alhambra affects people strongly: they hate it or adore it.

We quarrelled violently, and often. It is my belief and my experience that energetic and frequent sex breeds sudden storms of antagonism. Tolstoy wrote about this. So did D. H. Lawrence. Why should this be? We made love when we stopped the car in open and empty country, in dry ditches, in forests, in vineyards, in olive groves. And quarrelled. He was jealous. This was absurd, because I loved him. In a town in Murcia, where it was so hot we simply stopped for a whole day to sit in a café, in the shade if not the cool, he was convinced I was making eyes at a handsome Spaniard. This quarrel was so terrible that we went to a hotel for the night, because Jack, the doctor, said that our diet and lack of sleep was getting to us.

We drove from Gibraltar up the *costas,* where there were no hotels, not one, only a few fishermen at Nerja, who cooked us fish on the beach. We slept on the sand, looking at the stars, listening to the waves. Nothing was built between Gibraltar and Barcelona then; except for the towns, there were only empty, long, wonderful beaches, which in a year or so would become hotel-loaded playgrounds. Near Valencia, a sign said, 'Do Not Bathe Here—It Is Dangerous,' but I went into the tall enticing waves, and one of them picked me up and smashed me onto the undersea sand, and I crawled out, my ears full of sand and grit. Jack took me to the local hospital, where the two doctors communicated in Latin, proving that it is a far from dead language.

In high, windy Avila there were acres of wonderful brown jars and pots, standing on dry reeds. I bought the most beautiful jar I have ever owned, for a few pence.

What struck me most then, and surprises me even now, is the contrast between the wild, savage, empty beauty of Spain and the stuffy stolidity of even the cheap hotels we could afford, between the poverty we saw everywhere and the churches loaded with gold and jewels, as if all the wealth of the peninsula had come to rest in them.

We visited Germany, three times. The first was when I wanted to find Gottfried. Peter had gone the year before for a summer to visit his father. I had told Gottfried he must not have him do this unless he was sure he could keep it up. As usual he was contemptuous of my political acumen: of course he would be able to invite

Peter whenever he liked. I said I wasn't so sure; besides, Moidi Jokl said he was wrong. I turned out to be right. Germans who had spent the war abroad were suspect, and many vanished into Stalin's camps. I was angry, partly for the ignoble reason that I had been insulted and patronised by Gottfried for years about politics but in fact had been more often right, and he wrong. I was angry because of Peter, who had had a wonderfully kind father who had apparently dropped him.

Now I understand what happened. It was indeed a question of life and death. What I blame him for is for not smuggling out a little letter saying, I cannot afford to keep contact with the West; I might be killed for it. It would have been easy: there was a good deal of to-ing and fro-ing. Instead people would come back from some official trip to East Germany and say, I saw your handsome husband. He is a very important man. He sends you his love. 'He is not my husband,' I would say, 'and it is Peter who needs his love.' I hated East Berlin. For me it was like a distillation of everything bad about communism, but some comrades admired it. For years, right up to the time of the collapse of communism, they were saying, 'East Germany has got it right. It is economically in advance of any other communist country. What a pity the revolution didn't start in Germany.'

Another trip was to Hamburg. Jack wanted to find a friend who had disappeared in the war. He failed. Hamburg had been badly bombed and was still full of ruins. It was February, dark, very cold, with a bitter wind coming off the North Sea. Jack said there was a trade-union festival, a traditional one; we should join in. In the gaps between buildings, among ruins, burned great bonfires, and around them leaped and staggered or swayed very drunk people, with bottles in their hands, singing or rather howling songs from the war and traditional workers' songs. It was like Walpurgis Night. It was like Bosch. It was horrible. For years these scenes stayed in my mind, and then I returned to Hamburg after thirty years and told my publisher what I remembered, and he said, Impossible; nothing like that has ever happened here. You must be thinking of Berlin, or Munich.

And indeed I saw the ruins in Berlin, miles of them, and I stood where the Brandenburg Gate had been. Much later, thirty years later, I went back and there was not a sign of ruins; you'd think the war had never happened. I met people who had been children just after the war in Berlin, and apart from being permanently hungry, what they remembered was playing in the bombed houses. They thought that was what a city was—streets sometimes whole, sometimes in ruins. Later they went to undamaged cities. One of these, who as a child had been half starved, had survived because his mother was working for the Americans; he saw a film with Orson Welles in it and said, 'One day I'm going to eat as much as I like, and I'm going to be as fat as Orson Welles.' And that indeed came to pass, and then he was in trouble with his doctor and had to go on a diet.

I went on a trip with Jack to southern Germany. It is recorded in 'The Eye of God in Paradise'. The mood in Germany was so bad then, so low, so angry. The experience depressed me, and so did writing the story. Some Germans have reproached me for writing it, but the point of the story is not Germany but Europe: it was all of us I was thinking of, Europe building itself up, knocking itself down, building, destroying, building . . .

The nastiest of my recollections of Germany was of a woman coming up to me on a railway platform to complain that Germany had been divided. Her fatherland was cut in half. Did I know of this injustice? Was it fair? What had Germany done to be punished in this way? Other people came to join her, all assaulting me with voices full of the insincerity that goes with a consciously false position.

Jack went to Germany partly out of political conviction. As a Marxist he refused to believe in national characteristics, national guilt, but this was the country that had murdered nearly all his family.

I was full of conflict. I had been brought up on the First World War, and a good part of that was my father's passionate identification with the ordinary German soldiers, who were victims of their stupid government, just like the Tommies. I had been married to a refugee from Hitler's Germany. I had been brought up to believe that Hitler and the Nazis were a direct result of the Versailles

Treaty and that if Germany had been treated with an intelligent generosity, there would have been no World War II. I believed—and still do—that the Second World War would have been prevented if we, Britain and France, had had the guts to stand up to Hitler early and had supported the anti-Nazi Germans, whom we consistently snubbed. Being in Germany then was so painful: I was divided, sorry for the Germans, and yet hearing German or seeing a sign in German still reminded me of the fear I felt in the war, though I believed this reaction to be stupid and irrational. There was a day, or rather a night, when, standing on a railway platform in Berlin and realising that every person on it was a cripple from the War—legless men, armless men, eyeless men, and all drunk, in that particular way of being drunk in war or bad times, a bitter drunkenness—I said to myself, Enough, stop tormenting yourself: this is like voluntarily rubbing one's nose in one's own vomit. What am I doing this for? What good does it do to me—or the Germans? And I did not go back to Germany for decades. And then Germany was whole again, and that landscape of misery and destruction had vanished. Please God, for ever.

And now I have to record what was probably the most neurotic act of my life. I decided to join the Communist Party. And this at a time when my 'doubts' had become something like a steady, private torment. Separate manifestations of the horror that the Soviet Union had become were discussed, briefly, in lowered voices—the equivalent of looking over one's shoulder to see if anyone could hear. I do not remember one serious, sit-down, in-depth discussion about the implications of what we were hearing. Rather, sudden burstings into tears: 'Oh, it's so horrible.' Sudden storms of accusation: 'It's just anti-Soviet propaganda anyway.' Marital quarrels, even divorces.

People complain that old Reds 'try to justify themselves'. These are nearly all young people, for older ones understand exactly why it was natural to be a communist. To explain, to 'bear witness', is not to justify.

To spell out the paradox: All over Europe, and to a much lesser extent the United States, it was the most sensitive, compassionate, socially concerned people who became communists. (Among these were a very different kind of people, the power-lovers.) These decent, kind people supported the worst, the most brutal tyranny of our time—with the exception of communist China. Hitler's Germany, which lasted thirteen years, was an infant in terror compared to Stalin's regime—and yes, I am taking into account the Holocaust.

The first and main fact, the 'mind-set' of those times, was that it was taken for granted capitalism was doomed, was on its way out. Capitalism was responsible for every social ill, war included. Communism was the future for all mankind. I used to hear earnest proselytisers say, 'Let me have anyone for a couple of hours, and I can persuade him that communism is the only answer. Because it is obvious that it is.' Communism's hands were not exactly clean? Or, to put it as the comrades did, 'There have been mistakes'? That was because the first communist country had been backward Russia; but if the first country had been Germany, that would have been a very different matter! (The fact that the Soviet Union had inherited the oldest and most successful empire in the world was decades away from being noticed.) Soon, when the industrially developed countries became communist, we would all see a very different type of communism.

I have been tempted to write a chapter headed 'Politics', so that it could be skipped by people who find the whole subject boring, but politics permeated everything then; the Cold War was a poisonous miasma. And yet it is hard from present perspectives to make sense of a way of thinking I now think was lunatic. Does it matter if one woman succumbed to lunacy? No. But I am talking of a generation, and we were part of some kind of social psychosis or mass self-hypnosis. I am not trying to justify it when I say that I now believe all mass movements—religious, political—are a kind of mass hysteria and, a generation or so later, people must say, But how *could* you believe . . . whatever it was?

Belief—that's the word. This was a religious set of mind, identical with that of passionate religious True Believers. Arthur Koestler and others wrote a book called *The God That Failed,* and now it is a commonplace to say that communism is a religion. But to use that phrase is not necessarily to understand it. What communism inherited was not merely the fervours but a landscape of goodies and baddies, the saved and the unredeemed. We inherited the mental framework of Christianity. Hell: capitalism; all bad. A Redeemer, all good—Lenin, Stalin, Mao. Purgatory: you can't make an omelette without breaking eggs (lagers, concentration camps, and the rest). Then paradise . . . then heaven . . . then Utopia.

Yet I was far from a true believer. For one thing, Jack, the most serious love of my life, embodied the conflicts or, if you like, the 'contradictions' of communism: eleven of his closest friends, his comrades, his real family, had been hanged as traitors. When I said to Jack I was thinking of joining the Party, he said I was making a mistake—and it must have hurt him most horribly to say it. Yet he knew, having been through all those mills himself, it was a waste of time saying it. 'You'll grow out of it,' was what I could have heard.

Arthur Koestler said that every communist who stayed in the Communist Party in the face of all the evidence had a secret explanation for what was happening, and this could not be discussed with friends and comrades. Some of the communists I knew had decided that yes, the reported crimes were true—though *of course* not as bad as the capitalist press said—but that Comrade Stalin could not possibly know about what was going on. The truth was being kept from Uncle Joe. My rationalisation, my 'secret belief'— and it certainly could not be discussed with anyone but Jack—was that the leadership of the Soviet Union had become corrupt but that waiting everywhere in the communist world were the good communists, keeping their counsel, and they would at the right time take power, and then communism would resume its march to the just society, the perfect society. There was just one little thing: I didn't realise Uncle Joe had murdered them all.

And then there was this business of Britain's class system. It shocked me—as it does all colonials. Britain is two nations, all right . . . though it is a bit better now—not much. When I first arrived, my Rhodesian accent enabled me to talk to the natives—that is, the working class—for I was seen as someone outside their taboos, but this became impossible as soon as I began talking middle-class standard English: this was not a choice; I cannot help absorbing accents wherever I am. A curtain came down—slam. I am talking about being treated as an equal, not of the matey, rather paternal 'niceness' of the upper classes. And then I found that people who had suffered out the thirties on tea and bread and margarine and jam, who had been for years unemployed, who lived in filthy slums, voted Tory.

An incident: One of my RAF friends from Rhodesia took me to lunch and said, 'You could learn to pass. Women are good at it.' This was meant kindly: he had taken me out to lunch to say this. He did not understand when I said that I had no intention of learning to 'pass'. People did not necessarily admire his kind. Only six or seven years later, with the advent of the (so-called) angry young men, that generation, it would become unnecessary to justify this stand, but then it was necessary. Uncomfortable, embarrassing for both sides.

An incident: With another man, also ex-RAF, I went into a pub in Bayswater. It was the public bar. We stood at the counter, ordered drinks. All around the walls, men sat watching us. They were communing without words. One got up, slowly, deliberately, came to us, and said, 'You don't want to be here [rather, 'ere]. That's your place.' Pointing at the private bar. We meekly took ourselves there, joining our peers, the middle class. This kind of thing goes on now. Foreigners, returning natives, complain about the class system, but the British say—both classes—You don't understand us, and continue as before. The working classes, the lower classes, have 'internalised' their station in life.

When in this mood, a bitter criticism of Britain, my set of mind was identical—but I saw this only later—with that of the people who became communists in the thirties: because of that grim and grimy poverty. And, too, with the people who went off to the Spanish Civil War, because of anger when the French and British governments refused to supply arms to the legitimate government, while Hitler and Mussolini armed Franco. A deep shame persisted in many people I met then. (Does this kind of shame, over the behaviour of one's government, still exist? I think not—an innocence has gone.) This shame caused some people to become traitors, and spies. The Spanish Civil War had left a painful legacy.

People have forgotten how badly the refugees from Spain were treated, kept in camps near the border for years, as if they were criminals, to be punished. Well into the sixties, there were a couple of pubs in Soho where intensely poor Spaniards met to talk about how the world had forgotten them, and yet they had been the first to stand up to the Nazis, to the fascists. There are cynics who say that that was their crime.

And so I joined 'the Party', which is how it was generally referred to. I hated having a Party card. I hated joining anything. I hated and hate meetings. I merely record this . . . a tangle of contradictory, lunatic emotions and behaviour. Later, so very much later, quite recently, in fact, an explanation of why so many people stuck with the Communist Party, long after they should have left, came to me. But for now, enough.

There was another thing: I had seen too many of the kind who run around saying, 'I am a communist,' but wouldn't dream of joining the Party. I despised them. Quite soon, in London, there would be a new generation of young people saying, 'I am a communist,' to shock the bourgeoisie, to annoy mummy and daddy, to give themselves and others an enjoyable frisson.

I was interviewed by Sam Aaronivitch, cultural commissar. He was a very young man, lean, stern, military in style, with the grim, sardonic humour of the times. He had been a very poor boy, from the East End. The Young Communist League had been his education but not his nursery, because he was a Jew and one of a people of a Book. I have several times been told by children of the Jewish East End how they listened to fathers, uncles, elder brothers, even mothers, argue politics, philosophy, religion, around meal tables on which there might be hardly enough to eat. Why had 'the Party' chosen a young man who had read nothing of modern literature, and was not interested in the arts, to represent culture? The interview was in the Communist Party headquarters in King Street, Covent Garden. ('King Street says . . .' 'Those idiots in King Street . . .' 'I was summoned to King Street, but I told them that . . .') He heard me out, like an officer interviewing a rookie, and said he was intrigued to meet an intellectual who wanted to join the Party, when most of them were leaving it, and he looked forward to reading my denunciations of the Party when I left. Then he took me on a tour of the East End, where he had grown up. Sam does not remember doing this, but it is one of the vividest of my memories of those early days in London. He was showing me a culture already dead, which he regretted, because of its guts and its cohesiveness. Sam has had a various life, or perhaps one should say lives: one of them as 'the Balliol Marxist'. Sometimes we meet, when he is sprinting and I am ambling across Hampstead Heath. We reminisce: I remember this, he remembers that—for instance, that Peter used to spend weekends and play with his daughter Sabrina. He is now helping the Bangladeshi community who live in the streets where he grew up. The Bangladeshis in East London are people of a Book, but for some reason theirs does not do for them what the Jews' Book did for them, producing the passionately polemical, intellectual, clever people who were able to rise above their poverty to invigorate the worlds of learning, business, and the arts. The children do not grow up hearing fathers, mothers, uncles, elder brothers, argue about religion, politics, literature; they do not hear poetry and bits from great novels quoted in support of arguments. When they go to school they do not do brilliantly, as did the poor Jews who lived before them in those streets.

One of the reasons some found it hard to leave the Party was precisely because there were so many colourful, extraordinary people in it. Good people, generous, kind, clever.

I shall mention two out of many. Once, when I was so short of money I didn't know what to do, thought I would have to give up trying to live on my earnings and get a job, I got a letter quite out of the blue from people I did not know, communists, who wrote to say they had heard I was hard up, they liked my books, and enclosed one hundred pounds. That was a lot of money then. They did not want me to return it, but when I had enough, they would like me to send it on to someone who needed it, with the same request: to hand it on to someone in need. I shall be forever grateful to these people, whom I never met.

A bit later, when feeling imprisoned by the stratifications of the class system, I asked the Communist Party to arrange a visit for me to a mining community. I found this village, Armsthorpe, near

Doncaster, grim, depressing; and yet it had been recently built and the people in it felt themselves lucky compared with families living in some of the old villages. A miner, his wife, three adolescent children. He had been a communist for years, and so had she. The house was full of books: I saw no other books in the houses of the village. They listened to music on the radio, and plays. They talked about how Sybil Thorndike had brought a company to play Shakespeare to the miners in the middle of the war. Everyone in the community remembered this. These two had travelled to the Soviet Union and to other communist countries. That was before mass tourism; they were the only travelled people in the village. He was a father figure, or unofficial representative; people dropped in all the time to ask his advice. Everything he said about the mining community, about Britain, about his life—the usual story of bitter poverty in the twenties and thirties—was full of information and good sense. Everything he said about the Soviet Union and the communist world was nonsense. To have said to this man, What you admire so much is an illusion, and Stalin is a monster—that would have killed something in him: hope, a belief in humankind. This kind of dichotomy, on one side everything that was sound and sensible and honest, and on the other a mirage of lies, was common.

I used to lie awake, for the two weeks of my visit, in the living room on a sofa immediately under their bedroom and hear him coughing just above my head. He had lung disease from the pit, and he knew he would die soon. He wouldn't allow his children to go near the mines; it was a life for a dog.

Walking with him through the street, I saw a group of young miners, just up from the pit, wearing cheap best suits and red scarves, having showered in the pithead baths. They were off to Doncaster for the evening. They greeted my host, nodded to me. The old miner was full of an angry tenderness for them: what were they eating, they didn't look well, those scarves weren't enough to keep them warm. You could see their affection for him.

I used this experience in a short story, 'England Versus England.'

★ ★ ★

My Party card was in fact delayed. I had been invited to go to the Soviet Union for the Authors World Peace Appeal: that kind of inspirational organisation flourished then. It had been started by Naomi Mitchison and Alex Comfort. Few people could be found who would go. The atmosphere was such that I got letters and telephone calls saying that I would disappear into a concentration camp. When I said that it was hardly likely that the Union of Soviet Writers would allow eminent guests to disappear—surely bad publicity for them?—I was told (like Moidi Jokl with Gottfried), 'You don't understand anything about communism. It would serve you right if you were bumped off.'

There were six of us: Naomi Mitchison herself. Her cousin Douglas Young, because he understood Russian. Arnold Kettle, a well-known Marxist literary critic from Leeds University. A. E. Coppard, the short-story writer. Richard Mason, the author of *The Wind Cannot Read,* a best-selling novel from the war, about a young English soldier in love with a half-caste nurse. And myself, a very new writer. This, we knew, was hardly the level of literary repute the Russians must have been hoping to attract for the first visit of writers from the West since the war—this was 1952.

There was a preliminary meeting, passionate and polemical, violent. Alex Comfort hated that there would be a communist on the delegation, Arnold Kettle, who would try to pull the wool over our eyes and feed us lies. Naomi refuted this. She knew Arnold, who was a sweet young man. A. E. Coppard, as innocent as a babe about politics, had gone to the Wrotslav Peace Conference and fallen in love with communism, as if he had been given a potion. The meeting developed into a plan with detailed instructions, from Alex Comfort, on how to outwit Arnold. I think Richard Mason was present.

Meanwhile the Party had decided it was not a good thing to have two communists on the trip; one was enough. They told me not to join, formally, until after I returned. This made me uncomfortable, put me at once in a false position. Deception was not, really, in my nature. An immediate, direct openness, often criticised as tactlessness, was more my line.

Discussing it later with the knowledgeable, I was told that this was typical communist tactics. I was from the very start put in a position where I was involved in a dishonest act and could be exposed for it. I believed that, but not for long, because I began to see something much deeper. Why was it that anywhere near the Party, facts became twisted, people said things which you knew—and they must have known—were untrue? The devil is described as the Father of Lies, a resonant phrase, suggesting other, older phrases, like 'Realm of Lies'. I have come to think that there is something in the nature of communism that breeds lies, makes people lie and twist facts, imposes deception. What is this thing? This force? One cannot believe one word that emanates from a communist source. Communism is indeed a realm of lies. Stalin, the great deceiver, was only partly responsible, because it was Lenin, the exemplar, who provided the blueprints. 'Disinformation' was—is?—only a crystallisation, a formalisation, of communism's deepest nature. But these are deeper waters than I know how to plumb: I am sure, though, that there is something here that lives well beyond the daylight world of common sense and simple causes.

We were an improbable assortment of people. First, Naomi Mitchison. She was one of the writers who had broken new ground for women in the thirties, particularly with the novel *The Corn King and the Spring Queen*. She was a town councillor in Scotland, a farmer, and, with her husband, Dick Mitchison, who was a member of Parliament, an energetic member of the Labour Party. A. E. Coppard wrote some of the best of English short stories, gentle, wry, humorous—and sharp-eyed, like himself. But unfortunately, falling in love with communism had not done much for his clarity of vision. Richard Mason claimed he was going to the Soviet Union because the year before he had gone to Lourdes and thought this would be a nice contrast, and as piquant an experience. But he was deceptive, played the role of philistine, a pipe-smoking tweedy Englishman, phlegmatic and silent. In fact, he was a romantic soul. Arnold Kettle was on this delegation because Naomi had invited him and because the Party had agreed to it. I had written a well-reviewed novel and short stories.

When we met at the airport, five of us looked with suspicion, or with wariness, at Arnold Kettle, but almost at once his calm and good sense made him the mentor of the group. This often happened: communists, seen as demons, seemed disproportionately sane when actually met.

Our opinions about the Soviet Union could hardly have been more diverse, but we were made one partly because of the hysterical attentions of the newspapers, which caused us to close ranks, and partly because of Arnold's insistence that we should present a united front, regardless of our differences. This had to be the party line, from King Street and—presumably—the Soviet Union. It surprised the 'right wing'—Naomi and Douglas—and upset A. E. Coppard, because he wanted only to embrace communism publicly and for ever on behalf of the whole British nation. The point was, he was quite unpolitical, had not been, as it were, inoculated against politics, and his first introduction to it had overthrown him. Richard Mason was unpolitical by nature and intention. So Arnold and I found ourselves holding the centre ground, which certainly suited my temperament and, of course, my sense of importance. I think now that if we had quarrelled publicly, in front of the Russians, we would at least have presented a fairer picture of British attitudes towards communism, but with every hour together we found ourselves feeling more and more British, and patriots. This united front was matched as soon as we met the Russians, for they were all old-fashioned nationalists. This sounds a simple statement, to be met now by: Well, of course! But nationalism of this sort had nothing to do with the purities of Utopian Communism, which planned the mutual love of all mankind. To listen to our hosts talking like Colonel Blimp made me remember, most uncomfortably, the hours we had spent in the group in Southern Rhodesia, trying to make sense of the twists and turns in the 'Party Line'. Masterpieces of dialectic, they were, and particularly from Gottfried, manipulating Marxist verities. If the Russians had known how local communists, all over the world, wove their airy structures of explanation of why the Russian comrades were doing this and that improbable thing, they would have laughed their heads off. How right I had been to say—and Gottfried too—that no real Communist party anywhere would recognise our idealistic vapourings. But to encounter this crude, simplistic nationalism here was not what I had expected, and yet why not? The Russians, or rather Stalin, had never made any secret of it. These mental discomforts I discussed with Arnold, for the others would not have understood us. We concluded that the war had been so terrible for the Russians that of course they had to retreat to nationalism. Russians had to be forgiven everything because of that war. They had lost more people in the siege of Leningrad than the British and Americans combined had lost in the whole war. This was why Czech Jack kept saying to me, 'You people here simply don't understand.' ['The Soviet Union' and 'Russia' were interchangeable in those days, improbable though that sounds now.]

I have to say that these memories of that trip are not shared—for instance, with Naomi, as I discovered when twenty-five years or so later I found we were not remembering the same things: it was not a question of remembering the same things differently but as if we had been on two different trips. This experience, which was shocking to me, began my attempts to understand the extraordinary slipperiness of memory: before that, I had taken it for granted that people with the same experiences would remember the same things. Particularly when they were as vivid as those during our trip to Russia. I did better with Arnold; our memories did match, more or less.

I have seldom been so torn, astonished, disappointed, alert . . . *alive,* as during that trip, and my memories of it are among the most vivid I have. There is a basic question about memory: why do we remember this and not that, particularly when *this* is not necessarily important, is on the contrary mere trivia. We remember what we do, I think, because for one reason or another we were particularly alert, paying attention, *present* in the occasion—because most often we are not present but thinking about what we had for breakfast, or what we will do tomorrow, or recalling what we said to So-and-so. Why we are more alive and awake at some times than others is a separate question, leading to very deep waters. Well, I was certainly present, every minute, during that trip, and that is the reason for my memories of it. I had often decided to write about it but then decided not. What was the point? Anything said or written about the Soviet Union was bound to be greeted by emotions so violent, so enraged, or so partisan that no calm judgement could be expected. Besides, what I remembered was not necessarily flattering to my fellow delegates. Of course, this was bound to be true of what they thought about me.

But now all there is left is the music of the distant drum. . . .

Our official host was the Union of Soviet Writers, headed by one Alexei Surkov, whose name was soon to become synonymous with the oppression of decent writers by Soviet ideology. He was an ordinary-looking man, in the style Soviet officials used then to convince: bluff, open, take-me-or-leave-me, honest-John Surkov, the friend of friends of the Soviet Union. Behind him was the KGB, monitoring and directing every word and action. Did we know this? Yes, but our view of the KGB was naive, to say the least. Also coloured by arrogance. We joked, in our hotel rooms, that the KGB would be tapping our telephones and the concierges examining our belongings, but it was of no concern to us; we were from the West and did not go in for that sort of thing. We did not see ourselves as useful tools for the KGB. Correctly, as it turned out, though they would have been pleased if we had become their tools—after all, so many did. From their point of view we were the first delegation of 'intellectuals' from the West since the war, the 'Great Patriotic War'—a phrase which caused us discomfort and highlighted our differences from them—and were to be humoured and pampered.

Behind them were the horrors of the Great Famine, deliberately engineered by Stalin, the Purges, the Gulag, the crushing devastations of the war, the killing of the Jews during the Black Years— not over yet—unspeakable injustices, torments, murders, tortures. While writing this, I read that the mass graves recently discovered and acknowledged were because Stalin, continually imprisoning hundreds of thousands of his people, was told the prisons were overcrowded, did not feel inclined to waste money on building more, and solved the problem by having the prisoners shot and then beginning again. Behind the Russians we were meeting was this history. And Stalin was still alive, watching like a spider from his Kremlin. We did not know then, but Stalin read everything

not.

68

published in the Soviet Union—novels, short stories, poems, and all play and film scripts. He had caused songs to be written, with prescribed words, suitable for different stages of the war and even for battles. He certainly believed that the artist is the engineer of the human soul—as he was always being quoted as saying. The opening of the Soviet Archives has fleshed out the character of dear Uncle Joe.

Their visitors must have seemed to them like not very bright children. I have oftened wondered if this visit contributed to remarks—by ex KGB, GRU, and other intelligence agents—like: 'The Western communists and fellow travellers are like naive children, and when the Soviet tanks roll over them they will be crying, Welcome, Welcome.' No, the still innocent would be crying, 'But, comrades, stop your tanks; you are making a terrible mistake, and you are sullying the glorious name of communism.' As late as the 1960s, a Jew from Israel, not a communist but left labour, was arrested and imprisoned in Prague and charged with being a fascist-Zionist agent of international imperialism—decoded, this meant a Jew—and when in prison pleaded with his torturers and jailors, 'Comrades, how can you soil the hands of the working class in this way, how can you hurt yourselves and all the decent people in the world by such behaviour?'

Our first official engagement was around a long table in a formal room, and there were twenty or so of us. Surkov opened with a florid official speech, which set the tone for all their succeeding speeches.

The gulf between the Soviet writers—or rather the official party line—and the British contingent was unbridgeable. This was evident from that first speech, and the distance between us widened rather than narrowed throughout the visit.

Naomi opened for our side. A middle-aged woman, in appearance not unlike a friendly terrier, she said she had been in Moscow during the twenties, she had had the most wonderful love affair, and why had the Soviet Union become hostile to Free Love? She remembered bathing nude in the Moskva River with her lover, and all kinds of good times. Once, the Soviet Union had been a beacon of progress in matters amorous, but 'you have all become so reactionary'. Needless to say, Arnold and I were burning with shame and embarrassment. The seriousness of the occasion! Our responsibilities as representatives of our country! Now I wonder if this wasn't a pretty good way of dealing with all the rhetoric and bombast, with an impossible situation.

Then Douglas Young demanded to put the case for the exploited colonies, speaking 'for Scotland, England's vassal. He wore a kilt at times during the trip, for dramatic emphasis. (He was very tall and very thin, and a kilt was even more dramatic on him than on an ordinary man.) On every possible occasion he stood up to speak for downtrodden and oppressed Scotland. I have no doubt he was a sincere Scottish nationalist, but he had his tongue in his cheek. The communists were obliged to rise to their feet and cheer him whenever he spoke of oppressed nations, so waves of noisy insincerity were continually disrupting whatever meeting we were having.

The details of what both sides said have gone, but not my emotions. I was feeling a direct continuation of the emotions fed into me by my parents, particularly my father: You don't understand the awfulness of . . . in this case, the Second World War as experienced by the Russians, by the Soviet Union—their feeling of isolation, which nobody could understand who had not been part of it. This was shared by Arnold, for very personal reasons. Emotionally, then, we were both identified with the Russians. Certain arguments—discussions they were not, rather the stating and restating of our so different positions—were repeated. They attacked with their creed: literature must further the progress of communism, the Communist Party's right to decide what should be written and published, the Party's responsibility for the glorious future of all humankind. We defended ours: the integrity of the individual conscience, individual responsibility, the duty of artists to tell the truth as they saw it. (No, this debate is far from over: the Communist position is represented now by the defenders of political correctness.) The Russians—most of them were Russians—put themselves beyond the possibility of serious debate when they said there was really no need for official censorship. 'Communist writers develop an inner censor, which tells them what they may write.' This inner censor seemed to us a terrifying thing: that they should defend it—no, boast of it— shocked us.

Another problem was their attitude to Stalin. Stalin's name could not be used without a string of honorifics—the Great, the Glorious, and so on. This was because the slightest whisper of criticism of Stalin would put them in a concentration camp. No, we did not understand this. We said that when we read in the reports of their assemblies that Comrade Stalin had spoken for five hours and the applause lasted for half an hour, we were incredulous. In our culture—we boasted—there could not be this kind of reverence for a leader. In fact, the very word 'leader' was an embarrassment. Decades later, with what chagrin did I read, during the reign of Thatcher, 'wild applause for fifteen minutes'. Thus does Time punish our arrogances.

A couple of coordinating meetings were attempted, by Arnold, between the members of the delegation: the 'right wing'—Naomi and Douglas—and the left wing, Coppard. Arnold and I would confer—hastily, for we were worn out by the intensity of the experience—in my room, late at night. Naomi wanted to issue a statement, on behalf of all of us, condemning the camps and extolling democracy. If she did this, A. E. Coppard threatened, he would demand his right to say—on behalf of all of us—that the Soviet Union was the hope for all the world, and the British people had been told lies by their government about the real nature of communism. Arnold undertook to take on Naomi and say that if she did what she wanted, we would all resign and go home. At the same time he would tell Douglas Young, who would be in Naomi's room, that he must stop playing the jackass in his kilt. I must explain to Coppard that if he did what he wanted, we would all resign and Naomi would issue her statement. I did and he was terribly distressed. Our conversations went on in my room, or rather suite, which looked like a blown-up version of a Victorian parlour, all heavy plush tablecloths, heavy velvet curtains, ornate mirrors, thick carpets. He sat on one side of a vast table, I on the other. Alfred Coppard had been a poor boy, had always hated 'the ruling class', or 'that lot up there'. He saw Britain as being run entirely for the benefit of the few; the formulations of communism

71

seemed to him the merest common sense. He had become a Utopian Communist, as I had, ten years before. I felt for him. More, I loved him. He was a pure soul, incapable of understanding evil—if I may use that word at all. I have known few people as loveable as he was. Ever since the Wrotslav Peace Conference, which divided the world for him into two camps, good and bad, he had been in a kind of ecstasy.

But something must be said about the World Congress of Intellectuals at Wroclaw* August 25–29, 1948. It was the first of the big 'peace' congresses, and they went on in one form or another until the collapse of the Soviet Union, which inspired and stage-managed them. They were all the same, because there had to be total disagreement between the communists and the rest. I include here two cuttings from the *Times,* and from these can be deduced what all the other congresses, conferences, and meetings were like.

INTELLECTUALS AND PROPAGANDA
ACRIMONIOUS CONGRESS

WROCLAW, Aug. 27—The aggressive opening day's speech of the Soviet writer Alexander Fadieev, in which he delivered a bitter attack of a political nature on American imperialism and certain facets of western culture, continued to plague the World Congress of Intellectuals to-day.

Mr. Fadieev's speech set the tone for the entire proceedings, which have developed to a large extent into the usual futile acrimonious exchanges of Soviet and western viewpoints. To-day, for example, there was only one speech among nearly two dozen that held to the intellectual rather than the political level established by Mr. Fadieev. This was delivered by the French writer M. Julien Benda, who urged that educators and historians should cease to glorify warmongers, 'whether they won or whether they lost.' Literature should concentrate on glorifying civilization, justice, and those who oppose destruction.

Otherwise the day was filled by protagonists of one side or the

*Wroclaw: Wrotslav, or Breslau.

other, and was noteworthy for a strong answer to Mr. Fadieev by an American delegate, who said things of the Russians that are ordinarily not said in public in present-day Poland. He is Mr. Bryn J. Hovde, director of the New School for Social Research in New York. Mr. Fadieev's speech, he said, if made by a responsible member of a Government, was of a kind that would be made 'to give propaganda justification to a premeditated military attack.' Mr. Hovde said that Americans thought that, since temptations to imperialism went historically with wealth and power, the Soviet Union was 'no more immune than we ourselves,' and when it came to demanding her own way in the world, Americans thought that the Soviet Union took a back seat to nobody.

The British speaker to-day was Professor J.B.S. Haldane, who said he agreed that the main threat of war came from America and the dangers of American imperialism. He criticized the Russians for failing to make available 'full information on the facts of life in the Soviet Union,' which he said was necessary in order to influence British intellectuals.

INTELLECTUALS' CONFERENCE
SOVIET WRITER'S OUTBURST

The World Congress of Intellectuals dedicated by the French and Polish organizing committees to find a road to peace opened in anything but a peaceful manner to-day. After the Foreign Minister, Mr. Medzelewski, had welcomed the delegates, the Soviet writer, Alexander Fadieev, launched the work of the Congress with the usual bitter diatribe against 'American Imperialism' and for this occasion extended it to include 'reactionary aggressive' elements of American culture as well.

Mr. Fadieev also attacked schools of writing which 'bred aggressive propaganda,' and, naming T.S. Eliot, Eugene O'Neill, John dos Passos, Jean Paul Sartre, and André Malraux, he said: 'If hyenas could type and jackals could use a fountain pen they would write such things' as were produced by these men. The Soviet writer's outburst drew a temperate but firm reply from Mr. Olaf Stapledon, the British author, who, reminding Mr. Fadieev of the purpose of the Congress, said that if they were to reach any agreement they must all make a special effort 'to enter into the other point of view.'

Mr. Stapledon said that no side could lay claim to all the truth and that both sides, not just one, were guilty of using 'instruments which pervert the truth.' He answered Mr. Fadieev specifically on Mr. Eliot, saying that while they might not agree with his politics he certainly was an important figure in British poetry.

Mr. Stapledon arranged a private meeting to-night between the British and Russian delegates to enable them to get to know each other better.

The delegates from Britain were Sir John Boyd Orr, the dean of Canterbury, Professor J. B. S. Haldane, Professor J. D. Bernal, Professor C. H. Waddington, Professor Hyman Levy, Richard Hughes, Olaf Stapledon, Louis Golding, Rutland Brougham, Bernard Stevens, Felix Topolski, Dr. Julian Huxley, A. J. P. Taylor, Denis Saurat, Edward Crankshaw. A starry list. (The *Times* list.)

As for our Authors World Peace Appeal: Very late at night, after those interminable, exhausting banquets, those speeches, trips here and there—collective farm, children's holiday camp, museums—Albert Coppard and I sat in my room and exchanged talk which must have had the ears of our invisible listeners curling with disbelief. No, I said, no, you must not go on the radio and say that Stalin is the greatest man who ever lived, no, nor claim that Britain is a tyranny worse than any communist country. Do you really want us all to quarrel publicly and make a field day for our newspapers? 'I don't see why we shouldn't quarrel publicly,' he said, 'if that's how we feel.' From time to time he tried to kiss me, or fondle me. My stern sense of duty forbade amorous dalliance. Besides, he was *old*.

It was also my duty to visit Richard Mason in his room and tell him that he simply must not announce on every possible occasion that he had never read Tolstoy, Dostoyevsky, Gorky. Our hosts had read all of British literature—the writers among them really had—and he was shaming us all. 'Who is Turgenev?' he might drawl, if the name came up. I thought he was putting it on, that this was his equivalent of Douglas Young's kilt. But he really had not read anything much. He claimed that he had become a writer by accident. A very young lonely soldier, he had lain wounded in a hospital in—I think—Burma, had fallen in love with his beautiful brown nurse, had written the story, as much from boredom as for anything, and it had become a best-seller. He claimed he found great literature boring. Was this true? But his phlegmatic, philistine persona concealed all kinds of sensibilities. Like us all, he was upset by what he saw in Moscow: its dreary streets, its empty shops, the bad clothes, its atmosphere—this was just before Stalin died. We used to beg our minder, one Oksana, a beautiful Georgian girl, to be allowed to wander about the streets as we pleased, but she was evidently afraid. We did manage little guilty trips when she wasn't looking, but were recalled by her anxious scoldings: 'What are you doing? You are not allowed . . .'

In those streets of almost empty shops there were two exceptions. One was the bread shops, wonderful, redeeming the ugliness, crammed full of different breads, brown, white, black, great fat crusty loaves that smelled so good we wanted to eat them then and there. The other surprise was corset shops. There were scarcely any clothes, the shoes were flimsy or clodhopping, there was nothing frivolous or nice, or piquant, or fashionable, or colourful. But there were corset shops and, in each, one or two enormous bright pink or purple corsets, with stays like girders, and shiny pink ribbons. Not a bra in sight, though.

Scenes, little bright-coloured scenes, which I wrote down when I came home after the trip, and used to come on, among ageing papers and old notebooks. 'Good God, all that happened, it *did* happen. . . .'

We are in the Tretyakov—an art gallery—surrounded by vast pictures of grazing cows, happy peasants, agreeable landscapes. Naomi, a collector of modern art, stands in front of a herd of cows. 'That is a very fine cow,' she drawls in her Oxford voice, which for some reason is emphasized in Russia. Our guides, the museum officials, gaze at the cow. 'A fine cow,' she drawls, 'but surely she needs milking?' The official meets her innocent gaze, but it is more than his life is worth—literally—to laugh. 'Soviet cows are well treated,' he says severely. Naomi says, 'I've got a cow in my herd just like that brown one.' We, coming on behind, are smiling, and even risking a laugh, but the look on the man's face stops us.

It seems that the Soviet artists, who were allowed to paint only 'healthy' pictures, softened their situation, at least a little, by this ruse: A picture having been completed, they deliberately painted in a dog or an obviously out-of-place figure. When this picture was set in front of the officials who would say yea or nay, they were bound to criticise it, to cover themselves in case of criticism from high up. At which point the artist would come in. 'Comrades, I've just seen—it's that dog. I was wrong to put in that dog.' 'Very well, then, comrade, take out the dog.' And the picture was passed. This sort of stratagem has turned out to be quite amazingly useful to me, in all kinds of contexts: suitably modified, of course.

While on a trip to a collective farm, the official cars having turned off onto the farm road, Naomi asks if we may stop. Our cars, four or five of them, stop. We all get out, about twenty people, and stand on the track, looking across fields. It is August, very hot, the grain already harvested. 'That's a very nasty bit of erosion,' says Naomi, pointing. And indeed, it is. 'But our grain harvest for last year was very good on this farm.' 'Well, you won't be getting good harvests for long, if you allow that kind of erosion,' she says. In this way did her frustrated need to criticise much worse show itself.

It was at this collective farm that I witnessed the bravest thing I have ever seen in my life.

We, the six of us, and our hosts, headed by Alexei Surkov, stood facing a crowd of collective farmers. We were being introduced. An old man, dressed in a white peasant smock, like Tolstoy, stepped out and said he wanted to speak. At once the others attempted to hustle and scold him back into the group. He stood his ground, said he had to speak to us. A silence. Oksana was clearly frightened. The old man spoke. Oksana interpreted, and Douglas Young, our Russian speaker, stopped her. 'No, you are not interpreting properly,' he said, blandly, like a professor. The old man addressed him, and Douglas interpreted, while Oksana squeezed her hands together, as if she were praying. 'You must not believe what you are told. Visitors from abroad are told lies. You must not believe what you are shown. Our lives are terrible. The Russian people—I am speaking for the Russian people. You must go back to Britain and tell everybody what I am saying. Communism is terrible—' And he was pulled back by the others and surrounded, but he stood among them with his burning eyes fixed on us, while the others scolded him. That was remarkable—they scolded and fussed at him; they didn't shrink away from a pariah. And throughout the long, toast-filled meal that followed, he sat silent, his eyes on us, while they scolded—affectionately, there was no doubt about that. Yet at that time people vanished into the Gulag for much less than what he had done. No crime could be worse than to say such things to foreigners. He would be arrested and disposed of, and he knew that this would happen.

During this meal Coppard was enjoying himself flirting delightfully with the collective farm's teacher and nurse. He loved charming young women, and these two were pretty and warm, and flirted with him.

I try and imagine this as a scene in a film, but it is truly too terrible. There is a long, loaded table, flowers, wine, a banquet. There, the special people chosen from the farm to represent the Soviet farmers. There, we happy delegates, elated and pleased with ourselves, the way you get on such trips. There, the party officials, all affability. There, the old man in his smock, never taking his eyes off us. Albert Coppard is flirting. We make speeches. Douglas Young reminds us all of the sufferings of the Scottish farmers. Naomi talks about British farming practices, contrasting them severely with what we saw while driving through the fields.

In the lavatory there is a framed copy of Kipling's 'If'. We are told that this is everyone's favourite piece of poetry and they all know it by heart.

The next time I saw 'If' on the back of a lavatory door was on a large rich farm in Kenya, where there were photographs of the Queen everywhere.

We were taken to a building filled with presents to Stalin from his grateful subjects. It was sad, because they were mostly hideous, derivations or fallings-off from some genuine peasant or folk tradition, like carpets with his face occupying all the middle of them, or carved boxes or metalwork—all with his face. I left the others at it and went to sit outside. It was there I decided to try and write a story according to the communist formula, because I was becoming uncomfortably aware of our smugness and superiority. It would have very good and very bad characters in it, like Dickens. I wrote it. It was called 'Hunger.' It was about a youth from a village in Africa, risking his fortunes and his life going to the big city, this being a basic plot of our time, not only in Africa. The background came from Africans I knew, who would describe, when I asked, exactly how this or that was done in a village, how things were in the locations and shebeens of Salisbury. This story has been much translated and reprinted, and yet I am ashamed of it. Quite a few of my early stories I would like to see vanish away. What is wrong with that tale is sentimentality, which is often the sign of an impure origin: in this case, to write a tale with a moral.

Naomi and I and Oksana are standing in St. Basil's Cathedral in Red Square, and Naomi is lecturing Oksana about the Russian lack of taste. Naomi suffered aesthetically throughout that trip. Everything was ugly and second-rate. If Arnold and I murmured something about the war, she would say, Nonsense, they are producing new materials and furniture, and they are hideous. She showed Oksana the patterns on the walls and ceilings and said, Why, when you've got this, do you put such *hideous* patterns on your dress materials? Oksana was confused. She did not know the patterns on the new cottons and silks were hideous. When Naomi showed her the Liberty skirt she had on, Oksana did not see why it was any better than the bales of cotton she had showed us that morning. She thought the patterns on the cathedral walls were old and old-fashioned. She asked me afterwards why, if Mrs. Mitchison was a rich lady, she wore cotton and not silk. For of course, if you could afford it, you wore silk all the time. Oksana's best dress was silk. 'And very nice too,' said Richard Mason gallantly. Arnold and I discussed how Naomi patronised our hosts and apparently did not know it, and how we could stop her. We actually took her to task. 'Naomi, you've got to stop hurting their feelings like this. We won't have it.'

'But I simply cannot understand it,' Naomi said, that voluminous voice booming. '*Why* can't they take good models for their furniture instead of that rubbish?'

'But, Naomi,' said intellectual Arnold, 'that's what happens when a peasant tradition is smashed: they model themselves on something modern. They had taste in the old ways, but they have to develop taste in the new.'

'Well,' drawled Naomi, 'but I'm going to have my say. This delegation is supposed to be bridging gaps: I'm jolly well going to tell them about their atrocious taste.'

'Then when we get home we're going to tell the press that you spent your time patronising the Russians about their aesthetic sense.'

'But, Arnold, my dear boy, you surely can't be serious.'

'*You're hurting their feelings,* Naomi,' said Arnold, his eyes full of tears.

In Leningrad they asked Naomi and me if we minded sharing a room. We thought this odd; it took me a long time to see that probably they wanted to overhear our conversations. It being August, the nights were not completely white, but almost; there were only a couple of hours of real dark. Exhausted, I flopped into bed, a double bed, and there was Naomi, prodding me, because she wanted me to tell her about my love life, so she could tell me about her lovers in the twenties. I thought this was like being back at school, naughty conversations in the dorm. She said young women these days had become real stick-in-the-muds. I went to sleep.

Leningrad was a sad city, grey and elegant, full of watery perspectives, its walls pocked with bullet holes or cracked because of the attritions of the siege, in which ten years before one and a half million people died. We moved from palace to palace, all built in the style I know some people adore, all gilt curlicues and cupids, rosy flesh, pink and blue ribbons, medallions, a very festival of pouting and dimpling architecture. This was because Russian royalty had adored France and imported the style for palaces, and so even when we went to the Children's House, it was a former palace, and the thought of sandpits or swings seemed in rather poor taste.

We had a formal encounter with the Leningrad branch of the

Soviet Writers, and there we were, in another of these frivolous rooms, for an occasion as sombre as any I remember. Naomi had said she was going to insist that the Leningrad writers produce the writer Mikhail Zoshchenko for our inspection. There were rumours in the West that he was dead—murdered. Arnold and I were horrified. First, why should any writer anywhere be produced like evidence in a law court? And then we did know that writers were, as it is now put, keeping a low profile—trying not to be noticed—and perhaps it would be the last thing he would welcome, being made a test case by the West. But Naomi insisted.

I cannot remember the names of our hosts. The opening speeches were all sound and fury. Already we were weary of them, to the point where we were saying, Thank God we are going home soon; one more speech and—

'Or one more toast.'

'Or one more banquet.'

After a while you literally cannot listen to these speeches. It is as if the rhetoric numbs your brain: the words—the sound—a narcotic. Speeches of this sort went on for the hours of the meeting but were interrupted by a young poet who, like a Quaker, from time to time feeling an impulse he could not disobey, had to jump to his feet and recite an ode to Stalin. Obviously, no one could object, at the risk of being accused of *lèse-majesté,* so that every time this happened, all the officials smiled benignly at the inspired infant and even clapped. Against this background Mikhail Zoshchenko was brought in and sat in the middle of the room, the Russians on one side, we on the other. He was a little thin man, yellow-skinned, and he looked ill, and was being brave, and dignified. Just as with the defiant old man at the collective farm, it was as if the atmosphere itself put protective arms around him. These officials, no matter how much they were vassals, lackeys, arse-lickers, were all under threat themselves, had seen many writers, friends or not, disappear into exile or the camps. Zoshchenko had been under official criticism—and that meant from themselves too—for a long time now. He had written small, very funny, very popular stories about the mishaps and anomalies of the lives of citizens living under communism, and a wonderful novella called, simply, *People*—and for a while had been officially applauded, but that did not last.

While sitting before us, he agreed, when prodded by the chairman, that he certainly did still exist, was well and well-treated, and had seen the error of his ways; he had repented of his negative and critical early work, but he was now engaged on a three-volume novel about the Great Patriotic War, which he hoped would atone for his former crimes.

Mikhail Zoshchenko died quite soon, of illness, not in a camp; so he was more fortunate than many Soviet writers. Arnold and I, discussing the death, tried to hope that what we had thought was a grotesque and silly intervention in his life perhaps in the end had protected him. But I do not think Stalin, who decided these matters, cared about the opinions of "useful idiots." (Lenin's description of Westerners like us.)

By now there was no pretence that we were a unit. Naomi and Douglas spent their free time, such as there was, together.

Coppard wanted to be with me, to be reassured. He was disturbed by the grimness of Moscow, while delighted by the multitudes of visitors—delegations—from everywhere in the communist world.

But I was mostly with Arnold. We talked, and we talked. How ridiculous it does seem now—that we took ourselves so seriously. Don't forget that on the shoulders of communists rested the future of the entire world. Communists and 'progressive forces'. It occurs to me now that all adolescents believe this: everything lies in their hands, because adults are such a disaster. Is it possible that this so fundamental belief of the communists was no more than delayed or displaced collective adolescence?

The stress, the pressures, our disagreements, the lack of sleep, the strenuous pace of our engagements, were reducing us to our worst selves, or at least to the extremes of our natures. Richard Mason became more solitary, silent, and exaggerated his philistine pose: 'I'm sorry, I never go near a theatre or a concert.' Coppard always found in any gathering that sympathetically pretty woman, or untrammelled soul, with whom he talked about how in his youth he had walked by himself all over England—this was often Samuel Marshak, who had walked over Russia as a young man.

Coppard told everyone that he loathed politicians, hated the ruling class of his country, loved communism. Douglas Young's enormous height and kilt called forth storms of applause as he talked, whenever he could, about the ground-down Scots. Naomi's upper-class drawl become more intolerable with every day. 'But the poor things, they simply *must* learn better.' Arnold became more emotional and was often in tears. There was every opportunity for tears. They took us to a dance hall, to see how the people enjoyed themselves. This was Moscow's main amusement hall. It was an ugly, poor place. A band played 1930s dance music. And not a man in sight, not one, only women and girls, dancing together. 'Why no men?' we asked, stupidly. And Oksana said, 'But the men were all killed in the war.' For she had no man, nor expected to marry: just like my mother's generation, whose men were dead.

Arnold wept, and I became bossy-boots, more so with every hour.

Arnold and I, sitting in my plushy suite, every word we said monitored, decided it wasn't good enough, we could not stand any more of the official rhetoric; the trouble with the Russians was they hadn't had enough contact with the outside world, they did not know how to talk simply, in a human way. What we had to do—we decided after long discussion—was to frame a question which would force Alexei Surkov to answer truthfully, bypassing the jargon. And this was the question we came up with: 'Always, in every society, even in the most rigid, new ideas appear, are usually regarded as reprehensible or even seditious, but then become accepted, only to be swept aside in their turn by ideas at first considered heretical. How does the Soviet Union allow for this inevitable process, which prevents cultures going rotten, or stultified?' If these were not the exact words—I believe they were—this was the sense of the question. Arnold and I found a moment when Surkov was not surrounded by henchmen. We said we wanted to put a question that was of the greatest importance to us. He listened carefully, nodded (with the sternness demanded by the Soviet style), and said, 'Yes, that's a very good question,' and he would give us our reply tomorrow, when we went to Yasnaya Polyana.

This was Tolstoy's estate, a place of pilgrimage. We did actually expect a real answer.

We drove, several cars, out into the country, and on the roads were local people selling wild strawberries. The officials all bought them, and particularly Boris Polevoi, who though not an official was with us in Moscow. He was an applauded writer of novels about the Great Patriotic War. Konstantin Simonov was also there. He had just produced a volume of love poems, officially accepted, though love poems were considered daring and Stalin himself had said he thought that such effusions should surely be confined to the bedroom. This remark was being quoted often, as a sign of the great man's paternal interest in the arts. Boris was an attractive man, boyish, enthusiastic, and he went everywhere on a motorcycle, which fact was rubbed in at every opportunity: here is this important and honoured writer, but he is not too good to go about on a motorcycle. At Tolstoy's place we saw his house, which, if you think that this man was an aristocrat and a member of Russia's top society, was astonishing, because it is not large and yet it had in it so many relations, children, servants, visitors. Above all, it is poorly furnished, and the sofa on which the countess gave birth so often stands in an ordinary public room and might have been designed for maximum discomfort.

The woods and fields are wonderful. The table for lunch was long, for about thirty people, and set out under the trees. Surkov's daughter was there, a merry, pretty girl, her father's pet: he could not take his eyes off her and showed her off to us. She remarked she was going on a trip to polar regions, and the romanticism of the communist imagination at once seized Arnold, who asked if she was going on an expedition to the North Pole, for no less could be expected of a Soviet maiden. She laughed prettily and said no, she was going with school friends to visit some picturesque place. It is only when I recall moments like this that I can put myself back into that atmosphere of heroic expectation which was the air of communism.

Arnold and I were waiting for Surkov's reply, and when nothing had happened and it was time to leave, we invited him to come aside with us. But he stood his ground. Not moving even a step away from his officials, he raised his voice, so that everybody in sight had to turn and look, and, lifting his clenched right fist, orated, 'The Soviet Union under the guidance of the great leader Comrade Joseph Stalin will always make the correct decisions, based on Marxist principles.' He did not meet our eyes. This, obviously, was what he had been told to say, after the KGB, having listened to our earnest prattle, had worked out a formula of no danger to Surkov or to themselves. He was also saying something about his own position, but that I am afraid only too obvious fact I did not see for some time—years.

Arnold and I discussed this reply and decided we had expected too much. We were part of an official delegation, and he was the main representative of the Party during this visit.

We discussed, too, whenever we could, Stalin and their attitudes to him. This was a time when a version of the following appeared constantly, in short stories, novels, reminiscences: 'My tractor/motorbike/harvester/car had broken down. I was standing by the road, wondering what to do, when suddenly I saw standing in front of me a simple-looking kindly man, with honest eyes. "Is something wrong, comrade?" I pointed at the machine. He indicated the carburetor/engine/brakes/tyres. "I think you'll find the cause lies there." He smiled, with stern kindness, nodded, and walked on. I realised this was Comrade Stalin, the man who had sacrificed his life to be of service to the Russian people.'

My attitude towards Comrade Stalin by that time was less than reverential. But Arnold could not bear to hear a word against him: he was one of those who believed the truth was being concealed from Stalin by his colleagues. Arnold was suffering because of the many 'mistakes' the Party was making. He was a man who needed to respect authority, just as I needed to oppose it. He was a homosexual, he confided—hardly a surprise—and said that before this trip he had gone to Harry Pollitt, the Communist Party boss, and told him he was worried, visiting the Soviet Union as a homosexual. Harry Pollitt had consulted with his mates. Their decision was that it was all right, the Party would stand by him, but any approach by spies, pretty boys, and so forth should be at once reported to them. Arnold was emotional about this. It was then illegal in Britain to be a homosexual: people could and did go to prison. Many years ahead was the tolerant attitude we take for granted. That 'the Party itself' should stand by him was, I believe, why Arnold remained a Communist when other people left in droves. I admired Harry Pollitt and his colleagues too: it could not have been easy for these conventional, respectable working-class men to accept Arnold.

Almost the last place we were taken to was a summer holiday camp for children. We knew it was a show place. Oksana and the others insisted that every child in the Soviet Union went for six weeks of the summer to a camp just as good as this one. It was a pretty well-run place, full of charming girls, in pinafores and braids, and well-mannered boys. What struck us was the library, stocked with Russian, English, and French classics. Everywhere on the little beds, and in the public rooms, lay Tolstoy, Chekhov, and translated English books too. 'Our children read only the best.' And this was true all over the country? Yes, we were assured. Of course we discussed this. It was true that everyone we met knew as much about English literature as we did and that people could be seen reading their classics on the underground. The 'contradiction' was this: these people lived in a country where every moment of their lives was governed by a senseless brutal rhetoric. Yet they were being brought up on the humanist tradition. A single volume of Tolstoy would contradict everything they were officially being taught.

I think that literature—a novel, a story, even a line of poetry— has the power to destroy empires. *'And their packs infest the age.'*

Once upon a time, there was the Russian intelligentsia, cultivated in music, art, and literature: we know about it from a thousand novels and plays. Viciously and consistently attacked through the communist era, these people survived, carefully conserving their heritage. But, it seems, this is no longer true, for when communism collapsed, in flooded the worst of western products, pornography and violence, and what remained of the heritage collapsed too. A unique culture has gone, one that truly inspired the world.

We were invited to go to Samarkand, but Naomi said she had to be back at a council meeting in Argyll. This had the deliberate frivolity, cocking the snook, of Douglas Young's kilt, or Richard Mason's 'I think on the whole I preferred Lourdes.'

There was a touch of the surreal about that invitation, but what could match, for improbability, the great sky-high propaganda banners decorating Red Square: DRINK MORE CHAMPAGNE! For as always, the government was trying to combat the demon drink, and champagne was considered a step up towards health from vodka. Or the overheard chat among the officials, during those interminable banquets, about the superior charms of holidays on the Black Sea. 'My wife just *adores* the way they do the sturgeon.'

It was not all collective farms and People's Palaces and speeches. There was *The Red Poppy,* a ballet of political exhortation, but hardly boring, for its hypocrisies included a scene of a decadent capitalist nightclub, enabling the audience to enjoy what it was ordered to despise: those faces, avid, envious, condemning, as they watched the writhing nudity. But the audiences for the opera *Ivan Susasin* were a different matter: here was the other Russia, preserving itself. What singing, what music! But for us the production already had the charms of the past, for it was realistic to the point where you could count the leaves on the trees. In this opera, the hero, a peasant, a man of the people, defies the invaders of Mother Russia and dies to save his Czar. Some of the audience wept quietly throughout, and of all the impressions of that fevered fortnight, it was this one that spoke direct to the heart about the Great Patriotic War and what it had meant to these people.

There was an evening at the flat of Frank Johnson, a British newspaper man in Moscow. All foreigners visited that flat. He made no secret of his Soviet sympathies, and it seems he was KGB all the time. He was an affable public man. His wife was a Russian beauty. It was there I heard from the Russians, including her, remarks like 'I hate black people' and, like any white madam in Southern Africa, 'I wouldn't drink out of a cup a black had used. I'd disinfect it.' Also Russian talk about their non-Russian republics—Georgia, Uzbekistan, the Baltic States, and so forth— just like Southern African whites: 'They'd be nothing without us.' 'We support them.' 'They're very backward.' 'I don't think we ought to let them into Russia.'

When we were being driven back to the airport, at night, this happened. In the back of our car were Oksana, Arnold, and I, while Douglas Young sat by the chauffeur. A man staggered out into the headlights on a half-dark road. The car swerved but hit him. We all jumped out. A peasant lay bleeding, spread-eagled. He was very drunk. Oksana, transformed into an angel of vengeance, said we should leave him on the road, to punish him. We insisted on bringing him into the car, where he lay in Arnold's arms, dazed, incoherent, bleeding. Arnold wept, while cradling him with a passionate protectiveness. It was all of the Soviet Union he held there, the millions of the dead, the women without men, the pathetic war-wracked streets. I knew this was what he felt, because I did too. Oksana kept up a high, vindictive scolding all the way to the airport: 'How dare you do this, these are distinguished foreign guests, how dare you insult our great country, you will be punished for this, you should be ashamed.' Douglas Young translated, in a satiric voice. This was the most bizarre of all the scenes on that trip, a summing-up and a caricature—the drunk, bleeding man, the Soviet nanny-shrew, Arnold's weeping, Douglas's Scottish voice, deliberately exaggerated, full of bitterness, full of anger, an indictment, and I interrupting Oksana: 'But you will take him to the hospital when we get to the airport, promise? You will, won't you?'

At the airport, there was Boris Polevoi, who had come on his motorcycle to say goodbye to us, all smiles and good comradeship. A friendly fellow, he was, and he promised to see that the drunk was taken to the hospital. 'A likely story,' we agreed. 'Lucky not to be shot,' said Douglas, and Arnold did not protest.

We were delighted we were leaving, we all concurred.

We stopped off at Prague for two days on the way back, to go to the Karlovy Vary Film Festival and to visit a picture gallery. I remember very little about Czechoslovakia, probably because I was exhausted by then, but there is one incident: The six of us were trailing through the gallery, when I was left behind in a room by myself, looking at a picture I liked. The attendant came up to me and whispered, 'I love you. I must marry you. Take me to England.' He was desperate, pleading; he clutched my arm and said, 'Please, please, tell them you love me, take me with you.' And then in came the interpreter to retrieve her charge from this dangerous straying from the flock, and the little attendant—he was old, or so I thought then, thin, sad, all anguished dark eyes—quickly pointed to a picture as if explaining it to me. His eyes followed me as I went out; there went his chance of escape from his life, intolerable for some reason I would never know. When I told Jack about this later, he said, with that mix of bitterness, pain, anger, that was his characteristic, 'Poor bastard, poor little bastard.' And then, 'Well, why not marry him. But don't imagine you'll get rid of him so quickly.' Jack had married a girl in Czechoslovakia to rescue her from the Nazis, in a scheme organised by the Party, but afterwards she was difficult about divorcing him. At last she agreed to meet him, and he reproached her: 'I was doing you a good turn, and you've given me so much trouble.' She said to him, with bitterness, 'But you didn't even take me out to lunch after the wedding. I'll never forgive you.'

'Just think,' said Jack. 'If I had the foresight I'd have given her a rose, or some flowers, and saved myself all this trouble.' This was a reference to an early very famous Soviet story. Sentiment at weddings had been banned, and a pair of young lovers, like all Soviet couples then, went through the minimalist registry office ceremony. Despite their allegiance to Soviet principles, they felt sad, bleak, deprived. Someone gave them flowers: a defiant gesture. Everyone felt better.

As soon as we reached London, the six of us became a unit again. This was because of the press conference. It is truly impossible to re-create the snarling, hating atmosphere of the Cold War. We were confronted by journalists who hated us so much they could scarcely be polite. They demanded to be told 'the truth'. The inevitable reaction was that we defended, where we could; Naomi and Douglas too. If they hated us, we hated them. This was by no means the only time in my life I have reflected that journalists can be their own worst enemy.

After that I refused invitations to go on Peace or Cultural Delegations—it was the beginning of the era of delegations to all the communist countries. I remember invitations to China, Chile, Cuba, others. Writers considered sympathetic, or at least not hostile, to communism were always being invited. The trouble is not that you fall for the official Party Line but that you like the people you meet, become one with them in sympathetic imagination, identify with their sufferings. This must be a version of what happens when terrorists capture hostages, who soon become one with their hosts, by osmosis. The communist governments always used the prestige of their visitors to impress their captive populations, but the said populations were in fact too wise to be impressed. Debates about whether one should or should not go to oppressive countries as official visitors went on then, go on now. When I went to China for the British Council in 1993, with Margaret Drabble and Michael Holroyd, Western journalists who operated in the East approached me to say I was wrong to go. But some Chinese, in London including one who had been in Tiananmen Square, did not understand when asked if I should go. 'Why should you not go?'

'Because the people will think we admire the Chinese government.'

'No one will think that. But it is important for the writers and intellectuals to see writers from the West. They feel isolated.'

No sooner had I got back to London than I was sent my Party card and approached by John Sommerfield to join the Communist Party Writers' Group. By now I was regretting my impulse to join the Party. I did know it was a neurotic decision, for it was characterised by that dragging helpless feeling, as if I had been drugged or hypnotised—like getting married the first time because the war drums were beating, or having babies when I had decided not to—pulled by the nose like a fish on a line. Going to the Soviet Union had stirred up emotions much deeper than the political. My thoughts and my emotions were at odds. I was a long way off seeing, as I do now, that 'supporting' the Soviet Union was only a continuation of early childhood feelings—war, the understanding of suffering, identification with pain: the knowledge of good and evil. I only knew that here was a deeply buried thing which was riding me like a nightmare.

What I was *thinking*—attempts at cool objectivity—was something else. I told an ex-Party friend of mine this experience: On parting with Oksana, so poor, so hardworking, with so few clothes or trinkets, I wanted to give her a little gilt-mesh bracelet, from Egypt. It was nothing much. She went pale with . . . could that be terror? Surely not. She stammered out frantic fearful refusals. What was that all about? I asked my expert friend, who said with the furious impatience we use for people who are still in positions we have just outgrown—he had only very recently left the Party, 'Don't be so naive. If she was seen with that bracelet, she would be accused by the KGB—who were of course instructing her every day—of taking bribes from the decadent evil Western capitalist world. It could get her sent to a labour camp.'

And why was it so many of the writers we met insisted on talking about the royal family? They went on and on: how interested they were in our Queen, such a good institution—for Britain, of course, not for them—and how much they admired us. Why on earth should writers in the Soviet Union care about the British royal family? 'Obviously,' was the reply, 'they could not say openly how much they hate communism. They said it indirectly, hoping you would have the gumption to understand.'

The Writers' Group was about to fall apart under the weight of its contradictions. Ah, with what nostalgia I use that old jargon . . . but how useful were those *contradictions,* always on our lips, while we tried to keep hold of the roller coaster of those days.

Remarkable people, they were. First, John Sommerfield. He had fought in the Spanish Civil War and written a book, *Volunteer in Spain,* describing various actions he had taken part in. It was dedicated to John Cornford, his friend, who had died there. He had also written good short stories, *Survivors.* He was a tall, lean man, pipe-smoking, who would allow to fall from unsmiling lips surreal diagnoses of the world he lived in, while his eyes insisted he was deeply serious. A comic. He knew everything about English pubs, had written a book about them. It was he who took me to the Soho clubs, saying that their great days were over, the war had been their heyday. He was married to Molly Moss, the painter. Like everyone else then, they had no money. They bought for a couple of hundred pounds a little Victorian house in Mansfield

Road, NW3, and filled it full of her paintings, and Victorian furniture and bric-a-brac which could be bought for a few shillings because everything Victorian was unfashionable. This cherished little treasure house, a jewel box of a house, was pulled down with hundreds of others in those great days for architecture, the sixties, and replaced with some of the ugliest blocks of flats in London. During one hard winter, when the Sommerfields were broke, their big tomcat caught pigeons for them, which they stewed, giving him half of what he caught.

The meetings were held in my room because, since I had a child, it was hard for me to go out. Also because I had informed John Sommerfield that I loathed meetings and had had enough of them to last my life. He said, In that case we'll come to you and you can't get out of it. John had said that when you joined the CP it was a good principle to say that there was something you couldn't do, like taking buses or being out at night. Why? To let *them* know they couldn't put anything over on you. 'But no, you cannot say you won't go to the meetings.' *Them?* The Party, King Street.

All the writers shared this attitude to King Street, not much different in spirit from David Low's cartoon trade-union horse, a great lump of obstinate stupidity. The loyalty that they could not feel for 'the Party' was deflected to the Soviet Union, which of course could not be anything like as stupid as King Street.

Montagu Slater was a smallish, quick, lively, clever man, and many-sided. He had done the libretto for Benjamin Britten's *Peter Grimes*. He was under pressure, because he had written a book about the Kenyan war, then at its height, exposing the machinations and dirty tricks of the British government against Jomo Kenyatta, and was being reviled by the newspapers: 'What can you expect from a communist?' Everything he said was true, but soon it didn't matter, because Kenyatta won the war in Kenya and in no time at all had become a Grand Old Man, revered by everyone, not least the whites in Kenya.

Jack Beeching was a poet, with a wife and new baby. I visited them in Bristol, with Peter. They had no money and were in an old, run-down flat in a terrace now beyond the means of anyone not rich. Enormous, beautiful, freezing rooms. I haven't said much about the cold in those days, when houses were often heated with a bar or two of tiny electric fires, sometimes no heat at all. The five of us—Jack, his wife, the new baby, Peter, and I—huddled like refugees under sweaters and blankets in the centre of the great room, where the draughts blew about like cold winds. Jack is still alive in Spain, writing poetry and history.

Jack Lindsay, the Australian, was perhaps the purest example I know of a good writer done in by the Party. He was a polymath, knowledgeable on a variety of subjects, and wrote two kinds of novel. One was party-line orthodox, factories and workers and the proletariat, the other fanciful, whimsical, novels, like Iris Murdoch, but nothing like as good. They might have been written by two different writers. He also wrote biographies.

Asked by some researcher about Randall Swingler, I said he was not a member of the Writers' Group but later found he was. I simply did not remember him. Perhaps he was never there: I was told as I wrote this that he had said the Writers' Group was nothing but a sink of lost talent. What did impress me about him was that he and his wife bought a cottage in Essex for five pounds, without running water, light, telephone, heat, or toilet. A paradise in summer, but in winter? There they lived, solving the problems of poverty, for years. Then Essex cottages became fashionable. . . .

Soon after our return from the Soviet Union, there was the last of the great fogs. Truly you could hardly see your hand in front of your face. Naomi was having a reunion for the people on the trip, in the Mitchison flat on the Embankment. I was standing on the Embankment, unable to move, having lost my way. I was submerged in fog as in dirty water. Suddenly a man bumped into me. It was a Soviet official—Surkov,* I think—in a state of ecstasy because of the fog, because all foreigners adore Dickens's fogs and to this day will say, 'Your terrible London fogs . . . ' 'But we don't have them any longer; we have the Clean Air Act.' It is a disappointment. You can't sweep away potent symbols so easily.

When I was a member of the Communist Party I did not go to the ordinary meetings. Much later, many years, when I was no

*On a Peace Delegation, probably.

longer a communist, I was invited to address a Communist Party group, a real one, of the rank and file. It was a house in a poor street in South London. I was appalled. Here was a room full of failures and misfits, huddled together because the Party for them was a club, or a home, a family. But—and this was the heart-break—there, too, were the village Hampdens, inglorious Miltons, often self-taught, with original and questioning minds on every subject in the world but communism.

A visit to a Communist Party meeting in Paris was a very different affair. I told King Street I was going to Paris, would like to see what the French CP was like. I was told to contact Tristan Tzara. He was a Party member. A likeable man. King Street had had to get permission from the top brass in the French CP, who instructed Tristan Tzara. The local branch on the Left Bank were ordered to receive me, but they said only on condition that I left when they began discussing policy. We had lunch. Only politics were discussed. This was the communist Tzara, not a sign of the anarchic surrealist Tzara. I said to him, What did the Left Bank local branch of the French Communist Party expect? That I might blow them all up? He did not find this amusing. I said that in Britain someone thinking of joining the Party might drop in to a meeting to see how he liked it, but Tristan's silence confirmed that this was no more than what could be expected of British comrades. I insisted: what was wrong with that? He asked: how did you guard against infiltration from hostile elements? I said that there is no way to prevent spies or hostile elements from gaining entry anywhere they like, if they set their minds to it. He said, with an efficient air, that I was wrong: vigilance is essential. The exchange, classic for this kind of situation—and how often so many of us had it!—did not prevent good feeling, but he was truly disappointed in me. He made it clear that the French CP despised the British CP.

Tristan took me to a building somewhere near the boulevard St.-Germain, on the Left Bank, just beginning to be touristland. Guards at the door inspected us, and then we were checked again inside—I had been given a temporary pass. We entered a large, drab room, with a small table at one end for the officials. A hundred or so communists, and they all looked like recruits for an army, for everyone wore at least one item of war dress, probably army surplus. Certainly they all saw themselves as soldiers in a war, men and women, for that is how they carried themselves, how they spoke, cold, clipped, and responsible. No one smiled. Perhaps they were in imagination still in the great days of the Partisans, the Occupation, the Free French. They might look as if they expected war to begin tomorrow, but what they were talking about was a fund-raising event in the *quartier*. After an hour or so, I was requested to leave. Tristan asked how I found it, and I said I thought it unsurprising that the French and English have such a hard time getting on. Did they really need such a military atmosphere? After all, the German Occupation had ended getting on for ten years ago. He said gently, forgiving me, that I underestimated the strength of the enemy. When I reported this visit to the Writers' Group, they said that one must expect this kind of thing from the French. They have to dramatize everything.

I think there couldn't have been more than ten or so of these Writers' Group meetings. Discussions about literature did not defer at all to the party line and were critical of 'socialist realism'. As for me, I was told by the comrades, as a summing-up of my contributions to Party thinking, that I raised questions none of them had thought of before or which had such obvious solutions no one would dream of wasting time on them. My trouble was that I couldn't see the difference.

And now the Communist Party Writers' Group put me into a truly ridiculous situation. Montagu Slater and John Sommerfield told me that they had gone to the Annual General Meeting of the Society of Authors.* This, they said, was an authoritarian, undemocratic organisation, run by a self-perpetuating oligarchy. No member ever went to an AGM. They had put my name forward to be on the management committee. I was furious, said I had meant it when I told them I hated meetings. I would not go. Too late, they said airily, and after all, I did have to do something as a Party member. I

*The Society of Authors is something like a writers' trade union.

94

could regard it as my revolutionary duty. They did speak with the sardonic relish for incongruity which I understood so well. I therefore found myself in that charming Chelsea house, at a meeting, to help run the affairs of the Society. They, of course, knew that I was a communist, having been proposed by two well-known communists, and they saw me as a beachhead for an invading force. They expected from me the dishonesty and double-dealing characteristic of the comrades. After all, they could hardly be innocent of the ways of the Party, since some of them were bound to have been in it, or near it. I cannot remember who they were. A young woman announced that she was a Conservative. She was there as a counterbalance to this subversive person, and scarcely took her satiric and knowledgeable eye off me. How I wish I could remember who she was. As for me, I was depressed and discouraged. I knew nothing about the policies of British literature, and did not care much, being so absorbed in the difficulties of trying to write when so beset with the problems of money, my child, my mother, my psychotherapist, my lover, and—not least—wishing I could slip unnoticed from the Party. For this was a time when, if any public person left the Party, it was to the accompaniment of press furore: 'So-and-so has left the Communist Hell.' 'Communist Party Secrets Revealed.' You were always meeting ex-comrades apologising: 'I'm terribly sorry, I didn't say that. They made it all up.' (Then, as now.)

I was a year on that committee, hating every minute.* Accustomed as I am to being in a false position—sometimes I think it was a curse laid on me in my cradle—this was the falsest. A false position is when people around you believe you think as they do; or that you stand for something quite different, and they assume this difference is what they have decided it is. Or when you have found this position or that oversimplified, a mere set of precepts, and this means that in any gathering your mind is supplying a running commentary, amplifying what is being said or assumed. I have always done this, even as a child. When I was young, this opposing commentary was irritable and intemperate, but the older I get, the more weary: 'Oh God, I suppose it has to be like this?'

*I left 1953.

There was another problem, which I do not have to explain to any ex-colonial (which includes here Canada, Australia, South Africa, and all the other indisputable ex-dominions) and to most foreigners. All your life you have been used to seeing the Brits working in difficult places, often isolated, coping with all kinds of deprivations and savageries. You know that the British are never happier than when on the top of some dangerous mountain, or crossing the Atlantic in a cockleshell, or alone in a desert, or deep in a jungle. Indomitable is the word. Self-sufficing. Solitude-loving. And yet a group of these same people, in England, seems cosy, seems insular, and, confronted by an alien, they huddle together, presenting the faces of alarmed children. There is an innocence, something unlived, often summarised by: 'You see, Britain hasn't been invaded for hundreds of years.'

There is a dinkiness, a smallness, a tameness, a deep, instinctive, perennial refusal to admit danger, or even the unfamiliar: a reluctance to understand extreme experience. Somewhere—so the foreigner suspects, and for the purposes of comparison, while writing this I am one too—somewhere deep in the psyche of Britain is an Edwardian nursery, fenced all around with sharp repelling thorns, and deep inside it is a Sleeping Beauty with a notice pinned to her: Do Not Touch. One Christmas, when I had a child visitor to entertain—and this was the seventies—the following were on offer in London: *Peter Pan. Let's Make an Opera. The Water Babies*—child chimney sweeps. *Alice in Wonderland. Toad of Toad Hall. Pooh Bear.* To sit through a matinee of *Pooh Bear,* while the young mothers, not the children, weep bitterly, makes you think a bit.

Two episodes stand out among memories of that unlucky year as a committee member. One, a discussion of *My Fair Lady,* derived from Shaw's *Pygmalion.* Shaw actually wrote a future for Eliza. She accepts her rich, effete suitor, to save herself from her background and from her tormentor, Higgins, but then takes charge of her life. The makers of the musical insisted she should settle for Higgins. And so there is yet another masochistic woman in literature happy to bring a man's slippers and lick his hands. The Society of Authors acts as agent to Shaw's estate—10 percent. I was shocked at this then and am shocked now. I could not believe then and find it hard now that when Shaw made his intentions so clear, they should be overridden for the sake of the money. It was this incident which told me how out of place I was among those people, who could see nothing wrong with what they were doing. The other bad moment was when Dylan Thomas was off to New York and wanted to use the Society's contacts there. He was by then very drunk and destructive, and it was agreed that people in New York should be warned. I was shocked then—an artist's sacred right to anarchic behaviour: that kind of thing—but think differently now, having seen not a few poets and writers allowing themselves every kind of licence and expecting other people to clear up after them.

Another experience which I suppose could be called communist was when I took Peter down to Hastings during one of his holidays, to a hotel run by Dorothy Schwartz for communists. Oakhurst provided lectures, courses, and the usual amenities. I found the place dispiriting. It was the atmosphere of us and them, of the faithful against the ignorant world. For someone used to sun and large skies, Hastings is not easy to love. I keep meeting people now who you would never think could have been communist, such pinnacles of respectability they are, but they were there, listening to or giving lectures, and in one case actually working as a waiter. What I did find intriguing was that Aleister Crowley had lived just down the road in the sister house, Netherwood. In the twenties and thirties, flamboyant occult groups flourished in Britain, and not all of the participants were negligible: Yeats, for instance, and the New Dawn. Crowley had a reputation, even in the fifties, of dazzling arcane accomplishments, but at the end of his life he was a pitiful figure. He had died in 1947, but they were still saying of him in Hastings, 'Supposed to·be a magician, was he? Then why was he living like an old tramp?' The hotel, Dorothy's place, was reputed to have been the house that Robert Tressell used as a setting for *The Ragged Trousered Philanthropists*. The living room had a beautiful ceiling, and all guests were shown it as a possible work of Tressell's hands.

The Ragged Trousered Philanthropists, a classic of working-class life, had been published several times, first in 1914, but only in a truncated form. Fred Ball, who had been researching Tressell's life for many years, managed to locate the original manuscript and bought it, with the help of friends, for seventy pounds. Some people doubted its authenticity, but it was genuine. It was difficult to get the full version published, because the abridged version was still in print and several publishers felt that the full text was too much of a socialist tract. Eventually Maurice Cornforth at Lawrence and Wishart, the communist publishers, were persuaded to publish. It was very successful. Jonathan Clowes, who was to become a well-known literary agent, was working as a painter and decorator then. He was a friend of Fred Ball, helped him with advice, and was able to place his biography of Tressell with Weidenfeld—a mainstream publisher, not a socialist one. Lawrence and Wishart did not want to publish the biography, because Fred Ball discovered that Tressell, probably the son of a well-off Irish RM, was not working class. This was about the same time as Joan Littlewood had a big success with a 'working-class' play about building workers called *You Won't Always Be on Top,* by Henry Chapman, also Jonathan's friend—described by the press as the Hastings bricklayer. Much to the disgust of the Communist Party cultural commissars, Henry also turned out to have impeccable middle-class origins.★

During this time, when almost all the people I met saw themselves as the vanguard of the working class, the only person I knew who was a genuine representative, unredeemed and unpolitical, was—classically—the woman who came to clean my flat once a week. What interested me most about her was that she was just like the Scottish farmers' wives I had grown up with. She was Mrs. Dougall, about sixty, thin, pale, unwell, never without a cigarette, but if Fate had taken her winging across the seas to Southern Rhodesia? Instead she was as downtrodden as anyone I've known, but a willing accomplice in her exploitation. She was on the books of a firm employing cleaning women, which charged us the maximum per hour, paid her half. It was no use telling her that if she set

★Jonathan was actually acting as an agent for talented but impecunious friends, some of whom later became world best-sellers, before realising that that was what he was.

up for herself she would earn twice as much. 'They've been good to me,' she would sigh. She had an unsatisfactory husband, whom she often had to keep. She loved him. My little splinter of a story 'He' was suggested by her. When not talking lovingly of her husband and kindly of her employers, she brooded about 10 Rillington Place, just up the road, the scene of horrific murders.

She had been sent there to work but had not been found suitable. 'It could have been me,' she would mourn, taking from her handbag fresh cuttings about the murders. 'I could have been that corpse they found, couldn't I, dear?'

HOW WE WERE THINKING: THE ZEITGEIST

First of all, the National Health Service, the Welfare State. What pride in it, what elation—and what confidence! The best thing was still the young doctors setting up group practices. Most but not all were socialists of various kinds. Memories of the thirties were close, documented by The Stars Look Down, Love on the Dole, The Citadel, *novels which everyone had read. Whole families could be brought low because of the illness of one member. That terrible poverty in the 1930s, that cruel indifference to suffering on the part of Britain's rulers—but now there was the welfare state. Pensions meant old age was no longer a threat. (Forty years later a government can say blandly, But we can't afford it—and cut benefits that the citizens imagined they had been paying for. Has anyone ever thought of suing a government that reneges on its promises? But perhaps a more important question is, What state of mind could we have been in, to trust the promises of governments? But that is easy: a romantic, Utopian, idealistic mood, where every good seemed possible.) The 'Dole' was gone, and so was the Means Test, which could mean, and often did, that help was refused to poor people down on their luck. I knew, when she was old, a woman who told me that when she had nothing to eat for days but stale bread begged from a baker's, the Means Test officials refused her help, because she had not sold the rug on her floor. No one remembers now the bitter resentment even the words 'Means Test' could arouse.*

Mass observation, particularly during the war, was the first manifestation of an attitude towards ourselves now common. Sociology was being

99

born, the ability to look at our society, our own behaviour, as an alien might see it. Now this seems to me the important thing, but it was the welfare state that filled our imaginations, as citizens.

Harry Pollitt, the general secretary, or leader, of the British Communist Party, stands outside Pontings, an emporium in Kensington High Street. Compared with the riches of our shops now, it was a poor thing: compared with shops like Harrods or Selfridges then, it was a village shop. He raised his clenched fist and shook it, then lowered it to point an accusing finger: 'When we take power, we're going to pull all these places down.' Meaning, this shocking luxury. So much for the Communist Party beating to the tune of the heart of the masses, who, clothes rationing having just ended, dreamed of nothing but a little fashion, a little glamour. There is a strand in British thinking exemplified by this anecdote. It is deeply puritan, pleasure-hating, with a need to control and suppress.

When I told John Sommerfield this story, he said, 'If you want to understand England, just remember that we are the nation that bulldozed down Nash's Regent Street for the sake of a few pounds' profit.'

French food. Our food then was so bad, but just over the Channel there was France, real food. This was a decade before Elizabeth David. How we grumbled and despised what we had. The delicatessen shops were our consolation, the French and Italian food shops in Soho. Soft white bread was the symbol of everything bad about our food. (In the nineties, this hated bread is the choicest new thrill in Paris, where they cannot get enough of our white-bread sandwiches.) No, baguettes, croissants, brioches—and Gauloises and Gitanes: this was civilisation. Food is always much more than itself. To return from Soho with a decent bit of Brie or Camembert, or a French pastry, was a victory over barbarism. Now I wonder how much this passion for food—certainly fed by the deprivations of war, inflamed by our little trips to France, to Italy—contributed to our present obsession with food: whole pages of recipes, and talk about restaurants and chefs, reviews of cookbooks, which we read like novels. There is more space given in our newspapers or on TV to food than to books these days.

Charity was gone for ever. The Welfare State had ended this bitter insult to the poor, for ever. Besides, soon there wouldn't be any poor.

'At least we'll never again have to put our hands into our pockets for handouts.'

Marghanita Laski wrote a play, The Offshore Island, *whose theme was that Britain had become a dependency of the United States. U.S. military bases were positioned everywhere over Britain: the price we paid for the United States rescuing us when we 'stood alone' against Hitler. She was reviled as a communist, which she was very far from being. Anyone who criticised 'the establishment'—a phrase only just coming into use, replacing 'the ruling classes'—was a communist and by definition a traitor. Now this seems to me the worst of the consequences of the Cold War: so much legitimate and useful criticism was dismissed with, 'It's only communist propaganda'.*

Picasso came to London. He was openly, not to say disdainfully, a communist: take it or leave it. It was he who had drawn the Peace Dove that adorned communist peace campaigns all over the world. His welcome was far from wholehearted. Along with the encomiums went anger: 'We don't want this communist here.' Riots were threatened. His reputation was not as unchallenged as now. Charlatan, trickster, mountebank, subversive—another Grand Old Man in the making.

In cinemas and theatres, we stood up for the national anthem.

As often as we could, we went to see French and Italian films at the two art cinemas in Oxford Street, Studio One and the Academy. The National Film Institute had not yet been born. Happy hours we spent there, and we often said, 'I'm going off to get a dose of sunlight.' In French and Italian films we could touch for an hour or two the grace and charm that we so lacked.

Television: Our children's minds would be rotted by this monstrous new invention. What could we all do to save ourselves?

British was still best: everything British.

People from abroad said how civilised our streets were, so gentle.

In the CP Writers' Group we were joking that the perennial difficulties of understanding between Britain and the Soviet Union would be easily resolved if we and the Russians remembered Britain was still like Dickens's novels, and Russia like Dostoyevsky's.

So far this has mostly been a record of outward events: trips, meetings, the Writers' Group, politics—and so it will go on. A scaffolding, a framework, into which fits the interior life. But suppose it was the other way around—the framework being the writing and the thoughts that go into it? Impossible to describe a writer's life, for the real part of it cannot be written down. How did my day go in those early days in London, in Church Street? I woke at five, when the child did. He came into my bed, and I told or read stories or rhymes. We got dressed, he ate, and then I took him to the school up the street. But soon I put him on the bus, and he took himself the two stops to the school. I suppose now one couldn't do this. I shopped a little, and then my real day began. The feverish need to get this or that done—what I call the housewife's disease: 'I must buy this, ring So-and-so, don't forget this, make a note of that'—had to be subdued to the flat, dull state one needs to write in. Sometimes I achieved it by sleeping for a few minutes, praying that the telephone would be silent. Sleep has always been my friend, my restorer, my quick fix, but it was in those days that I learned the value of a few minutes' submersion in . . . where? And you emerge untangled, quiet, dark, ready for work.

Often when Peter went to the Eichners' for a few days or the weekend, or my mother had taken him off somewhere, I simply went to bed, sliding into that restorative underwater state where you lie limp, rising towards the surface, just reaching it, sinking, rising. . . . You are not really conscious when you are reaching wakefulness, and the sleep itself is lightened by the half-knowledge you are asleep. An hour . . . a day even, if I had become too frenetic. As I grew older, and became cleverer at managing my emotional economy, I began to wonder if the condition of being awake accumulates some kind of substance, which jangles and vibrates, making you tense and sharp, and that this is exaggerated a hundred times if you are writing: but even a few minutes' sleep, the merest dip into that other dimension, dissolves it, leaving you calm again, newborn.

And now, on the little table that has been cleared of breakfast things, replaced by scattered sheets of paper, is the typewriter, waiting for me. Work begins. I do not sit down but wander about the room. I think on my feet, while I wash up a cup, tidy a drawer, drink a cup of tea, but my mind is not on these activities. I find myself in the chair by the machine. I write a sentence . . . will it stand? But never mind, look at it later, just get on with it, get the flow started. And so it goes on. I walk and I prowl, my hands busy with this and that. You'd think I was a paragon of concern for housekeeping if you judged by what you saw. I drop off into sleep for a few minutes, because I have wrought myself into a state of uncomfortable electric tension. I walk, I write. If the telephone rings I try to answer it without breaking the concentration. And so it goes on, all day, until it is time to fetch the child from school or until he arrives at the door.

This business of the physical as a road into concentration: you see painters doing it. They wander about the studio, apparently at random. They clean a brush. They throw away another. They prepare a canvas, but you can see their minds are elsewhere. They stare out of the window. They make a cup of coffee. They stand for a long time in front of the canvas, the brush on the alert in their hands. At last, it begins: the work.

There are no attempts to write when the child is there, for that only results in irritation on both sides. He is read to, we play board games. He listens to the radio, which he adores, grown-up plays as well as the children's programmes. Supper. If Joan or Ernest are there he goes down to see them. He is put to bed at eight, but he has never been a sleeper, and he will lie awake until nine or so— later. Meanwhile Jack arrives. We eat. We talk. Jack works very hard at the Maudsley Hospital. This is the leading psychiatric hospital in Britain, and it is a time of ferment and discovery. Many psychiatric beliefs and practices we now take for granted were being established, then. Jack was the kind of doctor probably now obsolete. He illustrated the Maudsley theories and practices, or incidents

103

with patients, with comparisons from music—for he knew a good deal about music—or from composers' lives, or incidents from literature. A poor man from London's East End would be matched with a character from Dostoyevsky, a mad girl with a story from opera. He suffered over the sufferings of his patients. He was often dubious about the experiments that went on. He described, for instance, experiments in hypnosis. If you take someone—anyone—hypnotise them, and ask them to say what happened let's say on the second of May in some far-off year, when this person was ten years old, or twenty, they will come up with a complete account of that day. 'I woke in a bad mood, I quarrelled with my husband, I went to the shops, I cooked supper . . . ,' and so on. It is all stored in the mind somewhere. What we call memory is a tiny part of what is in our brains, and it is easy to think of it as a kind of overspill from the full, real record. 'What right have we to intrude into another person's mind like this?' He told me how he stood in front of him a line of people chosen at random and went along the line, snapping his fingers, and—'They're out! Just like that! You can do what you like with them. No human being should be treated like that.' He was always saying that human beings should not be treated like this, or like that. He may have been a communist, had been a Stalinist, was still, he said, a Marxist, but he was an old-fashioned humanist, and that was true of all communists with the literary tradition in their blood.

And then we went to bed. The dark, and love.

In the morning he was often off as the child woke. 'I have to pick up a clean shirt from home,' was the formula.

'You could always keep your clean shirts here.'

'Now, come on—why should you have the bother of my shirts?'

This exchange, archetypical between man and mistress, went on, in one form or another, for the four years we were together.

So that's the outline of a day. But nowhere in it is there the truth of the process of writing. I fall back on that useful word 'wool-gathering'. And this goes on when you are shopping, cooking, anything. You are reading but find the book has lowered itself: you are wool-gathering. The creative dark. Incommunicable. And what about the pages discarded and thrown away, the stories that were misbegotten—into the waste-paper basket, the ideas that lived in your mind for a day or two, or a week, but haven't any life, so out with them. What life, what is it, why is one page alive and another not, what is this aliveness, which is born so very deep, out of sight, fed by love? But describing a day like this: I got up, the child went to school, I wrote, he came back, and the next day was the same—that is hardly the stuff that keeps the reader turning pages.

I think a writer's real life is understood only by another writer. And a few other people. These used to be publishers. The publishing scene has changed so much that it is hard to believe the heart of it was once the relationship between the publisher, as an individual, and the writer. In the fifties, every publishing firm had been started by one man—then it was men—in love with literature. They had often risked everything they had, were usually undercapitalised, and yes, they were sometimes bad businessmen. They were on the lookout for new writers, cherished them, kept books in print that might sell only a few hundred copies. The present dispensation, when everything is geared to a few weeks of intensive selling, was ushered in by a joke which—as so often happens—soon became no joke at all, but an accurate description, used by everyone in publishing: 'This book's shelf life is, or was six weeks . . . two months.'

Here is an example of the opposite of what we are now used to. In 1949 a man called Frank Rudman took his demobilization pay of one hundred pounds and began to publish sixty titles a year from three attic rooms in Bloomsbury. This was Ace Books, the very beginning of the paperback revolution, and his list included all the fine writers of that time, from Europe, America, the Caribbean. I should imagine no one made much money. Frank Rudman liked to conduct his business when possible from the nearest pub.

A first novel, or collection of short stories, was kept alive, not remaindered. The second novel, always a tricky moment, was similarly nursed. But a reputation was growing in the literary world. A third book, perhaps a fourth. None of these may have sold more than a few hundred copies. Then a book takes off, for some reason. It wins a prize—there were only a few then—or is mentioned on radio. More likely, I think, an invisible hoard of goodwill is growing, and there is a moment when the scale is tipped: the writer now has a steady readership, a constituency, who look out for a new book by her or by him. It can be a slow process, but it is organic, with a life in it: books recommended, books lent, a reputation growing mostly by word of mouth. And now the new book may at last sell ten thousand, twenty thousand. All this time the writer has been living frugally, or has an office job, or subsists on reviews, a radio play, an article sometimes.

At the heart of this process was the close relationship between the writer and the publisher—the firms being small, it was usually the publisher himself. They didn't move around then, they stayed. The writer relied on a steady, developing friendship, which I am sure has depths not yet acknowledged. It must be confessed that writers are all childish, at least in this department of their lives. On to the publisher—or editor—are projected a whirl of emotions: need, dependency, gratitude, resentment at being needy and dependent, a fighting, contradictory affection, which nourishes the work. The publisher's passionate love of literature feeds into the writer's work, and the discrimination that comes of reading so much helps in criticising the book, insisting on its being better. Yes, this is an exemplary relationship I am describing, perhaps the most famous being Thomas Wolfe's (not the journalist, but the 1930s novelist) with Maxwell Perkins at Scribner's. This was a fruitful and sustaining relationship, for the writer and for the publisher. There are few such publishers or editors left.

I did not have this relationship with Michael Joseph, who never cared about literature in that passionate way. His associate, Robert Lusty, took me out to lunch and confessed he never read books, only watched television. In the early days of television, it was rather despised. These two men hated each other and, unable to confer in the usual way, communicated by notes carried back and forth from one office to another (next to each other) by the secretaries. I do not know if this affected the efficient running of the firm. During this time I relied for support on Juliet O'Hea.

What has happened to publishing exemplifies the rule that things often turn into their own opposites. The antipodes of the slow and reliable growth of a reputation, meaning that books are bought by people who have a personal stake in them, is this: Last year I was interviewed by a young woman from the *New York Times,* and a shallow and superficial article resulted. The publisher rang a couple of days later to say that this interview had sold one thousand five hundred copies of the book (*Under My Skin*) to a certain big chain, which does not mean that this number was read. A feature of our scene now is that books are bought but not necessarily read. The impulse to buy has come from outside—a prod from an interview or a TV appearance—but this kind of stimulus does not mean the reader will like a book. Impulse buying does not necessarily mean serious reading. The root of the trouble is that publishers are managed by accountants, who are interested not in the literary quality of a book but only in how much it sells, and writers are judged only on their sales. But some writers—and they can be the best—never sell more than a few hundred or a couple of thousand. Yet they have a strong, wide, deep influence. The real, the good books, those that in fact set a standard, or a tone, for the whole country or culture, have been, always will be, for a serious minority. No amount of 'promotion' can change such a book into a best-seller; it will result only in unsold books piling up in the warehouses, to be pulped.

These enormous publishing firms, the international empires, are very good for the big blockbusters, the best-sellers, and even the serious and already well-known writers, who are well-treated and cherished. I am one of them and I am grateful for it. Tucked away among the accountants and the moneymen are people who care passionately about literature, but they tend to develop a hunted look and may be heard to murmur, "I *used* to care passionately about literature, but these days I have no time to read." For they are badly overworked. Good books are published, good writers survive, but all the pressures are against the small, or rare, or special books. Every one of us who care about literature cherishes a list of books that are out of print, or not published at all, or published but the editors have not troubled to sell them. In the long run, the neglect of these difficult-to-sell books will badly affect publishing as a whole. Once upon a time the publishers knew very well how important these difficult books were, a little spring of bubbling vitality. Some of us remember wistfully the days when a publisher might say: 'Neither you nor I will make a penny out of this book, but it should be published.'

The other big change is 'promotion'. Writers sadly joke that having written a book, we then have to sell it. This is no joke. It took three and a half months of my life—of writing time—to 'promote' *Under My Skin* in Britain and in America, in Holland and Ireland and France. The old publishers understood that writers need peace, quiet, need to be left alone, not expected to be public people. So now we develop split personalities. One, the real person, stooges around in our rooms, as always, wool-gathering, dreaming, dredging substance out of our own deepest selves. The other puts on a smile and goes forth to be 'a personality'.

The change began with the stinginess of publishers, who did not want to spend money on advertising. They relied on reviews. Then writers were asked for interviews. These cost the publishers nothing. Newspapers and magazines need to fill space. It was a snowball process. Writers became known for their lives, their personalities, became celebrities. The more this happened, the more we were in demand for interviews, for 'profiles'. About ten years or so ago, the literary festivals took off. They are a success, and there are new ones with every year. They frankly rely on the writer as personality. To them come thousands of readers, not all of whom care more for the books than for the personality. It does not mean that the reader, having sat through a talk by the celebrity, at once goes off to buy the book: one often substitutes for the other. The obsession with the autobiographical element in a writer's work here reaches its fulfilment: having seen Shelley plain, what need to read the work?

Then there are the signings, the most irrational of all the phenomena associated with promotion. You give a lecture, conduct a seminar, then you sit at a table while long queues patiently wait for a signature. They value this signature yet must see that it is as valuable as anything that comes off a mass production line. They know that this writer must be signing hundreds, thousands, of books a year. They at last arrive in front of the writer, hold out a book, which they may or may not have just bought—for often they bring in copies from their libraries—and say, Please put For Marie, For Bobbie, For Marcelle, For Jack, please put Happy Birthday Pat, Happy Christmas Jorge. The writer, who has begun with a fierce concern for the honour of literature, and who might even once have refused inane messages, since she has never heard of Marie, Bobbie, and the rest, is broken down by the demand, will do anything to put an end to the miserable business. She, he, is privately thinking, for the sake of sanity, that once writers shyly signed a book for a good friend: Cassandra, from Jane. Dorothy, from William. What would *they* have said to these production lines? I have been asked to sign six thousand copies of a new book: I refused. But I did sign three thousand once. What for? Secretly I think, If I sign enough copies, if we all do, then quite soon the readers will see the ludicrousness of it. A couple of summers ago there was a joke going around the Oxford students: 'I have the only unsigned copy of . . .' How can anyone possibly value these signatures? You think of the long patient lines of people waiting for a signature who have actually seen the author sitting there, speaking for almost an hour, they have heard her take questions. They know, after all, that they and the author share the same human frame, that she must be utterly exhausted and secretly cursing them. But on they come.

In a hotel in Sicily, the manager stood behind the desk, held out one of my books in front of me, ordered, 'For my mother, Maria. Then put, With respectful wishes.' Meanwhile he held his hand over my room key: I would not be given it until I signed.

In Washington I spoke for a most serious literary organisation. Invited to supper afterwards by the committee, I had not even sat down when in front of me appeared a pile of my books, and I heard, 'You are going to have to sign for your supper.' A jest.

In the mid-fifties, this happened: Michael Joseph sold his firm to a big conglomerate, but only on condition that if it was resold, the people working for it must be consulted. Shortly afterwards the firm was sold to—I think—the *Illustrated London News,* and the first the staff knew about it was when the news came through on the ticker tape. Some resigned. We all thought this was outrageous. Now we have reached the point when dozens of editors, of people, can be axed from a publishing firm and given a couple of weeks to leave. No thought is given to the tenuous relationships being built up between writer and editor. These days, the editors working in a publishing firm are treated as roughly as any writer has ever been.

It is an interesting fact, perhaps the most revealing of all, that writers are never consulted when firms change hands. We sign contracts with one firm, perhaps on the basis of its reputation, or of liking for or trust in a certain editor, but this counts for nothing. We are so much baggage now, commodities like the books we write.

In those early days it was a rare thing to get this letter, soon to become common: 'I am afraid I must tell you that I am leaving this firm and going to ———. I am sorry, because I have so much enjoyed working with you. I hope you will soon have lunch with me. I would like to think that one day we may work together again.' At the very beginning, before publishing firms were bought and sold like bags of groceries and editors moved from firm to firm, writers were expected to stay 'loyal' to a publisher. But writers, very soon seeing what was going on, became as loyal as their publishers and moved to suit themselves, usually after an editor with whom they had built up trust. But when that 'loyalty' went, something much deeper than a legal contract was being undermined.

The worst thing that has happened to literature was when the very rich, multimillionaires, took a fancy to owning publishing firms. A power trip: which of them cares about literature? And at once they forced publishing to become like any other branch of industry. None of the great publishing empires make much money, so we may hope that the very rich men soon lose interest and with luck—or am I merely dreaming?—these unnatural associations of publishing firms fall apart again. In this realm, small is indeed the most beautiful. Perhaps we may return to a state where publishers care if the books are well produced and even properly copyedited. Readers will have noticed that books are not as they once were: they are full of errors. This is because, cutting corners as they have to now, under orders from the accountants, publishers often neglect to employ a copy editor, unless a writer takes a stand and insists.

It certainly does not do anything to feed the confidence and self-respect of the writer, knowing that it is of no interest to the publisher that the print is full of errors, the paper and the format of the cheapest.

But it is not just a question of money. Somewhere here is something dark and dubious; an unacknowledged need is being fed. Humiliation cannot go much further than being sent on a trip to some bookshop, let's say in Manchester (or Detroit), to be sat in front of a pile of books, but no one turns up to buy a book, let alone have it signed. I have seen young writers put through this misery.

Or take a Book Fair. Each publisher has a row of writers waiting to sign books. The well-known writers will have their queues. But the less well known—and they can be just as good—sit for an hour, two hours, with no one coming near them. What is that about? Not to sell books, surely? No, it is that a publisher is displaying his writers to the other publishers: Look what I've got in *my* stable.

At the Harbourfront Literary Festival in Toronto, I saw this: I came into the reception area and saw Michael Holroyd, one of the best of our literary biographers. He was white, dazed with exhaustion. His publishers had flown him on three separate trips from Toronto to different cities in the States, to 'promote' his Bernard Shaw books. A TV interview had been cancelled in one, but he knew about it only when he arrived in the studio. At the second, he was interviewed by someone who wanted to know about Lynne Reid Banks: but he happens to be married to Margaret Drabble. At the third, the interviewer did not know what he had written. It was an interview of more than usual imbecility. This kind of exploitation—and humiliation—of the writer is taken for granted.

Only last week it was reported that someone said: 'They should crawl along ditches and through mud.' Meaning authors promoting books. And now there it is, plain and out in the open. Publishers, even the best of them, have moments when they find it irritating, even unbearable, that that quality in a writer which produces good work is uncontrollable. Everything else can be controlled but not that. But you can send these writers who are so pleased with themselves trotting about signing books or giving idiotic interviews. You can jump them through those hoops and put it in the contract too. Publishers often try to dispense with writers altogether. They come up with schemes where novels are concocted to a formula, from plots fed into a computer. But oddly enough, these novels do not have the juice or essence which is the basis of all their publishing. They cannot bear this. The fact that writers themselves find it pretty irritating, often enough, that their best work is elusive does not console them.

A scene: A group of powerful New York publishers sit around the dinner table in a fashionable restaurant. They forget that a poor little writer (not me) is present. They are boasting about their power. 'We make them and we break them.' Or perhaps they haven't forgotten about the author: they need a witness to their displays.

A most famous New York publisher nursed a fantasy of how he would have 'his' authors all safely immured in a line of little cottages, like horses. We would be locked in all day, to get on with our work, and allowed out for three or four hours in the evening, to pursue our unimportant little lives, but locked up again at twelve. A joke!

Yet the will-o'-the-wisp, that firefly, creative excellence, remains elusive. The film industry tries to buy it. Since films began, the process has gone on. There is a novel with this quality. The film-maker buys the novel. The writer, if already seasoned by experience, may smile a little. The film-makers heap compliments on the writer. This marvellous astounding wonderful original book . . . just trust us, you'll see. The writer continues to smile, and cherishes her own thoughts. The writer reads the first draft of the film. Just for the sake of the thing, she or he may say, But that doesn't have much to do with my novel, does it? At this point the film-maker will start to murmur about compromise. The word *integrity* appears: 'The essential integrity of the story . . .' If the writer is an innocent, she (or he) will ask, truly bewildered, But why buy my book at all, if then you don't use it, or only make a travesty of it? Why not write a script of your own, from scratch? But—and this is the point—film-makers, the whole industry, are really believers in magic, though they don't know it. The novel has a certain something—what can it be?—a presence, a fascination, and they have bought the book to get their hands on it. They think that even if they change the story, or idea, so that it has little to do with the original, some of the charm, or power, will stick. And sometimes they are right.

Do they understand this? Probably not. These powerful wheelers and dealers are remarkably ignorant about their own processes. One thing they don't understand is that their industry runs on high-octane emotional energy which they themselves create. Anyone coming from the sober world of literature into films will be astounded by the crises, the tears, the threats, the hysterics, the telephone calls at three in the morning, all the unreal melodramas that accompany film-making. What is it all about? They are manufacturing their own fuel, that's all. They don't understand, either, how they wastefully use it.

A writer may, and often does, experience this. On the fax machine or by express messenger will arrive ('Very Urgent, Immediate Delivery') yards of print, thus: 'I have just read your wonderful marvellous fantastic novel. I was kept up all night . . .' And this will go on for hundreds of words. But the emotion of enthusiasm has already gone into the message, has been used up. The sender, a week later, will pick up the novel, turn it over. 'I've gone off it. Funny.'

When Bob Gottlieb advised me, as a youngish writer, 'The only advice I can give any writer is this: "Take the money and run"', I thought it cynical. But he was right. Unless you fancy an excursion into that phantasmagoric world where nothing is as it seems.

It may be thought that I have gone on too much about publishing and publishers. But how may one write about the life of a writer without it? There are two very great difficulties about writing this book. If it is hard to convey the atmosphere of the Cold War, which was like a poison affecting everything, and which now seems like a sort of lunacy, then it is as hard to describe the difference between the atmosphere that pervaded publishing when I began writing, and what it is now. Young writers—or readers—can have no idea of what you are talking about, if you say, 'In those days publishing was governed by a respect for real literature.' 'What do you mean?' demands this imaginary interlocutor. For they do not know what you mean, since nothing they have experienced can have taught them and many really do not know the difference between a good and a bad book. A single example of the change: in those days periodicals like *The Observer* would review only serious books, would be ashamed to give room to reviews of the second-rate. If this young person who has never known anything different sees in a newspaper described as 'A quality paper' columns of review space for some bodice-ripper or a sex-and-violence epic and one paragraph for let's say a reprint of Flaubert's *A Sentimental Education,* then he or she will know what to think.

I shall repeat an essential, *the* essential fact. There are books that can be only for a minority, and no amount of puffing and promotion will change that, but these are the best, and—secretly, quietly and unobtrusively—the most influential, setting a tone and standard for the time.

I was now on the invitation list of the Soviet Embassy. On occasions like the Anniversary of the Revolution, Red Army Day, and so forth, there were enormous receptions. I went to about five or six of them. I did not enjoy them. Why did I go, then? A revolutionary duty can be a continuation of the duty parents and grandparents owed to the church. Now I can hear my father's 'Oh *Lord,* do I have to go?' when my mother wanted to go to the church service at Banket. A comrade: 'Are you going to the Soviet Embassy, Doris?'

'I suppose so.'

Inside an ornate room—amazing how the representatives of the insulted and injured have to be housed in glitter and glamour— were waiting for us an inordinate number of Soviet officials. They were nearly all spies, but we did not know that then. There were also Party members and fellow travellers. These included some remarkable people. One was D. J. Bernal, the scientist, who had made original contributions to crystallography and had inspired a generation of students, communist or not, who revered him forever as a teacher. As early as the late 1930s, he was exhorting British communists to comprehend that there was a gap between the arts and the sciences and how damaging it was. This was one of the major themes of communist discussion. There were many debates, lectures, and study groups. I think I even gave a talk myself to the group in Salisbury, Southern Rhodesia. This idea was later taken up by C. P. Snow, who made it his own. The process is of much wider interest. Again and again, ideas that have been confined to a minority, particularly if it is an attacked and beleaguered one, take wing and permeate a whole culture. Within ten years, phrases born in communism had become part of general currency: concrete steps—we must take concrete steps—intrinsic contradictions, demos, fascists, all the rest of the dreary jargon, could be found in editorials in the *Times*.

J. B. S. Haldane, Naomi Mitchison's brother, wrote pieces for the *Daily Worker* explaining new discoveries in science. It was he who thrilled us all with 'The universe is not only queerer than we suppose; it is queerer than we can suppose.' I knew people who bought the paper for these articles and read not a word of the rest. Later he went to India, where he educated a generation of Indian scientists. People like these were originals and, like all their kind, shared the characteristic that when they talked about the Soviet Union, every word was rubbish. A question: Do some people need to be identified with a hated minority position in order to flower in other ways? There were colourful characters like the Red Dean, Hewlitt Johnson, who had written a meretricious book called *The Socialist Sixth of the World* and was one of the brightest feathers in the Party's cap, since he was at the heart of the religious Establishment.

No one could say the guests were a boring lot, but I found the atmosphere oppressive. I hated the smugness that went with being in this position—we, the clever minority, supporting the defamed and unjustly attacked defender of the world's working class. But then something happened that put me off going again. A couple of men in military uniform came and said I was to be introduced to a very important visitor from Moscow. They took me, one on each side, to stand in front of a general—I've forgotten his name.

Around him were aides I thought of as military staff, but of course they were KGB. He was a squarish, solid man, with eyes like ice, and he was talking entirely in communist jargon: 'The working class . . . fascist imperialists . . . peace fronts . . . exploited masses . . . advancing the cause of communism.' I wasn't really listening. What was wrong with me? Was I going to faint? I was cold, and my palms sweated. There was the queerest sensation at the back of my neck—the short hairs there were standing up. I was scared. I was terrified. He was frightening me to death. This has never happened to me since. I think this was where I came closest—touch close—to the murderous horrors of the Soviet Union. I did not discuss the incident with anyone. It was too 'subjective', as the comrades said about anything not at once explainable. Unfortunately, some of the most important encounters in one's life, changing you, can seem so minor they are hardly worth mentioning. I did not go to one of these big receptions at the Soviet Embassy again.

I went once with Jack to the Czech Embassy and was as bored as I usually am at such affairs. An unlikeable young man stuck to us, kept bringing us drinks, and, when we said we were leaving and would find a taxi, insisted on driving us both back to Church Street. Uninvited, he nevertheless insisted on coming upstairs with us. There, he boasted about rich and powerful friends, invited us to all kinds of parties, tried to wring promises from us to see him again. When he left we joked that no one in his right mind, rich and powerful or not, would voluntarily spend half an hour with this pathetic little name-dropper. His name was Stephen Ward. Later it turned out that he was not only some kind of pimp for the rich and powerful but also involved in espionage. He was Christine Keeler's friend or lover. When he got into bad trouble, the people who had been making use of him dropped him, and he committed suicide. Similarly, you would meet people who had met the fascinating Christine Keeler at dinner parties—'She's such good value. . . . She's so witty. . . . She's so clever.' But these admirers did not come to her aid when she needed it.

What else did I do that I would not have done, had I not been a communist? I went to sell the *Daily Worker* and canvass for some council election in a big block of flats. It was daytime. It was women who opened the doors. 'I leave this kind of thing to my husband.' They invited me in, because they were lonely. Women and children, shut into dingy, meagre, poor rooms—this was well before the explosion of affluence described as 'You've never had it so good.' At once I was in an only too familiar situation. What they wanted was advice about hire purchases,* about child allowances. They did not know what was due them, or how to obtain it. Whereas in Rhodesia, leaving such scenes, I had only to telephone someone: 'The woman in number 23, she needs . . . ,' now I scarcely knew the rules myself or whom to telephone. I told the Party that these people were not interested in communism; they needed a social worker. I did this only once. Anything to do with the Party was grim, was depressing, and not only because of my being in my usual false position.

I went to Hull University, to lecture on Southern Rhodesia. There were about fifty Nigerian students. Now, that was an experience which taught me a thing or two. They literally could not understand me: that is, take in the fact that a tiny white minority—about 150,000 people—kept in subjugation a million and a half blacks. 'But why don't they tell them to leave?' 'Why do they let the white people tell them what to do?' 'Tell me, please—I do not understand what you are telling us.' I said that Southern Rhodesia had been physically conquered, by force of arms. 'But we would not allow ourselves to be turned into—what did you call it?—hewers of wood and drawers of water.' I have never had a more uncomprehending audience.

I was asked to speak to the IRA about conditions in Rhodesia—their invitation. About fifteen people, all young men. I learned it was usual for IRA members to be arrested without a warrant, imprisoned without trial, and kept there without being sentenced and without hope of release, except at the whim of the British. The war between the IRA and the British had far older roots than most people think now.

I was asked to put the Party Line on literature to a meeting organised by the Kensington communists. I didn't agree with the

*Instalment buying.

Party Line, I never had. But I went—as always—partly out of curiosity. The proposition demanded that Graham Greene must be dismissed as a reactionary. I admired Graham Greene. I was, however, well able to expound the Party Line on literature. Why did I do it? It was, I think, the only time in my life I did this. I began stammering. I have never stammered. I could hardly finish my speech. I did not have to be told by Mrs. Sussman that I had stammered because I did not believe what I was saying. 'Don't you think', said she, 'it is time you learned to say no?'

All these activities went on to the accompaniment of commentaries by Mrs. Sussman, by Jack, and, as well, by my mother, who was frantic, sorrowful, bitter, reproachful, and kept saying I should think of the future of my son. When was Jack going to marry me? Why did I run around with communists? Who was this Mrs. Sussman? Why was I prepared to listen to a foreigner and a stranger, and not to her?

Meanwhile there was an undercurrent in the Party—at least in the circles I was in—of talk about the news coming in from the Soviet Union and Eastern Europe. That is, not the news in the newspapers, which we automatically discounted as lies, but word-of-mouth news. This talk went on in bewildered, frightened voices: the arrests, the disappearances, the prisons, the camps, all summed up by 'a pity the Revolution didn't take place in a developed country; then none of this would have happened.' The Party—officially—denied that anything was happening, even when Party members went in to see them in ones and twos, or in delegations from branches. 'Capitalist lies.' Unofficially . . . that was a different matter. There was a phrase current then: 'knowing the score'. A bitter acknowledgement. Still not the whole truth; far from it.

The phrase *knowing the score* admitted you into an élite of political sophistication.

A great deal has been said about the financial corruption in high-level Communist circles in Britain but I think money was the least of it. They prided themselves, the top brass—and all the Party members would boast—that these officials' pay was never more than the average working man's wage. Did they take handouts from the Soviet Union that there was no record of? No one could say they lived luxuriously. Trips to the Soviet Union and other communist countries there certainly were, but these wouldn't be thought of as perks, I am sure, more as visits to their alma mater. No, it's power—that's the drug, that's the lure. Having inside information, having the ear of the powerful, knowing the score. It is my belief that a lot of people stayed communists, long past the time when they should have left, because of belonging to this élite privileged to know the score. The need to belong to an élite is surely one of the most basic needs of all. Aristocracy, the dictatorship of the proletariat, the Garrick Club, secret societies—it is all the same.

About then I met my aunt Margaret, my mother's brother's widow, and her sister. This was my mother's world, another élite, the upper middle class, the one she admired and wanted me to be part of. Yet she had never liked her sister-in-law. It wasn't that I disliked them, these two conventionally dressed ladies, with their careful hats, their gloves, their fox stoles. It was a world I had nothing to do with. Even to come near it was like being threatened with prison. I felt I had turned my back on it years before, yet now my mother was urging me to take my place in it, among 'nice people'.

I did try and meet my father's brother Harry. It was he who had left his wife, Dolly, after thirty years or so of marriage, saying he had stuck out an empty marriage for the sake of their child and had found at last the love of his life. She was, said the family, 'a red-haired hussy'. If you are red-haired, among 'nice people', the epithet is always imminent. She was—they said—a barmaid. She wasn't, but a red-haired hussy of a barmaid was too good to resist. My father, who had never liked his brother, found at last something to admire and pleaded for him, but it was no good. I wrote to my uncle Harry, said I was not like the rest of the family, could we meet? He did not reply. I tried again—no. His daughter, Joan, came to see me and spent an hour reviling her father. I did ask if he didn't deserve some credit for sticking out decades of a bad marriage for her sake. I did not want to see her again.

In fact, I did not see many people, and those I did were mostly for the sake of the child. This is true of most mothers with small children.

For instance, the Bulgarian Embassy held a weekly folk-dancing evening. I took Peter. Many parents who were not communists went because of their children.

In a garden on the canal known as Little Venice, now very smart, then dingy and run down, there were held ceilidhs, where Ewan MacColl sang, and there was the usual extraordinary mix of people to be found in Communist Party cultural circles. The house belonged to Honor Tracy, an upper-class young woman whose education had destined her for a very different life, and her husband, Alex McCrindle, who was Jock in *Dick Barton, Special Agent,* a radio series of immense popularity. There were people from the worlds of radio, music, and nascent television, and, of course, women with children. Most of them were communists, but none of them were communists ten years later, except for Alex. And Ewan MacColl, the communist troubadour and bard.

I found these occasions pretty dispiriting, all these people doing Scottish folk dances, often in a cold drizzle.

At Guy Fawkes, and on any occasion that gave an excuse for them, there were bonfires on the bomb sites, and the parents with their children came from all the streets around. I contrasted these occasions, with their air of amiable amateurishness, with the great Walpurgis Night bonfires I had seen on the bomb sites in Hamburg.

My initiations into the hardihood of the British in the realms of cold were many. Basil Davidson⋆ invited Peter and me to his cottage in Essex. There was Marion, his wife, and his three children, and the cottage had one electric heater in it, with a single bar, and most often it was not on. Their attitude was that it was summer, and therefore one didn't need extra heat. Mine was that it was freezing. We all wore carapaces of jerseys, and I, for one, wore a blanket. Then they said, We need some fresh air, and we got into the car, drove to a hillside where the wind swept in melancholy

⋆Basil Davidson later became known as an expert in African affairs and of African history.

blasts. We must find a sheltered spot, they cried. This was done, a mild hollow, where the wind blew no less, carrying sharp stinging raindrops. There we huddled, eating sandwiches and drinking tea out of flasks. 'Mad,' I was saying to myself. 'These people are mad.' But now I don't think so, and find cold rain no reason to stop me walking, and am just as mad myself.

The Party often organised marches on weekends to protest about this or that—Hyde Park to Trafalgar Square, usually. Peter adored them. Most children did. They were like picnics, family occasions, people ringing each other up to meet, or go to a pub before or after, or discuss CP business en route. I was privately thinking they were a continuation of church picnics. These marches, or 'demos', whether large or small, were affirmations of togetherness, we are in the right against the whole world. And in those Cold War days people could shout abuse, even throw things at us, confirming our willing martyrdom. Every time the organisers would claim that there were so many hundreds, or thousands, or tens of thousands, the newspapers would say there had been half that, or even less. The truth lay somewhere between. There was an occasion when we were protesting against reductions in funding for education, the 'Butler Cuts', and the children marched along gaily, singing, 'Down with the Buttercups'. The fact that it is so pleasurable to march, demonstrate, protest, even—for some people—riot and fight with the police, is seldom acknowledged. For many people, these 'demos' were their social life.

In fact, occasions for my revolutionary duty were few. Partly, they were limited to what I could do, with a small child; partly, the Party wasn't going to ask too much of me: 'intellectuals' were leaving the Party all the time.

Once, I went to lobby at the House of Commons and waited with a couple of miners who had come especially from the Welsh pits to lobby their member of Parliament, an old mate, who had been a miner with them. They sent their card in, and we waited. And waited. A long time; a couple of hours. We became friends. I told them about my experience in the mining town near Doncaster, but they said their conditions were much worse. At last we three stood in the great ornate hall, with its flunkeys, its statues, its grandeur. The Welshman who came to see his old friends, now his constituents, who had voted him there, was affable and a mite embarrassed. He asked after wives and parents. He said he might be coming back home in a month or so. He could spare only a minute now; he had to be in the House. Yes, he agreed that the government policy was . . . And off he went. The flunkey indicated that we must leave. We stood for a moment, looking around. Then one of the miners said, not bitterly, not angrily, but with the deadly what-can-you-expect, 'Now that I've seen it, I understand what happens to them when they come up here. Not many could stand up to this'—indicating the marble halls. And then, another: 'I won't waste my time and money coming again.'

This was the period when the Soviet Union sent circuses, concerts, dancers, to London. The Russian clowns were wonderful; we had—or have—nothing like them. About the treatment of the animals, that is another matter. The concerts, the choirs, the dance troupes, were all distinguished by a certain coy whimsicality, a sentimentality. Monstrous cruelties produce these qualities in the arts. Sentimentality and cruelty are siblings: cruelty often wears a simpering smile. Jonathan Clowes says he was on a bus and saw a discarded magazine with what he thought he recognised as Soviet art. On closer examination, these heroic figures turned out to be in a feature on Nazi art. On another day he was reading the *Daily Worker,* and the painter David Bomberg, who also used the number 36 bus, told him how barbaric the Soviet system was and said he should read Arthur Koestler, particularly *Darkness at Noon.* Jonathan did, but it was the similarity between Soviet and Nazi art that clinched it for him.

A Soviet cute or heroic maiden was indistinguishable from a Nazi maiden. The empty eroticism of a naked youth striving towards the future could be Communist or Nazi. Ditto the banal cheerfulness of heroic soldiers who could not wait to die for their fatherland/motherland. Ditto the fruitful mothers with overflowing breasts. Both the Soviet Union and Nazi Germany went in for military parades with columns of healthy, bouncy-breasted *mädchens* and *devushkas,* all secretly yearning for the touch of Hitler and Stalin. Probably the most horrible thing I have seen on stage was a woman in a Soviet variety show, about forty, stout, ugly, in a short tight dress, being a small girl, coy, arch, sly, writhing with flirtatiousness, lisping baby language. This was what she was, this was no act, and it was because of the power of this unnatural thing, a middle-aged woman being a winsome child, that she was able to earn her living on the stage.

To offset all this communist propaganda, my mother took Peter to the changing of the Guard, to Royal Tournaments, the Tower of London, the Boat Race, museums in South Kensington, and similar wholesome fare.

There were wonderful children's concerts at the Queen Elizabeth Hall on Saturday mornings, organised by Sir Robert Mayer. Peter and I went most Saturdays, and Joan sometimes came too. More than once, Benjamin Britten's *Let's Make an Opera*, for children, was put on. Packed audiences of—of course—middle-class children. Well, better some than none. What could children from poor streets or—soon—the council housing estates have made of these tales that have as their matrix the Victorian nursery, nanny, servants, mummy and daddy?

What Peter enjoyed most of all was Naomi Mitchison's place in Scotland, where we went three or four times. This large house on the Mull of Kintyre had been bought by Naomi during the war, as a refuge for the family. At Easter and at Christmas, and in the summers, it was full of people. Naomi's sons were doctors and scientists, and their wives were all remarkable in their own right. They all invited friends. The famous divide in the culture between science and the arts did not exist here, because Naomi's friends, writers and journalists from London and from Edinburgh, came, and politicians too, since Dick Mitchison was one. Naomi had begun her association with Botswana, where she soon became adopted as a Mother of a tribe, and so there were Africans. The local fishermen—Naomi owned a fishing boat—and town councillors mingled with guests from London. Naomi has not been given her due as a hostess, for surely this was an unusual achievement, mixing and matching so many different kinds of people. Above all, there were children of all ages, since this was a fecund clan. These days I meet people in their forties, their fifties, who say that the holidays in

Carradale House were magical, the best times in their childhoods. How could this not be so? The enormous house, full of rooms and nooks and corners and turrets; the soft, mild airs of West Scotland, which might suddenly begin to rage and roar, buffeting and whining through all those chimneys; the miles of heather and fields, where they could run and play unsupervised and safe; the beaches and the waves of the Mull of Kintyre, just down a short road. There could be thirty or forty people tucked into the house somewhere, or into annexes. The atmosphere was boisterous, noisy, not only because of the children. In the evenings, astonished foreigners might find all these eminent people playing 'Murder' or 'Postman's Knock', like children. The next minute there was chess, or a noisy game of Scrabble. Voices were often loud, and sharp. The daughters were jealous of Naomi, their exuberant and uninhibited and clever mother, and were bitchy. I would think, Well, if you don't get on with your mother, why don't you leave, as I did, instead of making use of all the amenities and then giving her such a hard time? But I was seeing the beginning of a new era, when children criticise, bitch—but stay.

'Am I really as awful as they say I am? Tell me—no, tell me what you think.'

'Of course you aren't, Naomi.'

'If I'm only half as bad as they say I am, then I must be the biggest monster in the world.'

'Oh, take no notice. It's just mother-and-daughter stuff—you know, happy families.'

'Sons are best,' she would say. But I think she longed for a nice amenable friendly daughter. She treated me like one. She was kind, generous, curious about my doings, hungry for female gossip—which was not my style—and full of good advice, which I listened to with the kind of patience I should have achieved with my mother. Yes, I was indeed aware of the ironies of the situation.

She relied for support on her sons. But this was a clan, and when it was threatened from outside, they closed ranks. Once, the daughter of an eminent American scientist, who had fallen in love with a Mitchison son, was mournfully and tearfully present: the clan had decided against her. I had not seen such cruel, cold exclusion since I had left school. This all went on unconsciously, I think, like a cuttlefish expelling clouds of ink. The thing was, I had never known a clan before. All these people as individuals were charming. But I was giving thanks that I had not been part of a large family.

An incident: Naomi asked me to take a certain inarticulate young scientist for a walk. 'And for goodness' sake, get him to say *something*—his tongue will atrophy.' His name was James Watson. For about three hours we walked about over the hills and through the heather, while I chatted away, my mother's daughter: one should know how to put people at their ease. At the end of it, exhausted, wanting only to escape, I at last heard human speech. 'The trouble is, you see, that there is only one other person in the world I can talk to.' I reported this to Naomi, and we agreed that it was as dandified a remark as we could remember, even from a very young man. Quite soon he and Francis Crick would lay bare the structure of DNA.

An incident: Staying for a night or two is Freddie Ayer, the philosopher. He is with his American mistress, soon to be his wife. She comes down to breakfast wearing a scarlet flannel nightgown trimmed with white broderie anglaise lace. Her style and dash overwhelm the dowdy scene—the rest of us being snuggled into layers of wool. The United States, in those days, was continually and in a thousand ways inspiring envy and emulation.

If the talk one overheard about science, or took part in about politics, was irresistible, the same could not be said about literature.

'Oh, *silly* old Dostoyevsky,' you'd hear. 'Boring old Tolstoy.' There was only one poet, Auden. Yeats? Oh, poor old Yeats. Eliot? Poor old Eliot. Hopkins? Who's he? I thought this was just another little sample of the British philistinism I was encountering so often, but later I understood that here I was tapping some buried layer of past literary culture, a deposit. Sometime in the twenties or the thirties, in some corner of the literary world, or briefly in all of it, a wave of opinions worked their way across, and they were all saying, Auden is the only poet, poor old Eliot, poor old Yeats.

Philistinism is endemic in Britain, and most particularly in London. As I write, the favourite pastime at the dinner tables is to recite—with pride—the list of great books you haven't read and have no intention of reading. A major newspaper, the *Independent,* has a weekly feature, 'All You Need to Know About the Books You Meant to Read,' where the plot of, let's say, *War and Peace* is briefly given. (What, can't you take a joke?) It is all too easy to imagine the triumphant smile of the man writing these little résumés, reducing some masterpiece to the level of an answer in a school examination.

Sometime in the seventies I wrote a humorous piece for the *Spectator* where I used quotes from Meredith *(The Ordeal of Richard Feverel)* and—I think—D. H. Lawrence to show how certain of their purple passages could have come out of any popular romance. This was taken as denigration, and at once in came the letters rubbishing the great. Goethe? How German! Cervantes? What a bore—a favourite epithet. Stendhal? Oh, what tedium! The slightest excuse, and in they rush, these dogs who cannot wait to tear the body of literature to pieces.

Rebecca West, a clever and cultivated woman, said that all of Goethe's philosophy amounted to 'Ain't Nature grand'. And there it is, the authentic grunt from the swamp.

What the British—no, the English—like best are small, circumscribed novels, preferably about the nuances of class or social behaviour.

I said to Naomi that she and her family had an instinctive preference for the second-rate—meaning in literature. It is amazing what rudeness colonials and lesser breeds without the law can get away with: we don't know any better. There was a sad day when I realised that I could no longer get away with it: I and my tongue had to learn to prefer silence.

Why did I go to Carradale when I didn't much enjoy it? Because of the child, of course.

It was the Mitchisons all together as a clan that I disliked, but met separately, that was a different thing. I used to meet Naomi for lunch at her club in Cavendish Square. What I enjoyed about her was the vitality, the exuberance, of her enjoyment of life, and her lack of hypocrisy as she told me the latest instalment in her love life. Naomi had been sent by her father, the great scientist John

Scott Haldane, to the Dragon School in Oxford. It was a boys' school, and she was the only girl. I think this probably set the course for her love life. Aged sixteen, when, as she said, 'I was still at school with my hair down my back,' they affianced her to Dick Mitchison, a handsome young soldier. She hardly knew him. Their marriage, I thought, was the essence of good sense and civilised behaviour. She had her love adventures, and he at least one long-lasting love. These two were the best of friends. A good many people watched this marriage, admiring it, and young people particularly saw it as good. I remember a conversation at Carradale between two girls, both resisting marriage. 'But there has always been this kind of marriage; nothing new about it.'

'Yes, but it is all in the open. No hypocrisy, no lies.' For, being so young, hypocrisy and lies were the worst of the bad things they saw when surveying the adult world.

Of the people I went with to the Soviet Union, Naomi was the one I saw most and for longest—over years. I met A. E. Coppard and his wife several times. He was less and less at home in a world increasingly commercial and rushed. He was a countryman, a man for villages, fields, woods, long rambles. A vanished world . . . I did not see Douglas Young again but heard of him through Naomi. Sometimes I had lunch with Arnold Kettle, but he was never able to sever himself from the Party. Richard Mason I did see. He lived with his wife, Felicity, just down the road in Chelsea. Felicity was a truly beautiful woman, as befits a Muse, for she saw her role as the inspirer of genius. Before Richard there had been one or two, but as soon as she saw him, she knew what would be her destiny, and his, and informed him accordingly. She decided that a little house in Chelsea and a quiet life were what he needed to create. Every morning she made him go upstairs, while she kept from him the telephone, the results of the doorbell, visitors, or any manifestations of ordinary life. This is of course what many writers dream of, not least myself, when much beset by care, but for Richard it certainly was not the recipe. I was present at a painful and very funny evening with several guests, all of whom had been following this drama to its inevitable end with sympathetic curiosity, when Richard told Felicity what it was he needed, and she told him what she was determined he should have. 'What I want is to go to some exotic place, and there I will fall in love with a coloured girl. She must be poor or ill or something like that. Then I will write my next book.'

'Nonsense, darling. What you need is peace and quiet,' said this blond goddess, energetically tidying the room.

'Peace and quiet are driving me mad,' he said. 'Felicity, I can't go on.'

'You've just got a writer's block, darling.'

'Yes, I know I've got a writer's block. It's because I can't stand this life.'

He would lean out of the window upstairs and wistfully watch the vivacity of the street, or even sneak out of the house when she wasn't looking, for a guilty hour or so in a pub. It could not last. It didn't. He went off to Hong Kong, where he wrote *The World of Suzie Wong,* an instant best-seller, about a girl who was tragically afflicted by Fate, not in one way, but in several—tuberculosis, for one—like the romantic heroines of the past. Felicity sensibly went off to find another writer in need of a Muse. Richard became at least temporarily lost in the world of films. One tale he told was of how he and his director went off to look for a perfect Suzie Wong, in Honolulu or some such romantic island, but found the entire population lined up to welcome the ship, singing 'Onward, Christian Soldiers' and wearing gym slips.

For a couple of years I saw a good deal of a young woman with a child Peter's age. We collected the two boys from school at the same time every day and to fill the hours between then and bedtime went to Kensington Gardens to sail little wooden ships, or walked there while the boys ran about. We both lived in places too small to suit the wild energies of six-, seven-, eight-year-olds. There were sheep then in Hyde Park: country in the town.

She was a quiet, reflective woman, and her child was a tough little redhead, combative, explosive—this was not a match of temperaments. She had some job that enabled her to leave work at four, and was, like me, always tired. Her story was unusual then and commonplace now: She became pregnant by a man who said he would stand by her, but he had gone off. In short, this was a single-parent family. When she got pregnant her parents would not help her. She was given shelter by some nuns, who went in for this kind of philanthropy and who kept her washing and scrubbing twelve hours a day; put her, like a poor girl from Dickens, on a hard pallet in a cold room; fed her badly. She was one of half a dozen pregnant girls. When in labour, she was told her pains were the result of her sin. She and the others were reviled all day: sluts, whores, children of the devil. This was just after the war. She had to stay there because she had nowhere to go. I was full of indignation at her treatment. I think she was amused by me: her attitude was: What can you expect? But if acceptance of social ills is a sign of maturity, what becomes of progress? Four or five years later, and she would have been rescued by the Welfare State. The story has a happy ending. The man came back and accepted responsibility. He was not easy to live with, and she put up with a good deal for the sake of the child. They had two meagre rooms, with few amenities.

This ill treatment of pregnant girls, and unmarried mothers, is the same in every culture, always. We have just seen an outbreak of it in Britain, with these young women who have to struggle so hard in everything ritually insulted and denigrated, this time as cunning thieves determined to get an easy life out of the Welfare State. You'd never think that their children were due anything, worth anything: no, their mothers have done wrong, and they must be punished too.

When I visited my Aunt Daisy and her sister, Evelyn, at Richmond, I entered a world so different from the rackety makeshift one most of my friends lived in that for me it was a trip into the past. It was a sizeable house, shabby, needing paint, in a wonderful garden, full of birds. Old houses greet you with reserve, watching you through discreet windows as you go up the path, and when you ring the bell, it is as if inhabitants, some of them ghostly, move into position ready to deal with this intruder. The inhabitants of an old house for someone like me, knowing all about England through the pages of a hundred novels and plays, exchange lines of dialogue from novels they may never have read or even heard of.

I had to brace myself to be a disappointment, because Aunt

Daisy was my godmother, and it was she who had sent me books about Jesus and the Apostles all through my childhood, and here I was, an atheist and a communist.

I rang the doorbell—it was very loud. Was Aunt Daisy or Aunt Evelyn deaf? I rang again. Slowly the door opened, and there stood two tiny old women, smiling. Each wore a best black dress with a flowered apron over it. The aprons meant that they did not have a servant, and I had to jettison Patrick Hamilton's novel *Slaves of Solitude,* set in this part of London and in a house like this one. For it was about the middle classes and their servants, and I had intended to use it as a guide. I kissed two papery cheeks that were presented to me, first Daisy, then Evelyn. The little boy put up his arms for an embrace, to Daisy, but she was slow, through age, and so he put out his hand to be shaken instead, but then he was engulfed in embraces from both of them. The two stood admiring the healthy child, and Aunt Evelyn, the missionary from Japan, said, 'What rosy cheeks little English boys do have.' Peter looked up at me, confused: he thought he was not English, or so he had found out at school.

'I suppose little Japanese boys don't have pink cheeks,' said Daisy to her sister, and Evelyn said, 'But that doesn't mean they aren't as healthy as English children.'

It was eleven-thirty, and in the living room stood a tea trolley and on it waited scones and jam and two kinds of tea. The aprons came off, with apologies. 'I'm afraid we can't afford a proper servant these days. We have a woman who comes in once a week, so everything is neglected.'

Nothing looked neglected. The room was full of Victorian furniture, bought when Aunt Daisy was young, when it would have been only the sort of thing available in the furniture shops. Now they were antiques, though not worth anything because so unfashionable. Peter sat fidgeting, trying to be well behaved, and Aunt Daisy said, 'Perhaps he would like to go out in the garden? I'm afraid we don't have any porcupines or lions or elephants, though.' Peter went out and could be observed through the windows, wandering about among the shrubs with the look of anxious boredom children get when they know they have to put up with hours of grown-ups talking above their heads.

Meanwhile, while making conversation with Aunt Daisy—Aunt Evelyn had put on her apron again to go to the kitchen—I tried to see in this tiny frail old lady the Daisy Lane I knew so much about. She had been a probationer at the old Royal Free, when my mother was ward sister, a martinet with a heart of gold. When Daisy became ward sister in her turn, and level with my mother in that jealous hierarchy, the two women became close friends, and remained so, and it was to Daisy that my mother wrote her long weekly letters, pages of blue Croxley writing paper, with postscripts and post-postscripts, and sometimes 'crossed' in the Victorian manner, the lines running perpendicularly as well as down—which then was for thrift but on the farm was because if the writing paper ran out, then you had to wait until you got some more from the store seven miles away. Daisy Lane was for my mother the England she was exiled from, and the letters were a chronicle of exile, to which Daisy, now an Examiner for Nurses, returned regular but shorter letters. 'I'm sorry my news cannot be as exciting as yours, dear, I can't regale you with tales of snakes and forest fires.' She wrote to me, most conscientiously, when she sent her good books, not only her thoughts about Jesus, but about her sister's life as a missionary in Japan.

'But I suppose you know more about missionaries than I do,' she would write. 'I know that our church supports a Mission in Kampala.'

She certainly knew more about my mother's thoughts and feelings than I was ever likely to. When my mother came to England after all those years and the hundreds of letters, she stayed with her old friend here, in this house, for a week. A London house was what she had been dreaming of, but surely not of a too large house, slowly going shabby because of no servants, and two old women, their active lives a long way behind them, spending their days in cooking and housework. How did that visit go? I wondered but did not ask, for surely it could not have gone well. For one thing, my mother and Evelyn did not see eye to eye. 'Maude was always one to speak her mind,' Daisy said mildly, but with a nervous look at her sister.

And that was all I was to find out about that week, that anticlimactic week, when my mother and her closest friend met at last, in Richmond.

An hour after we arrived, sherry came in on a silver tray, with Bath Oliver biscuits. 'Do you think Peter would like a glass of milk?' enquired Daisy.

'Perhaps he would like some sherry?' said Evelyn.

'Now that really is absurd,' said Daisy. The child was lying on his stomach on the neglected lawn, his head on one arm, while he poked at something with a twig.

'No,' said Evelyn firmly. 'Let sleeping dogs and contented children lie.'

We drank sweet, thick sherry, and Aunt Daisy, doing her duty, enquired about Peter's religious health. 'Then I'll go and dish up the luncheon,' said Evelyn, 'and leave you two to arrange Peter's spiritual life.'

'Japan has given Evelyn some quite unorthodox ideas,' said Daisy. 'I really don't know what our vicar would say if he knew of some of them. But let us discuss the little boy. Maude tells me you did not have him baptised?'

'She had him baptised.'

She sighed. She was distressed. She made herself face me, this intransigent one, and, supported by her long years of service to me, as my godmother—and for which I am now grateful—said, 'But that means he has no godparents.'

I said, 'But you know, Aunt Daisy, people can take on children and be responsible for them, just the same as a godparent; you don't have to be religious for that.'

'But my dear, where is his duty to God—who will tell him of it?'

The conversation laboured on parallel lines, and then there was lunch.

Roast beef on a vast china dish, with a well in it to hold the good juices, which were spooned over Peter's vegetables, to make a man of him. Roast potatoes, carrots in white sauce. Cauliflower in white sauce. The beef was truly wonderful. And so were the puddings, suet pudding with golden syrup, and jam tart. Cheese, biscuits. The old ladies had tiny appetites, and most of this meal was taken out, presumably to be eaten up during the week. We all longed for sleep, after the sherry, the heavy food, but there had to be coffee, a weak grey coffee, and we sat around in the living room in that particular agony, needing to sleep when it is out of the question. Aunt Evelyn spoke about the Japanese understanding of Jesus, not at all like ours, she said, and sang us 'Rock of Ages' in Japanese, keeping time with a teaspoon. Just like my missionary Aunt Betty so long ago in Tehran, but she had sung in Mandarin.

Aunt Daisy said that nurses were not as they had been, so she was told by younger colleagues still not retired. 'No one these days wants to do a job for the sake of it,' she said. 'And look at these modern girls—they won't do housework any longer.'

'No,' said Evelyn, 'they prefer factories. Who in their right mind could possibly prefer a nasty factory to working in a nice house like this?' Here the ghost of Patrick Hamilton hovered for a few seconds.

At four o'clock the tea trolley came in again, the aunts putting on aprons to prepare it, taking them off to consume it. On the top tier were scones, butter, jam, crumpets, honey in a comb, little cakes, biscuits of various kinds, while on the bottom tier were two large cakes, one a sponge with fruit and cream, and the other a fruit cake. And now this was serious eating. Lunch, yes, they had done that, because luncheon, and a Sunday luncheon at that, had to be done properly; but this is what they enjoyed. I could see this was the serious meal of the day, and they ate and ate, and pressed on me and Peter more and more, and they drank many cups of tea, Earl Grey for Daisy and Ceylon for Evelyn, oh do have just one more little piece, and then on went the aprons for the washing up, and then it was five o'clock, and we could leave. And as Peter and I went off to the bus stop and waved goodbye, and waved goodbye again, I heard, from Evelyn, 'And now, Daisy, you just sit down and take the weight off your legs, and I'll get the supper.'

Peter said, 'Do we have to go and see them again?'

Taking him to see the aunts was part of my trying to preserve at least a sketch and a scaffolding of family life. But now it was done, and no, he did not have to do it again.

They moved to Salisbury (England), and I went to see them

there. Another little old house, and a garden full of bees and birds and butterflies. They occupied themselves with arranging flowers for the cathedral and diligently kept up the fabric of middle-class life, with meals all day, and good works, for they visited the poor, with cheerful words and little gifts of home-cooked cakes and sweets. Then Aunt Daisy said she was coming to London to spend the day with me. She could not be asked to climb those precipitous stairs, so I took her out to lunch, but it was hard now to find the kind of restaurant she was used to, with nice English food. All over Britain in provincial towns, yes; not in London. I took her to Derry & Tom's roof garden. I took her to tea. Then, unexpectedly, Aunt Daisy asked me to help her get into a good old people's home. I was so surprised, so taken aback, that I sat there, numbed and dumb. It is useful, this kind of memory, for when you are older and full of competences and know-how, you forget it wasn't always so. Now, if someone said, Please arrange for me to go into a home, I would know how to go about it, but then it was as bad as if she had asked me to push her on a wheelbarrow from Land's End to John o'Groat's. I was still so much on the edge of life in London, just clinging on with my fingertips—so it felt. An immense dismay seized me, a tiredness, and this tiredness was my enemy, for so much of my life I wasn't doing what I would have liked to do, or enjoyed doing. How was it that Aunt Daisy, who had been in my life since I was born, could not see that she was asking too much of me? Besides, how was it that this woman who all her life had lived in London and for most of it at the heart of what we now call the 'caring professions' needed this kind of assistance from me? And what about Evelyn? Were they not sharing their old age? For my attitude was still the common one—the lazy one: 'Here are two old ladies; how nice for them to live together.' (And look after each other, so that I don't have to.) But perhaps they don't get on? Perhaps Daisy and Evelyn, these sisters who had seen so little of each other, for one had been all her adult life in Japan, didn't like each other?

I was sitting there, silent, and knew I was a stand-in for my efficient and energetic mother, Maude McVeagh, and was thinking that the heart of the relations between the two women was revealed in this request. My mother had been the dominant one, the competent one, but she had gone back to Rhodesia, but here was her daughter, the goddaughter, a successful writer, no less, and so she would cope just as Maude would have done.

Now I said to her, or blurted out, my voice not only shocked but incredulous, meaning, How can you put this onto me when I am so burdened already? 'I'm sorry, Aunt Daisy. I can't. I don't know how to begin.'

Soon she wrote that she was going into such and such a home, but I don't know what happened to Evelyn. I didn't see either of them again, but Aunt Daisy sent me Christmas presents, as she had when I was a child: a postal order for perhaps two and sixpence, or a linen handkerchief with a pressed flower in it. I sent her boxes of chocolates, and my books as they came out.

A long time later, years, it occurred to me that Aunt Daisy had been asking in this indirect way if she could live with me. It did not enter my head, at the time, that she could want to share a life with this rackety atheistical Red. She could not have heard one good thing about me for years. My mother's letters to her must have been a steady week-by-week indictment of this terrible daughter. 'Everything you do is *deliberately* designed to cause your father and me as much hurt as possible.' Yet if Aunt Daisy was not wanting to live with me what was it all about? I brood about this sometimes; there is something hidden and painful and impossible here, probably the story of two sisters, very unlike each other, who had spent their lives apart but in old age were expected to live together and share their tiny pensions.

It is hard now for younger people to understand what a poor country this was, after the war. Between then and now are decades of money flowing about, things rapidly getting better, 'affluence'. Even poor people now live better than a lot of middle-class people did then. Few people had central heating: we were a laughing-stock in Europe because of our attitude towards it, for somewhere in a corner of a puritanical national soul there is still a feeling that to be comfortable and warm is self-indulgent. We had gas or electric fires, fed by coins put into a meter. This meant that people returned from work into freezing rooms. Refrigerators were only just becoming common. I had a food safe on a wall and bought milk and meat as I needed them. Most floors had rugs or mats on stained or painted boards; wall-to-wall carpeting was still to become general. You could go into a house or flat full of good old solid furniture, but there was no heating, no refrigerator, the kitchen was still furnished by a china sink and wooden draining boards, and chilly floors shivered under beautiful rugs. A lot of furniture was still 'Utility', because of the war. During the war, Utility furniture and Utility clothes were all that could be bought new, and both seemed designed to prove just how ugly necessity had to be.

An average young person taken back to stand in a quite unremarkable home of then, the early and mid-fifties would be ... well, what? Embarrassed, probably. All too recent for comfort: the world of their grandparents, a threadbare, cold adequacy in everything.

None of the writers or artists I knew had any money. Attitudes have changed: now young writers demand exaggerated advances and worry about security. For us to worry about what would happen to us was felt to be shameful, 'bourgeois'. Probably it was the war that destroyed a belief in security. It was not shameful to be poor or to live shabbily: all that was simply not an issue. As for me, I can say with equal truth that I did not worry about money, because I knew things would come right in the end, and that I was always worried about it, short term. My basic optimism, which I think is an affair of the nerves, the flesh—a disposition, a temperament—was just what the situation needed. I did not expect to be rich, for that was not the point; I simply knew I was doing what I had to do, which was to write. And that meant managing my resources so that my time was not invaded by the unnecessary, my energies were not used up wrongly. Easy to say, easy to write—but this is the crux and the heart of the writer's task. When we go about, having temporarily become talkers, standing on platforms and holding forth, we are always asked, Do you use a word processor, a pen, a typewriter; do you write every day; what is your routine? These questions are a fumbling instinct towards this crucial point, which is: How do you use your energy? How do you husband it? We all of us have limited amounts of energy, and I am sure the people who are successful have learned, either by instinct or consciously, to use their energies well instead of spilling them about. And this has to be different for every person, writers or otherwise. I know writers who go to parties every night and then, recharged instead of depleted, happily write all day. But if I stay up half the night talking, I don't do so well next day. Some writers like to start work as soon as they can in the morning, while others like the night or—for me almost impossible—the afternoons. Trial and error, and then when you've found your needs, what feeds you, what is your instinctive rhythm and routine, then cherish it.

Now, looking back, I am quite amazed, I am impressed, at how I balanced my way between demands—the child being, of course, the main one. Intense concentrated work, when I could, with always an eye for the energy-eaters.

The first novel, *The Grass Is Singing,* had done well for a first novel in Britain, America, and Europe, had been much reviewed, and was reprinted. But few serious novels make their authors rich. My second book, *This Was the Old Chief's Country,* got good reviews, sold well for short stories, and individual stories from the collection were printed in anthologies and abroad. *Martha Quest* and *A Proper Marriage* sold well enough and got published in Europe and America, but neither was the stuff of best-sellers. All my books continue to sell, steadily, are in print, but not until the seventies did I earn big money on advances. In 1958 I calculated that I earned on an average twenty pounds a week, the working man's wage.

Like all authors, I survived from cheque to cheque. Joan did not mind my weekly rent being paid two weeks or three weeks late. Once, the debt ran on until it was five weeks, and this made me sick with worry, because she did not have much money either. These little sharp memories correct generalisations, like: 'Having no money did not worry me.' (I was actually saying this for a time.) There were times when I was worried, all right. I was walking down Church Street, having dropped the child at school, and I was crying because I couldn't buy food. A man walked rapidly up the street towards me, stopped, and said, Why are you crying? I said, I haven't any money. He said, Well, cheer up; you will have by this time next week, won't you? This being true enough, since money always did turn up from somewhere, I did cheer up. I sold my mother's jewellery. Giving me her heavy gold chain, her gold brooch, her gold bracelets, some Victorian trinkets, was a ritual: mothers hand on their good jewellery to their daughters. I did not want it, asked her to keep it, but she insisted. When I took it to the jeweller's I was positively asking to be cheated, to be done down, so low was my morale. The jewellery was not fashionable. I remember even pointing this out, apologetically. I was paid less than thirty shillings for what ten years later, when Victoriana became fashionable, would be worth hundreds of pounds. Similarly, I had a Victorian sewing table, from my aunt Daisy. It was very pretty, full of little drawers, fretwork compartments, padded pin-and-needle cushions—a gem of a piece. There was an antique shop downstairs. I begged them to buy it. They refused, said there was no market for it. Soon it was worth a lot of money.

The vicissitudes of a writer's life mean complicated tax returns. One year I had no money to pay tax The year before I had earned well. The income tax official came, was sympathetic, but it was no good: I had to pay it. How? I don't remember. Probably I asked for books to review. I don't think there were allowances then for women in my position—a child, and no support from the father. If so, I would have scorned to take them: a question of pride.

If you are thinking, But you had a lover; why didn't he help? I always paid my way with Jack. That was a question of principle. Besides, he had a wife and family to support. Yet, if this was poverty, I can't remember really going without anything much, pining for something I couldn't afford.

And we ate well. Joan and I both cooked wonderful meals and invited each other. I made good use of that standby for people during hard times, the soup-stew which was continually added to and became better as the days passed.

Sometimes I must have despaired, though, because I applied for a secretary's job in Mayfair. Seven pounds a week. I said to the employer that it wasn't a living wage, and he said apologetically: 'I am afraid we expect them to live at home.'

I sent short stories to *The New Yorker,* sold them two, neither of them my best. Nadine Gordimer had had a short story accepted, told them to look out for me. (We had not then met.) I sent back a batch they had just returned, and they took one.

Round about then Stalin died, and I wrote a little story called 'The Day Stalin Died'. King Street—I was told—were not amused.

Isak Dinesen in Denmark was working for broadcasting, and she accepted a couple of short stories.

I did not do much reviewing. It is hard work, for very little money—that is, if you actually do read the books, and think about them, which cannot be taken for granted in reviewers.

Another false start was when I agreed to be Donald Ogden Stewart's secretary. One of the writers who had left the States because of Joseph McCarthy, he was well known then as a play-wright, and a screenwriter: *The Philadelphia Story* was his work. He was married to Ella Winters: she had been one of the well-known left-wing journalists who had seen the future working in the Soviet Union.★ Both were strongly pro-Soviet still. They had a flat in the Finchley Road. Of all my attempts at getting regular money, this was the silliest. He paid me seven pounds a week, the minimum. To go from Church Street, Kensington, to the Finchley Road took almost an hour by bus. Don worked very slowly. He walked about or stared out of the window, while I sat waiting to write down the results of these long thoughts. Then it came out: 'But it takes three-quarters of an hour to get to La Guardia Airport.' Was this how successful plays got themselves written? I was going mad with boredom. Meanwhile Ella was popping in and out, and finally said that if I wasn't doing anything I might as well go shopping for her. It is common for an employee to be competed for by a husband and wife. I stuck it for about three weeks, and we parted amicably. I decided I should try and write for one of the radio soap operas, *Mrs. Dale's Diary,* and submitted an episode, but they said it was too extreme. The subject was a delinquent child, so soon to be the stuff of so many run-of-the-mill radio plays and serials. I then

★'I have seen the future and it works.' —Lincoln Steffens, an American jour-nalist in love with the Soviet Union in the thirties.

decided that all these attempts to earn money in ways other than writing seriously were a mistake.

Juliet O'Hea was my support. She was remarkable because of the range of people she represented. She was a Roman Catholic and a Tory. She looked after at least three communists, one of them myself, and she hated and despised communism. She had other serious writers and, too, writers of romantic novels and adventure stories. She dealt with us on our individual merits, was fair, was kind, and a good friend. I can't remember her ever giving me bad advice. Since then the world of publishing has been in turmoil, has changed completely, and through it all I have been supported by my very good agents, first of all Juliet O'Hea, and then Jonathan Clowes. He still is my agent, and my friend.

Now my social life changed, because for a time I was part of a group of Canadian and American writers. Most were in London as exiles from McCarthy. Reuben Ship had made *The Investigator,* a gramophone record ridiculing McCarthy. No one had dared laugh at this man, and the explosions of laughter now all across the United States because of this record were probably the beginning of his downfall, or contributed to it. No one now remembers *The Investigator.* Its high point was when the devil allots places in hell to applicants for heaven. Reuben had been working in Hollywood and was escorted to the aeroplane in chains because of his dangerousness—which much impressed his family, who, Reuben claimed, were all crooks by profession and had despised him for going straight and being that unprofitable thing a writer. But the chains had redeemed him. Was this true? But Reuben was a very funny man, and who cares about details of the truth when you are laughing? No scion of an ancient family ever made better use of his ancestors than Reuben did of his criminal family, one a Mafia boss.

Ted Allan had been working in Hollywood. He wanted to write the greatest play, or greatest novel, ever written, which was the style in those days of writers from the other side of the Atlantic, and he did write some good things, but his talent surely was for talking: he was a storyteller, taking incidents from his life and blowing them up into monstrous and very funny inventions.

Some of the group had come from Canada because it was at that time hard to earn a living as a writer there.

Stanley Mann wrote scripts for films.

Mordecai Richler was the baby of the group. Probably hundreds of thousands of young men—millions?—all over the world were casting themselves as imitators of James Dean, a thoroughly unpleasant person, as it turns out, but does that matter? After all, how many millions of communists had pledged themselves to be worthy of Stalin and other brutal oppressors, but as they tried to match themselves to their imaginations of greatness, they acquired all kinds of stern virtues. Mordecai would stand with his back to a wall, a glass in his hand, inarticulate or almost stammering, lovably modest, genuinely so. He would confront me, or Ted Allan, or Reuben, all of us weighed down with responsibility and children, with the earnest and urgent query—straight from the flaming heart of the bohemian myth—Do you think an artist ought to get married and burden himself with children? Surely that destroys talent? Later he married Flo, the wife of Stanley Mann, and had four children, besides taking on Stanley's son.

At first it was Mordecai and his then woman, Cathie, I saw most of, for he was living just down the road in Church Street for some months. It was the informal colonial style, dropping in and out, making impromptu meals. Cathie was a loud, forthright, clever woman, and there was a running joke that though she was a shiksa, she cooked better Jewish food than any Jewish woman. A lot of jokes, a lot of drink, a lot of good food. Later it was Reuben I saw most of: we were friends for years.

This 'group' was in rapid change. For one thing, marriages and liaisons were breaking up—Ted Allan's, Reuben's, soon Mordecai's. The wives or girlfriends who had shared early hard times and acted as agents and counsellors, even earners—out. When this happens so often, is so common, what is the point of moral indignation? It seems to me that men have to fight so hard to free themselves from their mothers, but then circumstances and their natures make their wives into mothers, and they free themselves again: not always—far from it—swapping an old model for a younger one. Young women taking on young artists or men with futures should know from the start that this may turn out to be a labour of love.

It was a hard-drinking crowd. Now, I had hardly drunk at all since leaving Rhodesia. In Denbigh Road I had no money, and no one drank. At Joan's we drank wine, but not regularly. With these North Americans, it certainly was not wine they drank, and a great deal of competitive expertise went on about the right way to make this or that cocktail. 'Only one drop of vermouth in the gin, or better still, merely pass the cork over the top of it.' That kind of thing. And competition about pills, for some of them took amazing amounts. Later Clancy Sigal and Reuben would hold out palms to each other, on which were arrayed their daily quota, while one taunted the other about how their own were stronger, weaker, reliable, dangerous, only just invented. I used to be shocked at the style of their jesting, though I enjoyed it. This was the hard, aggressive North American humour, often cruel. Later Donald Ogden Stewart wrote a play, *The Kidders,* put on at the Unity Theatre, where the characters 'kidded' themselves and each other into violence and death. It was a good play, but the Unity Theatre was then unfashionable.

The jokes were mostly about which of them was a CIA agent. With these McCarthy exiles, I don't think there was an agent at all, but did it matter? There wouldn't need to be an agent, even a part-time one, for groups of exiles to damage themselves with suspicion of each other. This was my first group of exiles, and so I didn't know paranoia has to be the rule. Soon there were the South African exiles. I was never part of that crowd, because I didn't want to succumb to the South African weakness, which is that they tend, when away from their homeland, to meet only each other. I am pretty sure that the South African government, efficient about espionage, would have ensured that there was an agent or two around, but suppose they hadn't? It would have made no difference, from the point of view of the level of paranoia and the cruel suspicions and persecutions of each other.

Later still I was in Paris and met, briefly, some of the exiles from the Soviet Union. That was a truly poisonous atmosphere. They distrusted each other, knew that every French person they met was an agent for the KGB, were obsessed. I can say with confidence that I can think of no worse fate than to be one of a group of political exiles.

Now, as I look back, what interests me about the McCarthy exiles was their 'contradictions'—the same as communists everywhere then, but concentrated because of their insecurity. They had been communists, or fellow travellers (not Mordecai Richler; he was the odd one out), and by definition believed—surely?—in the violent overthrow of the capitalist state. Yet obviously they could not really have believed this article of faith, for they greeted with genuine derision the idea that they were or could have been any danger to the United States. This was partly because no one could believe that that powerful country could have been threatened by such a small number of people. But if you believe the ends justify the means, then why not Reds under the beds, why not Moscow gold? But no one I met believed that the Soviet Union financed communist newspapers, or Soviet-loving organisations, like the British Soviet Friendship Society and its American equivalents. The communist jargon was put into inverted commas: for instance, 'capitalist lies'—this was partly because by now everyone knew these capitalist lies were true. Above all, what these people felt was that they were innocent: they hadn't done anything. Well, they hadn't, had only talked. McCarthy was ludicrous, making a fool of himself. And when his lieutenants, Cohn and Schine, came on a trip around Europe, spreading McCarthy's message, everyone had to laugh. But McCarthy was frightening enough to his victims, as a hundred memoirs have testified—that is, the people who came up before his committees. And, too, then and later I met, or was told of, how quite small and unimportant rank-and-file Reds in the States were visited regularly by the FBI and threatened, lost their jobs, could not get employment, a steady year-in, year-out persecution. But I don't believe there were many American communists who experienced this. I think that the life of the average Red in America, as in Britain, was about as exciting as being a member of a Women's Institute or a church. That was certainly true of most British Reds, but things were bound to be worse in America, because Americans are an extreme people. No one ever seems to notice this, or comment on it: they always take whatever faith or crusade or persecution they go in for to extremes. But then the hurricane passes and is forgotten. Here, even the worst time of the Cold War was mild compared to the United States.

The most interesting thing that emerges from the now plentiful books about the CIA and the FBI is the ignorance of the heresy-hunters about what communists were really like. This is probably because spy-catchers took their information from defecting Soviet spies, or professional agents, all of whom seemed to live in lurid worlds of their own. They certainly had no idea at all of how they looked to more sophisticated parts of the world, or they could not have sent those pathetic clowns Roy Cohn and David Schine out around Europe to represent them.*

From the time I met him, I was under pressure from Jack to get myself my own place. 'You are a big girl now.' He said Joan bossed me about, but I knew his attitude to Joan was to do with some 'unresolved conflict' of his own. The ways in which I had or had not turned Joan into my mother were of course discussed with Mrs. Sussman. I thought Jack missed the point, which was that it was good for Peter to be in Joan's house, for he loved her, and she him, and Ernest was as good as an older brother. Surely Jack could see this. He was a psychiatrist, wasn't he? This was truly naive, but in those early days psychoanalysts and psychiatrists were considered infallible or at least given credit for insights in ways that would be impossible now: we know they are mere human beings, like the rest of us.

Now, there is no woman in the world whose lover urges her into leaving all others to find a place of her own who does not *feel* what he says, even if her mind is saying something else, as a promise. I was seeing less of Jack than I had. I thought I would see more of him when I achieved my own place.

I was missing the essential thing. It was not only me but other

*In the United States, Cohn and Schine were serious and admired politicians. Cohn had been one of those who sent the Rosenbergs to their death. In Europe, they seemed only ludicrous, because of their pompous hysterical oratory, and they were a gift to the comedians.

woman friends of his who were being told they must get their own homes. This was a man who had been very poor all his childhood, in a country and culture where security was a chimera. For a poor person, the first step into security is a roof over one's head. Decades later, when I was involved with some very poor old women, I heard all the time: 'a roof over my head'; 'I got a roof over my head'; 'You must keep the roof over your head.' Jack's advice to everyone was to find a house or flat in an unfashionable area, get a mortgage, and be sure there is enough space to let a room or two, which will cover expenses. This is the recipe for survival in hard times. But I had never thought like that, had moved so many times in my life I could no longer remember when or where, felt nervous at the thought of staying in one place. I had been in Joan's for four years—1950–1954.

It was not that I had not tried. I had been urged to buy a vast house in Blenheim Crescent, in bad repair, going for £2,500, ludicrously cheap even then. I asked the bank manager for a loan, but he said that house prices were so unreasonably high they were bound to fall, and he would not advise his wife or his daughter to make such a terrible mistake. *Experts*. (For a time I kept a file, 'Experts', but I lost it in one of the moves.) If he had given me this loan, my years-long, decades-long worries over getting and keeping a roof over my head would have ended right at the beginning of my time in London.

Suddenly there was a telephone call from Pamela Hansford Johnson, who asked me why I had not put in for the Somerset Maugham Award. It was then £400, with the proviso that it had to be spent travelling for at least 3 months. This was because Somerset Maugham felt that English writers were provincial, knew only England, and should travel. It was before the tourist explosion. I said that since I had been brought up outside the country, I thought I didn't qualify. Never mind that, said she. She was always kind to younger writers. (In my experience, older writers are kind to the young ones.) And so I won the Somerset Maugham Award, but I had to promise to spend the £400 out of Britain. This was like being handed an apple when you are starving and told to eat it next month. I needed that £400 badly. This proviso of Maugham's taught me that if you are going to give something, then don't make conditions. Previous recipients, also desperate for a roof over their heads, or to eat, had cheated. One had fulfilled the letter of the law by putting the money in a bank and travelling round Italy for three months with his guitar, singing for his supper and sleeping rough. Or with kindly girls.

There was a flat going in Warwick Road, controlled rent, for £250. It was large enough to let rooms. I gave this sum as a deposit to an Australian mother and daughter going back home. I was getting all their furniture, 'such as it is', included. I would go to Paris for a month. Peter would go to the Eichners' for a month, my mother and Joan would cope for a month. Then in his holidays I would take him to the Mediterranean for a month.

Jack was with me when the telephone call came that I had won the Somerset Maugham Prize. I was afraid to tell him—rightly, as it turned out—for he at once exclaimed, 'And that's it, that's the end.' It came from his depths, from his deep dark male depths. I was so shocked. I was so frightened. I expostulated. I begged. I appealed for justice, but that was the end, and I knew it.

'You don't love me; you only care about your writing.'

I am sure there is not one woman writer, ever, at any time in the world's history, who has not heard these words from her man.

It was unjust. Far from being like George Sand, who rose from the bed of love to write all night by candlelight, while her lover lay alone, I never put writing before love, or before Jack; was infinitely amenable to any suggestions from him, giving up any writing plans for him; and in short was like Jane Austen, writing . . . well, if not under the cover of a blotter, then only when he was not around or expected. But we do touch here on something deeper. A woman writer, putting love before literature, when love lets her down will then make literature out of love. *'Well, whose fault is it!'*

I put myself in a cheap hotel on the Left Bank and set myself to spend as little money as possible. Twenty-five—that's the age for Paris; young, fancy-free, unworried. I was in my mid-thirties. I spent my days writing, but I was not living the life of a writer in Paris. I sat in cafés trying to understand the talk around me, got into clumsy conversations with strangers but made no attempt to make friends. I was low and sad, and worried, waiting for Jack to arrive, when he would see that I was not having mad passionate love affairs with all and sundry. It is no good saying now I wish I had—what a waste of Paris! Jack came for a weekend. There could scarcely have been a more misused visit to Paris than that one, but it cost very little, which was the point. Then Peter arrived, by plane, and we went down to St. Maxime for the other month. I found an extremely cheap room at the bottom of a house, large and cool, with nothing in it but a couple of mattresses on the floor, two hard chairs, and an electric plate. Small black ants were everywhere. I have never been more bored in my life, but the child, of course, loved every second, because we were out on the beach from six or seven till the sun went down. We ate picnics in our room. There were other children, but they were French and not interested in an English boy. The much reprinted and anthologised story 'Through the Tunnel' comes from that holiday, so you could say it paid for itself. Also a little sour story called 'Pleasure', about enjoying oneself.

Back in London, it was time to move. Mrs. Sussman was supporting me. She always did. I do know how lucky I was to find her, having since seen in action therapists who do more harm than good. She told me, when I said I was worried about Jack, whom I was seeing so much less of, just as I was preparing to share a home with him, 'But you *are* married to him.' I will skip reflections on what being really married means. But probably he was married to more than one of us, apart from his wife. Like me, he had a talent for intimacy. The Shona people say that it may take years for a man and a woman to be really married. By definition, that must mean: within a framework of polygamy.

Going to Mrs. Sussman twice or thrice a week, which I did for about three years, saved me. I knew that then; it has not taken the passing of time to tell me. She was a friend. Perhaps if I had had a good older friend, I would not have needed Mrs. Sussman. I didn't care about the ideologies—Freud, Jung, and so forth. When she started 'interpreting' according to whichever creed it was, I waited for her to finish. For one thing, I had always been at home in these realms.

Joan reached me where it hurt when she said moving would be bad for Peter. I knew that, but the flat was too small. By then he was a vigorous boy of eight. He needed more room. But what he needed most was a father, and Ernest was at least a big brother.

Before leaving Joan's I wrote to Somerset Maugham, thanking him for the £400. I got a grudging letter back, saying that, first, he had nothing to do with the choosing of prize winners and, two, he had never read anything I had written and, three, no one before me had ever written to thank him. So much for good manners. 'You must always write bread-and-butter letters saying thank you.' Or, 'Doddis is a *good* little baba.' (*Under My Skin*) This letter from Maugham hurt. It was meant to. But I owed him a roof over my head.

Before committing myself to the new flat, I asked my accountant, and my bank manager, if the law was likely to change. I did not want to spend my precious £250 on a protected tenancy and then find I was out on the street. Certainly not, they both said; there is absolutely no possibility of the law changing. Well, it did, or that part of the law which affected me. *Experts*. But not for four years.

Warwick Road
SW5

—∾∾∾—

THE FLAT WAS IN WARWICK ROAD, A SINGULARLY UGLY STREET, where lorries thundered all day and most of the night. It consisted of a large kitchen, a very large living room, and upstairs two decent bedrooms and two small ones. A 'maisonette'. This was the first place I could call mine, of all the many rooms, flats, houses I had lived in. It was all brown wood and cream paint, twenty years later to be the last word in chic, but then the very essence of dowdy provincialism. I could not have lived with it. I painted it white, all of it, and that took two and a half months. I balanced on ladders, and windowsills, on contraptions of ladders and chairs and planks, even over stairwells: I now shudder to think of what I did. A painter dropping in from downstairs, hearing that this female was usurping his place in the economy, looked at the paint rollers, just invented, and said no decent workman would use such rubbish. 'No one can do a good job with rollers.' *Experts*.

The furniture that came with the flat was quite awful. I painted some of it. I put up cheap but pretty curtains. I dyed the ancient carpet green. A friend told me the other day that when she came into the flat and saw I had a black cover on the bed she was shocked. But it was red, surely? I remember dyeing a 'brocade' bedcover dark red. At first I took one of the tiny rooms as a bedroom, but then when Jack ditched me I moved downstairs, and the big living room was where I slept, worked, *lived*.

When I went into this flat or 'maisonette', which was really like a little house, was my approach much different from someone conquering a bit of wilderness? This flat was *mine*. I was not renting a corner in someone else's home. We put our mark on new houses, flats, with curtains, colours, furniture, but I did not have the money for all that. What I hung at the windows was not what I would have chosen. It was the dazzling skin of white over every inch of the walls that was my mark. I had thought my kitchen was mine— blue linoleum floor, white woodwork, a red wallpaper—but Jack stood in it, smiling, and said, 'What a colour box! You share more than you know with my wife. She's got the same wallpaper in her kitchen.' In those days there wasn't so much choice as now, not hundreds of possible kitchen wallpapers, so this was not really so surprising. But deflating, yes.

I could not have afforded this flat without letting a room, at least when I began. The rent was very low, but no one could let such rooms these days, even in the provinces. There were merely adequate beds, dressing tables, and wardrobes; painted board floors, everything bright and cheap. The bathroom and lavatory were shared. Peter had one of the big rooms. There was a succession of tenants: I had entered that world of the lost, the lonely, the misfits, the waifs and strays that drift from one let room to another in big cities. It was a nasty experience. It didn't help that I was a youngish woman, by myself. My highest social point as a landlady was when a couple of minor diplomats from the French Embassy took a big room and a small one. They were charming, affectionate in the caressing French man-to-woman way, and that was certainly good for my morale. They brought me flowers, offered to do all kinds of little jobs I found difficult, like moving heavy furniture. They were good to Peter. They were fascists—I mean, real ones. This was when the French were fighting the rearguard action in Vietnam, and they called the Vietnamese little brown scared bunnies. The two handsome young men staged a rabbit hunt through the four rooms upstairs, frightening Peter because they were violent and vicious, though they were making a joke of it. They were anti-Semitic, in a conventional way. They complained about the black people in the streets: 'They should go back where they came from.' So depressing was this experience of letting rooms that after a few months I decided I would chance it and live on what came in, hoping it would be enough. It was, more or less.

Peter was not happy. He had done well at his first school, had enjoyed it, or seemed to, and when it came to choosing the next school, I thought, Well, why not stay with what has worked well up till now? Most of the children from the junior school moved up to its senior school, which was next door, near Notting Hill Gate. Peter at once became sullen and miserable and was at the bottom of the class. Then he said the headmaster had beaten him. No one had ever so much as smacked him before. I went to see the headmaster, who was an unpleasant little bully. He said, Spare the rod, spoil the child, and called Peter 'Lessing the Blessing'. I knew that Peter was earning—far from the last time in his life—punishments for being my son. The children of the successful can have a hard time of it. The worst thing about this man was his cold, sarcastic, cutting voice, the voice which, when I was a child, shrivelled me up. He made drawling envious remarks about my books. There followed two unsuccessful schools. I thought that this most gregarious child was suffering from being so much of the time alone with me; he still did not sleep until nine or ten, still woke at five or six. He went to a school as a weekly boarder, coming home at weekends, but he hated it. He hated Warwick Road, as much as I did. During the time I had lodgers he was resentful and suspicious of them. He was used to a household with a lively family atmosphere—Joan's— and now he had to be quiet for fear of disturbing these strangers who were in his home. I made a mistake and refused to buy a television, though he begged for one. Bad enough, I thought, the 'comics' which he read for hours every day. So he used to go after school to friends' houses to watch their television. We became engaged in a battle of wills on this and it seems on every other issue. I knew that what he needed was a father. When Gottfried dropped him, just like that, and he was so unhappy, I made a point of creating a picture of Gottfried as a brave, heroic figure fighting for the poor and dispossessed. This was hardly the truth, but I believed it would be bad for the child to know too much about the failures of communism. I made up stories about how he—Peter— and Gottfried tackled all kinds of difficult and dangerous situations, from solving housing problems in slum areas to fighting landlords (this was the time of the landlord Rachman whose name is still synonymous with the wicked exploitation of tenants) or routing whole divisions of Nazi soldiers. Later, in his teens, when Peter went to visit Gottfried, he found that his father was vilifying me in every way he could and that he had been doing so for years. This is not at all uncommon, where one partner in a failed marriage, usually the woman but not always, builds up a 'positive' and flattering portrait of the absent one, only to discover that he, or she, is being made to look a villain to the children.

How to make better this bad situation? Meanwhile what saved us both was the Eichners, there in East Grinstead, in their old farm-house among the rocks, and the other children there, a real ordinary family, mother, father, and the children, and it did something to balance me, who lived without a husband—much rarer than today—this unconventional mother, this writing mother, and he was at the age when children are most in love with respectability and the commonplace. The Eichners took their own children and visiting children on all kinds of trips, over Britain and abroad, to France, Spain, and Peter went too.

At the Eichners', Peter was part of an instructive effort. Fred Eichner was a bit of a genius. He had invented something he called plastic foam, in two forms: one, blocks of substance full of minute bubbles, like sponges; the other, globules in various sizes. He had a small factory. He thought the stuff could be used in packing and by florists. As this caravan of adults and children travelled around and about Britain, Fred Eichner was trying to get some business or bank or forward-looking financier to back him, but when I knew him he constantly failed. Perhaps in the end he succeeded.

The oldest son, Michael Eichner, was Peter's friend, and he came to London and they went about together. I took Peter on holidays, once to Spain for a month in the summer, and he loved it, but I didn't, much.

There was a child in the flat downstairs for a while, a boy Peter's age. The parents hoped the children would be friends, as parents so often do, but they did not like each other. One day this happened: I had started Peter off on a stamp album; we bought stamps, sent for stamps, he swapped stamps. The little boy down-stairs took the album and stole half the stamps. Peter was miserable, in that frantic resentful way of children who feel themselves trapped by circumstances. I asked the mother to get the stamps back for Peter, but all she said was: 'Poor little boy'—meaning her son. Peter was hurt by the injustice of it, and I felt an only too familiar cold discouragement—that so often things went wrong for him and I could not put them right.

I will leave this theme here. Women who have brought up a son without a father will know how difficult it is, and those without the experience will have no idea of it. One may easily describe a single dramatic event—like a traveller arriving at the door with a present for Peter from his father, a plastic whale, for instance, but there was no word from his father, no letter, nothing. One may describe the pain of that for the child, his bewilderment and the mother's anger, but not the day-in, day-out slog of it all, trying to be what is impossible, a father as well as a mother.

When Jack finally left me, we were in Paris. He was going to some hospital abroad somewhere. I knew he had arranged it to break with me. We both knew this was the end but were saying things like: 'Well, it's only six months.' He was off to the airport, but he went with me to the ticket office at the station, where I would buy my ticket back to London. We embraced. He left. I stood immobilised, tears flooding. The young man at the ticket window made sympathetic noises. No queue. Seeing I had a packet of Gitanes in my hand, he nipped out from his little office, put a cigarette in my mouth, lit it, clicked his tongue, Tsk-tsk, patted me, said *'Pauvre petite'* several times, and nipped back to serve a customer. When I finally was able to ask for a ticket, he said love was a very serious matter, but cheer up, I'd find another lover soon.

It was very bad. The 'affair,' which had lasted four years, was in fact a marriage, more of one than either of my two legal marriages. I had been uncooked, raw, not involved with more than a small part of myself. But with this man, it had been all or nothing. How absurd that was: he had never ever said he would marry me, made any promises. And yet I had been committed to him. This was the most serious love in my life. So little did he understand how it was for me that he turned up later, three times in all, the last being in the seventies, to say that since we had done so well, we should start again. And with a look at the bed. That was where we understood each other. . . . But surely in a good many other ways too? In *Under My Skin,* I describe leaving two small children, and I earned criticism for not going into what I felt about it. It seemed to me obvious that I was bound to be unhappy and any intelligent reader would understand that without ritual beatings of the breast. Now I feel the same. There is no one who hasn't suffered over love at some time, and so it should be enough to say that being thrown over by this man was bad for me. It was the worst. I was unhappy for a long time. Men fell in love with me, but it was no good, I could not care for them. And then I did something foolish, after misguided reflection. My two marriages I did not think of as having been chosen by me: the first was because of the approach of war, always as good as a marriage broker, the second was a political marriage. My great love, with Jack, had ended badly. Why did I not do as people have been doing for centuries—choose a man for compatibility, similarity of tastes and ideas (at that time these had to include politics)? Among the men interested in me was one who could not have fitted the bill better, as well as being amiable with Peter, who liked him. We embarked on an affair. This was a bad experience for him. He was in love with me, but seriously, and I had to bring the thing to an end. I felt suffocated by him. There was no rational reason, and I have never understood it. We'd meet, with pleasure, talk, walk, go for a meal, I found him delightful— and then it would begin, an irritable need to escape, get away; and in bed it was the same, though on the face of it there was nothing wrong. I couldn't breathe. It had never happened to me before, and it hasn't happened since. I was shocked at myself for letting him in for such pain, because he was badly hurt by it.

And now my mother: the cruel story continues. She had been four years in London, that Elysium about which she had been dreaming for all the years of her exile, and she had spent them in a dreary little house, looking after yet another old man, who was not even her relative but my father's. She had more than once come to Joan's house to be with Peter while I was away. All this time she was saying, 'All I want is to be of use to my children.' When I left Joan's to get my own place, she suggested—without much confidence—

that she should come and live in it with me. 'You need help with Peter.' I did, most desperately, but not from her. She went to see Mrs. Sussman, to get her to make me see reason. Mrs. Sussman said, in a variety of conventional phrases, that young people need to live their own lives. Afterwards my mother complained that Mrs. Sussman was a Roman Catholic. I did not know what to say. She could have said that Mrs. Sussman was Jewish, that she was not English, was the very essence of European culture, was subjecting me to exotic un-British influences like Jung and Freud. But that she was a Roman Catholic? I knew there was nothing I could say that my mother would respond to, or even hear.

By now Peter was finding the Eichners', that paradise for children, more attractive than my mother's outings. I tried to suggest that a very energetic nine-year-old boy was bound to find a place full of children of various ages more interesting than the company ˙ of adults.

'Who *are* the Eichners?'

'They have four children of their own, and they have children at holiday times.'

'Yes, but *who* are they?'

'They are Austrians. They came here as refugees.' Never had I heard from either parent the slightest hint of anti-Semitism, so when she said, 'But they're foreigners,' she didn't mean Jews. 'They aren't Roman Catholics, are they?'

'I don't know. I never asked.'

Why Roman Catholics? Was it that Emily Maude McVeagh had had her childhood affrighted by Roman Catholics because her stepmother was the daughter of a Dissenting minister? But if Roman Catholics were so terrible, why had she sent her precious daughter to a Dominican convent? All of it incomprehensible, exasperating . . . *impossible*—as usual.

When, on one of the trips to the south coast, she had Peter baptised, she told me later. Defiantly, but she knew she was in the right. It wasn't the baptism I was angry about—as far as I was concerned, it was something not far off a pagan ritual—but that, as usual, what I thought didn't count. 'And now you're going to have to take him to church,' she ordered. As it happened, he was going to church, because it turned out that he had a beautiful voice and he was singing in the choir. 'And you could ask Joan to be his godmother.'

'But how could she be a better friend to Peter than she is, if she were his godmother?'

She came to see my flat soon after I got into it. She stood there in her good hat, with its little veil, in good gloves, her fox stole, her polished shoes, and she looked at my ugly furniture.

'You didn't buy that stuff?'

'No, it came with the flat. You know, they went to Australia.'

'You'd better have mine; I'll take it out of store.'

When the stepmother died, my mother had the furniture from the Victorian house put into storage, and paid to keep it there, year after year, even when there wasn't money for the grocery bills. When at last they 'got off the farm' and went back to England, there might not be a place to live at first, but at least there would be a houseful of furniture. This was not because she liked the furniture. On the contrary, she had hated the heavy dark house she had been brought up in, and everything in it.

Now she could not see that for me to fill my flat, the first place I could say was really my own, with her furniture would be like putting myself into her power, into a prison of the past, into a shirt of Nessus.

'I don't want it, Mother. Sell it.'

'You can't, you *can't* prefer this rubbish. . . .' And she looked at what filled my rooms, and then at me, and we looked at each other, in our usual hopeless, helpless misery. She could have cried out then, as she had when I was a girl, 'But why do you hate me so much?' Or I, to her, 'But you never liked me, did you?'

What had liking and disliking, hating or loving, to do with anything now?

For God's sake, Mother, just go away and leave me alone. No, I didn't say it. And that is what she did. First laying briskly on the ugly desk some papers. 'These are the receipts for the furniture. Do what you like with it.'

And she went back to Southern Rhodesia. To her son.

The furniture was, of course, Victorian. The mere word *Victo-*

rian then earned a superior or a contemptuous laugh. Very soon indeed it would be worth a great deal of money. I did not want to be bothered with it. I wrote to my cousin, my aunt Muriel's son, and asked did he want it. He came to see me, said he had no use for any old furniture. He does not remember coming. He was very hard up then.

So I told the furniture storage to sell the stuff and send the money to my mother. It was hardly worth sending, there was so little.

There is a mystery here. For a quarter of a century, my mother had been writing to her great friend, Daisy Lane. When my mother was in London, about which she had been dreaming all those years, she needed a place to live, and as it turned out, so did my aunt Daisy. Why then did they not live together? At the time, I thought of it with the bewildered exasperation that went with all my thoughts of my mother: I could make no sense of it and so did not think of it much. But now I put two mental images together. Aunt Daisy, younger than my mother, a tiny little bent woman in heavy black, was an old woman. But my mother, at seventy, could be taken for fifty, was vigorous and healthy. To whom was my mother really writing for twenty-five years?

You have to be grown up, really grown up, not merely in years, to understand your parents. I was middle-aged when it occurred to me that I had never known my father, as he really was, as he would have been, without that terrible war. Young, he was optimistic and robust, played football, played cricket and billiards for his county, walked and—what he enjoyed most—danced at all the dances for miles around, thought nothing of walking ten miles to a dance, dancing all night, walking back again. The war had killed that young man and left a sombre, irascible man, soon to become a semi-invalid, and then a very ill man. If I had ever met that young Alfred Tayler, would I have recognised him? And, similarly, my mother. Yes, I knew that the war had done her in too, not least because it killed the great love of her life, so that in the end she married one of its victims—and spent the rest of her life nursing him. But it took me a long time to see something else. This was the girl who had defied her father to become a nurse, standing up to years of his refusal even to speak to her. This was the woman who impressed everyone she met by her vigour, her competence, her independence, her humour. I cannot imagine that had I met the young Emily Maude McVeagh I would have had much to say to her, but I would have had to admire her.

I think what happened was this: When she arrived on that farm, which was still virgin bush, with not so much as a field cleared on it, not a house or farm building—nothing; when she knew that this would be her future, a lonely one, because of her neighbours, with whom she had nothing in common; when she knew that the forward drive of her life, which had been towards some form of conventional middle-class living, was blocked; when she knew her husband was an invalid and would not be able to keep his grasp on life—when she knew that nothing she had hoped for could ever happen—then she had a breakdown and took to her bed. But words like 'breakdown' and 'depression' were not used then as they are now: people could be suffering from neurasthenia, or low spirits. She said she had a bad heart and probably believed it, as she lay in bed with her heart pounding from anxiety, looking out over the African bush, where she would never ever feel at home. She lay there for months, saying to her little children, 'Poor mummy, poor sick mummy,' begging for their love and sympathy, and that was so unlike her it should have given me reason to think. And then she got out of bed, because she had to. But *who* got out of that bed? Not the young Emily Maude (she had become Maude by then, the Emily had gone—she had dropped her mother's name) but a woman who kept telling her children she had sacrificed her life for them, that they were ungrateful and unfeeling and . . . all the litany of reproaches that are the stock-in-trade of the female martyr. A creature I am sure she would have hated and despised when being herself and still young—and undamaged by war.

She went back to Southern Rhodesia, after four disappointing years in England, told her son and his wife—again—that she would devote her life to them, and—again—her daughter-in-law said to her son, Either her or me. And she began on a round of visits to friends. In the letters she wrote, she said, I hope I shall make myself useful; I don't want to be a burden.

The nicest result of the visit to the Soviet Union was that I became a friend of Samuel Marshak, one of the prominent Soviet writers, a winner of the Stalin Prize for Literature. He was a poet, translated Burns and Shakespeare, wrote children's stories. At that time writers unable to write what they wanted, because of the persecutions of serious literature, chose to do translating work: this is why the standard of Russian translation was so high. I had not noticed him more than the others, when I was there. But suddenly I got a telephone call from the Soviet Embassy. That must have been 1954 or '55. Would I visit Samuel Marshak in his hotel in Kensington. Things were loosening up, because Stalin had died, but even so, I was on my guard. After that, when he came to London, which he did several times, I was telephoned—and I went. I would arrive at about nine or ten, when the child was asleep, and leave probably about one or two. In between, I listened. That was my role. As a very young man, he had been in London with his first wife. That was before the First World War. They had no money, but they were in love, with each other and with London. Those were the happiest times in his life, he told me. He wanted to talk about that old London: the British Museum, trips to the country, the parks, the bookshops. I reminded him of that wife, he said. But then she died, and there was another wife. She died in the Second World War, of hunger and cold. He liked talking about what that war meant for Russians.

I sat in one armchair, and he in another, and he talked into the past. Sometimes he would slightly raise his fingers from the wrist of a hand, which rested on the arm of the chair, and that meant there was more he could say but he was afraid of invisible listeners: the KGB bugged all hotel rooms their protégés were put in.

The day-by-day struggle to live during the Second World War, or the Great Patriotic War . . . I sat and thought that it was not easy for anyone in Britain to imagine such hardship, such cold. Later he loved another woman, who worked in the Hermitage, in Leningrad, but he was living somewhere outside Moscow. It was hard to get permission to travel then, even for a prominent writer, but he did sometimes take the train to Leningrad—Anna Karenina's train, he reminded me—and she got the day off from her work. She had survived the siege of Leningrad, and she was very thin and weak, and not well. In her room they sat together all day and talked or were silent, and then he took the train back to Moscow. There was no need even to talk, he said. It was enough to be together. That was how that love went on, but she died too.

He also talked a lot about politics, about the times under Stalin. 'I never betrayed anyone,' he insisted, over and over again, raising his voice and giving angry looks at the telephone, where he believed the KGB bug must be. 'We were all compromised, every one of us. You don't understand, people like you in the West. There was no possibility of saying no to them. But when I was interrogated I would not speak about other writers—and that was what they wanted. They wanted to frighten us, that's why they interrogated us, even if *he* had decided not to send us to prison.'

He also wanted to warn me about the dangers of politics for writers. 'You are still young. I was young too, once. I was a boy genius. I was a peasant boy. Gorky noticed me. He said I was a genius. He and I were alike. We were both from poor families. We both liked to walk by ourselves through the villages. He walked all over Russia, and so did I. Sometimes I was months by myself, walking. The peasants fed me. But later Gorky was destroyed— they killed him—and so was I, but in a different way. I have spent my life on committees. That is where my genius went. I always tell young writers, Don't go on committees, they'll finish you. And that's what I am telling you too.'

'Ah, but you see, I learned that long ago.'

'That's good. That's very good. But it's easy for you. You can say no. It is hard for us to say no.'

He told a story of how, when he was on a country road in some province, Gorky saw him, stopped his car, made him get in. 'I want you to see something. You'll see an important man today.' Some writers were meeting in a country house, and Stalin had sent word that he would drop in. He did. He listened to their delibera-tions, all flattering to him. Then Gorky stood up and spoke directly to Stalin, telling him that everything that had been said was false. Conditions were terrible for the people. 'We were sitting there in that fine house, but all around, people were suffering. And the writers were suffering too. The Party's ideas about literature were wrong and not good for writers.

'We were holding our breaths,' said Marshak. 'We were all of us white with terror. I was shaking—I was a very young man, and these were all big, important people to me, and Gorky was treating them as if they were just naughty children. And no one ever defied Stalin. You don't understand, you people here. Then Stalin stood up, very deliberately, and he said he was glad there was one honest man present—Comrade Gorky. "All the rest of you are liars, and you only say things to please me." Then he went off with his guards.'

I have heard this story about other dictators. Clearly, we need to hear about this 'one honest man'.

I was fond of Samuel Marshak, and I think he was of me. But what he needed was someone to listen to him, pay him attention. He was lonely. Yet this was an important Soviet writer.

He wanted to meet Peter. Next time he came, we met in the daytime, had tea in a park, went shopping to buy Marshak some shoes, for all the visiting Russians bought shoes and good clothes. He loved Peter, and Peter liked him. He gave Peter a very fine knife and some of his children's poems, in Russian. He wrote some verses for Peter, but I don't know what happened to them. Later Marshak's son, a physicist, used to come, and I was telephoned from the embassy: would I take him shopping for shoes and clothes?

I do not see how any writer could have a worse fate than Samual Marshak's. To be a peasant boy with genius—or even talent—at that time, was to be seen as the inheritor of a glorious future. To be Gorky's protégé was to be accepted by the most famous writer in Russia. Gorky steadily fought Lenin over the inhumanity of his policies, procuring the release of hundreds of political prisoners, and then he fought Stalin too: it would have been easy for Marshak to feel allied with the good side of the Revolution, for it was then still possible to think there was one. Slowly he was absorbed into the structure of oppression, but hardly knew it was happening. By the time he knew he was trapped, it was too late. Easy to say, for people who have never lived with the experience of political terror, 'He should have opted out.' How? He would have been sent to die in the Gulag, like dozens of other writers. 'I never wrote what I should have written,' he said. 'I could have been like Gorky. Really my talent was for realistic writing. I should have written what I was seeing around me.' Samuel Marshak, to this day, arouses the most extraordinary degree of contempt among Russian intellectuals. They seem to want to spit (a very Russian expression of contempt, enshrined in the language) at the sound of his name: he was a Stalin Prize winner, he was synonymous with Soviet power. They are reluctant even to allow that he made good translations of Burns, Shakespeare, others. But surely the sad and humble old man I knew was as much a victim as Maxim Gorky, who was murdered by Stalin?

An incident not without its comedy was when the cultural attaché said he would like to meet me and discuss . . . what? Probably literature. I behaved as I would with anyone and asked him to lunch. When he arrived he found me alone, with the table laid for two—this was still in Joan's house. He had expected other guests, a real luncheon party. He surveyed the heaps of books and papers everywhere and said, 'You are a real writer, I can see that.' He was nervous, and I pretended not to notice. I was thinking, I'm damned if I'm going to change my ways to fit in with their stupid ideas. 'I cannot have lunch here with you alone,' he said. 'It might be misunderstood.'

'Oh, why?' said I, disingenuously. He was a nice sort of man, not at all like an official. I took him to the French Pub, which had a good restaurant upstairs, and told him the story of the Free French and this pub, and how on the Fourteenth of July people danced in the street. He liked all that. He didn't want to talk about literature at all and confessed that he was bored by culture; he hoped I didn't think the worse of him. What he liked was the circus. He went as often as he could. He was glad I was not shocked, for he knew that as a cultural attaché he should know about books. When we parted he said that he was sorry, but he had to inform me that I was not a communist at all, I was a Tolstoyan. No, this was not a compliment.

And now an occasion that gave up its full flavour only later. I was invited to the Soviet Embassy for lunch to meet Paul Robeson, the singer, a very public communist and having a bad time of it in the United States. As usual, I went thinking, Oh, Lord, I suppose I have to. There were as many Soviet officials as there were guests. About sixteen people sat down to lunch including Pamela Hansford Johnson and C. P. Snow, who, if not actually a Party member, was much trusted by the Russians.* James Aldridge was there with his wife, Dina. James Aldridge's novel *The Diplomat* was regarded in the Soviet Union as a great work of literature, but James was not much known in Britain. *The Diplomat* was full of what used to be known as 'progressive ideas' and was not a good book. The sad thing was that he had written a beautiful little novel called *The Hunter,* about the wilds of Canada, where he had been brought up. But this novel, the real one, the good one, was mostly ignored in the Soviet Union, and ignored here because he was such a public communist.

I was sitting next to Mikhail Sholokhov, the author of *And Quiet Flows the Don,* and *The Don Flows Down to the Sea.* The first is an epic novel of the fighting in the civil war between the Reds and the Whites, a wonderful book. I had read it as a girl, when still on the farm. The only word for this man is *macho,* positively a comic-opera he-man. Vibrations of dislike instantly flowed between us. He asked me if I had read his books. Yes, I did. Did I like them? Yes, but I preferred *And Quiet Flows the Don* to the second novel. Why did I? Since he had paid me the compliment of asking for my opinion, I told him I thought the first was full of vigour and invention, and the love story was wonderful, but the second didn't come up to the first. Suddenly he was furious. He said that if he had me in his country he would get on his horse, tie me behind it, and make me run until I fell down, and he would drag me behind him until I cried for mercy, and then he would have me flogged. That was the treatment for women like me. I said that I didn't doubt he would do all that. We exchanged this kind of jest for a while. It was only later I discovered that he had stolen the first novel from

*He was trusted by the Americans, too. I don't know any other writer in this position. It was because of his evident honesty.

some unfortunate young writer and, when it turned out to be such a success, read with admiration throughout the world, had tried to match it with *The Don Flows Down to the Sea.*★

Over coffee I talked with Paul Robeson and his wife. I decided they were both stupid, because they were talking entirely in communist jargon: capitalist lies, fascist imperialists, running dogs, democratic socialism (the Soviet Union), peace-loving peoples. Not one word was said in normal speech. But I hadn't understood something, which was that this language was often employed either deliberately or instinctively, at moments of threat, even for days or weeks at a time. He was at the Soviet Embassy, officials were hovering about, and he was dependent on the goodwill of the Soviet Union because his own country was treating him so badly. When politics and public life become as polarised as they were then, then people may seem stupid. So I can say that I have met and talked with one of the great singers of our time and, with equal truth, that I didn't.

Talking to Robeson taught me how different the American Left was from the British Left. But as I've said, the Americans are a people of extremes. I do find it odd that this is never admitted, let alone discussed. Some kind of national 'image', or sets of images, get in the way: the poor boy, or girl, who can become president . . . young people from indigent backgrounds working their way through college to become rich and famous . . . a chicken in every pot (now that is a cheapened symbol of plenty) . . . Jefferson, Lincoln, and all that. But it is a country that catches fevers and runs high temperatures. When we talk about the 'shared language'— English—as a barrier, because of some differing (though not very many) word usages, that is surely itself another barrier, obscuring the truth, which is that the barrier is national temperaments, or dispositions. At the moment, a suggestion that there can be national temperaments or characteristics may hardly be said aloud in the United States, because of political correctness. And that proves my point.

★This business of the theft of the young writer's book: sometimes it is claimed as true, other times denied. I don't know what the position is now.

The American communists were more communist, fanatical, party-line, and paranoid than anyone I ever knew in Britain. They produced more of what the Communist Party itself called the 'one hundred and fifty percenters'—and certainly not with admiration, for they knew that the extreme communist flipped over easily into his or her opposite, the communist-hater. No British communist was ever treated with the harshness the American government used towards Paul Robeson and some other American communists.

And now enter Clancy Sigal. As if off a film set. He was in the style of young Americans then, jeans, sweatshirt, a low-slung belt where you could not help but see a ghostly gun. The lonely outlaw. The lone sheriff battling against the bad men.

Someone had telephoned to say that this American was in town, he needed a place to stay, could I let him a room. I said my career as a landlady had not encouraged me to try again. Comrade Who-ever-it-was said wasn't I ashamed not to help a comrade out, when I had an empty room?

He was unlike the Americans I had met to date, most of them publishers or film people. They were then formal, correct, hair short-back-and-sides, and as if inside invisible armour. They watched their words. They spoke slowly. The phrase *stiff upper lip* might have been invented to describe Americans then, particularly the men, for it seemed a spell had been put on their mouths: they could hardly move them. You would see an American a hundred yards away, and from the set of his lips you would know him. Was this because of McCarthy? Had he frightened them into a tight-lipped and general conformity, even if they had nothing to do with left-wing politics? But soon this type of American disappeared, and they all became loose and laid back—as a style.

Clancy was a heroic figure, made one not only by a thousand film epics and the heroes and heroines of the Left, who inhabited his imagination like close friends, but, too, because of the great figures of American history. He had recently made that journey which was obligatory for young Americans, traversing the United States by car, by himself, crazy as a loon, conversing with Abraham

Lincoln, Clarence Darrow, Sacco and Vanzetti, Jefferson, Mother Bloor, John Brown, as well as Rosa Luxemburg, Speransky, Bukharin, Trotsky, and anyone else who turned up.

Clancy was a mirror of everything I was beginning to be uneasy about in myself. Only beginning—and that is the difficulty. Coming events cast their shadows before. But looking back from the perspective of those events, it is easy to be dishonest. Some tiny passing shade of feeling, a mere cloud shadow, may ten years later become a storm of revelation: about yourself, about others, about a time. Or may have dissolved and gone.

What I was beginning to be unhappy about was left-wing romanticism, not to say sentimentality, by no means confined to communists, and in fact it permeates the left wing. It is the sentimentality that so often accompanies the extremes of brutality, or can lead to it. Attitudinising. The Red Flag carried to fire-storming heights by dying heroes. The Storming of the Bastille, the Storming of the Winter Palace . . . both these last mythologized out of any resemblance to the truth. I could fill a page or two here—what am I saying?—a volume, several volumes.

What was, is, important to this layer of the Left was always the dramatic, indeed, the melodramatic, never some small sober unremarkable work or effort. There are in the Left (and elsewhere) people labouring for a lifetime to improve some small aspect of life for everybody, but never in the Left I had been part of. Clancy's history of the United States was all heroic battles, and often bloody confrontations with government. Miners against callous mine owners—no, I'm not saying there were not callous mine owners, and people have forgotten just how brutal they often were. John Brown's mouldering body. The courtrooms where Clarence Darrow fought for liberalism and the truth. The soup kitchens of the Great Depression. Clancy's vision put them in the centre of the stage, excluded anything else.

There is a history of Britain that is all heroism and big events. Clancy knew it as well as he did the American saga, and in neither was the story of some woman or man working for years to change some small law or other.

My 'doubts'—and these were separate from the 'revelations'

from the Soviet Union—have to be recorded here, though they were then so uneasy and so unsure of themselves.

Sometimes I survey my current thoughts and wonder which of them—some of them new, with the overemphasis of outline that befits an untried idea, still not worn into shape by events, some astounded at their own effrontery—will turn out to have been the ones I should have been listening to, developing. Which of them will seem absurd, and even pathetic, in a decade or so?

Clancy was pretty ill when he arrived, just about holding himself together. He had come from Paris, where a close friend, an American woman living in Paris, told him he was crazy. People had been telling him he was for years. 'Clancy, you have got to face up to it.' He had just decided that there might be something in what they said. He made no secret about finding in me a good substitute for a psychotherapist. He was younger than I was.

By the same cold but useful gauge I used for Jack, Gottfried, and others, Clancy and I were ill suited emotionally—that above all—and sexually, but that was because the cool, cut-off distancing of so many Americans then from emotion was inhibiting; but intellectually it was a match, all right, for a time. First of all, he had read everything. His mother, a Russian immigrant to the States, a very poor woman, saw herself—as did his father—as heir of the world's great revolutionary movements, and by definition that included literature. Both father and mother were labour agitators and trade union organisers, often losing their jobs and having to move on. Bringing up their child had always taken second place to the Revolution. In short, Clancy was a survivor, one of the extremest I've known. 'No wonder you're screwed up,' I'd say to him, and he'd say to me, 'Lady, I'm not screwed up; everybody else is.'

He was a Trotskyist. This had made him doubly an outlaw. First, as a revolutionary in paranoid America. Second, as a traitor to communism—and to the Communist Party. That meant he was a minority in a minority. It was his mother who had decided that if the Soviet Union was Stalinist, then she was a Trotskyist. At university, he had been execrated and reviled for years by the Stalinists. Now he was coming into his own. Very soon all the revolutionary youth of Britain, and anywhere in Europe, would call themselves Trotskyists.

A word about these ancient schisms, for they are rapidly being forgotten. The communist parties everywhere were Stalinist, and Trotsky was a traitor and heretic. But the new youth believed that if Trotsky and not Stalin had won the battle for power in the Soviet Union, then communism would have become that Utopia it was meant to be. Isaac Deutscher, historian of the Soviet Revolution, wrote two books about Trotsky, *The Prophet Armed* and *The Prophet Disarmed*. I recommend them. Here is an account of the political battles of the time, seen in the light of the struggle between Stalin and Trotsky. But it is hard not to see that the two often changed positions, one taking his stand where not long before he had accused his rival of treacherously or misguidedly being. It is like watching a dance of puppets. And these little straw men are being swept down a great waterfall. The Bolsheviks, having studied the history of the French Revolution, had agreed that they would not turn on each other, accuse each other, kill each other, as the French revolutionaries had done. But that is exactly what they did.

Isaac Deutscher thought Lenin, one of history's most ruthless murderers, was the Perfect Man. Interesting, that: it is a concept from spiritual traditions.

One of Lenin's contributions to the happiness of humankind was the concept of Revolutionary Vigilance—which in practice meant that Communist Party members must be regularly and steadily murdered, tortured, imprisoned, and sent to camps, so as to keep them on their toes. This policy was most faithfully carried on by Stalin.

I had a glimpse of what it had been like as a Trotskyist in America when I introduced Clancy Sigal to Reuben Ship, Ted Allan, and the rest of the group. They all had been Stalinists. They met with ironical, or sarcastic, understanding and at once began bitter debates. But after all, they were talking to each other, and quite recently no Stalinist would have considered a Trot worthy of a hello—more suitable, rather, as recipient for an ice pick in the brain.

I was thinking back to the Trotskyist group in Salisbury. I had secretly thought them a more lively and interesting lot than we were. There was such a thing as a Trot by temperament: anarchic, spiky, fiercely aggressive, funny.

In the Party, in the fifties, there was a joke that Stalinists and Freudians were of the same stuff, conforming and conservative, and Jungians and Trotskyists were similar: all rebels. Things have changed, so that it is hard now to explain how Freudians seemed then: they were a church, a priesthood, the possessors of a revealed truth; they persecuted opponents or people who strayed from their path. They were humourless. They were paranoid. I cannot say that I find Freud the most loveable of human beings, any more than I find Marx, but surely he—they—both—would have hated their inheritors? Surely people who have original ideas, start movements, must be haunted by what they know must happen: they will give birth to a generation who snarl and snap over their remains, turn them into icons, become fanatics and bigots.

I found I agreed with the Trotskyist Clancy about politics, and that was when I was a member of the Party, though thinking of ways to leave it without a fuss. Surely that was remarkable, for the official party line about Trotsky was unchanged. On the Left, everyone always spent a lot of time defining exact intellectual positions. A private individual 'line' need not be the party line—seldom was. Clancy and I spent hours: What do you think about this . . . and this? Do you think this is true or that is true? There would have to be a revolution—well, of *course*—but certainly the present communist parties, in Britain and in Europe, could not lead it; they were too compromised.

Clancy had an immediate, intelligent understanding of women, not as females, but of our situation, our difficulties. This was because of his mother's long ordeal, bringing him up, very poor, without help from his father—who went off and started another family. Women easily responded to him. In *The Golden Notebook* I call it 'naming'. He 'named' us. Every woman he ever met he got into bed, or tried, and as a matter of principle. The style of the Lone Ranger. He told me about his journeyings around America, north–south, east–west, and he seldom spent a night alone. I do not think these women lost out, even when he was ill, for when he left the next morning they would feel themselves supported, simply because he had understood them.

I remember with shame at my stupidity that when he came into my bed—I think on the first night he was in the flat—what I *felt* was that the loneliness I had been living in since Jack took off was over. There is no fool like a woman in need of a man. A man, that is, to have and to hold.

No, I was not stupid for long. Here was another man who made no secret at all of the fact that he was merely passing through. Both Jack and Clancy are in *The Golden Notebook*. Not necessarily facts, but emotional truth is all there. *Play with a Tiger* too. Later Clancy wrote a novel and put me in it, but I didn't read it. Usually I don't read books about myself, unless it is a supposedly factual book and I have to check facts. I don't read them because the temptation to burst into protest and altercation might prove irresistible: one could spend one's life at it.

'But I didn't say that.' 'Oh yes, you did!'

'I didn't, I tell you.' 'But I tell you you did.'

'Didn't.' 'Did.' 'Didn't.' 'Did.'

'That never happened.' 'I know it did.'

'I know it didn't.' 'It did.' 'Didn't.' 'Did.' 'Didn't.' 'Did.'

Most disagreements of this kind are usually not on a much higher level. What's true for you isn't necessarily true for me.

Clancy is now living in California, with a new young wife and a baby. He has had a first wife and a lot of women on the way. When I knew him, domestic life, intimacy, everything that comes so easily to me, was to him not merely a trap, as young men so easily see it—and particularly then; it was the mode—but a betrayal of the pure, the good, the decent, a submission to a bourgeois morality—than which, of *course,* there could be nothing worse. He would relate how he had walked out of a friend's house in the States because the man had got married—the ultimate submission—and there were contraceptive gels in the bathroom cabinet. This was evidence of the most disgusting moral backsliding from the standards of the young knights they had decided to be. Travelling around the States on his farewell trip, he had found half the friends of his youth married and with incriminating bathroom cabinets. 'That's when I knew that was it, I had to leave.' Domestic squalor—he could scent it on walking into a house.

We were together, if that is the word for it, for three years or so.

I really don't have much to say about Clancy's accounts of London, except that he claims that in London he was forced to eat in cheap hamburger joints. The fact is, he was cooked for by some of the best amateur cooks in London. If he did find himself in a hamburger joint, then it was on some nostalgic trip to the brave hardships of his poverty-struck youth. London was very good to Clancy.

He was a romantic man, Clancy. The Left was then romantic, heroic, monitored by the ghosts of heroes and heroines. Of the darker side of this, more later.

Now, I met Clancy just as the romantic—the sentimental—attitudinisings of the Left were beginning to shock me. I had fed on them, for years. They had been my fuel, my impulse towards better things. It is a strange business, how one may go along comfortably but with unease, at first which is at best slight, then more and more, and then a rush of dislike of what you are, have been, as the scales fall from your eyes. And then you dislike what you have been much more than it deserves, but you have to, for it is still a threat.

Clancy was emotionally young for a man in his late twenties. I was older than my years in experience. And so right from the start there was this between us—and when he accused me of being too down-to-earth, practical, 'sensible', it was not a compliment.

Clancy caused as severe a dislocation of my picture of myself as ever in my life. I had always been seen as a maverick—tactless, intransigent, 'difficult'—and now, all at once, I was accused of being an English lady. It was no good saying that any real English lady would at once repudiate me as a bogus sister. This English lady was ignorant of the harsh realities of life, which meant, for him, the struggles of the poor. Clancy was never one to spare unfavourable comment, and I was tongue-lashed, but I gave back as good as I got. I had only just learned the art of not saying what I thought when I thought it and I found I was defending hard-won social graces against this savagely angry social critic.

'Jesus, but the English kill me. Why don't you ever say what you think?'

At once he undertook my education into the realities of life, and he began with jazz. For which I shall always be grateful to him. To me until then jazz had meant the 'kids' of the Sports Club in Salisbury apeing Satchmo when they were drunk at the climax of some dance, or the smooth melodies of Cole Porter.

He went with me to buy a record player and twenty or so records, each one in some way special, a landmark in jazz, or the best of some artist. It took me years to appreciate just what a perfect little collection this was. No one may be immersed in real jazz, and the blues, without a change in sensibility. As Clancy knew. He was nothing if not an educator. He saw it as his task to re-form and re-shape every inadequate soul in his path. He instructed me in the history of jazz, of the blues, how to listen to different instruments, how to tell false from true, how to appreciate the way a group plays together, the instruments as a family. He insisted that I, like him, should own only the purest tastes. Later, his tutelage removed, I allowed myself less rigorous standards, a guilty Duke Ellington perhaps, an Eartha Kitt.

I listened to jazz, particularly the blues, for four years or so. What did it do for me? If the yearning, longing, wanting, you-are-out-of-reach music of the war years—'I'm Dancing with Tears in My Eyes', 'Smoke Gets in Your Eyes'—predisposed me, and all of us, to romantic love, whose essence is to be out of reach, then I think jazz, and particularly the blues, inclines us to suffering, the enjoyment of the pain of loss. I am oversimplifying, but in my case, listening to the blues, Billie Holiday, Bessie Smith, or the heartbroken fragmented cries of Bird's saxophone, went together with a time of pain, and the one reinforced the other. The richly enjoyable melancholies of adolescence can deepen into something dangerous, a poison.

Clancy taught me the code of honour of the working-class American, but surely it was influenced by the working people of Russia and East Europe and the shtetl too? Clancy always knew exactly what was right and what was wrong. This was as inflexible a code of behaviour as I've ever heard of.

First of all, if a friend, even an acquaintance, even someone you had only heard of, lost a job, then your first duty was to get her or him another. A priority, put before any of your own interests. This was a legacy from the unemployment in the thirties.

Secondly, you hated the police as a matter of course, always and everywhere. You always defended your friends or mates against the police, and any lie about the police was good, for they lied about the workers, or the poor. Clancy, walking in the southern states of America, from town to town, or hitchhiking, had been run out of town as a vagrant, taken beyond the city limits and dumped, or put in prison, suspected of all kinds of crimes. To say one word in defence of the police was to prove that you were middle class and an enemy.

Third, if any friend or comrade, or the wife or girlfriend of a friend, was down on his or her luck, then you rallied around with money and food.

Fourth, if anyone was on the run, or in hiding, for any reason at all (except of course if he was a political opponent), you sheltered him, hid him, without asking questions. I think this last surely was a legacy from slavery—hiding runaway slaves.

Clancy's education of me included his explorations into London, the squalid parts, for his instinct led him to them as if it is only in the lower depths that the truth can be found. For instance, I had not known that on a certain street corner in Soho a poker game went on every day under the noses of the police. Clancy used to go there, chancing his luck, when short of money. He talked a great deal to prostitutes. I was exasperated by his attitude to them—more romanticising, more glamorising of crime and poverty. Americans then were all fascinated by prostitutes, just as if they had none of their own. Any American who came to see me in those days would at once ask where he could find the girls. I directed them to Soho, where the girls would line the streets every evening, or Bayswater. But shortly that was illegal, and then I directed them to the newsagents' boards.

Soon Clancy became friends with Alex Jacobs, a large, friendly, instantly likeable young man, one of the people who would coalesce into the New Left, then in the process of being born. Alex was not the only person I've heard say that being forced to lie in bed with nothing to do for months was the best thing that ever happened to him. In his case, it was TB. He read all the time he was in the sanatorium, and came out looking back with pity on the ignorant youth he had been. He was a journalist and intended to write. The two young men took themselves around and about Earls Court, Notting Hill Gate, Soho, anywhere something was happening—crimes, scandals, protests, 'demos'—and sat about in pubs, cafés, bus shelters, cheap restaurants, the coffee bars just opening everywhere, and they watched people, talked endlessly, listened, reported minor injustices to the authorities. They were both outsiders, both outside by that unwritten law that says that the two great divisions of British society should be impenetrable to each other. Clancy's American accent and Alex's working-class voice, which he exaggerated when on these adventures, made them acceptable to what are known as ordinary people. They could go where people like me could not. It was all right for me when I still had my Rhodesian accent, which put me outside the system, but that had gone, and now, as is the way in these islands, I was judged by how I spoke. I discovered quite by accident that I had lost my early freedom here when, in Devon, I was walking towards an ironmonger's shop and saw the shopkeeper watching me. He stood in the doorway, hands on his hips, and he was doubtless thinking, She looks like them, the clothes . . . but there is something not quite . . . He waited for me to speak: Do you stock . . . whatever it was, and his posture subtly changed, he dropped his arms, and then, 'Yes, madam, if you'll come inside.'

Clancy and Alex used to breeze in, elated, after some excursion and tell me all about it, over coffee or a meal. They were accepted as honorary members by some groups of boys, young men, really, since they had left school. Fifteen was the age you left school then. Both men identified with these 'kids' who had little or no education, had nothing to do with themselves now except hang about the streets. This passion of protectiveness for the deprived: I knew what I was looking at, all right—what I was being invited to share.

One evening they brought a youth who sat for a couple of hours talking about his life, while Alex and Clancy encouraged him. Their understanding of his situation gave him much more coherence and clarity than normally he would have bothered with. He was not against his parents but did not want to be like them. He had been educated by films—there was not yet much television—into wider horizons, and he did not want to settle for (a phrase much used by Clancy, meaning a compromise with the second-best) the life of his parents. But he knew his education had not fitted him for anything better. He said he didn't have a job because he wanted more than what he'd have to accept. But soon he would get something, because he didn't want to live on his parents, and then he would marry, someone like his sister, and as soon as he married he would be trapped. This would be the only time in his life he'd have a bit of freedom, and he was enjoying it while he could. Once married, then that was it, that was the end. In other words, how he was thinking was the precise opposite of his sister, for she was waiting for the wedding, and then life would begin—as he pointed out. The visit was about a week before the Notting Hill Gate race riots, when white youths beat up blacks. The youth who had spoken so intelligently about his life was arrested and shortly tried at the Old Bailey; I attended with Clancy and Alex. They knew exactly what had happened that night, because they had been there, dodging about, watching. I knew what had happened because they had told me. We sat there in the crammed court, while the police lied, the witnesses lied, the defence lawyer lied, and of course the accused lied, to save themselves, but it was no use: they were sentenced to prison. I sat there watching the jury, thankful I wasn't among them, for if I hadn't been told, I wouldn't have been able to say who was lying and who wasn't.

Clancy and Alex pursued their researches, even after the New Left had become a social entity, a tribe, and met mostly only each other. One day they said they had found a young girl being kept prisoner by a Greek restaurant proprietor and they were going to rescue her and bring her to my flat. She was a plump fair frail beauty, with hazy blue eyes. She was eighteen years old: the

Greek's mistress. Her parents, she said, didn't like her. The Greek had a wife and children. He would not allow her out of the room he kept her in during the day. She was bored, she said. She was afraid of him, she said.

It seemed Clancy and Alex believed that all I had to do was to say, 'Now come on, my girl, pull yourself together, this won't do.' For whatever I said, no matter how I put it, this is how it would sound to her. She wasn't very clever, unlike the young man doing time in prison somewhere, but she did know she wasn't going to marry a boring man like her dad and then slave away for him. What was she doing now if not being a slave to her Greek? I did enquire, but she only smiled—her lazy, knowing little smile. It was perfectly clear to me that she had agreed to escape with the two young heroes because what she had *heard* was that they were promising her a future. Glamour. Posh people. Exciting times with this famous writer—so they had told her I was. She hinted she would like to be a model, a film star. I was a disappointment to her. She fingered books with my name on them, asked, had I written this? When I said yes, then she gazed at me, all baffled enquiry: then why are you living like this, why aren't you in a place like the ones we see on the telly? What had Clancy and Alex promised her, exactly? A general betterment, it seemed, improvement, enlightenment. They would breeze in, to see how this process was going, and find us gossiping in the kitchen over cups of tea. And stronger—she liked a bit of gin, or sweet liqueurs; she was used to going out with her Greek to drink with him and his friends in the evenings.

She made free with my clothes, for she had brought none with her. She pushed the clothes she was prepared to consider to one side of my cupboard, despising the others, and dressed herself up. In those days I wore a lot of black. 'Why are all your things black?' Clancy had asked the same question, and I had replied, 'Obviously, I am in mourning for my life,' but to her I said, 'Because black suits me.' She put on me a red shirt, a white one, tried this and that garment, said I was right, I should wear black, but she thought my lipstick . . . She made me up with her make-up, then shook her head and said yes, I should stick with what I had. Absolute concentration, this inspection of me, my clothes. But that did not last long, and she was bored. She was waiting for something to happen. Clancy and Alex came, and when she asked—shyly—what they had brought her here for, they said, had she thought about going to school, getting this or that certificate, perhaps university? I was amazed at them, the way women are with men when they can't see something obvious. There she sat in my cherry-coloured dressing gown—she hardly took it off during the ten days she was with me—smoking, while they admired her breasts, for she allowed the gown to fall open to her waist, and her white knees emerging from the cherry-coloured folds, and she said she didn't think school, no. Then, they said, Doris would make enquiries about being a hairdresser. 'What do they earn?' she enquired languidly, her beautiful blue eyes heavy with boredom.

She was too short to be a model, by several inches. Asked if she fancied modelling bras and underwear, she said she didn't think her Dimitri would let her. She didn't want to upset him. He said he would marry her one of these days. Well, perhaps he would; miracles happen. Yes, she did like him. She liked being hit about a bit—'He never bruises me, Mrs. Lessing, don't think that'—and then thrown on the bed. One day she did not come down from her room, which she usually did about midday, and when I went up I found my dressing gown laid out on the bed, which she had made neatly up, like a good girl, and on the pillow was a note: 'Ta a lot. Don't do anything I wouldn't do. Ha Ha.' So she had gone back to her Greek, and after that, who knows. By now she must be a fat, dyed old woman, probably a lush, and the thought hurts.

In Warwick Road I used to go walking at night, late. Now it would not be late, but people went to bed so much earlier then. The streets were still empty by eleven, as they had been when I first came, and there was nothing of what we take for granted now, as if it has all been going on for ever: animated streets long after midnight, lively groups of mostly young people in search of pleasure and adventure. I would go out only when Peter was at school or at the Eichners'. This was not because I feared to leave him alone: there were people living downstairs, and at the beginning, when I was still being a landlady, people in the flat, then later Clancy was there, and his typewriter would be going like a machine gun. No, Peter was fearful for me, because one parent had disappeared, and so I might too. He never spoke about this fear, but I knew.

Walking around and about the London streets was like my nocturnal wanderings in Salisbury; when I set off, the houses would have lights in them, and by the time I got home again they were dark, and the radios, which had been spilling music from house to house, were silent. But now it was the small flickerings of the televisions on curtains that were extinguished as I walked.

What was I doing? What was I looking for? There was the need to move, for I had all that physical energy, earned by the ritual needed to write, when I walked around the room, blind to it, wrote a little, working up into a crescendo of effort so intense it was exhausting and sent me off into a few minutes' sleep, and then up again into walking around and about the room. This process might go on for hours, the stints at the typewriter and the little restoring sleeps, yet all that, mysteriously, did not discharge physical energy but left me with energy that I needed to use up.

It was not into the streets I knew in the day that I came down from the upper part of the house. This nighttime London was a foreign land, and I did not think, as I walked, This is Kensington High Street; This is Earls Court. I tended to avoid the big streets, because I felt them to be alien, with a hard self-sufficiency that excluded me. This is how a child experiences a certain street, or even a room: turning a corner to be met by an unfamiliar row of shops where a scarlet postbox seems hostile and the little public garden across the road is full of unknown streets and shrubs—yet there are children playing there, as if they recognise nothing dangerous—or opening a door into a new house where the furniture is standing heavily about in an ordered arrangement that says Keep Out, and then coming suddenly on a chair that welcomes you, or into a doorway in a shop where there is a woman who raises her head to smile at you ... There are no street names, no house names or numbers, in this geography, and no grown-up person would recognise the way a child knows a street, a house, a room, even the corner of a sofa. And the inhabitants of a city cannot share a newcomer's apprehension of it.

There were streets where I went quickly, to get through them, for I did not like them, others where I dawdled. When I came on the great warehouse-like buildings of Earls Court, standing about all darkened, silent, indifferent to me, I went by fast, not wanting to provoke them into attack, for they seemed full of incipient violence. When I found I had come upon the Albert Hall, which perhaps an hour ago had been as crammed full of people as a box with toys, its sober rotundities reassured me: yes, you are welcome here; but I went on perhaps a short way down Kensington High Street, as deserted as if the plague had struck. Yet it was only midnight. Perhaps there was someone waiting at the all-night bus stop, and I went slowly past, seeing the glow of a cigarette illuminating a face that took no notice of me, for a red bus was trundling along from the West End, headed out to a suburb that I thought of as I might Far Tartary, but not with the glow of pleasure you may get from thoughts of places you may one day visit; no, a vast darkened semi-city, made up of little self-contained and self-satisfied houses in tidy gardens—that was what I envisaged while the sole passenger trod up onto the platform and the bus bore him away. How London's enormousness does dismay its newcomers, and I was still that, six, seven, eight years after my arrival, for I was always trying to come to terms with it, take it in. A practised dweller in London learns to subdue it by living—that is, with heart and mind and senses—in one part of it, making that a home, and says, 'London is a con-glomeration of villages,' and chooses one, blanking out the frightful immensities of the rest, and waits for the greeting from the woman across the street, or a wave from the man who owns the vegetable shop, or a miaow of welcome from the cat at number 25, or the turn into the road where year after year in spring a certain tree appears in glittering white, or in autumn a shrub decorates itself with scarlet.

There was nothing convivial in the streets I walked through those nights, not a restaurant, not a coffee bar, and the pubs had closed long before. If I had got out early, before the pubs shut, then each one would be an island of enjoyment, closed off from the street behind its glowing windows, full of people who knew each other, for pubs are like clubs, without the benefit of rules and membership: the same people go there, making little communities, a companionship. But once the pubs had shut, only ill-lit streets and dark houses. Along one street, turn a corner into another, then another, whose name I never looked at, for I did not care where I was, though when I moved from one little knot of streets, or even one street, into another, it was moving from one territory to another, each with its own strong atmosphere and emanations, bestowed by me and by my need to understand this new place. Not to know its name, so that I could find it again, for I am sure I often walked along the same streets, past the same houses, but did not know it, for the capacities and understanding I brought with me were different on different nights. And besides, even in daytime a change of light or a shift of perspective will create a new view. You use a certain underground station often, you walk down the steps onto a platform you know as well as you do the street outside your house, but when you stop at the same station after your excursion, on your way home, you go up steps from a platform quite different from the one you set off from, ten paces away.

I might walk for two or three hours, not afraid of getting lost, because I was bound to pass an underground station I knew, or a police station. I'd go in. 'Well, you're a good way from home, aren't you?' the policeman would reprove.

'Yes, I lost my way,' I'd say brightly, offering my incompetence as a fee for his help.

'You can catch the all-night bus at the corner there.'

'No, I'd rather walk.'

'Right, then,' and he would come out to the door. 'You just go along there, and then turn left, and then . . .'

It seems a long time since we could wander at all hours of the night in London, or, for that matter, in any big city, without it once occurring to us to be afraid. I took my safety for granted.

At a suggestion I might be raped, which is what young women think of now, I would have said, indignant, 'Don't be ridiculous.' But women have changed. Sometimes—but in the day as well as the night—some sad man in a furtive coat or a mac would suddenly

There are very few photographs in this volume.
I hated being photographed and also we thought that being photographed
was really rather petit bourgeois and self-indulgent.

Peter in Church Street.

My mother and Peter.

Peter in 1954.
He was eight
years old.

The six members of the Authors' World Peace Appeal delegation. From left to right: A. E. Coppard, Naomi Mitchinson, Douglas Young, me, Arnold Kettle, and Richard Mason. Taken outside Tolstoy's house at Yasnaya Polyana.

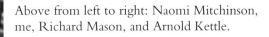

Above from left to right: Naomi Mitchinson, me, Richard Mason, and Arnold Kettle.

Naomi Mitchinson.

At Tolstoy's grave.

Boris Polevoi.

A. E. Coppard.

Taken on a trip to Salisbury, 1956.

Carradale, Naomi Mitchinson's house on the Mull of Kintyre.

Clancy Sigal.

From left to right: Me, Ernest Rodker (standing behind), Samuel Marshak, Joan Rodker in 1954.

With Clancy Sigal.

With Peter.

Gottfried Anton
Nicolai Lessing.

John Wisdom in
Canada.

Jean Wisdom,
early 1960s.

From left to right:
Me, (unknown),
Michael Hastings,
and Kenneth Tynan, 1957.

Clancy and me on the bus
to or from Aldermaston.

Aldermaston rally in Trafalgar Square.

On an Aldermaston March.

Mrs. Toni Sussman—
Mother Sugar in
The Golden Notebook.

The kitchen, Charrington Road

part it to show ... but I had walked on, thinking, Poor thing. If a car slowed to see if I was for sale, I shook my head and walked on, faster. It never occurred to me to feel insulted. Is it a good thing that women have become so squeamish, so easily shocked—and resourceless too? Like Victorian ladies (or so we are told they did, though I have never believed it), contemporary women scream or swoon at the sight of a penis they have not been introduced to, feel demeaned by a suggestive remark, and send for a lawyer if a man pays them a compliment. And all this in the name of the equality of the sexes. I was never once in danger, not in all those nights of walking, and sometimes in the most unappetising, shadowy streets, where, if I felt threatened, it was only because of my inability to understand what I was seeing. It is a long time since I have felt that kind of cold exclusion, in London or anywhere else in the world—the same as a small child's feeling when taken into a room full of very tall solid falsely smiling adults sitting on chairs and sofas that have become alien, though when the room is empty of strangers, they are friends and familiars, where you play and hide.

When I got home, perhaps at two or three in the morning, the rooms of the flat—in particular the living room, which was in fact quite large, and the kitchen, a large room too—seemed small and overbright and banal. Where had I been? I did not know, did not care. My mind was full of dark streets and buildings. And if, suddenly, a light had come on in a house where the windows had been reflecting a dim street light, then it had been as if the place had raised its eyes to look at me: *Who are you?*

That was the night, when what London's streets really were was hidden. Daylit London was not the city I had arrived in, so grey, so battered, so colourless. Already the war was becoming history, buildings were being painted, and the new coffee bars enlivened the streets. When I first came, every person I met had talked of this or that battlefront—the war in North Africa ... Egypt ... Burma ... India ... France ... Italy ... Germany—and of the bombing of London. The new young ones did not talk about the war, which had ended ten years before; they wanted to have a good time. And they wore clothes a million miles from the dreary wartime Utility. Now there were Indian restaurants opening everywhere, rescuing us from that choice: eating in an expensive restaurant, which most of us couldn't afford, or eating at home. The Cold War was still blasting us with bombast and rhetoric, but inside the Left—and I would say left-wing attitudes permeated thinking that did not even call itself left—all kinds of new thoughts were growing. It was that stage in a process where ideas, opinions, fresh opinion—all critical of a predominant cast of thought—are building up behind a dam and will shortly burst it open . . . to become a new conformity.

It was already hard for me to remember how dismayed I had been when first in London, how any time I left the little protective shell I lived in, and ventured forth, I needed an inner stiffening of defences: No, I will not let myself be depressed by it.

And now my first cat, in my home, my place. My responsibility. I had loved most fiercely the cats on the farm, long ago, but I did not know much about them. My mother cared for them. A good place for a cat, someone said, desperate to find a home for a kitten. You've got two floors, and outside your front door a wooden staircase down to a yard, and a large flat roof too—of course you must have a kitten. And that is how we acquire a cat. What's a cat—a mere cat? A creature without rights, living as it can, where it can, and when in our houses often ill-treated through ignorance. I did not know how to look after a cat. On the farm there were indoor cats and outdoor cats, they drank water from the dogs' drinking bowls, were given milk when the pails came up from the milking, caught their food in the bush and were given leftovers and tidbits. They died easily: a cat wasn't worth a vet, who was so many miles away and who in any case dealt with serious animals, working animals, like dogs and cattle, and the horses for the gymkhanas. They easily went wild with the real wildcats; they were bitten by snakes or went blind from a cobra's spitting into their eyes and had to be 'put down'. There were innumerable litters of kittens, and most were drowned at birth.

With this apprenticeship, I acquired a cat, a black and white cat, your basic moggy—plump, sweet, rather stupid, and dependent, for she would have liked to be with me every second of the day and night.

She did not like tinned food and slowly persuaded me she should have calves' liver—in those days, before the culinary revolution, liver, kidneys, any 'offal', was so cheap that its price alone attested that it was not worth eating. She liked steak. She liked a bit of fish. She was fed too well, for I did not know then that a diet of liver and steak and fish was not good for a cat. I hope I had a bowl of water down for her and her kittens. Most cats like plenty of water and don't like milk all that much. No, she did not get ill, she flourished, but did not live for long, because she fell off the flat roof and broke her pelvis—in this way at least continuing what I knew from the farm, where cats used up their nine lives so quickly.

She was kindly treated, she was fed, she was taken to the vet, she was petted and fussed over, she slept on my bed. But it was only later that I learned to appreciate cats, as individuals, each one different, just like humans. Later there were cats who impressed themselves on me by their force of character, their intelligence, their bravery, their fortitude when suffering, their sensitiveness to what you are thinking, their care for their kittens—in my experience, this is true of male cats too. But this cat, my first as an adult, was, simply, just a sweet cat.

I had to learn how to observe a cat, interact with it and its emotional life, its loves, its affections, its jealousies. For like humans, cats are jealous creatures, want to be first in your affections. From a cat you get back what you give to it—rather you get back a hundredfold—in the way of attention, observation, above all, observation, so that you know what the cat is thinking and feeling. All this is missed by people who think that cats are all alike, are 'independent' and 'don't care for people' and 'are only interested in you because you feed them'.

How often do you see that sad thing, an intelligent cat in some house with ignorant owners, trying to persuade these blocks of insensitivity that here is a loving creature ready to be a real friend—but yet again it is rebuffed, roughly thrown off a lap or even hit, and it goes away, sullen but patient, a captive of stupidity.

Now I know I missed a whole range of responses and affections with that first cat, because I had decided she was sweet but not very bright. If you look at it from her point of view: this very dependent cat, who by nature should have been with one person, night and day, found herself in a flat with a mistress who would not pay her attention when she was working, who was always walking restlessly about or lying down for short naps, from which she jumped up, dislodging her. This friend went away often, once for six weeks, and how very long that must seem to a cat, probably the same as our years. Yes, she went away for years at a time, leaving her with people who might or might not love her. When this mistress came home, and once again the cat could look forward to a warm place on the foot of the bed, then that might not happen, for it was by no means certain there was only one person in the bed, and often she had to retreat to a chair, make herself small, not be a nuisance. There was a young boy, and he was kind, but he didn't have time for her, and he came and went all the time. The currents of feeling in that place where she had found herself taken—no choice of hers—they were disturbing, very often they were frightening: cats pick up every nuance of feeling. This was not a calm and reassuring place; all the people in it were restless, or anxious, going and coming, and that was why this cat always wanted to be with this mistress, who might disappear altogether—if she could vanish for years, why not for ever?

The cat, like everyone who came into that flat, did not have much faith in the roof over her head.

And now, simply for the pleasure of writing about it, a marriage made in heaven. A young communist idealist, a Russian woman, met in Moscow Bill Rust, the editor of the *Daily Worker,* the British communist paper. He was there on some official trip. Well known and well liked was Bill Rust, respected outside the communist world, for within the limits of the communist imperatives he was a forthright and independent editor. Because of his position, permission was given at once for her to leave the Soviet Union and marry him. Some hopeful brides languished for years, no permission forthcoming. Soon Bill Rust died, and Tamara was left a widow. She was by temperament and belief and training a communist activist. She was also still very Russian, an exotic for the insular British workers. The Party gave her the job of activating the peasantry in Britain. (This formulation was very much the Party's idea of a joke.) On a trip to the West Country, Tamara met Wogan Phillips, the eldest son of a lord, a gentleman farmer near Cheltenham. His father, furious that he was a communist, cut him off without the proverbial penny but could not deprive him of the title, which in due course he inherited. Wogan wanted to marry Tamara. Understandably. She wanted to marry him, but the doubts inseparable from committing oneself to that enormity, marriage, caused her to spend some days before the wedding in acutest conflict, most of them with me. 'How can I,' she demanded, 'Bill Rust's widow, marry an English lord?'

'Easily,' I said. (At that time a joke in the Party was that the CP might not be able to get anyone elected to the House of Commons but it had no difficulty in attracting lords. There were three communists in the House of Lords, and quite soon there would be Wogan. Another communist aristocrat, Ivor Montague, was in love with Communist China. He introduced table tennis to that vast empire, where it flourishes to this day.)

Tamara wanted to marry Wogan. Understandably. He was probably the handsomest man I have ever known. He had all the virtues of an aristocrat and not one of the vices. He was, but truly, a lovely man, and I've never met anyone who didn't think so. But she was of good communist Russian stock and . . . 'Of *course* you should marry him,' urged this romantic, unable to bear that true love was being thwarted by mere politics.

There was a wedding in a house in North London somewhere. A not very large room, and not many people in it. Wogan was imperturbably affable and kind, Tamara was in a fizz of elation, love, and doubt, and there, too, was Harry Pollitt, general secretary of the British Communist Party. If he was not actually giving Tamara away, he was representing the approval of the proletariat of both countries. He had with him a lieutenant. These two, short stubby men in stiff Sunday-best suits, held their own by force of character in these most improbable circumstances. Who else was there? I can only remember two tall, fair youngsters leaning against a mantelpiece and looking benignly on, shedding charm generally over us all. These were Sally, Rosamond Lehmann's daughter by

Wogan—two beautiful people had produced a girl who is remembered by everyone who ever met her as a rare and lovely creature—and Patrick Kavanagh, the poet and man of letters. They were either already married or about to be. She was to die quite soon and suddenly. Sally and Patrick should, like Wogan and Tamara, have lived happily ever after for many many decades.

I went twice or three times with Peter to visit Wogan and Tamara on their farm. He might have been cut off without a penny by his father, but luckily there must have been a halfpenny or two from somewhere or other. Their life was a dream of Englishness, all affability and kindness, on a gentleman farmer's farm, and Peter loved going there, and so did I.

Tamara and Wogan used to drive into Cheltenham, a city that could not have known a seditious thought since the Civil War, and sell the *Daily Worker* on the streets to astonished citizens. I was remembering equally quixotic attempts in Salisbury (Southern Rhodesia) to sell the communist *Guardian* newspaper around suburbs populated entirely by white kaffir-haters. Their revolutionary duty done, Wogan and Tamara went to their favourite pub, where farm labourers, some their employees, bought the *Daily Worker* because they liked Wogan.

Wogan had been left an estate in north Italy and decided to divide it up and give it to the peasants who worked it. Very soon they came and begged him to take it back or at least administer it, because they were being cheated by the surrounding landowners. Tamara and Wogan couldn't see anything funny about this, or about selling the *Daily Worker* in Cheltenham, or if they did, they weren't going to admit it.

Another wedding was Arnold and Dusty Wesker's. All Arnold's family were there, from well-off businessmen to people still not far from the East End. Dusty's family were farm workers and small farmers from Norfolk; Arnold used them in his play *Roots*. There were also actors, directors, and writers from the Royal Court Theatre, a couple of dozen of us. Blond, large, slow, ruddy-faced farm people, quick, dark, dark-eyed Jews, and us, the job lot from the Court, this improbable mix of people sat in three separate parts of a big room, eyeing each other until at the end we all became one soul, united by dancing the hora, around and around, and on and on.

Not all my associates were dedicated to social progress. A visitor from Canada stayed for some weeks. She gave me a yellow silk umbrella, a little graceful umbrella with an ivory handle. It came from an altogether different life. It leaned against the wall in my kitchen, and I thought, If I use that I'll have to buy different clothes, live in a different kind of flat and certainly in another part of London. The umbrella reminded me of a wonderful short story, in *New Writing*. It was from that post-war time in London when high-minded refugees from everywhere lived their precarious lives in cold shabby flats and scarcely knew where their next meal was coming from. A certain poet—Hungarian, I think—said to a friend, 'If you're going to throw that coat out, give it to me. I'm freezing.' The coat was elegant, if threadbare. He wore it day and night. His comrades said, 'We're not going out with you in that coat; we've got our reputations as serious people to consider.' The poet wore the coat to a publisher's party, and the publisher's daughter noticed him. He said to his own girlfriend, 'Why don't you buy yourself a new dress?' She said, 'Once you loved me for myself. Now you've become just another rotten bourgeois.' He had to get a new job, which he despised, to support a new wardrobe and new friends, and then he moved to a new flat, with the publisher's daughter. His comrades spoke of him as a lost soul, but he was merely ahead of the times.

And now, again, the tricky question of time: I had been in London for nearly eight years. What's eight years? I would say now. It's nothing at all, a mere breath; but I was still living in young-adult time, and it seemed I had been in London for an age, packed and crammed with new people, events, happenings, ideas. I was being urged to go back to Southern Rhodesia by friends there—Mrs. Maasdorp, the Zelters, the comrades generally, but certainly not my brother, with whom I exchanged polite letters—to write articles 'which told the truth'. I needed to go back, because my Rhodesian years seemed so distant, so cut off from me, and I was dreaming every night, long sad dreams of frontiers and exile and lost landscapes. There were, however, two reasons I couldn't easily go back. I had no money, and there was Peter, who could hardly be left with the Eichners for as long as I needed. Six weeks. I began with the money. *Picture Post,* a wonderful magazine, one of the first to use picture reporting, always fighting the proprietor, who was timid, was edited by Tom Hopkinson, who was brave. In the end, cowardice defeated courage. Meantime *Picture Post* could be relied on. I went to see Tom Hopkinson and asked if *Picture Post* would pay my travel expenses to Southern Rhodesia. The way I saw it, I was as well equipped for this as anyone. I had been listening to nonsense about Southern Africa ever since I had come, though about South Africa the truth was becoming known—partly, of course, because of people like me. Now there was something called the Federation of Central Africa, which was uniting Northern Rhodesia and Nyasaland—both had always been Colonial Office Protectorates, with the interests of the natives paramount—and Southern Rhodesia, which had always been modelled on the iniquitous laws of South Africa. Everyone in Britain, and all the newspapers, including the dear old *Guardian,* were in love with this federation: there is something about high-minded formulas that the British find irresistible. Only two newspapers, the *Tribune* and the *Daily Worker*—both at the extreme left—were pointing out that oil and water could not mix and that 'unrest' was inevitable. 'Unrest' was already breaking out everywhere in Nyasaland and Northern Rhodesia. As I and some others had foretold. I told Tom Hopkinson that I could travel from person to person in all three territories, friends or contacts, that I would cost his magazine only the airfare, and that I was in a much better position to come up with news than the real journalists. He was cautious, said he thought yes but would let me know. He wrote to say no, he was sorry. What had happened, obviously, was that he checked with the secret services, whose members were bound to be chums of his, because this is true of nearly all the male Establishment, and had been told not only that I was communist—which of course he knew—but that I was dangerous (this was the Cold War). I did not know then that I had been made a Prohibited Immigrant in South Africa and in

Southern Rhodesia too. Meanwhile Mervyn★ and Jeanne Jones had generously offered (on their own impulse; I had not asked them) to take Peter to be with their own children for six weeks. All I needed was the airfare.

And now I thought things out, carefully and soberly. I went to the Soviet Embassy and asked to see the cultural attaché—another one—and said why didn't they get some Soviet newspaper to pay for my airfare, treat me as a correspondent? Of course I knew this was an enormity and that I was inviting accusations of Moscow Gold, at the very least. What was outrageous was my casually turning up and inviting them to behave like a Western newspaper, just as if this was normal. Yes, I was finding it funny, enjoying it. But I was also very angry. What I *felt* was that I had given my own side the chance to employ me, they should have done, so it was their fault. And I knew I would give value for money. I was in an ambiguous relation with these Russians. True, I was a Party member—and they could hardly know how I was thinking seditious thoughts about the Party and that I intended to leave it. But I was not, like James Aldridge, 'one of theirs', the Russian formula, still very much in use: So-and-so is 'one of ours'—*nashe. Nashe* and therefore good. *The Grass Is Singing* had been slammed by their reviewers as 'Freudian' and revealing a hundred non-communist faults, which I cannot now remember. The short stories were paternalistic and lacked a feeling for the proletariat. The mere fact that I had gone to them without even checking with the Party was proof of a serious lack of revolutionary understanding.

I went ahead with my preparations, trusting to luck. Something like a week before I left, when I was getting panicky, not least because all the comrades were telling me that this had never been done and wouldn't be done now, I got a cheque from the Narodny Bank for, I think (I've forgotten), a thousand pounds. Perhaps it was five hundred pounds. It was a lot of money. I could pay my airfare and a good bit over. On enquiry, by telephone, to the Soviet embassy, I was told the money was for royalties. (The Soviet Union was still pirating my books and never paid royalties—you

★Mervyn Jones is a novelist and journalist.

had to go there and spend the money. Not a few writers did, holi-daying on the Black Sea, living like rajahs—or like commissars. I never did this. My feeling was that the publishers should pay writers what was due and not go in for emotional blackmail: 'You know our terrible difficulties; we feel sure you will be happy to help us by coming here, taking your money in Moscow, and spending it with us.') There was never any written confirmation that this money was for royalties. When I asked what newspaper I would be writing for, they said I should send the articles to the embassy and they would find a newspaper.

And now my real unforgiveable naivety: It never occurred to me that my articles would be 'creatively' translated to make the situation in Central Africa worse than it was. This little tale illus-trates why the people dealing with Soviet officialdom all had ner-vous breakdowns or had to leave the work. First, although the Embassy had been told my trip depended on them I didn't get the money until the last minute—people organising trips to the Soviet Union often got the visas the night before or even on the morning of departure, guaranteeing maximum anxiety for everyone. Then, I was not formally told for which of my books these royalties were being paid. Writers were never told when their books were pub-lished in the Soviet Union. Someone would return from a trip and say, 'I saw your book for sale in Moscow'—but that was the first I had heard of it. To this day I don't know which of my books and stories were published there. Then, when I sent in the articles, after my trip (the same as were printed in *Tribune* here and in left-wing papers in Europe) I was not told what Soviet papers printed them.

Meanwhile something else had happened. The Communist Party of the Soviet Union held their Twentieth Congress. No young person now will react to 'Twentieth Congress of 1956', but everyone, not only on the Left, interested in politics at all from those times will remember that this was when Khrushchev 'came clean' about the crimes of Stalin. The effect of these 'revelations' on the faithful was as if the Communist Parties of the world had been blown apart by a bomb. All over the world were people (and there are still a few left) who knew that everything bad said about the Soviet Union was a lie, an invention of the capitalist press, and that communism (of course, there had been 'mistakes'), headed by the great and good successors of the great Stalin, was the future of the world. Comrades were indignantly refusing to believe the 'revelations', saying that Khrushchev was a traitor, he had been bought by the CIA, or that he was exaggerating, or that if what Khrushchev said was true, then someone else, or a clique of conspirators, had been responsible for the crimes and Stalin had never known anything about them.

To write all this in the nineties is not easy. Gone—I hope for ever, but let's not be too sure—is the climate that made these events possible. I'm writing about mass social psychopathology. I was part of it. But things were not as clear-cut as this all sounds: the edges were blurred. As Arthur Koestler once remarked, every communist had a private agenda of personal beliefs. I was among those few who were disappointed by the Twentieth Congress for opposite reasons. These few knew by then that Stalin's crimes were a thousand times worse than Khrushchev said. Why was he not telling the whole truth? We—these few who discussed these things privately—believed that though everything the 'capitalist press' and the émigrés from the Soviet Union and the by now many refugees from the communist countries of Eastern Europe said was true, there must remain inside the Soviet Union a hidden number of pure souls who would 'at the right time' emerge and say, 'Yes, everything that has been said about us is true, but now we shall put Soviet communism back on the true path.' If I use the word 'believe' here, then it was a half belief, for with every new book about the Soviet Union, or every conversation with someone who had been living there, this belief had faded. Slowly. Losing faith in communism is exactly paralleled by people in love who cannot let their dream of love go. Now I knew that everything I had been clinging on to was nonsense. I cannot say it was a heart blow, for my psychological eggs were not all in that basket and never had been. But I knew people who had invested everything, heart and mind, had made sometimes bitter sacrifices, who had lived only for the golden communist future, and they were breaking down all around me, or suffering violent conversions into their own opposites. These were dramatic: soon there was a joke around the Left that having been a communist was the best possible education for becoming a very successful businessman.

Having shed all faith in the Soviet Union, and in communism, did not mean relinquishing revolution. Implicit was the idea that revolution was necessary to save us all. Hard now to put a term to it, but I would say revolution as a basic tenet of a creed was around for at least another twenty years. Perhaps more. It was implicit: no need to justify or spell it out. Revolution was good. The temporisings of socialism were bad and also despicable symptoms of cowardice, like a belief in God.

It was—is?—part of the structure of our minds and of our thinking. Take South Africa. When I became aware of South Africa politically, I was twenty or so, and it was taken for granted by us that there had to be a bloodbath, a 'night of the long knives'. Again, this was so much part of how everybody concerned saw things that it needed no explanation. When, in 1992, Mandela and de Klerk agreed and the "inevitable bloodbath" was no longer on the agenda, decades of political belief simply evaporated.

In 1956 I was in a most familiar situation: I could not say what I thought, except to a very few people. I certainly could not say to comrades whose hearts were breaking, who were ill with shock, that what Khrushchev said at the Twentieth Congress was just cowardice: he should have told the whole truth.

Before leaving on my trip I was approached by the Party to ask if the artist Paul Hogarth could go with me. I did not particularly want this, but why not.

About this trip I wrote a short book, called *Going Home,* and it is there in print if anyone is interested.

I was in the Zelters'* house for a few days, discovering that in England there is always a hard tight little core somewhere near the solar plexus, on the alert to resist cold and damp, and it never really relaxes. The wonderful dry invigorating heat of Salisbury's altitude began with my bones, then took over the rest of me, and I did not really want to begin work. But I had arranged to stay with

*See *Under My Skin.*

Bram Fischer,* in Johannesburg, who had arranged people for me to see and told Paul where he could go to find scenes most visitors never suspected were there. It was the time when South Africa was making a Prohibited Immigrant of any person critical of them, and we were joking that I might find myself put back on the plane that took me to Jan Smuts Airport. And that was what happened. I had told Paul that if I was stopped by the Special Branch, then he was not to know me; but while I was being led off by the policeman he was waving and shouting, Where are you going? I pretended not to know him. Their long experience of safety has made the British incapable of understanding how breeds without the law have to live. There was a joke in Party circles then that if a British communist photographer, journalist, or artist was travelling under the aegis of the Communist Party in any country with a repressive government—let's say Greece—his progress could be followed by a trail of people arrested and flung into prison: his contacts, the brave people prepared to help him. This trait is by no means dead. On the television you see being interviewed people who have demanded anonymity, for they fear arrest or reprisals. And there they are with an inch or two of geometrical dazzle in the very centre of their faces, ensuring that they will be arrested or even murdered the moment the programme is shown. But journalists and TV programme makers have the *right* to do as they like.

I was not really upset by being turned out of South Africa, for I had no emotional stake in the place. I was taken to the plane I had come on by two officials, and on the flight back sat by myself while people looked at me, imagining God knows what crimes.

Back in Salisbury I was postponing all the business of being a journalist, not really my favourite occupation, and sat around on verandahs, gossiping. Then there was a call from the Prime Minister's office, saying, Don't you want to interview Garfield Todd? It had not occurred to me. What for? I was after very different sources of information. But off I went to the Prime Minister's office, and there was Garfield Todd, a tall, handsome man striding

*Bram Fischer was perhaps the best-known, bravest of the South African communists. He was a lawyer. He spent years in prison.

about like Abraham Lincoln, for you could see walls and ceilings irked him and he would rather have been out-of-doors. And there I was for about three hours. As usual, I was in a thoroughly false position. Garfield Todd, a noble soul, was in love with the Federation of Central Africa, that noble idea that ignored every reality. He said, 'I have let you in . . .' or, rather, 'I have stretched my hand out over you, my child'—he was a missionary—and this was because he intended me to write nice things about Southern Rhodesia and the Federation. The foreign journalists always gave it a bad press, he said. He had told his publicity men to give me every facility, because he knew that when I saw 'with my own eyes' what was being done, I must be impressed, and I would write nice articles. I said I had been brought up in the country, I knew it inside out and back to front, and there was no way I could write 'nice articles' about it. What can be more extraordinary than what one doesn't hear, doesn't 'take in'? Because it was *emotionally* impossible for me to be excluded from the landscape I had been brought up in, I couldn't hear what he was saying. The fact was that I had been made a Prohibited Immigrant by Lord Malvern (Dr. Huggins, the family doctor) when I left Southern Rhodesia eight years before: 'I wasn't going to have you upsetting my natives.' But I had not been told I was Prohibited. They were embarrassed about it when, weeks later, I went with a lawyer to Rhodesia House in the Strand. They prevaricated, they wriggled, they lied, but in the end they admitted I was Prohibited, saying, 'Drat it, you've forced our hand.'

Meanwhile, on being told by the Special Branch that my name was on the passenger list, Garfield Todd had intervened to allow me in. I told him he was putting me in an impossible position. He said he had confidence in my fairness of mind. I said it obviously had nothing to do with fairness of mind, since we both had fair minds but disagreed. We went on to debate about the bases of federation. I said that its inflammatory nature was surely shown by the fact that it had given birth to the two African National Congresses, of Northern Rhodesia and of Nyasaland. (It had also given birth to the still invisible National Congress in Southern Rhodesia: I had already met clandestinely two men who lived permanently on the run from the police of all three countries, smuggling into Southern Rhodesia leaflets and information from the two northern countries.) Garfield Todd said he loathed and despised the leaders of the National Congresses. He said they were loud-mouthed agitators. Of course they are, I said. Quite soon he was to become the good friend of all the black leaders.

I spent the rest of my time in Southern Rhodesia being courteously escorted around by his publicity people but at the same time pursued by the Special Branch, who had a rather more realistic view. They turned up in the most surprising places, such as in the middle of the bush near the Zambesi, where Paul was drawing a Coca-Cola stall; at the next table in the Karoi Hotel, trying to eavesdrop: he had the bad-tempered look characteristic of these people when forced into unwilling proximity to their seditious charges; in the next car at a drive-in cinema—but he went to sleep.

The painful part of the trip was going to see all my old comrades, the Reds. To hold views about the society you live in not shared by the people you live among, to preserve them coolly and sanely, to remain unparanoid and unbitter . . . well, it is not possible. In the old Southern Rhodesia, before the advent of Reds and kaffir-lovers, there were one or two such souls, one of them Arthur Shearly Cripps, the poet, who was supported by religion, but on the whole it was impossible. Eight years had passed. The Cold War still gripped, and because of the birth of the National Congresses up north, white attitudes had hardened. I found my old friends had become paranoid, had taken to drink, or had turned into their own opposites, defending White Civilisation in ways they would so recently have found pathetic. Or they were having breakdowns. All these people had been sustained by a vision of that beautiful and true Utopia over there in Russia, but they had just read in the *Observer* the full text of the Khrushchev speech, and they were angry, disbelieving, bitter. I met little groups or the isolated person in some mining town or in a house in Bulawayo or Salisbury, and they were in despair, and their hearts were broken. There was one thing I could not say: 'Not only is the Khrushchev speech all true, but the real truth is a hundred times worse.' 'Yes, it is true,' I said. 'Yes, I am afraid it is true, Khrushchev's speech is true.'

I was looking—and I knew it—at what I would have become had I stayed in that first marriage, a civil servant's wife in that society. I would have been a lush, had a breakdown, at best become bitter and neurotic.

I saw my brother, for a couple of days, in his house in Marandellas. It was uncomfortable for both of us. He was entertaining this wrong-headed kaffir-lover, who had written these unfair books. I was with a man whom you could not even describe as 'reactionary', for his attitudes on any subject at all were always at an extreme, like caricature.

I saw my mother for an afternoon. She was staying with her old friend Mrs. Colborne, and we met with our usual politeness, and under this surface were worlds of grief.

I went to see Lord Malvern, head of the famous Federation, and said I wanted to go to Northern Rhodesia and Nyasaland, for Garfield Todd had warned me I would have to get permission. He said, 'How long do you want to go for?' and, when I said a week or so, 'I suppose you can't do much harm in that time.' I still didn't know he had Prohibited me.

There is a certain charm about all this, an amateurishness: it is because I was white. Had I been black, the South African Special Branch would not have had one second's embarrassment about deporting me. Had I been black, with my views, I would have been on the run, hiding, like the National Congress men, or pretending to be a house servant.

The best part of the trip was being alone, in the bush, driving for hours absolutely by myself, the only person on the road, stopping from time to time simply to sit on the edge of space and stare into the great skies. Once, on the road north to the still building Kariba Dam, I saw in front of me on the side of the road an apparently broken-down car. In it were two American anthropologists, whom I had met the night before in Salisbury. Could I help? I asked. They were pale, they were trembling, they were in a funk. What could be the matter? It was all this space, they said. They couldn't stand it. They couldn't bear to look at it. I stood by them, as they sat huddled in the front seats, and I looked at all the magnificent emptiness and at the blue distances above, and I asked what it was they were afraid of. But for them, that landscape was full of menace. They begged to be allowed to follow my car, so as not to be the only car on that road. Which they did, until the turnoff to Kariba, where they sent me pathetic smiles and waves, as they drove slowly onwards by themselves.

On that trip I drove through a forest more wonderful than any I have seen anywhere—tall, noble trees and clean yellow grass, animals and birds everywhere, even elephants, for I saw them quite close, on a little hill. Thirty years on, it had gone, the forest had gone, there were only wrecked trees and erosion.

Going to Northern Rhodesia was exciting in ways not due entirely to present 'unrest'. In those days no one went there unless they had to—mining engineers, civil servants, miners in search of work. Northern Rhodesia was the Copper Belt, Lusaka unimportant. Then, as now, most of the black people were in the towns, not in villages in the bush, unlike Southern Rhodesia and—now— Zimbabwe, where most people are still village people. It was a hard-drinking, rough place, like an urban Wild West. The hour's flight to Lusaka was from a modern and developed country to a backward one. All of Northern Rhodesia was aflame, with people rioting, throwing stones at white people in cars, setting minor buildings alight—the pathetic weapons of people without power. In the old days—the thirties and forties—the public figure in the news was Roy Welensky, the miners' trade-union leader: white miners. He was noisy, effective, and crudely anti-black. 'A rough diamond,' opined the whites of Southern Rhodesia. Recently he had toned down his racism, to match the times, but the blacks distrusted and hated him. He had been made prime minister of Northern Rhodesia, one of the pillars of Federation. This was a stroke of such brilliant stupidity that even now one has to marvel. It was as if the authorities were deliberately saying to the blacks: You are absolutely right; federation means you will be put into the hands of black-haters, not only Southern Rhodesians but your best-known local one, Welensky.

I went around and about a good bit, but all that is in *Going Home*. Three events stay in my mind. One was visiting the headquarters of the African National Congress, a little brick house in a suburb. In the front room, Kenneth Kaunda, a clerkly man, every inch an intellectual, sat reading the *New Statesman*. In the back yard, a small crowd gathered to greet Harry Nkumbula, the then leader of the Congress. He had been on a trip to see the River Tonga, who were being thrown forcibly off their land to make way for the great Kariba Dam. The Tonga were a major political issue then, used by the National Congresses to accuse the whites. But once in power, none of them gave a damn about the suffering Tonga. I was a sentimental soul in those days and was moved by this outcry. Harry Nkumbula, who had spent some days in the bush, dodging the police, and had hardly slept, returned, found the crowd in the yard, stood on a box, and harangued them. He was a magnificent orator. His lieutenant, Kenneth Kaunda, continued to sit in his shirtsleeves, reading.

In Ndola, a Copper Belt town, they gave a party for me. I was the main course. This could hardly have been an unambiguous pleasure for them. On the one hand I was a writer and a celeb, and they were short of excitements of that kind, but on the other I was a known sympathiser of the blacks, and a Red, and an enemy. All through the evening I was the target for sickening racial remarks. These people were feeling threatened, because of their no longer obedient blacks, who were throwing stones at their cars and shouting insults, and they defended themselves that evening with spite, malice, and vindictiveness. If they could have killed me slowly, and with maximum unpleasantness, they would. Meanwhile, and all evening, they listened to Eartha Kitt records and sentimentally sang along. They loved Eartha Kitt, brown sugar, little black rabbit; they simply couldn't get enough of her. Oh, my compatriots, my white compatriots, how I did dislike you, what a nasty lot of people you were. That is to say, whenever the racial nerve was touched, because at other times you were charming, just like anybody else. Who were they all that evening? Managers and senior technicians from the mine and representatives of the big mining companies, Anglo-American and the Rhodesian Selection Trust. More men than women, for women were always in short supply on the Copper Belt. During my time there I was a fizz of angry energy. The

Copper Belt had a raw violent energy, and hating something fills you with energy too.

And now the third event. On the plane from Ndola to Lusaka, I was sitting next to a likeable young man who was—improbably—a policeman. He had been on some stint of duty on the Copper Belt, and he was returning to his mother and his sister, with whom he lived. He talked about his little pigeons and his rabbits. He said I should go with him and meet his mom and his sister. He said we should get married, we would get along fine. Now, that plane trip lasted less than an hour. I was shocked. I was shaken. Attractive young women are used to inconsequential proposals of marriage. Love—that's a different thing; nothing surprising about invitations to love, at a moment's notice. But marriage? More than once, when young—but it was during the war—I had sat with other women and we had marvelled—uneasy—at the casual way men will propose. But this young man was rather sensible, I thought. He was not drunk. He was not high on anything—except, probably, dreams. He had never left Northern Rhodesia. Here, sitting beside him high above the earth, was this woman; a journalist, she said. She lived in London. This sweet young man—he was younger than I was by a good ten years—was in a dream of some kind. A figure from the girls' magazines his sister bought had come and sat beside him on the aeroplane, and when she went off at the airport, waving goodbye, he was full of loss, as we are when we wake from a dream of our heart's desire and find our arms empty after all.

But it was such an odd little event, or happening, so bizarre, I could not forget it. I brooded about it, then let it go, but came back to it and fitted it together with events of the same kind. It comes hard for any young woman with even minimal attractions to dismiss them as irrelevant, but at last I had to conclude that some women are like blank screens where people—not only men—project images. These women are not necessarily beautiful or even pretty. They may be plain. They attract proposals and offers of every kind all their lives and make a mistake if they think this is a tribute to their personal charms. I used to think, Well, we're good listeners, perhaps that's it. I conducted a quiet private survey among women of my age. Some would look at me, ready to be derisive: What *are* you talking about? But others knew at once what I was talking about.

Shortly after my return to London, there was a telephone call, that so frequent telephone call: You are not pulling your weight. The leadership of the Northern Rhodesian National Congress were in London. If they had stayed, they would have been put in prison. They had very little money, they were living poorly, please would I ask them around and see that at least they sometimes got a decent meal. So that is why, for some months, two or three times a week, I had an assortment of black exiles in my flat, in my big room. The most important one was Harry Nkumbula, the movement's leader. This then so well-known politician has long ago disappeared from view. Like many other Africans in exile then, he drank too much. Later he backed a line too moderate for the uncompromising mood of the blacks in soon-to-be Zambia and fell from grace; Kenneth Kaunda took his place. Harry went on drinking and did himself in with it. Sad; he was an extraordinarily nice man. The people who came to these evenings were not all from Northern Rhodesia. One was Orton Chirwa, from Nyasaland. He worked in London as a teacher. His classes were all white children. Every morning he lined them up, and sat in a chair, and allowed them to file past, each child feeling his hair and exclaiming over it. This ceremony had to take place, as otherwise his classes were continually interrupted: Please, sir, can I feel your hair? Orton was a kind and witty man, but that did not save him from a horrible fate. Another habitué was Babu Mohammed, from Zanzibar. He used to come early and cook with me, his contribution being great pots of curry, Zanzibar style. Others dropped in, but I've forgotten names. These men did not know they would soon be in positions of power. They were uncertain, low in spirits, and lonely in London. Later I looked back and thought uneasily about their so different fates. Orton Chirwa was to confront the tyrant Hastings Banda, and he was for many years in prison, where he was chained, tortured, then murdered. Kenneth Kaunda was the first black president of Zambia. Mainza Chona, the promising young poet of the assembly, full of charming idealisms, became minister for home affairs and presided over some very nasty prisons. He had eight children, as an example to his nation, because the idea that having too many children is a bad thing was merely another little plot by the whites. Babu, having worked in the post office, a refuge for many exiles, went back to Zanzibar, where he was imprisoned as an agitator by the British. In prison he said he had the disconcerting experience of reading *The Golden Notebook*—not the most likely prison fare. Later he became a minister in Julius Nyerere's government. He was one of the people responsible for the socialist villages—Ujamaa—in Tanzania, which wrecked that country's agriculture. Zanzibar had a tyrant, Karume, loathed by everyone except his immediate henchmen, and opposed by—among others—Babu. Someone assassinated him. Babu—among many others—was accused of it. He told me that he could not have possibly done this, because he was in a boat on a pleasure trip with some girls at the time. President Nyerere, about whom Babu had never had much good to say, put Babu in prison to keep him safe from the assassins of Zanzibar and refused to extradite him to certain death: they were torturing and hanging and imprisoning people by the hundreds in Zanzibar. Babu, one of the most gregarious men I have ever known, was for seven years in solitary, where he wrote his memoirs on lavatory paper, as is prescribed. He was fed and kept alive because the men who were his jailors admired and helped him. He said that being in prison under the British was a holiday camp compared to conditions in African jails. Babu was quite often described in the newspapers as 'the most dangerous man in Africa'. How they do love this kind of idiotic label. Dangerous to whom?*

On these evenings in my home, a great deal of sombre joking went on. They dreamed of how things would be when they were governing their countries. One evening I heard the Northern Rhodesians, Kenneth Kaunda included, saying it would be impossible to run their country, achieve real independence, because the Copper Belt was owned by international capital. Copper is Zambia's only asset, apart from abundant wild life. They would never be allowed to close down the copper mines. It would be best sim-

*Babu died in 1996.

ply to blow up all the mines, and then they would have independence. This idea was a serious, if wistful part of their programme, developed over more than one evening.

Kenneth Kaunda, Mainza Chona, Harry Nkumbula, returned to Zambia, where they were in prison for a time, but then the first two became Prime Minister and Minister for Home Affairs respectively, while Harry faded from view. Babu went off to Zanzibar and the British prison. Orton Chirwa went to Nyasaland, Malawi, and his terrible end.

I heard no more from the Northern Rhodesians. I was told that Mainza Chona was going about telling people to keep clear of me because I was a dangerous communist.

I did not mind this. For one thing, my evenings were my own again. Did I then feel—or do I now feel—resentment that men I befriended, gave money to, fed (though of course I was not the only hostess in London to help them), then became someone to be avoided? No. In politics virtue has to be its own reward, and anyone who expects justice and even gratitude is as stupid as a soldier risking his life in war who expects his government to do right by him—crippled soldiers were selling matches and bootlaces on the streets of London to survive before the war in The Trenches had even ended—or women who stand by struggling young artists and poets.

There was, in fact, very little communism, theory or practice, during those evenings. For one thing, the dogma, or Party Line, still was that black nationalism was an aberration, reactionary, and so forth. A black proletariat was still the only key to the glorious dawn in Africa. None of these men was interested in communism. Their talk was all of the repressiveness of the Colonial Office, of how they had been betrayed by Federation. Queen Victoria had promised their chiefs that their (black) interests would always be paramount, yet the Colonial Office had agreed to Federation, which would put them at the mercy of Southern Rhodesia. The bitterness of betrayal was the keynote of their talk.

A little event, which I still find touching. Someone in Whitehall decided it would be a good thing if a Royal could have these agitators to tea, because one never knew: after all, look at Kenyatta, look at Nkrumah, dangerous agitators and then noble leaders. In the Palace they probably said, 'Oh Lord, *no,* someone's got to ask a parcel of blacks out to tea. How about you?'

'No fear, can't stand the buggers.'

'How about you, then?'

'Not me.'

'I know, we'll tell Alice she's got to do it.'

So Princess Alice asked the future government of Zambia to tea in a palace, I don't know which, and these lonely and ignored men were so grateful for the attention and, too, for what they saw as a delicate reference to Queen Victoria's promise to their forebears, that half a decade later, when Zambia got self-government, President Kenneth Kaunda most especially asked if Princess Alice could be his official guest and open the big official ball with him at the Celebrations. And so there at the ball was this old frail lady, dressed in her jewels, with her pretty tiara, waltzing gently around and around with President Kaunda. . . . About politics there is nothing to be done, finally, but laugh.

By then I had become impatient with what I had decided were romantic and paranoid souls in the Party who were convinced that their telephones were tapped and their letters opened, but then something happened that convinced me my letters were opened. After Babu had returned to Zanzibar, he sent me a letter recommending a certain cousin, who would come to see me on such and such a date and would much benefit by attending the evenings— but by then they had ended. He wasn't interested in politics, said Babu, he was a good-time boy, and he needed instruction. When this cousin turned up, without having telephoned or sent a message, he was fearful, said he had come only because Babu had told him he must. He had been summoned by an official in Whitehall, and warned that he must keep clear of a certain Mrs. Lessing, who was involved in dangerous conspiracies with the Arabs. He must be careful to avoid this woman, or his time in London would be short. They knew he planned to visit me on such and such a date. So they must have opened Babu's letter. This cousin wanted to know who were these Arabs? I wanted to know too. The Arabs (which?) were not then noisy figures on the world stage; we hardly thought of them. I had not met any Arabs in London. The only time I had met an Arab was back in Salisbury, Southern Rhodesia, when our group conceived the brilliant idea of asking all our Jewish friends to meet the Arabs just let out of the internment camps, where they had been for the years of the war because they were pro-German. They were bitter and angry men, the Jews were bitter and angry. We had actually imagined that civilised discussion might clear the air. So hostile were the few first moments of their confrontation that we—the noninvolved—simply left them to it and went off to drink in the Grand Hotel, sending emissaries from time to time to see how things were going. Very badly, and they ended in violence. And that had been my sole encounter with Arabs of any kind. I was mystified, and so was the cousin, who said he couldn't afford to follow Babu's instructions and come to my parties, because he wanted to have a nice time in London and didn't want to be ejected from Britain. These mysterious conspiratorial Arabs were to reappear later. As for me, I shrugged my shoulders and thought, Well, what can you expect? Any encounter I've ever had with the famous British secret services—and they have always been slight—has had this flavour of the farcical, the surreal.

The creed most often discussed in that flat was not communism but anarchy—classic anarchy. Before Babu went off home to do his obligatory stint in prison, he was an anarchist, a friend of Murray Sayle, who was an anarchist because the labour movement of Australia was influenced by this most attractive philosophy—which has none of the disagreeable obligations of power. I remember saying to Babu, And when you have got into power, what will you do with the organisation that got you there? 'Easy,' he said airily. 'We will simply disband it and let natural forces operate.' It is only fair to record that when I reminded Babu later of his anarchist period he was shocked and said he was glad he couldn't remember that youthful irresponsibility. Meanwhile, irresponsible or not, it was all very entertaining. Babu came rushing into my flat one afternoon to say that he had a wonderful plan for changing the whole future of Africa. He had a cousin—another one—working on a boat that plied to and fro from London to Egypt. Cairo was then using a very powerful transmitter to saturate 'the whole of Africa' with propaganda. I have forgotten what. Babu said we should supply this radio station, where he had a friend, with material of a suitable sort, factual and sober, not the rhetoric employed by Cairo. How would we do this? Easy! We would give it to the cousin on the boat, who would give it to a contact in Alexandria, who would send it to Cairo. But, I said, by the time this valuable material got to Cairo it would be weeks out of date. And besides, surely the people running the radio programmes in Cairo would notice? My role, alas, was to dampen youthful exuberance. For how could I help responding to these attractive lunacies, even while I poured cold water?

Round about that time, I went to some meetings of the Movement for Colonial Freedom, Fenner Brockway's creation. They were always held in a big room in the nether regions of the House of Commons. The twenty or so people might include future prime ministers and presidents who either had just emerged from British prisons in their respective countries or were about to disappear into prison. I did indeed find democracy in practice likeable. These meetings, which hastened, or marked, the disintegration of the British Empire, went like this. There was a long agenda, a list of the names of the British colonies or protectorates in various stages of unrest: Cyprus, Northern Rhodesia, Nyasaland, British Guyana . . . and so on. Barbara Castle came down from above for these meetings: a most efficient and impressive woman she was. The names of the various countries were read out, and a report was given by someone on what was going on. Northern Rhodesia? Unrest. Riots. Stone throwing. Strikes on the Copper Belt. Harry Nkumbula and Kenneth Kaunda imprisoned. Nyasaland? Unrest, strikes, stone throwing, riots . . . and so on. But when it came to Southern Rhodesia, it was simply passed over. Nothing to be said about it. I asked why and was told that as Southern Rhodesia was a self-governing colony, Britain had no say in what went on. I really could hardly believe my ears. I said that Southern Rhodesia became a self-governing colony in 1924, but with two reserved clauses. One was Defence. The other was Native Policy. At any time since 1924, Britain had had the right to step in and protect the black population, forbid the passing of legislation, always copied from

South Africa. Britain had never done this, not once. It was not too late. The blacks of Southern Rhodesia loathed the idea of Federation, and Britain had the right to intervene.

Nothing came of my remarks. I was looking at the polite, armoured faces of people who 'didn't want to know'. Britain had never said no to the whites of Southern Rhodesia, and clearly it was being judged, in that room, as too late to start now.

This was a traumatic experience, painful. I had come to terms with the fact that when the colonies were being discussed, the House of Commons was always empty. No one was interested except the people in this room, who were known everywhere as defenders of freedom for the colonies and freedom inside colonies. These were the people who surely should have known that Britain had a responsibility to the Southern Rhodesian blacks. And now, reminded, they did not care. To them it was irrelevant. I was remembering how often I had been with Charles Mzingele and his friends, hearing them say, 'And when our brothers in England know how we are being treated, then they will support us.' The 'brothers' here . . . but this was a complicated concept. The 'brothers' did include the trade-union idea of brotherhood and, too, the brotherhood of the labour movement; there was all kinds of morally uplifting talk at trade-union congresses, and Labour Party congresses, about freedom for the colonies. But stronger was some old idea of Britain, or perhaps I should say England, embodying decency and fair play and—forgive the old-fashioned word—honour. Honour is not—or was not—an outdated concept to the Africans. When the blacks of Northern Rhodesia rioted and threw stones, when the blacks of Nyasaland took to violence, it was because they felt betrayed: Queen Victoria had made promises to their chiefs, and these promises had been broken. Similarly, Charles Mzingele and his mates could not believe that Britain would not ever honour the promise made in the entrenched clause: that no legislation damaging to the blacks should be passed in Southern Rhodesia. And somewhere or other I must still have believed in this old-fashioned concept of honour too, for something died in me at the moment when I realised that these people, members of the one organisation in Britain which cared about the colonies, were not interested in Southern Rhodesia and Britain's responsibility. How very careless, how lazy, how indifferent, the British Empire was, how lightly it took on vast countries and millions of people, not even bothering to inform itself about them. Yes, of course I had known that; yes, I had been working, in a very small way, against that indifference. But now I was in the basement of the House of Commons, and I learned, coldly and sharply and finally, just how careless and irresponsible Britain could be. And—I switched off. It was the enormity of it, the impossibility—matching Charles Mzingele's perennial 'When our brothers in England know . . .' with the indifference of the people in that room. I went home so angry that—no, I was beyond anger. I could have wept for Charles Mzingele and his misplaced hopes, his betrayed faith in his 'brothers'—but I was beyond tears. That was probably when I finally stopped believing in the possibility of anything decent in politics. And so I did not go to any more meetings. That was that. It was the moment when people who have been buoyed up by some kind of idealism or belief see it end and then take to violence or 'direct action'. Well, for me 'direct action' had been soured, as for so many others. But when the black people of Southern Rhodesia, shortly afterwards, allowed 'unrest' to turn into war, it was because that moment had been reached, the turning of the switch: *That's that.*

I would not have believed that I had cherished these sentimental expectations for my country.

But to finish with that climactic year 1956. The year of the Twentieth Congress of the Communist Party of the Soviet Union. The year of Suez. I was involved with the 'unrest' over that to the extent I was at a Trafalgar Square demonstration, but only as an onlooker. My dislike of crowds, which are always on the verge of becoming mobs, was growing with every 'demo' I attended. Nor did I have anything to do with the year's other big event, the Soviet invasion of Hungary.* I was noting, surprised, how many of our young activists went rushing off to Budapest to enjoy the thrill

*I wrote a passionate letter protesting about it to the Union of Soviet Writers and got a conciliatory letter back. Of course I had not expected to actually change anything.

of the thing . . . I was quite ashamed of my sour view, but really this was the beginning of a very different assessment of the excitements of revolution. Resignations from the Party became a flood. Soon certain 'revisionist intellectuals', as the Soviet Union put it, split away and started a rather attractive magazine called *The New Reasoner*. Edward Thompson—E. P. Thompson the historian—and John Saville were the moving spirits of this little rearguard action: for in retrospect it is easy to see it was not a new beginning, as we all thought then, but only one of the death throes of the Communist Party.

While writing this, I got a letter from Dorothy Thompson: would I like to have copies of the letters I wrote to Edward at that time? I had forgotten I ever wrote any. I read them with interest, to find out what I had been like then, for the mature and reasonable reflections, all passion spent, of my remarks about the Party are not untrue, but none of the emotions of that time are there.

First, the contradictoriness of it all.

Now it seems to me that what is most interesting about monolithic political movements, or countries with a state religion or creed, is not their uniformity, which is only apparent. When I was young, there was Nazi Germany, strutting and Sieg Heiling, as if a single mind governed it, but that is not what history sees now, which is something like a thirteen-year-long explosion. And that Nazi Party which so terrified us all, as if we were watching people hypnotised into a single mind, was nothing of the kind, rather a mass of disagreements, intrigues, plots. Then there was the Soviet Union, easy to see as a mass mind, a fortress mind, which a tiny handful of 'dissidents' hardly touched, but again, it was in fact all intrigues, plots, little futile rebellions, the mass murders of opponents. To go from the monstrous to the minuscule: inside the British CP, it was an only seeming homogeneity.

I am not talking about the fact that the Party was shedding members from its inception; the turnover of members was such that until recently there was a joke: 'Everyone has been in the CP, but no one is in it.' Inside, it was always a steady evolution of disagreements and adjustments. The Party Line was like that jagged line on a seismograph in a time of earthquake.

In 1956, when I did not regard myself as 'really' being a Party member, because of what I disagreed with, I still was thinking of how to save 'King Street' from itself, still seeing the CP as something that could be reformed and rescued from the baleful influences of the Soviet Union. If a map were made of my opinions, I would have to be described more as a Trotskyist—and in any communist country I would have been shot for saying a hundredth of what I thought.

Now I look at the great 'monolithic' fanatic movements, and what I am thinking is, So what is *really* going on inside there?

58 Warwick Road
London SW 5

19 October

The reaction to the Twentieth Congress has been expressed in party circles throughout the world in the phrase 'the cult of the individual'. That these words should have been chosen as the banner under which we should fight what is wrong with the party seems to me a sign of the corruption in our thinking. For they suggest that what caused the breakdown of inner-party democracy was an excess of individualism. But the opposite is the truth. What was bad is not that one man was a tyrant, but that hundreds and thousands of party members, inside and outside the Soviet Union, let go their individual consciences and allowed him to become a tyrant.

Now we are discussing what sort of rules we should have in the party to prevent the emergence of bureaucracy and dictatorship. A lot of worried and uneasy people are pinning their faith in some kind of constitution which will ensure against tyranny. But rules and constitutions are what people make them. The publication of the Constitution of the Soviet Union, an admirable document, coincided with the worst period of the terror. The party rules in the various communist parties are (I believe) more or less the same; but the development of the different communist parties have been very dissimilar.

I think that this talk about changing the rules is a symptom of the desire in all of us to let go individual responsibility on to something outside ourselves, something on to which we can put the blame if things go wrong. It is pleasant to have implicit trust in a beloved leader. It is pleasant and comfortable to believe that the communist party must be right simply because 'it is the vanguard of the working class'. It is pleasant to pass resolutions at a conference and think that now everything will be all right.

But there is no simple decision we can make, once and for all, that will ensure that we are doing right. There is no set of rules that can set us free from the necessity of making fresh decisions, every day, of just how much of our individual responsibility we are prepared to delegate to a central body—whether it is the communist party, or the government of the country we live in, be it a communist or a capitalist government.

It seems to me that what the last thirty years have shown us is that unless a communist party is a body of individuals each jealously guarding his or her independence of judgement, it must degenerate into a body of yes-men.

The safeguard against tyranny, now, as it always has been, is to sharpen individuality, to strengthen individual responsibility, and not to delegate it.

Doris Lessing

The calm, dispassionate, judicious tone of this letter is very different to anything being said privately then.

It was written in 1956 and was published in *The New Reasoner*. At once the CP responded, through Maurice Cornforth, saying to Edward that this must have been a personal letter and he shouldn't have published it. The fact that they could have thought this confirmed how little they understood the emotions raging in the ranks. There was a ferment of meetings, telephone calls, threats from King Street, and the batch of letters I have here would be fascinating, I am sure, to those who lived through all that, but boring to those who didn't.

The second letter: I had intended to write a satirical little novel, *Excuse Me While I'm Sick,* making fun of the new surly iconoclasts, Kingsley Amis et al. (Later John Wain became a good friend.) But I lost interest.

21 Feb. 1957

My dear Edward,

First, some practical points.

(a) Excuse me while I'm sick. Don't feel bad that I may feel bad because you don't like it. I've rather lost interest anyway. I think, were I to finish it, it would be a quite interesting small novel, which would appeal to a certain number of people; but quite obviously its mood is right out of key with what a very large number of people are feeling who would be its natural readers. Such a book, a sort of intellectual jape, is of value set against a background of accepted moral values. In the absence of any such background, perhaps it is better left. I think in one way it is a pity this book is not going to be finished. But a piece of polemical writing, even if on the surface a frivolous one, is half the magazine it is published in, and clearly the New Reasoner is not the magazine.

But of course our different attitudes over this are a reflection of a much deeper difference, which is why I am finding this letter so hard to write . . .

But first, about the suggestions in your, I think, second letter. I like the suggested article by Alex Werth. I would be interested in a piece by Hervé. I would very much like to read a bit of Not by Bread Alone, but you must be sure first that it hasn't been translated and published as a whole first—I shall be surprised if it doesn't appear here very soon. They always do publish this sort of thing fast. Like The Thaw, for instance. And they did the Visitors on the radio very quickly.

I think autobiography is a good idea. A really truthful bit of writing about experience in the C.P. at some stormy point would be invaluable, but I shall be very surprised if people are ready to be truthful writers or readers. The instinctive defence against being truthful is so very strong.

I think it would be interesting to have a serious description by someone like Kingsley Amis of his experience with the C.P.* It

*Kingsley Amis was not a Communist Party member.

would be typical of the experience of hundreds of thousands of people vis à vis the C.P. But these angry young men have nothing philosophically to utter. Why should they have? They are all artists, not philosophers.

But now my dear Edward—there are a lot of points in particularly your middle letter.

That poem 'Plea for the Hated Dead Woman'* was written ten years ago, and has nothing whatsoever to do with any recent political situation. It was written in a mood when I was hating my mother.

As for my recent novel, *Retreat to Innocence,*† I think it was a bad book, because I wasn't facing up to any essential issue—I wasn't being truthful with myself, although I imagined I was, and so it's soft-centred and sentimental. I don't hold with it. Though it's got some good bits in it.

But what I am trying to say is more complicated than all this:

Look, when I read your letters I feel as if you were reaching out for some kind of final word or statement from me; as if you wanted something of me, and I ask myself, why? And what is it?

But above all, our moods are very different.

I know full well that all my reactions now are because (if I may use this word I hate so much) I am an artist, and I've exhausted all the experience and emotions that are useful to me as an artist in the old way of being a communist. Someone said flippantly that people left the C.P. because they got bored. You know—Frank Pitcairn, always forget his real name. But he said it because he is an artist.

I shall wither and die and never write another word if I can't get out of this straitjacket of what we've all been thinking and feeling for so long.

But this is not a political attitude, and this is why I don't think you ought to ask me for clarification.

And I suspect you of being an artist, in which case you ought to be finding out what you think by writing it.

It seemed to me the other afternoon that you and Randall shared the same attitude, which was that unless you could present yourselves

*Printed in the *New Statesman*.
†I suppressed this book.

214

and justify yourselves as you have been during the last fifteen or whatever years it is, you would have let yourselves down? But all of us have been involved in this thing that has been so corrupting, and there is nothing to justify that which interests people who have not been involved in it. You, Edward Thompson and Randall Swingler don't stand or fall by your explanations now. . . . If you think this is a very emotional way to take your demand for philosophical clarity, then I retort that your attitude is at bottom not at all a demand for a philosophy, but a terrible need to explain yourselves.

You have been a pure and high-minded communist, and until recently wouldn't accept the evil in it, and your idealism is hurt and your picture of yourself is damaged.

Get thee to thy typewriter, dear Edward. You can communicate your experience in art, and as such it can be communicated. But what has your lost feeling got to do with philosophies?

We are living in a time, I am convinced, when there aren't likely to be any philosophies one can pay allegiance to. Marxism is no longer a philosophy, but a system of government, differing from country to country.

Which is a good thing. Any philosophy which lasts longer than fifty years must be a bad one, because everything changes so fast.

I know I am a socialist, and I believe in the necessity for revolution when the moment is opportune. But whether the economists like Ken and John, or the historians are right as Marxists, I don't know. How should one know? It seems to me that a great many of the concepts we have called Marxist and which are shared by people who aren't Marxists are simply the reflection of the pressures of the time we live in.

I don't want to make any more concepts. For myself, I mean.

I want to let myself simmer into some sort of knowledge, but I don't know what it is.

Do you think there is something to be said for the point of view that being a communist has never been (except for a very few people) a question of intellectual standpoint, but rather a sort of sharing of moral fervours?

I haven't got any moral fervour left. No one who feels responsible for the bloodbaths and cynicism of the last thirty years can feel morally indignant about the bloodymindedness of capitalism? I can't, anyway.

What I feel is an immense joy and satisfaction that the world is going so fast, that the peasant in China no longer starves, that people all over the world care enough for their fellow human beings to fight for what they feel, at the time, to be justice. I feel a sort of complicated gigantic flow of movement of which I am a part, and it gives me profound satisfaction to be in it. But what has this got to do with political attitudes?

I want to write a lot of books.

And the stale aroma of thirty years of dead political words makes me feel sick.

I know quite well, since you are looking for something from me, this letter will make you feel let down. But I can't help it. You shouldn't go asking people like me for certainties.

I feel as I've been let out of a prison.

But above all I am convinced you should get yourself in front of a typewriter and ask yourself what you think.

Love,
Doris

The background to all this was the issue: Should Edward Thompson, John Saville, and the rest get themselves expelled from the Party? I obviously thought not. Yet while all this went on, my conversations with Clancy and others were the purest 'Trotskyism'. Somewhere we 'revisionists' still believed that the Party could be purified and reformed. Edward was demanding meetings—open meetings with the leadership to get 'everything out into the open', which was very much a keynote of the time. Hard to believe now that as late as '56, '57, it could come as a revelation to these intelligent people that 'King Street' lied, rigged meetings, manipulated votes. All kinds of people were going to King Street demanding the truth and nothing but the truth. There was Haimi Levy, who had gone to the Soviet Union, having told King Street he was going whether they said yes or not, and there met with the infamous Suslov. Haimi wanted to discuss the treatment of the Jews in the Soviet Union. Hundreds—hundreds of thousands—had been murdered, tortured, persecuted. Suslov continued to repeat, throughout the interview, that there was no Jewish question in the Soviet Union, because there were no Jews. Haimi returned to London, demanded that the Party should publicly 'come clean', and when they refused, he joined Edward Thompson, John Saville, and others.

I clearly wanted the 'revisionists' not to put themselves in a position where they would be kicked out, because the Party would then be even worse than it was.

Before these letters came from Dorothy Thompson I had forgotten I went to see Gollan. Now I do remember I found him unimpressive. John Gollan succeeded Harry Pollitt as leader of the Communist Party. Pollitt was solid, honest, in so far as it was possible to be, and respected outside the CP. He was a product of the British working-class movement and its struggles against the very hard times of the twenties and thirties. Gollan was a product of the Communist Party—not at all the same thing. I never met anyone who did not respect Harry Pollitt, but people did not have much time for Gollan.

Yet while all this was going on, I was wondering how I could leave the Party without a fuss. That was because journalists lay in wait for defectors, and there would be headlines: So-and-so reveals the truth about the Communist Hell—meaning the British Communist Party. I wasn't going to provide fuel for any headlines, if I could help it. So what was I doing busybodying about, going to see Johnny Gollan and writing letters to Edward Thompson, some at least in the tones of an affectionate but rather bossy elder sister? Alas, the truth must be: the enjoyment of political intrigue, being at the centre of things—in short, power, even in this minuscule way.

Facts: There were several meetings at my flat, a convenient venue for people coming in from outside London. The people I remember clearly are Edward Thompson, John Saville, Haimi Levy, Randall Swingler.

I remember nothing about those impassioned debates, but the atmosphere remains with me, vigorous, often acrimonious, and of course full of the enjoyment of political battle. Of course we would have talked about the invasion of Hungary, but this has become, with the passing of time, *the* event people remember now. For us, living through all that, Hungary was the culmination of a series of ugly events, one being the Soviet suppression of the uprising in East Berlin in—I think—1953.

I was sick, because of the tension of it all, and was not the only one.

I wrote a short story for *The New Reasoner,* 'The Sun Between Their Feet', which I think is one of my better stories. I saw it then as my comment about the failures of communism, but now rather as on the vanity of human wishes.

I had nothing to do with the grind and effort of running the magazine, for that was left mostly to Edward and John.

We all still believed in Revolution as an article of faith.★

A ferment of change . . . a gale . . . a hurricane . . . began with the dramas of 1956. Rather, the rapid changes that had been going on, mostly out of sight, certainly out of public sight, became visible. The Youth were back. Those of us who had complained of the indifference of youth towards politics now found young people vociferously everywhere and often knocking—no, banging—at our doors, to get our support for a hundred wondrous political plans. At a complaint that they were finding you lacking in fervour, you might murmur, 'You see, this is far from my first Dawn—and I'm sorry, but I've learned to distrust fervour.' An unattractive posture, as I knew, for I had only to look back at my own first dawn—and surely that could not have been only fifteen years?—and see one's own flashing eyes, and burning beliefs, and dislike of temperate and temporising and humorous elders.

'They're all Trots, you know,' one of us might say to another, perhaps on the telephone, announcing news to some former Stalinist. 'Well, fair enough,' he or she might stoutly say. 'After all, they could hardly be Stalinists these days.' 'Why do they have to be any sort of *ist?*' But that was going too far.

But for some people this was not at all a time of euphoria and

★Which Revolution? Against whom or what? Why? When? But we are talking about a mass social psychosis.

renewal. Let us take Haimi Levy, who went to confront 'the Party itself in Moscow' about the fate of the Jews. He was a poor Jew from the East End. The Young Communist League and then the Communist Party had been everything for him and for many like him—university, education, rescue from the kind of poverty that does not exist now anywhere in Britain. He had a brother, equally clever. The family could afford to support only one of them through university. The brothers tossed for it. Haimi Levy went to university and became the brilliant and respected professor of mathematics at Imperial College, while his brother went into business and also did well, supporting Haimi financially and otherwise with the utmost tenderness. The brothers helped each other all their lives. For Haimi the collapse of communism was no mere temporary blow. He died soon afterwards, I am sure from the pain of disillusionment. And there were others like him, with broken hearts.

A Meeting

General de Gaulle was restricting the freedom of the French Press. There was a protest meeting in London: de Gaulle was becoming a dictator. It was an afternoon meeting, and I remember it for two reasons, one because it was there I had a glimpse of the past. Isaac Deutscher was speaking. He wore clothes of a military sort, and he strode onto the platform, looking sternly ahead into the future, and stood orating in a heavy rhetorical style, while his right fist rhythmically punched the air. Lenin himself! we were all thinking; here was the Old Guard incarnated. What did he say? I have no idea. The other reason the occasion stays in my mind is that as I took my place on the platform to defend democracy, a man shouted from the audience: 'Have you just got out of bed?' Sympathetic laughter. I was indignant, having worked hard all morning. But I was wearing a red skirt and a black shirt, and doubtless fitted a template. Ah, La Pasionaria. Ah, Rosa Luxemburg. How the ghosts of these and similar women haunt the minds of left-wing men! (Not so much the women.) But I was then becoming more uneasy every day about our heroic imaginations, the intrepid postures. Who else was on the platform? I only remember Spike Milligan, day to Deutscher's night, who made a humorous mild sensible speech deprecating excess. I felt with him, because I knew he was there although he hated politics. As we speakers went to the door, there was Spike Milligan beside me, a hero to me as to everybody else because of *The Goon Show*. Seeing that I was about to say something invasive of his privacy, he shot out a hand: 'And so we meet again'—sharply withdrew it—'for the first time.' This startled my mental machinery into dislocation, and I could say nothing. I determined then and there to use the same technique when attacked by fans, but one has to be Spike Milligan for it to work. The point is, it isn't humiliating, as when, newly arrived in London, at an occasion at the PEN Club I found Eleanor Farjeon towering beside me and told her that her tales had meant so much to me when I was a child. At which she murmured, 'You see, I wrote them especially for *you*.' I swore then that I would never ever be as unkind myself to some respectful fan, and I hope I never have been, despite temptation.

Another Meeting

The newly formed *New Left Review* organised a meeting almost certainly called 'Whither Britain' or 'Britain at the Crossroads'. I was on the platform with some others, speaking my thoughts, when a man stood up in the audience and asked, 'How can you justify standing there giving us your opinions when you and your lot have been so wrong about everything?'

A very good question. One answer could be: 'Why are you sitting there listening to us?' Or, 'But there is a lot we have been right about.' Or, 'But everyone was a communist.'

But we were bearing witness. Why? This can only be because we felt we were representative of others. 'This has been my experience and that of many other people.' Is it that we do not trust our own experience until we know other people have felt it too? Surely that is because we live through times of such very great and often sudden change. You want to know what friends are thinking these days, for it goes without saying that they are not thinking what they did last time you met. ('How do you see it all now?') Yet there have been societies, so we are told, when everyone thought the same for centuries. There probably still are pockets of such people. An American friend, Uzbek by inheritance, went to look up her roots, as we all feel impelled to do, and found that the clan or tribe, from where her grandparents had come, were living exactly as they had done, were traders and shopkeepers and were much involved with horses. Their lives centred around long, companionable communal meals where people sat talking. A relaxed sort of life, and surely beneficial, otherwise it wouldn't have gone on for so long. But meanwhile she, a little splinter from the clan, had been like a leaf in a whirlwind of modern people, with nothing staying the same for five minutes.

There are public figures whose fame is mainly because of how often and thoroughly their minds have changed about everything. 'The winds of change blew into my head, and just look how it rearranged the furniture.' We bear witness. 'I used to think this, now I think this.' As if ideas were anchors.

On the Shelf

John Wain and I remembered we had enjoyed dancing 'when we were young'. Surely it goes without saying we were not thinking of ourselves as much more than young. I was not yet forty, he about that, I think. We took ourselves to the Jazz Club in Oxford Street, where Humphrey Lyttleton played his saxophone with his band, and found that all the young things were being very kind to these oldsters, who really had no right to be there. We jogged sedately about, inhibited by the tolerant but humorous stares, and then danced our way to the edge of the dancing floor—and off and out to drink coffee and to lick our wounds.

Salutary Occasion

John Berger had decided it was a bad thing that writers met only writers, painters painters, architects—their own kind. He was right. There should be a central meeting place, as existed in Paris, where there were cafés one could go to, knowing that there could be found artists, writers, thinkers. But not for the first time—and I am sure not the last—we all came up against the size of London, which can never be like Paris, so much more compact and centred, and the Dôme and the Flore and the Deux Magots ten minutes away. And then, in London, there were the licensing hours, for pubs closed at eleven. But John decided it was worth a try. He hired the large room over a pub a minute away from Oxford Circus—surely central enough—and invited a great many different kinds of people, to break down those incestuously defined barriers. Everyone was there. The place was full, it buzzed, it jumped, it vibrated. What a good idea, we all thought, how clever of John Berger to have thought of it, and of course there must be many more such occasions. And then John called us to order and made a speech. It was a good cause of some kind, political. At once it was observed that the painters, having exchanged looks, were making for the door. They went first, as people remarked, 'They always did have good sense.' And then the others left, one by one and in groups, while John spoke bravely on. What was the good cause? Who knows now, who cared then, for we were leaving. 'Not *again*,' people were saying. 'We've been here before, too often.' And so ended a brave attempt; but if politics had not intruded, we would all be there yet. . . .

The Social Life of the New Left

This was lively. They created a new café, as energetic as ours had once been and enjoyed themselves painting and doing it up, and intended it as the centre of the new political life, but idealistic thoughts are no substitute for a business sense, and it went bust. There was Jimmy the Greek, who served cheap and abundant food in a vast basement restaurant in Frith Street, full of the new comrades, day and night discussing politics—and Jimmy's is there still. Various cheap places were being hired to house *The New Left Review* and associated organisations, and these were all being painted by the faithful, and a very good time they all had. Just as we did. In these places, and in the coffee bars and in the cheap restaurants, the new youth sat about, talking. Talking is what one does most of in a New Dawn. I took no part in all this, but Clancy did, and I heard how things were going on through him.

In 1957 my mother died. This is what happened. Having failed to find a home with me, and back in Southern Rhodesia, she stayed with this and that old friend, but knew this could not be her future. She then informed my brother that she would come and live in Marandellas (now Marondera again), so as to be near him. She proposed to devote her life to him and his children: 'What else am I good for, if not to be of use to others?'

My mother was in a decent and comfortable retirement place. She had a little garden. Nothing wrong with these arrangements—which she made herself. But she had nothing to do. She was a vigorous seventy-three. She played bridge and whist in her afternoons and evenings—she was an excellent player—and tried to persuade herself that she was usefully occupied. Really, she was waiting for a summons from her son: Monica is finding everything too much; please come and live with us and take over the children.

And then she had a stroke. Into her room came the priest—she was Church of England—to administer Extreme Unction. She tried to raise herself, tried to say No, no, no—with her thickened tongue—and fell back and died. She could have lived another ten years, if anyone had needed her.

I was grief-struck, but this was no descent into a simple pain of loss, but rather a chilly grey semi-frozen condition—an occluded grief. As usual I pitied her for her dreadful life, but this rage of pity was blocked by the cold thought: If you had let her live with you she would not have died. I drifted about the flat, returned to my very earliest self, the small girl who could see how she suffered but was muttering: No, I won't. *Leave me alone.* Clancy was intermittently there, and was kind. His feelings for his mother, whom he pitied and feared, enabled him to understand mine. The emotions I could not out of honesty allow myself, like simple tears, were expressed for me in blues music. For some weeks, or months, I listened to nothing else. 'St. James Infirmary', 'St. Louis Woman' ...Bessie Smith, Billie Holiday, others ... I cannot hear them now without covering my ears or switching whichever machine it is off. Listening, I was thinking, At what point during this long miserable story of my mother and myself could I have behaved differently? Done differently? But I had to conclude that nothing could have been different. And if she returned to life and came to London and stood there, brave, humble, uncomprehending—'But all I want is to be of use to others'—then I would say, and be, exactly the same. So what use grief? Pain? Sorrow? Regret?

It was a bad slow time, as if I were miles under thick cold water. Peter knew that his grandmother had died, but why should he care about an old woman who had been there for a while and then left? There are deaths that are not blows but bruises, spreading darkly, out of sight, not ever really fading. I sometimes think, Suppose she were to walk in now, an old woman, and here I am an old woman . . . how would we be? I like to think we would share some kind of humorous comprehension. Of what? Of the sheer damned awfulness of life, that's what. But most of all I think that I would simply put my arms around her. . . . Around who? Little Emily, whose mother died when she was three, leaving her to the servants, a cold unloving stepmother, a cold dutiful father.

The New Left was not the only manifestation of young politics. The other was the Royal Court Theatre, now seen as a little theatrical golden age, under the benevolent aegis of George Devine. True, but it was a time of young, talented, clever young men, mostly from the north, mostly working class, and intending to make their mark. Which they have done, every one, for soon they were working in the highest levels of opera and theatre—and film. Then they were mere sparrows to George Devine's eagle, except for Tony Richardson, who in fact ran the theatre for a while. He was full of irreverence for the established order, like all the young men of the New Left. He was shortly to make the films which put new life into British cinema, *Look Back in Anger, A Taste of Honey, Tom Jones, The Charge of the Light Brigade.* Meanwhile he was the Royal Court's cutting edge. He was a tall, bony, handsome young man, who had evolved a camp drawling style, full of darlings—dah-ling—which probably began as a parody, a style, but took over, as styles so often do. Tony Richardson's strength came from being the very essence of The Outsider, both in situation and in temperament. Not middle class, not southern English, but with the directness and lack of cant of the northern English, he took a good, long, cool look at cozy middle-class London and soon was dominating any scene he was part of. Now when I look back at the people in and around the Royal Court, he is the one that stands out most, and they were a quite extraordinarily gifted lot.

The Court was more than a lively theatre, with a brave history, where everyone of talent wanted to work. Its atmosphere, its ambience, was so strong that for a while it was more like an informal community. Around it grew workshops and 'happenings' of the kind which would be commonplace in the sixties. What need was it then, in the second half of the fifties, expressed by large numbers of people, all young or at least not old—some of them actors and dramatists but some not even working in the theatre—to spend whole evenings, weekends, being Trees, Walls, Rivers, or delineating Anger, Pity, Love, Compassion, and so forth? Some of these sessions were not unlike what one reads of Victorian drawing rooms, with their tableaux and charades. One house where this sort of thing went on was Anne and Peter Piper's★ on the river at Hammersmith, a wonderful fragile house, with pillared verandahs, giving it the air of a ship adrift on the tides. It was full of beautiful daughters, of all ages, so that it was impossible to be in it without dreaming that Renoir might return and paint the whole lot of them. While I—and Peter—loved visiting the Pipers, I cannot say I enjoyed the charades, neither there nor at the Court, despite its heady atmosphere. I did not like the togetherness, the family, the 'we against them'—the tribe; I had had enough of all that to last my life. I knew it would soon blow apart, for it always does, but it was charming while it lasted. And for a while I was a Royal Court writer. 'Oh, you're one of our writers,' they would say, giving me good seats, but meanwhile I brooded over betrayal: you made me a promise and didn't keep it.

I had written a play, about that time when the youth were certainly not interested in politics. For me, after years of political refugees, survivors of concentration camps, of the refugees from the communist countries, to hear some languid youth murmur, 'I'm afraid I have no time for politics'—it was painful. Kenneth Tynan was the exemplar of the time, for he was a dandy, wearing peacock clothes to annoy his elders, inspired by Max Beerbohm and Wilde. My lot were shocked and disturbed, for we thought, if you are not

★This was David Piper, known to his friends as Peter.

'politically conscious', then you get what you deserve—Hitler, at least. That some of the most politically conscious generations in history had got Stalin was not a thought we could yet accommodate. So that was the background to *Each His Own Wilderness,* that and watching a friend of mine, a communist, being harassed by her non-political son, week in and week out, for months, about her politics. Then she gave up politics, and he, overnight, became extremely, not to say violently political—everything he had criticised her for being. Even while I was writing it everything had changed, and Kenneth Tynan headed the new wave. I sent this play to the Royal Court, which meant to Tony Richardson, and was invited to lunch by him and by George Devine, who both enthused about the play. 'Just as good as *Look Back in Anger,* da-h-ling,' drawled Tony. Some prescient imp spoke out of me when I said, 'But you might change your minds.' I was assured by both men, with a thousand promises, that this could not happen. Months passed, and I dared write to ask what had happened to the run I had been promised, and got a letter from George Devine, beginning: 'There are still some things we like about your play.' Tony Richardson had gone to work in the States, and it was he who had admired the play. His successor as George's mentor was Lindsay Anderson, who was rigidly left-wing, and he did not approve of it and had told George not to do it. Instead of a run, the play was put on at the Court for a Sunday night, John Dexter directing.★ He was then still unknown, unsure of himself but not of his talent, was already a wonderful director. The Royal Court's Sunday Nights for a time drew packed houses. The play got good reviews. Had it been given a run, it would have done as well as many others, but it was unfashionable not only in subject but also in form. The Court despised the well-made play. They loathed their predecessors, Noël Coward, Terence Rattigan, Anouilh, particularly Priestley. One had only to mention them to hear the sound which is the equivalent of the noisily pulled lavatory chain.

Does it have to be thus? I mean, that a new efflorescence of young talent must despise its predecessors? Many are the New Dawns that I

★John Dexter was later a famous director of theatre and opera.

have seen, and all of them are engineered by young people who have to hate their elders. And looking back at my dawn, remembering the vigour of my contempt for those who went just before me, I feel discouraged, know why it is so—but persist in wondering: Surely it doesn't have to be like this? For it is a wicked waste, this cycle, the new energies leaping up, demolishing what went before . . . then slowly realising they may have been too hasty and learning to salute people who are only themselves a generation or so back. Meanwhile they are being rubbished by their successors. A sad, bad, stupid cycle.

The new plays given a run by the Court were mostly shapeless, not to say anarchic, and badly needed cutting. Few have survived. But to cut and shape and prune seemed to these innovators an insult to creativity. (This was not true of Arnold Wesker's plays, John Osborne's, or Shelagh Delaney's).

I don't want to make any great claims for *Each His Own Wilderness*. It was a nice little play, nothing special. It sometimes gets put on again. To see what it lacked, just think of *Waiting for Godot,* or Genet's plays, or Sartre's. Long after, when Tony Richardson came to see me, visiting London, he said, 'That was a good play.' He felt bad about what had happened. And he did something generous. He asked me to write a script of Faulkner's *Intruder in the Dust* for a thousand pounds. By then I understood enough about the film world to know that this film might never be made, and certainly not as I had written it, and only later understood that Tony was using this way to give me some money. My experience of Tony, about whom harsh things are sometimes said, was that he was kind, thoughtful, generous by instinct, apart from being very clever.

I saw *Look Back in Anger* with Miles Malleson and could not have had a more appropriate companion. Miles was distressed by the play, but he was far from being some old fuddy-duddy. Now we take Ibsen, Chekhov, Molière, for granted, but then theatre managers were wary of them. Miles had sometimes made new translations, put pressure on the managers, and acted in these plays. He saw himself as having been in the avant-garde all his life, a comparable figure to George Devine. But that night, in the feverish, uneasy audience, the young shouting enthusiasm, the older generation unhappy, Miles kept saying, 'But bad manners isn't social criticism.' Miles was a socialist, but not far from communist; perhaps he was a communist, I don't know. I met a daughter of his at the National Theatre not long ago, and she assumed my friendship with Miles was that of two old Party warhorses, but I never heard anything like the party line from Miles. Jimmy Porter, with whom so many young men identified, I thought was infantile and as self-pitying as the youths who killed themselves because of *Werther.* Miles saw him as the equivalent of a fart let off in the face of respectability, and as useful.

Why was Jimmy Porter so angry? There are two deaths in that play. One was his father, dying from the Spanish Civil War, which had made so many Britons ashamed of their government, and the other was an old working-class woman who was a survivor of the hungry, threadbare, grimed-with-poverty thirties. I identified with that anger. Yet the older people were demanding, What was Jimmy Porter—or John Osborne—so angry about? Surely that was what he—or they—were angry about. Acres of print then occurred about the reasons for that anger.

In 1951 had appeared *Angry Young Man,* the autobiography of Leslie Paul, a distinguished man of letters whose life and publications fill two fat columns in *Contemporary Authors.* I've never met anyone who has read this book, but its title probably inspired Osborne's title. The phrase was in the air. When at the Royal Court the publicity people were thinking of how to draw attention to *Look Back in Anger,* they said, to John Osborne 'I suppose you are an angry young man?' And fed it to the press. As we all know, to our sad cost, the press cannot let a good thing go, and for years every appearance of new talent was hailed as an 'angry young man'. 'Angry Young Men.' An astonishing phenomenon, journalists: you'd think they would sometimes try for a little originality. Recently we have seen the same thing with John Major, who was described early on in his premiership as 'grey'. For years, and until recently, John Major has inspired journalists to add 'grey'. Like so many programmed rats. Mrs. Thatcher: handbag.

And now enter Tom Maschler, very young—twenty-three—handsome, and ambitious, who arrived in my flat with the demand that I write a piece for a book he planned, called *Declaration.* I said I hated writing think pieces. He said reproachfully that his whole future depended on this book. I later discovered that this was how we all agreed: we could not withstand Tom's need. Besides, he had approached Iris Murdoch—he said—and she had said no, and he had to have a woman in it: I could not let him down. This is how I became an angry young man.

Tom was very much a war victim. His parents had come as refugees from Vienna when he was six, and if this was not bad enough, they separated when they arrived. His mother got a job as a cook in a big house in the country. Tom, having been a young princeling in Vienna, was a cook's son. He became the leader of a gang of delinquent youths, and about his exploits he was very funny and somewhat boastful. He also complained that being rescued by being sent to a Quaker school had ruined him by giving him a moral sense, because otherwise he would have become a second Onassis. His short career in the army had not been a success: he was not the only young man I knew who, outraged that anything so crass could happen to him, simply lay on his bed and refused to get up. He had been a tour guide—this was at the beginning of this kind of tourism. His knowledge of languages and his charm made him a success. All kinds of adventures went on, one being the smuggling of coffee across frontiers. (Good real coffee was a treasured commodity.) I, taking Peter to Spain, had been invited to take across a parcel of coffee for our engaging young tour guide; those were innocent days. Tom decided to be a publisher, got a job at five pounds a week at André Deutsch, and was now in McGibbon and Kee, a very junior figure. He proposed to become the best publisher in Britain, but he had to make a start. This book, *Declaration,* would be the start. Tom did become the best, certainly the most visible, publisher in Britain. He had a nose, a flair, an instinct. He showed his flair in whom he chose for *Declaration.* What we had in common was that we were visible at the time; we were 'names' with an aura of success or promise.

While waiting for the publication of *Declaration,* Tom became friends with us all. Some of us gave him advice. Since he wanted to be a publisher, then it would be a good thing if he read some books. Interesting that we all came up with roughly the same list of twenty books. He should also try to read a newspaper a day, for while he might not be interested in politics, he should know what was going on. Well, all right, then: if he didn't want to read newspapers he must get someone to tell him the news.*

Tom is one of those people who attract comment, much of it unfavourable. Some of this is of course envy, for he has been so phenomenally successful.

Once, I told him it would be difficult to write about him because some of the things he did were so appalling.

'For instance?' asks Tom.

'For instance this,' I say. My Italian publisher, Feltrinelli, rang me from the Ritz to ask would I have breakfast with him. How chic, then, was a business breakfast: I had never heard of them. There we sat in the Ritz, surrounded by the plenitudes of the Ritz breakfast, drinking black coffee, since neither of us ate breakfast. He was an agreeable man, Giangiacomo Feltrinelli, and a brave publisher. He was a communist, Feltrinelli was a left-wing house, and he published books like *Doctor Zhivago* and other novels damned by the Soviet authorities. For this, of course, he was reviled by the comrades. That morning Tom happened to telephone, and I said I had had breakfast with Feltrinelli. Tom said, 'I'm coming over.' He then got me to telephone Feltrinelli at his hotel to say that my friend Tom Maschler was with me and would very much like to talk to him. I did this. I am not saying what I felt about it. I listened while Tom chatted up Feltrinelli, who could not have been blamed for assuming that Tom was living with me. The conversation finished, Tom put down the receiver and turned to say triumphantly, 'I'm seeing him tonight.' Next day he rang and announced that he was invited to stay with them in their country house. And Tom became a close friend of the Feltrinellis.[†]

---

*Because the era when it was fashionable for the youth not to care about politics was only just ending, there were quite a few hopeful young men who had to be advised by their mentors that they could not expect to be movers and shakers of the nation if totally ignorant about what was going on in the world.

[†]Giangiacomo Feltrinelli was later murdered—a political murder; no one seems to know why.

'Well, what was wrong with that?' says Tom. 'That was just being enterprising.' Chutzpah, that was Tom's middle name. He had been at McGibbon and Kee for six months when Howard Samuels, the proprietor, summoned him for an interview, and said to this ebullient and engaging infant, whom he had after all chosen from so many hopeful applicants, 'You know Tom, I don't really mind you allowing everyone to think you run this firm, but I am afraid I do rather object to your behaving as if you owned it.'

But really it was only necessary to remember Balzac's Rastignac, the provincial determined to conquer Paris. London was full of young men, most, but not all, from the north of England, many working class, from the grammar schools, without the connections that are so important in this country, but with plenty of cheek and cleverness. Women have ever been useful to ambitious young men. Why not? It is part of the social mechanisms. But until we worked it out—some of us by remembering Rastignac—women then in the news were always being puzzled by how we were being embraced in theatre foyers and public places by young men we scarcely knew, whose attentiveness impressed the onlookers, if not us; or summoned by public address systems, at the same time as youths we scarcely knew, to hotel or airport desks.

And now a more general comment. It seems to be generally agreed that unpleasant facts about people are more revealing of their real selves than pleasant ones, but why? Nothing is easier than malice, and to find something discreditable about someone needs no more than a good look at him; besides, everyone alive has a root down into the mud: it is the human condition. We are skilled critics of our fellows, clever sniffers-out of moral weakness. Once, to be malicious was considered a fault; now it is applauded. Our current happy phrase 'dishing the dirt' says more about us than we ought to like: it is diagnostic of our nasty time. And now, if I write: Tom was for years an enterprising, a brilliant publisher; he brought Jonathan Cape from a moribund condition to being the liveliest publishing house in Britain; he found new young authors and cherished and supported them; he fought for books at first patronised or rubbished by reviewers, like *One Hundred Years of Solitude* and *Catch-22;* he has kept his friends loyal to him through thick and thin . . . but I am sure the reader's eye has slid over these encomiums, waiting to get to the dirt. *The truth.*★

My complaint now is more general: What happens to these glorious buccaneers when they get old? These youths who entertained us with their exploits? They get respectable: you meet some balding oldster whom you remember for his reckless adventures, and he is lisping away about imaginary youthful conformities, which in fact he would have despised from the bottom of his brave heart.

When *Declaration* came out, Tom Maschler at once became famous, as its originator, and it was described by every newspaper as a manifesto by the Angry Young Men, as if they were a movement or a group. In fact, as I soon found out, they divided into two main groups, with nothing at all in common. The real left wing was Ken Tynan—who had left his dandyish young self behind—and Lindsay Anderson. John Osborne was called a socialist by other people, but I don't think he ever said he was. John Wain might have written *Hurry on Down,* similar to Kingsley Amis's *Lucky Jim,* and to my mind as good, but he was a Young Tory if there ever was one.

I suppose they could all justly have been called angry, because of the state of the nation, but there were also three I thought of as the Metaphysicals, and they were not only not angry but had not even met their left-wing fellows, and in fact rather despised them for their shallow view of life. To call this odd lot of people a group, or a movement, was simply absurd. I asked the Metaphysicals to tea, separately. They were charming. One was Stuart Holroyd, a very young man, whose book *Emergence from Chaos* was in the news. Later he wrote: 'at twenty-five I had the temerity to publish an account of my own inner life and experience. This was in the late 1950s, when the British press made much of "the angry young men", and that was probably one reason why I ventured to write autobiographically: all the publicity we had received made us feel

★Later, when Tom Maschler ran Jonathan Cape, he was my publisher—most felicitously—for many years. In the States I was published by Knopf—Robert Gottlieb. I have been fortunate: two of the finest publishers of the time have been my publishers and my good friends.

that what we had to say was important.' Bill Hopkins had written a first novel, *The Divine and the Decay,* also acclaimed. He died very young. Both these young men were unlike the rest of the contributors, who tended to be combative, and concerned with social mechanisms: they were shy, sensitive, interested in inner experience, and well read in mystical and religious literature.

Colin Wilson had written *The Outsider,* which was acclaimed as a work of great significance, if not genius, by the literary establishment. If there ever was a rising star on the literary horizon, it was Colin Wilson, but then there was a reaction, as if the people who had lionised him were thinking, You aren't going to get away with *that* again. On the whole it is not a good thing for a first book to be wildly praised: there is nearly always an irrational reaction. If that first (good) book of Wilson's was overpraised, then his succeeding books have been unjustly ignored or dismissed. At least two—I haven't read them all—should have been commended. One was *Rasputin and the Fall of the Romanovs,* which rescued Rasputin from his reputation as a sort of hysterical charlatan and put him into the context of a tradition of Russian shamans and healers. The other was *The Great Beast,* about Aleister Crowley, equally balanced and sensible.

So there we all were. The Left-Wing Politicals, very fashionable. The Metaphysicals, unfashionable, but they would be the last word in chic only ten years later. And me, a female and ten years older than any of them.

Briefly and in passing: it is a sad thing that what is written has permanence, whereas what is said is often unnoticed. Something written is reprinted, becomes part of theses. Decades later it is quoted back at you. It is a millstone around your neck, and there is nothing you can do. 'But you said, on page 123 . . .' I like most of my piece, 'A Small Personal Voice' in *Declaration,* but emphatically dislike some of it. What is that nonsense I was writing about Camus, Sartre, Beckett, Genet? I am shocked at myself. I wrote nonsense about China and the Soviet Union. I am appalled at my sentimentality when I said that I had never met anyone who would throw the switch that would unleash what we then thought of as The Bomb. It seems to me now that anyone would, given the right programming. Still, it was a piece for its time, all right.

One thing I wrote about in *Declaration* is still true—and more so. I complained about the xenophobia and little-mindedness of Britain. Sometimes, when one has returned from a trip abroad, a session with the newspapers and magazines is like opening a door on to a room full of very clever argumentative schoolchildren. News about one another is considered important. Wars and famines can be raging, governments tottering, but what they are writing about is that one of the children is trying a new hairstyle, or pettishly refusing to have lunch with another. My father used to complain about the parish-pump mentality of Britain, which was why he was eager to leave it in 1919 and in 1924.

The Angry Young Men was a phenomenon entirely invented by the newspapers, the media. It went rolling on, year after year, gathering momentum, and all the time I was amazed no one seemed to notice that in fact they had very little in common. The media are the equivalent of yesterday's scientists, for today's scientists have seen that when they conduct an experiment they are part of it and influence results by their very being; the media can create a story, a scandal, an event, but behave as if they have nothing to do with it, as if the event or the reputation were a spontaneous happening and they haven't influenced the result, or invented it all in the first place. 'The general interest in ... continues and is growing.' Of course it is, since the journalists are fanning the flames, permitting themselves fits of moral indignation, excitement, concern. Meanwhile the public marvel at them.

I repeat: The Angry Young Men was a creation of the media, invented by the newspapers, and never had any basis in fact. But it is no good saying so; a thousand theses have been written and a thousand reputations made, and now people have a vested interest in the thing and it probably will never be allowed to die. When I was in Japan, some professor asked me about the Angry Young Men and their manifesto, and I said they had never existed and it was a newspaper bubble. His face ... but I saw on it that he was an expert on this revolutionary movement and the last thing he could bear to hear was that it was all a mirage.

The Angry Young Men (and I) were associated with the Royal

Court because of John Osborne and because of the Court's glamour then.

There is a famous photograph of the Royal Court people on some jaunt, on the top of a bus, lovely Mary Ure in front—she was every bit as fascinating as Marilyn Monroe, with the same fragility. The young lions and lionesses are laughing, and every young lion, and most particularly John Osborne (who would shortly marry her) and Tony Richardson, is watching Mary, who has her head back, laughing, but seems a bit panicky, from all the attention. It is a picture of wonderful gaiety, like children on a picnic, when they are overexcited.

A party to celebrate the publication of *Declaration* was planned at the Royal Court, but the management refused to host it, on the grounds that John Osborne had insulted the Royal Family in his piece. "My objection to the Royalty symbol is that it is dead, it is a gold filling in a mouthful of decay." The venue was switched to the Pheasantry, Chelsea, a great basement room, crammed with directors, politicians, actors, and of course, the contributors, everyone in the news at that time. Aneurin Bevan was there, with his entourage, just back from some conference, where he had allowed his famous fire to be flattened by a prevailing wind, and some of us tackled him and said that now communism had collapsed, he represented much more than the left wing of the Labour Party. He seemed surprised at what was expected of him. He was a politician, and revolution was certainly not on his agenda, whereas I would say that revolution, an abstract, inspirational, and uncompromised revolution, was part of how most people in that room thought. Not if you said to them, Do you think it should be this or that kind of revolution? No, nothing pedantically defined.

The din was incredible, but it was silenced by a loud voice from the top of the stairs that led down into the throng. There stood a young woman, dowdy, with floppy blond hair, a flowery dress— then the height of unchic—and disapproving pale eyes. 'And who,' she was demanding of her escort, in the ringing tones of her class, 'and who *are* all those furry little people?' For a good deal of slumming was going on, and the classes were getting a good stir round.

★   ★   ★

The people I was seeing about then came from very different worlds. The bliss of big cities is knowing people who may not care to know each other, and only those who have had to live in the provinces—like Salisbury, Southern Rhodesia—can appreciate the freedom of it.

For a time I saw a good bit of Miles Malleson. He had been in the theatre for forty years, and I loved hearing him talk about it. I went with him to the theatre, and to theatre restaurants, like the Ivy, and to the zoo, for he was a fellow of the Royal Zoological Society. Miles was fond of Peter, and Peter liked the zoo, where he could meet Miles's special animal, but I've forgotten what it was. I have known so many people who have supported tarantulas, sloths, scorpions, apes, and chameleons and they have blurred into a generic Zoo Pet.

We also talked about love, I with reluctance. Miles fancied me, but this was not a sentiment that needed much compassion from me, because Miles was in love with love. A product of the Twenties, he said he was: Free Love had been his emotional education, and he still thought this was the only way to conduct one's life and loves. Miles said he had never felt jealousy, or a need to own a woman, but women were sadly lacking in his largeness of approach. He thought one should be able to tell one's chief loved one about the fleeting fancy that had occupied a charming weekend, but his whole life, said he, had been a repetition of when he had gone ebulliently in to tell his first wife—I think; at any rate, a wife—about such an adventure and she had said, 'Now that's enough. Out!' Why did women have to be like that? he demanded, really expecting an answer. He said he believed that love between a man and a woman—that is to say, real love—could exist only on a basis of absolute frankness. But frankness caused unhappiness. Well, yes, I said, I had heard similar complaints in my past, but surely this was the basic and intrinsic and terrible dilemma at the heart of love. Why did he think he was going to solve it all, just like that? But he did think so, he still hoped so. He would speak about it in a voice full of the hot grievance of a lifetime. I put him in a story called 'The Habit of Loving'.

I saw Tom Maschler quite often too. He was rushing about

London, seeing everyone, for he operated on a high-octane energy. You don't often meet people like this, who make you realise just how slowly your own wheels revolve in comparison.

The journalist Murray Sayle was in and out of my life. He lived up the road, in Notting Hill Gate, with his wife Tessa Sayle. They had met in Paris, both poor, as everyone was, and had been the right age for that city. She was Austrian, aristocratic, a pretty, sprightly woman, whose chief characteristic then was a love of order. She was the tidiest woman I have ever known, and nothing in their flat was even half an inch out of place. Later, when she could afford expensive clothes, she would take them to pieces and put them together according to her exacting standards. Murray was Australian, affable, easy-going, and carelessly generous with his time. Here was another of those improbable marriages, and it didn't last. Murray lived inside an always evolving epic, populated with outsize characters, one of them Shoulders Moresby. Later I learned that this character actually existed—and exists—and I was disappointed. Sometimes you may hear about a friend's friend for years, until he or she has all the familiar charm of a character in a folk tale, and the last thing you want to hear is that they live in the ordinary light of day. One of the incidents in the saga was when Murray and his mates decided to renovate a boat on the Thames in order to sail around the world; they spent a year of weekends and holidays doing it, needless to say much to the disapproval of their women. At last they set off, accompanied by champagne and speeches. But it was rough in the Channel. They were all seasick, a hazard they had not once thought of. They left the boat in Cherbourg, where it might very well be to this day, and travelled home, not by sea. Surreal adventures of this kind entertained Murray's friends for years. Murray worked for a popular newspaper, like the *Sun* or the *Daily Mail*. One day, having pursued some scandal to its limits, he was sitting on a bench in the park, and as with St. Paul on the road to Damascus, the scales fell from his eyes. These are people I'm doing these terrible things to, he thought. What am I doing? I am supposed to be a lover of humanity. He resigned from the newspaper and came to tell his friends, with all the penitence of a criminal determined to reform.

The journalists on those scandal sheets were not exactly admired, but I don't think we loathed and despised them, as decent people do now, for their lies and dishonesty and their cruelty to their victims. They certainly hadn't evolved anything like their present levels of hypocrisy. We have indeed gone from bad to worse. It would be nice to report that Murray at once became the world-famous journalist he is now, but in fact he had a hard time at first, and virtue had to be its own reward. A novel he wrote got into trouble with the libel law and had to be withdrawn. His life loitered in the doldrums. For a while he was earning his living as a salmon putcher on the Severn Estuary. This is the person who takes salmon out of the traps when the tide falls. He was in a minute house and eating far too much salmon, as he complained, serving delicious salmony meals to his friends when we visited. The saga of adventures continued, with Shoulders Moresby an attendant knight. True or false, who cares? The storytellers of this world should not be held to account for tedious exactitudes.

A scene: Facing me across a low table scattered with ashtrays, cigarettes, and teacups sits Betty, a plain young woman frowning with earnest endeavour, her eyes all anxiety. Yet there is a certain little complacency there too, for she has on her string in the role of agony aunts, Tessa Sayle, Joan Rodker, and others. She holds on her lap a neat white handbag that looks as if it was bought at a church bazaar. She is a bishop's daughter: the daughters of bishops do seem far more often than most of us to flounder in mires of moral adventure.

If with Babu Mohammed and Murray Sayle, both younger than I am, it doesn't matter—for we are confreres in enjoyment and farcical conspiracy—with Betty my ten years' seniority makes me into a matronly adviser. Like Tessa, like Joan Rodker, and who knows how many others, I often sit listening to her dilemmas.

'You see, Mrs. Lessing, I don't know what to do, I don't know what to think. I can't sleep, I keep tossing about, because what I like is black men, ever since I went to that dance for Colonial Advancement and went home with Mahmoud. I got used to everything, Mrs. Lessing. He used to say, Now go home for the weekend, Betty, I don't want you around, I fancy a bit of boy. Yes, it's part of their culture, I know that, and I just said, I don't want to get in your way, and I went home to my parents, but they get ever so worried. They say, Have you thought of the difficulties of inter-racial marriage? but I don't like to say that marriage isn't on my mind. I'm very young, Mrs. Lessing, I'm only twenty-two, I don't have to worry about settling down yet, what do you think? But now I'm used to Mahmoud, and he's gone to fight against the British—that's us—in Zanzibar, and what shall I do? You see, I don't fancy white men any more.'

'Have you thought of getting yourself another black man? You could try another dance at Colonial Advancement.'

'Oh no, I know you mean well, but you see, I love Mahmoud. And that's what I meant to ask you: Do you think it's all right that I've booked my seat out?'

'But, Betty,' I say, telling her what she knows already, 'he has a new wife and a girlfriend too, and they are leaders of the Militant Women. And they are both beautiful.'

'Yes, I know, but when he sees me I know he'll remember what we've been to each other and he'll choose me.'

'Has he invited you?'

'But I've got just as much right to be there as he has, haven't I? I'm British, aren't I? Well, then. It's a British country.' And off she went, to tell her tale again.

Time passes. And again she is sitting opposite me, in her neat little blouse, her hair tidily done, her little handbag in front of her. 'I don't know what to do, Mrs. Lessing. I did go out there, but he didn't answer the message I left for him. He waved at me when he saw me at the rally, so I waited around for a month, but I've come home. I think my heart is broken, Mrs. Lessing. What shall I do?'

She thought of going to South Africa, for she could find a black man there, and I said, 'Don't be silly. It's a prison sentence for fancying a black man there.' But she did go to South Africa, where things were as I said, and travelled up through Africa and found herself in the middle of the wars in the Congo. Horrific wars: the whole world was shocked, appalled.

Once again we are drinking tea and sharing cigarette smoke and her news. 'I like Brazzaville,' says she. 'There were a lot of black men there. I had a good time.'

'But there's a terrible war on,' I say.

'I didn't see any war, not where I was.'

'So how are things going?'

'Well, I'm married now, and Daddy is pleased.' She met a crocodile hunter on the shores of Lake Victoria, and he had fallen for her. 'You'd think he'd like a black girl, wouldn't you? There were plenty of them around. But he liked me.'

The marriage had not succeeded. She was back with us, still dreaming that one day Mahmoud—now in terrible trouble, being one of those accused of assassinating his leader—would return to claim her.

John Dexter was a friend then. That was before the law about homosexuality was changed, and he was caught with a boy. I forget the details. He got six months and was sent to Wormwood Scrubs. All his friends visited him there. I went twice. The first time was frightening, not because of the prison being so grim and nasty, for I had expected that, but because John seemed to have turned into his own opposite, repeating that he deserved to be punished, the police were quite right, because he had done wrong. By the next visit he had gone back to normal, but meanwhile I was thinking how fragile we all are, poised so lightly on beliefs, on principles—on what we think we are. John had suffered no physical ill treatment, but he had been a target for newspaper insults, he had stood in court and been despised, been sentenced as an evildoer, then found himself in that grim place, being punished. No wonder people make false confessions and say, Yes, I am guilty. But I had not seen this before, and I did not understand it, and I was afraid, seeing what a frail skin civilisation paints over our pretences.

Long after this, I was giving a lecture about barriers to perception—what prevents us seeing more clearly—and one was guilt. At question time they were all, one after another, getting up to ask about guilt. Guilt, only guilt, as if nothing else had been said. I don't think this is at all a simple question.

I have just found this in a book, *The Prospect Before Her* by Olwen Huston. It is 1707. A Jesuit is preaching.

He presented to them (women and girls) the enormity of their sins and the abuses that they had made so very often of the blood of Jesus Christ (by taking communion in a state of sin). He put before them the image of Christ crucified reproaching them for their ingratitude and their perfidy. I would scarcely have believed the effect of this discourse had I not been a witness. They prostrated themselves face downwards on the ground. Some beat their breasts and others their heads upon the stones all crying for forgiveness and pardon from God. They vowed their guilt in the excesses of their grief. They took these excesses so far that the priest feared they would do themselves harm and ordered them to stop groaning so that he could finish his exhortations. But he could not silence them. He had himself to shed tears and to cease his discourse.

Little scenes, mere flashes:

It is afternoon. John Wain is there. And Robert Conquest. A mutual friend is about to marry. 'Memento mori,' says Robert Conquest, tragically. And John Wain says, 'Marriage can be undone; it is not like ordering a coffin.'

'Oh yes, it is,' says handsome Robert, looking at us women standing about.

I have hyacinths growing, but not yet in flower, in an earthenware bowl, and certainly they are an emanation from a world very far from the noisy flat and the thundering lorries. Clancy is standing staring at them, full of horror. 'What is the matter?' I ask. He is pale with disgust. I try to see them as he does, for he often sees the ordinary as monstrous or amazing, and manage a glimpse of something like a green mandrake, which might start hopping about or even screaming. 'They are hyacinths,' I say firmly.

'Put them where I can't see them,' he says. I had never known anyone so much a product of streets, buildings. (Later he was at ease in the country.) Since then I have known others. They get unhappy if they so much as step off a tarmac path in a park on to grass. Sometimes I make myself stop, switch off my usual ways of seeing, and look with neutral eyes at a configuration in a cloud, a hairy fold in a curtain, the way light falls on a railing, raindrops clustered like diamonds on a pane. I see it as a madman might, so full of threat or of intimations of otherness you have to switch off, reclaim your ordinary mind—and yet there are a great many people who live like this, with some climate of menace in their minds, that focuses like a spotlight on cloud, or fold, or the glitter of crystal drops, and they can never escape these enemies who are inside them, moving with them everywhere they go, even if they cross continents or oceans to escape them. My story 'Dialogue' is an attempt to portray this.

I have met an Indian somewhere, who takes it into his head that I need him in my life. He turns up at my door and is insistent about coming in. I throw him out. I realise afterwards that it has never crossed my mind that I must be 'nice' to him because he is a person with a dark skin, whereas when I first came to London I would have been full of colonial guilt. I realise I am cured of the sentimentalities of 'The Colour Bar' and I am pleased with myself. (The Colour Bar—now there's a phrase that has gone with the wind.)

One night I was standing at the kitchen window, looking down, and saw a man vault over the tall wooden fence and stand staring up at me. I moved back out of sight. I had seen him loitering about when I went to the shops, watching me. Builders had left a plank, and now the man placed the plank on some bricks, slanting up, laid himself on it, and began masturbating. I rang the police and said, There is a man in my yard, and he is annoying me. They came around, found a door in the fence. One said, 'Now then, old son, what are you doing? You can't do that kind of thing here.' They all four stood on the pavement, out of sight, but I heard a policeman say, 'Now you just run along and don't do that again.' I was impressed by how they handled the incident.

There was a Britain that some say has gone for ever, is nowhere to be found—like the readers of *John O'London's Weekly,* who made a provincial literary culture. Easy to believe that it has gone.

Reynolds News, a socialist Sunday paper read by labour support-ers, trade unionists, socialists of all kinds—but not, I think, com-munists—was a decent, sober, unexcitable, unscandalous paper, whose readers would have despised our lying sensational newspa-pers. It ran a short-story competition, and I was asked to judge. Hundreds were submitted. I was sent the final forty. They were of a high standard, of the realistic kind; Dickens, Hardy, A. E. Cop-pard, Somerset Maugham, Chekhov, and Gorky were their pro-genitors.

Most stories came with a letter describing the difficulties of the writer. This was a time of high employment, and the culture of leisure had not arrived. Not easy then for people who might have unsympathetic families, small children, long hours, to find the time and space to write. Some said they had written novels; would I read them? I read perhaps thirty. I had not done anything of this sustained kind before and was surprised by what I know now is common. First, these novels were all *nearly* good. All writers—I have not met one who is different—go through the stage when what we write is nearly good: the writing lacks some kind of inward clinching, the current has not run clear. We go on writing, reading, throwing away not-quite-good-enough work, and then one day something has happened, a process has been completed, a step forward has been taken: these clichés are here because it is hard to say what has happened. But the process of writing and rewriting, and of reading the best, has at last succeeded. Professional writers all know this period of apprenticeship. Amateur writers cling to their early uneven drafts and won't let them go. Every one of the novels I was sent was the work of a talented person. Every one needed to be rewritten, or put away and another attempted. There is some-thing I call the 'my-novel syndrome'. So much of the writer has gone into it, often there have been sacrifices made to acquire the time and space to write, and then the product of this investment of self and time becomes sacred; the author will not let it go and may spend ten years hawking it around to publishers.

To every one of these authors I wrote carefully, with advice, and saying, When you have rewritten this one or done another, send it to me. Not one of them was heard of again. There is a sad waste of talent going on. But things have improved; there are writing classes and courses, and above all, it is easier to find time to write.

I am remembering this because of the current sad query: Where is that England, that Britain? All the stories, all the novels, were about small, sensible, decent, hopeful lives, with no aspirations to be fashionable or sensational. After Richard Hoggart, so much a representative of that Britain, went on *Desert Island Discs,*★ he said he had seventy-three letters, all from people asking that question. Somewhere out there is still an honesty, an integrity—or so I believe—and a slight shift in our political fortunes would bring this face of Britain forward. At least, I hope so.

Now I see that overlarge flat which always had people coming through it as a continuation of the easy ways of the places I lived in with Gottfried: someone staying the night or the weekend, friends, the friends of friends. The 'bohemia' of the comrades (mostly now ex-comrades) was infinitely hospitable, undemanding, anticipating the youth culture of the sixties. Any number of young poets, promising playwrights, novelists, male and female, came and went, all moneyless, passed from hand to hand, from city to city, and sometimes from country to country.

For instance, and typically, there was Balwant, a young Indian, who arrived in London by way of the British Council. He had no money, was from a poor village, had written some good plays on timeless village themes: the wicked moneylender, the cruel parents, the brave lovers, the villagers confronting poverty. They had been performed in India. Joan Rodker, Tana Ship, Reuben Ship's ex-wife and I—we looked after him. My Three Graces, he called us, sitting smiling like a dear child, his head wagging, philosophically solicitous about our efforts on his behalf. Tana typed his work, Joan and I fed and nurtured and found him shelter. He was around for a couple of years, and then off he went, to find himself captured and married by a Polish woman who wouldn't take no for an answer. But that is another story. The trouble is, if you are a

★A radio show that has been running for years.

novelist, your typewriter is always longing to go clattering off after some tale.

A sad thing happened, a sad visitor, a black girl who came to my flat because of that by now so familiar telephone call: 'I hear you have an empty room.'

'I'm not going to be a landlady, never again. I'm sorry.'

'It's up to you how you settle with her. She's at college; she'll be out all day.'

Lucy was perhaps twenty, so clever she had attracted attention in some poor mission school in Southern Rhodesia, had been sent on a scholarship to a better one, and now found herself in gold-paved London, in a small room with grey rain slashing at the windows and, outside, a hideous street where the great lorries thundered day and night. She had come from a large family, sunlight, warmth, and a culture that did not understand the need for solitude. She was desperate with loneliness and homesickness. Now, my situation was that Peter had just gone to boarding school and for the first time, instead of fitting in my work where I could, I had a clear run of some weeks in front of me, and I planned to finish *A Ripple from the Storm.* I had worked myself gently into the slow, underwater state, where exterior events sound a long way off, and was ready to start—and there was this unhappy girl hanging over the banisters to hear when my typewriter stopped. It is amazing how little time students need spend at classes or lectures. She never seemed to be at her classes more than five or six hours a day. Many days she did not go in at all, and there were the weekends. She had no friends. 'Look, Lucy, I spend a lot of time just pottering about, looking out of the window, sleeping a few minutes—do you see? This is how I write.' Her wide anxious eyes fixed on my face: Is this the racial prejudice they warned me about? Is this white woman trying to snub me? she is thinking. And I am thinking, Oh, Lord, I hope she isn't thinking that. . . .

Normally I would walk from my big room along to the kitchen, look out of the kitchen window, wander back—the whole bottom floor of the flat was my field of concentration—but now I went into the big room, shut the door, and even took in vacuum flasks of tea there. All the time I was thinking of her upstairs, sitting on her bed, listening for me to stop. A too long silence, and down she would come, and I heard the little tap on the door. 'Doris? Doris? Have you finished working?' And we sat in the kitchen over tea, and I heard about her village, her family, her mother, whom she missed so that she had to cry when she thought of her, and her sisters and her little brother and her cousins ... I got to know her family better than I knew mine at that time. Within a week I had given up all thoughts of real work, did practical things in the short hours she was gone, and tried to stem the fever of exasperation and impatience that was poisoning me. 'Shall we go and visit your friends?' she would suggest hopefully, when she came back. 'Do you like looking at the shops?'

Writers, and particularly female writers, have to fight for the conditions they need to work, but this was the worst experience I had ever had, for I felt so guilty because of her loneliness.

'Do you have any friends at college? Have you met anybody you like there?'

'You're my friend,' she said, and put her two hands around my forearm and looked up into my face. 'You are my best friend in London.'

At last I rang her sponsors, and heard the cold disapproving voice. 'Surely you can set aside some time for her.'

'It's not a question of some time; it is all the time she isn't at college.'

'I must say I am surprised to hear this from you.'

'Look, I have to work, I can't work. . . .'

'But can't you work when she's at classes?'

'I'm sorry, you must find some place where she has a lot of people around her—a large family.'

'You mean a black family?' It was a cold sniffy self-righteous voice.

'I didn't say a black family. Any large family. She's used to a lot of people around her, all the time.'

'I don't see what I can do at the moment.'

'I have to work, I have to earn a living—I have a child to keep.'

And at last a family was found, with a girl her age, and off went the poor exile with her tiny possessions, feeling she had failed in

London, and I was left feeling a criminal—and counting the days of freedom left before the beginning of the school holidays.

About then my son John Wisdom came through London.* He wanted to be a forester, had gone to the University of Stellenbosch, but it was then very Afrikaans in feeling, anti-British, and no admirer of Southern Rhodesia, which had always taken its stand on being British. John, brought up to be British, could not tolerate this, and he left almost at once. In Vancouver, Canada, there were good forestry courses, and he decided to go there. He was not yet eighteen when I saw him for the first time since he had been eight or so. Although I was expecting him, when he walked into my room, I nearly said, Hello, Harry, for he walked, stood, held his shoulders, smiled, like my brother. He was in London for three days. He had expected the bright lights, and I did my best, but he was disappointed that I was not living better. A well-known author surely should be. . . . I don't know what he was expecting. We went to some good restaurants and to the theatre, and he enjoyed it all. He was a great enjoyer, John, all his life. We got on very well. We always had, after all. It is a strange fact that people can get on easily, instinctively, when they agree about nothing and their views on life are opposite. John had been brought up to believe that I was Hecate incarnate, a kaffir-lover, a communist. He had never heard anything good about me, and he had been forbidden to write to me. The letters and books I sent the children, the letters they sent me, had to stop. It could not have been easy for him to decide to see this problematical mother, but it all turned out well. He went off to the University of Vancouver, where he took his place in class—and, two weeks later, walked out of the class, the university, and Vancouver. In those days—and perhaps this is still true—there were men who lived hard and rough, earning good money for dangerous work, all through the winters, but in summer enjoyed life in the bars and on the water in Vancouver. This is what John did, for seven years. His first job was fire watching in the extreme north somewhere. The job is to stay at the top of a tower, set where a

*See *Under My Skin*.

247

great sweep of country can be seen, and watch out for the smoke of bush fires and then radio waiting firefighters. John listened to jazz from the Voice of America and to classical music from Moscow. He watched the wolves moving about in the snow beneath his tower, for they were as curious about him as he was about them. He admired them and claimed they all became friends. He lived like this for six months, completely alone; he had just become eighteen. Later he said this was one of the best times in his life. Then he got all kinds of jobs. He worked as a surveyor: though he had not studied surveying; he had watched a surveyor friend of his during a weekend and then proved to the employer that he knew the job. He worked in lumber mills. In summer he had a very good time indeed. He was not one of the world's letter writers, but I did get a couple of long letters, full of the small details of his life, always the most interesting, and, twice, a tape. Last summer he had lived in a little house with two Australians, they cooked this and that—John was a famous cook—they had parties every night, they sailed every minute they could in the bay, and the ice had just broken up, and he had run out into the raging and tumbling waters, balancing on the tablets of ice, and they all called him Mad Wisdom, but he was still alive, mad or not. He had been working last winter in a lumber mill, had caught his left hand in the machinery, the doctors had wanted to cut his arm off, but he wouldn't let them. He made them operate so as to keep his arm whole, although they said it was useless. But he had been proved right, he could use his hand for almost everything. 'I have been reading . . .' He read a lot of adventure and sea stories, war books. He loved the sea, but soon he would be living high and landlocked hundreds of miles from the sea. He had read my short stories. He liked the bits about the bush, he could see I knew what I was talking about, but he thought I was being unfair to the whites. 'We must have a good chin-wag about that.' Seven years went by. And then he turned up in London again on his way through. He said he had been in a bar, looking at the men who were ten years older than he was, had not left the life, were still living a tough young man's life, and they were not twenty-five, like him, but thirty-five and forty, and they were getting fat and soft and alcoholic, and he had got such a fright that he decided to leave Canada and go back home, though he was very sad, for no life could have suited him better. And he returned to Southern Rhodesia, to try his luck there.

Again, writing this, I am brought up short with: But all this is outward, you'd think my life was all politics and personalities, though really most of the time I was alone in my flat, working. The capacious flat in Warwick Road was a very different affair from the compact, low-ceilinged, intimate little place in Church Street. Only in one way were they alike: noise. The buses roared up and down Church Street, and along Warwick Road lorries banged and ground all day and most of the night. Now I live high in a house where I might as well be in the country, all trees and even a field, although this is London, and it is quiet except for the birds and the wind in the trees and around the chimneys—and absolutely silent all night. How did I bear those eight years of din? I now wonder. I swear that as you get older your eardrums lose successive layers of soundproofing.

This was almost a little house, with its upstairs and downstairs. Up, in one large room, was Peter, during his holidays; his things overflowed into the little room next to it. The other large room had in it Clancy, when he was there, and the little room had my clothes. Up and down those stairs I ran all day—not heavily, as I do now, holding on to banisters—and walked around my big room, or from the big room to the kitchen, back and forth, for, writing, I have to move. Just as, looking back at Church Street, I see Joan and me sitting at her little table in the kitchen, talking, gossiping, setting life, love, men, and politics to rights, the best part of my time there—one of my best times in London—so now I look back at Warwick Road and remember how Clancy, or some visitor or other, sat at the kitchen table with me and we talked. And talked. Politics and literature, but so much politics in that difficult time when 'everything' was falling apart; Now there have been a couple of generations who never talk anything but shopping or gossip, and when I am with them I wonder how they can bear it, this tiny, self-enclosed world they inhabit.

It was the big room, though, where I was most of the time. It had three tall windows, the bed recessed in one corner, the desk with the typewriter, the small table painted glossy black, with the ashtrays, the cigarettes, the mess and smell of the smoker, for I smoked so much that now I can't believe it. I walked up and down and around, and wrote a sentence, and walked some more, managed a paragraph, crossed it out, did it again, achieved a page that could stand, at least for a time. This process, this walking and thinking, while you pick up something from a chair and stare at it, hardly knowing what it is, and then let it drop, tidy something into a drawer, find yourself dusting a chair or straightening a pile of books against the wall, or standing at the window looking down while the lorries trundle past—this is the opposite of daydreaming, for it is all concentration, you are deep inside, and the outside world is merely material. And it is exhausting, for suddenly after an hour or two, with perhaps only a page or two done, you find yourself so heavy you tumble onto the bed and into sleep, for the necessary half hour, fifteen minutes, ten—and then up again, refreshed, the tension cut, and you resume the wandering about, the touching, the desultory tidying, the staring, while you approach the typewriter, and then you are seated, and your fingers fly for as long as they do—up again, movement again. How well I got to know that room, every fibre and thread of it, whose surfaces I had created: the plain white of the walls, the carpet I had dyed green, the floorboards I had painted glossy shiny black, the green-and-white curtains I had made on my Singer sewing machine, brought all the way from Africa.

While I was pottering, hesitating, tumbling into sleep and back, walking to the kitchen and back, I might hear Clancy's typewriter upstairs going like a machine gun, hour after hour, with never a moment's pause. And then long silences, then bursts of clattering sound, then silences.

In Warwick Road I wrote a lot of short stories, set in Africa, in France, in Germany. Some of them I think are good. Some are not up to much. If you are the kind of writer I am—that is, one who uses the process of writing to find out what you think, and even what you are—then it is surely dishonest to kick down the stepladder you came up by, but the fact is, I would be happy if some of the stories I wrote disappeared. Yet there are people who like the ones that I don't think much of. Isn't it a form of contempt to wish away what other people admire? I would be happy to be like those poets who at the end of their lives acknowledge a few survivors, rejecting everything but the best.

I wrote *A Ripple from the Storm,* which helped to put that frenetic time when 'everyone' was a communist into perspective. When it came out it was described by many of the comrades as seditious, 'fouling the nest', and so forth, but it has had a contradictory career. I still get letters from people saying that when they read it they thought it a betrayal of the Cause but later found they liked it. This book, which details the vagaries and dynamics of group behaviour—not merely political—caused a couple of young Americans as late as the early nineties to go off and join an extreme left group. I could not believe this when I was told about it, but apparently they were attracted to the intrigue and excitement. I am sure that is why many people join political or religious groups. They need the excitement. Regularly, through the decades, people have said to me that they were in this or that movement or group, and *A Ripple from the Storm* described their experiences—which was why they left the group, disillusioned. Later this was said of *The Good Terrorist.* 'It was just like life in . . .' a feminist group, a black activist group, Greenpeace, animal rights. A group is a group is a group—just as a mob is a mob. The machineries that activate them are the same, whatever the cause. If you've been in one, you've been in them all. It is amazing to me that now, when so much is known about the mechanisms and dynamics of group behaviour, there is no attempt, when one is being set up, to make use of this information about what is bound to happen. If there was ever a block in the mind—a barrier, a division—it is this one: 'We do not want to know' about our behaviour. But wait, there is one example of when people beginning something looked back at predecessors and decided to do better. The Bolsheviks agreed together that they would not be like the revolutionaries of the French Revolution: their own revolution would not devour its children, they would not kill each other. This noble aspiration, as we know, came to nothing, and they all murdered each other with rhetorical enthusiasm. So perhaps more is needed than a simple aspiration to do better.

How I felt about the reception of *A Ripple from the Storm* is in a letter I wrote to Edward Thompson. Here is part of it:

My dear Edward,

But Edward, I never said a word about policy, my attitude being entirely pragmatic, in other words, What About Me?

Seriously—I wrote a book all about the kind of politics which the *New Reasoner* has been theoretical about for the last two years.

As the reviews came out, I was more and more cross, though not surprised, at the way no one said what this book was about—either, that enigmatic girl, Martha Quest, at her antics again, or another jab at the colour bar. But no one could have deduced from the reviews that this book was about Stalinist attitudes of mind etc.

Therefore, since the kind of people I wanted to reach were obviously the *New Reasoner* and *The New Left Review* readers, I naturally hoped that either or both magazines would at least put in a paragraph saying that this novel was about current topics.

But not a word. Not a bloody word.

Meanwhile, both magazines, and particularly the *Reasoner,* print long and analytical articles about The Contemporary Dilemma. And both magazines ask me to write articles and statements about the C.Dil. The fact that I've seen fit to write 140,000 words about it, as a novel, is apparently considered quite irrelevant.

In a word, left magazines, like all other magazines, are not interested in what a writer says in his or her real work, but only interested to get ephemeral statements and articles, so that The Name will attract readers.

I wrote another book in Warwick Road, which I later withdrew. It was called *Retreat to Innocence.* So little do authors' wishes count that I often meet people who say triumphantly, 'I have a copy of that book you tried to suppress.' Like children in a playground: Sucks to *you!*

That novel was born out of being with Jack from Czechoslovakia, from Europe's bloody and fought-over heartland, and how inexperienced, how innocent—and unpleasantly so—he made me feel. He did not try to make me feel this. If you have the kind of knowledge about human behaviour that he had, then most of what people say that does not come from that area of experience must sound like babes prattling. As I write, the war in Bosnia goes on, and those who are part of it will think all their lives, Don't talk to *us* about civilisation. The two main characters in the novel are an older man, Jan, and a girl, Julia. It is a wonderful theme for a novel, but I didn't succeed. I wasted it. It is a shallow novel. But some people did like it, and some still do, and when they say so I feel the pain of an opportunity lost. What I could have explored is how the human mind—our minds—continually try to soften and hide bad experience, by deliberately forgetting or distorting. The way not only individual minds, but collective minds—a country's, a continent's—will forget a horror. The most famous example is the Great Flu Epidemic of 1919–1920, when twenty-nine million people all over the world died, but it is left out of the history books, is not in the collective consciousness. Humanity's mind is set to forget disaster. That was the contention of Velikovsky, whose story of our solar system's possible history is dismissed by the professionals, though surely some of what he said has turned out to be true. There is certainly nothing in the human consciousness of the successive calamitous ice ages, and we—humanity—lived through more than one. There are glimpses in old tales of great floods, but that is about it. In the book which I failed to write would be implicit the question: Is it a good thing that every generation decides to forget the bad or cruel experience of the one before? That the Great War (for instance), such a calamity for Europe, became the 'Great Unmentionable'—which made my father and other soldiers, of France and Germany, feel as if they were being nullified, discounted, were just so much human rubbish. That five or six years after that terrible civil war in Southern Rhodesia, the new young generation had forgotten and 'didn't want to know'. Well . . . it could have been a good book.

What else? I begin thinking about the scheme for *The Golden Notebook,* and I wrote *Play with a Tiger.*

For this play I used Warwick Road, as I experienced it, for a setting, the room with its typewriter, and the bed sheltering behind thin curtains, often seeming to lose its walls to the din and stink of the lorries thundering outside, the raucous groups of boys who late at night were forlornly drunk, mirroring Clancy's tales of his street-corner adolescence in Chicago, on the 'wrong side of the tracks', the prostitutes' house a diagonal glance away, where the girls sometimes emerged on to the pavement to attract customers or to quarrel.

By now Oscar Lowenstein was well into his career as successful impresario.* He did nothing but good for the British theatre and films, and he has not been given the credit he deserves, but he could have done better for me, personally. He liked *Play with a Tiger* but insisted on Siobhan McKenna for the lead. She was tied up for four years, and so that was the time we had to wait to get it on. I kept saying that there were other good actresses. But impresarios often have a streak of power obstinacy, and it was Siobhan McKenna or nothing. Jumping ahead then, to 1962, Ted Kotcheff directed brilliantly, with a sense for the play's flow and movement that meant, when watched from the dress circle, it looked like a slow dance. The male lead was another mistake. I said I wanted someone in style like Sam Wanamaker, but younger, but Oscar said, Over my dead body. He and Ted flew off to New York to audition and come back with a man's idea of what is attractive to women, a stud, like a cowboy. He was a good actor, but he had no feeling for ambiguity. He and Siobhan hated each other on sight, and this showed.

Siobhan was a kind of genius. She had that quality we agree to call charisma, but what is it? She flew over from Dublin, to be ballast during the auditions. It was a cold day, and the theatre was freezing. She was a bit drunk. She had a cold. She was inside layers of clothes. So as not to upstage the aspirant actors, she sat to one side of the stage with her back to us sitting in the auditorium: she was a generous actress and a kind woman. And yet we couldn't take our eyes off her, off that lump of a back with her dark-red hair

*Oscar Lowenstein died in 1997.

tousled over it. She was someone you had to look at; it was an effort to take one's eyes off her to watch the actors auditioning.

She was a fine actress but an undisciplined one, because somewhere early in her career she had been described as a wild Irish child, and so she lived up to it, all Irish impulse and whimsy, and she drank far too much. It was a tragedy that she had not learned discipline. On one evening she could be magnificent, unforgettable—and it was easy to see why Oscar wanted her—but on the next she was pathetic, forgetting her lines and moves, and evidently drunk.

We had a great supporting cast. Maureen Prior was sent the play and loved it so much she staggered from her sickbed, where she was ill, and came out in a bitter wind to the cold theatre to audition. 'I have to do this part,' she said, 'if I die for it.' She was perfect. Godfrey Quigley was good. They all were. The play was put on at the Comedy Theatre, and it ran for two months, but just under its break-even point. Harold Hobson, the most influential critic then, liked it, calling it 'the most troublingly poetic play in London'. T. C. Worsley said it 'ought to be seen by anyone interested in the contemporary theatre and indeed in contemporary living'. Milton Shulman said it was sensitive, sympathetic, and touching. Robert Muller said it was 'written with lacerating passion and truth'. But these remarks were culled from on the whole indifferent reviews—apart from Harold Hobson. Graham Greene liked it very much and generously wrote to tell me so. But he was not a critic.

The fact that it was so brilliantly directed was hardly noticed. Still, I am not the only person who thinks that when Ted Kotcheff left us for Hollywood, the theatre lost the best director working then.

What do I think about this play now? It is a good play but not a great one. It has a good shape and structure but needs the right director. It was of its time—why? That remark about 'lacerating passion' hints why. Lacerating passion is most unfashionable. The play for the times was *Who's Afraid of Virginia Woolf,* the sex war red in tooth and claw. *Play with a Tiger* has been put on here and there in various countries ever since, but mostly by feminist theatres, where it becomes an indictment of men, losing its balance and its humour. For it can, if done right, get not a few laughs.

I was hurt by its reception. I thought it deserved better. There was a sour and disagreeable note in the comment that I was to get full blast when *The Golden Notebook* came out. I believed it was due to anti-female bias, which can take many forms and may be far from straightforward. People known to me or not kept coming up and saying, But you put your own life into the play. Just as if John Osborne's *Look Back in Anger* were not direct from life, and as if Arnold Wesker's plays were not from life. No one had said to John or Arnold anything like the unpleasant things that were said to me. And I was probably oversensitive, for many more than were critical liked the play and wrote to say so. People still say now that they remember the play and how they liked it.

But there was no doubt that on the whole the play was a failure, and I was beginning to have thoughts about my career as a playwright that can only be described as unscientific.

At the Salisbury Playhouse, *The Truth About Billy Newton* filled the seats but did not transfer; to London and it had suffered improbable setbacks and fatalities. Then look what happened to *Each His Own Wilderness*. Then *Play with a Tiger*. To wait four years for an actress who was only intermittently satisfactory, and to be landed with the wrong leading man, and then all the fever and fret and the wounded pride—was it worth it? Later I wrote two more plays. One of them I read recently and thought—as I did then—that it would have done well at the Court, being a farce about the clash of the classes, but they turned it down. Joan Littlewood liked it, or said she did and came to lunch to say so, but Raffles, her manager, didn't agree. Then I wrote a modern version of the *Medea,* which for a couple of years kept getting itself cast on the highest level, but every time a star was secured, something terrible happened, until finally one of them died just as the contracts were being signed. By then I had decided that I was unlucky in the theatre, and I should see this and simply give up. But the end was when the National Theatre asked me to do a version of Ostrovsky's *The Storm*. I was asked because I was a woman and the play was seen by John Dexter as about the sufferings of womanhood. I should have said no, but my vanity was involved. A hundred plays would have interested me more than *The Storm*. It was played wonderfully by Jill Bennett and Anthony Hopkins, all grand passion and suffering, but in fact the play is about teenagers, as young as twelve and thirteen, being married off by cruel and greedy parents to secure their money and their estates. It is about the insufferable ignorance and stupidity of provincial Russia then. The understudies' production got the play right, heartbreaking it was, poor children enjoying a little flare of life before the lid slammed down on them. But no one saw this production.

I could go on about what was wrong with John Dexter's production—yet he was usually brilliant—and at the time I did go on about it, and just before the first night I was for an evening with Laurence Olivier and said what I thought about it all, much too forcibly, for I was drunk with despair. He was kind. I remember him all vitality, energy, sympathy—above all the vital energy (the same quality possessed by Charlie Chaplin, whom I met for ten minutes on a pavement with Miles Malleson in Leicester Square: he has left behind in my mind for ever an impression of quick forceful movements, quick intelligent dark eyes, humour, charm).

And that was when I sat myself down to do some serious thinking. Not one of my attempts at the theatre had gone as I wanted. I had put so much time and effort into plays. At least, when I wrote a novel, it was printed as I wanted it. The anguish, the tension, the sleepless nights, so many disproportionate emotions: and what for? I did not again write for the theatre but did for television, successfully and without disasters or misfortunes.

And so my passion for the theatre, my ambition to write for it, has been sublimated into the great pleasure of theatre-going, in that cornucopia of great theatre, London, and if sometimes I think, Oh, if only . . . , then I do not allow the moment of weakness to last.

My experiences in the theatre and later in opera went into *Love, Again,* my novel that describes a theatre group at work.

And now an encounter with the ex-comrades, which did not differ at all from confrontations with the comrades. Clancy Sigal had gone to a mining village, in the same spirit as I had five years before, but he, being a man, was at once part of the hard-drinking, pub and club culture of miners at leisure. He became friends with a young miner, Len Doherty, and spent a couple of weekends there. He wrote *Weekend in Dimlock* in three days, over my head, in Warwick Road, while I listened to his chattering typewriter. It is a brilliant little book. I have known no one in my life with Clancy's capacity for minute acute social observation. And then it was published and at once exploded that farcical shameful reaction that, alas, people on the left have seen a thousand times. Those people who you would think must welcome this book were those who did most to harm it.

Why is that? This book is no place for a little essay on literary criticism and its history on the left, but these push-button enmities have a long history, going back at least to the methods of the Inquisition, later adapted to the uses of communism. Every new writer, every new book, must if successful somehow survive the arrows of envy, but communism gave envy and jealousy a robe of respectability to wear over the nasty truth. Under names such as 'socialist realism', communist attitudes towards art and literature have been and in some places still are art and literature's deadly enemy. Again and again and in country after country, we have seen 'socialist realism' surfacing to rubbish respected writers, and this long after it was hated and despised by every working artist and writer in socialist realism's mother country as well as by readers. What happened in the countries of Scandinavia in the seventies is instructive: 'socialist realism' was used to discredit the well-known writers. And now, in country after country of the Third World, these primitive emotions are used against the successful.

Clancy's little book was greeted with a storm of accusations. One was that he had taken advantage of the good nature of the miners of the village in question. But he had shown the book to Len Doherty, who had cleared it for publication.

Then *The New Reasoner* asked Len Doherty to review it.

There followed an exchange of very heated letters between me and *The New Reasoner,* me and Edward Thompson. I certainly had a nasty little talent for invective. But then we all had, having learned in a nasty school. I shall quote only two little bits, relevant to my chief points:

'I'm sick to death of socialists knifing each other in the back,' I exclaim.

'. . . a resurrection of that destructiveness familiar to all of us who have been in the C.P.—if by any chance the left does produce some real creative talent then the first impulse is to squash it.'

I omit the really bad bits, but I told Edward he was a shit. He was equally uncomplimentary. This frank, brotherly-sisterly rough-and-tumble was very much the style of the comrades then. We remained good friends, when the storm, or stormlet, had blown over.

Weekend in Dimlock is still arousing irrational hostility among exactly those people you'd think would value it. 'Written by an American,' you hear. 'What does he know about our working class?' 'Written after a short visit.' 'He made use of the miners.' And so it all goes on, year in, year out, decade in and decade out. Once, I thought of making a list of the good and original work which has had to survive the onslaughts of the comrades, for it might be instructive. But then I thought this would be a major effort, take up a lot of time, and not change things, because the people who feel the need to attack new and good work do not know what their real motives are. Envy has always hidden behind moral indignation.*

*Three writers in particular should be remembered for their treatment at the hands of comrades. One is George Orwell, who wrote in *Homage to Catalonia* about what he had observed during the Spanish Civil War, the dirty dealings of the communists and, by extension, of the Soviet Union. As late as 1996 he was being accused, and had to be defended, when it became known he was working with British security forces against the Soviet Union—surely logical that he should, when he had learned the hard way about the real nature of Soviet communism and the blind support of the Left for everything it did. The influence of the comrades extended far beyond the Party: Victor Gollancz actually apologised publicly for publishing *Animal Farm*. George Orwell was systematically denigrated by the comrades until he died. Solzhenitsyn could not be dismissed by saying that he did not know firsthand what he was writing about, so instead they said he couldn't write—no talent. The third, Proust, has only recently been released from 'Oh, but he was such a snob.' No one has written more wittily about snobbishness, social climbing, machinations in pursuit of honours, how people's minds change under pressure of social opinion. But his scene was the aristocracy and its hangers-on, and so, 'He was such a snob'—that most vulgar of the critics' defences: identification of the writer with the material.

Clancy returned to 'Dimlock' several times and befriended Len Doherty, who was going through difficulties. A young man, in his twenties, with a wife and, I think, three small children, but the marriage was in trouble. Clancy brought him up to London, and he stayed in my flat, and Clancy and Alex took him around their London, which of course included the New Left and its precincts, and to Soho and similar enlightenments. Len came again and brought a friend, a miner, and came again and brought two or three friends. I thought their attitude to Len was paternal, they were concerned for him. He was a dark, much too thin, tense young man, who had found himself in the limelight. He emanated that moral exhaustion, like stale air, which is often a sign of physical illness. I remember an evening when he was in bed upstairs, for he had not been able to get up that day, having drunk himself silly the night before, and he was running a fever, and I and one of the miners were trying to keep him calm, for he was tossing his limbs about and throwing his head from side to side. 'It's too late,' he kept croaking, 'it's too late.'

He became a journalist on a local paper but later died, too young.

This little tale does illustrate the dilemmas of journalism, of 'the media'—what happens when a community has been made self-conscious, has been forced to look at itself through others' eyes. I do not think Len's fate would have been much different without *Weekend in Dimlock,* though perhaps he was made unhappier by being shown what must have seemed to him the glamours of literary London—for he had aspirations to write.

I took Clancy up to Carradale. Naomi asked me to: 'I hear you have a *fascinating* American.' The coach journey to Scotland remains as one of my nastiest memories. Clancy was ill then, a bit crazy. I felt sick, from the coach, but what he must have felt . . . He was pale, sweaty, sat with closed eyes, teeth clenched. I have known now not a few people who cope with periodic attacks of disequilibrium, and they are the bravest souls in the world.

I had told Naomi that Clancy should be inside the house, for he did not do well where he felt isolated, but she put him into a room right away from the house in an annexe. Interesting, too, that we were so thoroughly put apart. The whole clan hated him on sight, and he them. There was something about him, this maverick, this outsider, this deadly observer, that they could not stand. For the three days of our stay he sat quietly watching from the edges of rooms, while they patronised him or were rude. Oh, I do loathe groups, clans, families, the human 'we'. How I do dread them, fear them—try to keep well away. Prides of lions or packs of wild dogs are kindly enemies in comparison. Back we went to London on another coach, the cold rain streaming down the windows, and Clancy went straight upstairs to his typewriter, where he stayed for a day and then came down with some fifty or so sheets, which he handed to me. He sat at the kitchen table, watching my face as I read. I have never read anything in my life as clever, as acute, as minutely seen—or so terrible. For his hate had written that piece, and it was pure poison. Compare it with his writing on the miners' village: that was written from love and respect, but this, from loathing. For Clancy the word 'middle class' was already enough of a goad, but there was something about the Mitchisons . . . it was their safety, their security, their smugness because of their invulnerability—so this outsider was bound to see them—the way the clan was so tightly woven into society, that this outsider could not bear. I certainly learned a lesson from that. It is that nothing in the world is easier than malice. No, there was nothing easy about the brilliance of that observation, but one may switch oneself into the mode Hatred in the space of a thought. I don't know why we admire malice so much. It is often called 'wit'. One time when this flourished was the twenties—probably an emanation from that famous table at the Algonquin—and the influence percolated down through the decades, until some ancient lady erupts into cackling laughter and says, 'She's got a face like a potato' . . . and directs confident glances around to make sure this shaft is earning the admiration it deserves. 'He looks like a constipated frog'—oh, wot wit, as we used to say at school.

It's 1957, 1958 . . . I am deep in *The Golden Notebook,* and groaning secretly that every time the telephone rings there is something like this: 'Have you heard about poor Bob? He's taking it hard.' 'Mary's left the Party. She's training as a social worker.'

Are these ancient political passions of interest now? What I do think is important is the learning from them. We are still left with that (now) incredible and unforgivable fact that some of the most socially concerned, hopeful-for-the-future, dedicated souls connived at the crimes in the communist world, by refusing to recognise them and, then, by refusing to acknowledge them openly. Not ten, or a hundred, or a thousand, but many thousands, millions, all over the world. And this attitude—reluctance to criticise the Soviet Union, the great alma mater—goes on now and is shown by the way Hitler is put in the position of chief criminal of our times, whereas Stalin, a thousand times worse—and Hitler admired Stalin, quite properly seeing himself as a mere infant in crime compared to his great exemplar—is still handled gently in the imaginations of people on the left.

What is interesting, surely, is why. After all, this situation, a similar one, is bound to roll around again, in a different context, a different history. Everything does. And the next time, will we (humankind) recognise it and do better?

Like everybody in my generation, the one when 'everyone' was a communist, I have brooded, thought, wondered, allowed the pander memory to pretty things up, but have been left for years, for decades, with an unanswered question. Evidently it was a variety of mass lunacy, mass psychosis. Late, very late—quite recently, in fact—I began to see what I believe might be the reason for it all. Might be—that is all I claim.

Again, back we go to World War I, which is where the mass horrors of our time were brewed.

It is interesting to watch people with a vested interest in the national reputation soften and justify that terrible war. 'But we only lost . . .' so-and-so many hundreds of thousands of men 'in the trenches'. We—Britain. But this was a European war, and it was not only British soldiers who were left with a hatred and contempt for their government, or, if these words are too strong, at least disquiet, sorrow, and at any rate a loss of faith in the men who ruled them, because of their incompetence. My parents were not the only victims of World War I in the district of Banket, Southern Rhodesia. The woman we called Lady Murray because of her sad dignity had lost four sons and a husband to the trenches. Captain Livingstone, like my father, had only one leg. McAuley from the Ayreshire Mine had been badly wounded. There were others. All were lovers of the British Empire and their country, and all full of sorrow and anger because of the conduct of the war by Haig and by the British government. A German small mine worker with whom my father often reminisced had the same feelings about the German trenches and his government. The slaughter in the trenches destroyed something vital in Europe—respect for government. And from that stemmed communism, fascism, national socialism, and later terrorism, anarchy, and that attitude of mind which is now prevalent everywhere, the deadly 'Well, what can you expect?' Nihilism, cynicism, disbelief—for one's own side—and meanwhile all idealism, love, hope, dreams for a good world, put elsewhere, into Lenin, Stalin, Hitler, Mussolini, and, later, those other criminals, Mao, Pol Pot . . . there seems no end to them.

But there is a deeper emotion here, which I think is the point. The children of the soldiers of the First World War were brought up not only on bitter disillusion, and loss of respect for their own governments, but a feeling of being participants in an understanding denied to an unheeding, ignorant majority. It is the feeling expressed in that World War I song which my father remembered all his life:

And when they ask us,
We're going to tell them,
And they're certainly going to ask us . . .

Tell them—that is, the civilians—the truth about what was going on in the trenches. For in Britain, in Germany, in France, and the other combatant countries, the war cabinets whipped up the crudest national feelings—how glorious to die for your country—and suppressed the truth about the horrors of the trenches. So the soldiers felt misunderstood and unappreciated by their own people. The novels that came out of World War I testify to this bitterness the soldiers felt. *All Quiet on the Western Front,* Remarque, German, was perhaps the bitterest and the best. There was a Bairnsfather cartoon. A romantic girl in her nightdress, her hair down, loons out of her window at the full moon. 'That same dear old moon is looking down on him.' But the soldier she dreams of is, with a mate, standing up to his waist in water in a shell hole in No-man's-land, cursing the moon, which makes them visible to the enemy. A little encapsulation.

Them: the stupid majority; *we:* the initiates into the truth—and the truth is hard, painful, bloody, and the reality is pain and suffering, and the best people know this truth, and the worst are complacent idiots who refuse to acknowledge reality.

Truth was the preserve of a knowledgeable and experienced minority. Initiates.

Identification with pain, with suffering. This easily translated into 'You can't make an omelette without breaking eggs.' When I was on that trip to the Soviet Union, very strong was that emotion: Here is where the engine of events is, the painful heart of the truth.

I think it is likely that when young people became communists in the late thirties, flinging themselves into the war in Spain, it was because a pattern was being repeated. They were joining soldiers who were being betrayed. For the democratic governments, France and Britain, refused to come to the aid of the beleaguered Spanish democratic government, allowing Hitler and Mussolini to do as they liked in Spain, so that the fascist Franco won, and Hitler and Stalin were encouraged. The International Brigade were repeating their fathers' experience. And then the Second World War, where the Soviet Union took the brunt of the fighting. The Soviet Union lost eight million in the war. (Not twenty million—that figure is swollen to include Stalin's murders of his own people, cooking the books.)★ Swathes, multitudes of mowed-down people, and to identify with the Soviet Union meant to be part of the by then well-established emotion that in suffering is to be found the truth. Which after all was only a continuation of the religious love of suf-

★These figures are contested, but now the Soviet archives are open, the truth must soon be known.

fering, a pattern in the European mind long before World War I.

And that is why I believe people so easily became communists and why they stuck with it. Communism was being born in storms of blood and fire and bullets and explosions, and illuminated by the star shells of Hope.

'*Knowing the score*' meant being an initiate into the truth, knowing how things *really* work. And what could truth be but that unspeakable suffering is the price exacted by 'life itself' in its tortuous progress upwards—always upwards, it goes without saying. Life itself—the facts, reality, actual events, which are bound to be full of the nasty reality that disperses bullshit and the illusions that feed the innocent. The stupid.

A later generation used 'where it's at'. The truth, hard facts, the *real experience*—which, in the absence of war or revolution, was soon to be found in drugs, hallucinogens, illusion.

When people accepted the real situation in the Soviet Union, something deeply out of sight was confirmed, a knowledge of horror, of betrayal. A high price has to be paid: and with that knowledge goes a dark and greedy need for pain. The root of communism—a love of revolution—is, I believe, masochism, pleasure in pain, satisfaction in suffering, identification with the redeeming blood. The Cross, in fact. To leave 'the Party' was to give up the greater truth, give up being an initiate into understanding the real processes of life.

And here I think is an analogy with the reluctance of people who are in love to give up their ridiculous hopes. If you step out of that country of dreams, you are giving up the real experience, the knowledge of good and evil, you are tearing up your ticket to ride, you are relinquishing fructifying pain.

> But far within him something cried
> For the great tragedy to start.
> The pang in lingering mercy fall
> And sorrow break upon his heart.

That was the poet Edwin Muir, who, like so many others of his time, was a Red of some sort, and I put that quotation before one of the sections of *Martha Quest,* which is the first of the 'Children of Violence' sequence of novels. And right at the beginning of *A Ripple from the Storm,* the third, comes this quotation:

> There is no passion for the absolute without the accompanying frenzy of the absolute. It is always accompanied by a certain exaltation, by which it may be first recognised and which is always working on the growing point, the focal point of destruction, at the risk of making it appear, to such as have not been warned, that the passion for the absolute is the same as a passion for unhappiness.

That is by Louis Aragon, a French communist, who remained unrepentantly one and was that common mix, talking nonsense about communism and the Soviet Union, while the ferment of faith brought out in him original ideas on other subjects.

Now I look at those quotations and marvel at my younger self—and shudder, for I cannot yet laugh at it. To choose the Edwin Muir quotation meant that I did see I wanted sorrow to break upon my heart—but surely I should have been more disquieted than I was? And I did not see at all that to make *the growing point* an equivalent of *the focal point of destruction* was a pretty sick state of mind. I literally did not see it. Of course, if you are communist—and for many people not communist too—a growing point had to be a destruction, because you don't make an omelette without breaking eggs, and a revolution is—it goes without saying—a necessary preliminary to paradise.

The trouble is, you may see something clearly enough to use revelatory quotes to highlight parts of a story, but not clearly enough to be frightened at what you see. You can't see something in depth until you have lived your way into seeing it in depth.

This set of mind, this predisposition towards suffering, the unconscious belief that to understand life—or to know the score—means immersion in painful experience, shows itself in other areas than the political. It took much too long to see what I did about people becoming communists, but soon after came the thought, Wait a minute: take another look at what you've written—and then at what others write—for often enough a novel or story

266

chronicles a willed descent into extreme experience. Take, for instance, my novel *The Summer Before the Dark*. In it, the protagonist, Kate Brown, a middle-aged woman, is shown at a point of crisis, children flown, indifferent husband, life needing a new direction or at least understanding—and she allows herself a fall away from her own high standards into a sluttish and premature (and temporary) old age, permits herself a kind of breakdown ... though is this word, which we use so easily, really an appropriate one when Kate is so capably following her own inner line of growth, even if apparently in outward disarray? In allowing the forms of social life to disintegrate, Kate approaches self-understanding. Fair enough: a novel, to be interesting, has to have some sort of focus, and most novels report a concentration of experience of some kind. Around about the time that novel was written, in 1971 and 72 there lingered from the sixties the belief that to go mad is to receive the ultimate in revelation. Well, I have never believed that, though I might have added to it with *The Golden Notebook,* whose structure, at least, says that an over-aridity can be cured by 'breakdown'. As I had been observing so comprehensively during that period when communism cracked from top to bottom. It was the most rigid and dogmatic people who 'broke down' and were amazingly improved by the experience, emerging into the light of common day where live ordinary mortals like you and me. And Kate's self-immolation was analogous to a real experience of mine, not a literary one, when I deliberately drove myself crazy by not eating and not sleeping, out of curiosity. I did learn quite a bit, though I would not recommend it, for it is a dangerous little experiment. Its relevance here is that it was a willed submission to an extreme. I have not had the same experience I gave Kate Brown, but this raises an interesting question, for it feels as if I did. Again and again I have written about people mad, half mad, and in breakdown. I have never personally been mad or broken down, but I feel as if I have. The reason for my not having been personally mad or in breakdown is, I think—partly—that any inclination towards it has been staved off by writing about it. And, partly, because my life has always had in it people very ill—like my father; people who have had appalling childhoods; people in breakdown; or people who are—as we say—inadequate. But I do not believe that ultimate truths come from being crazy. I've seen too much of craziness. Schizophrenics have flashes of truth which in less knowledgeable times were described as divine inspiration, and they are certainly startling insights. The last-ditch depressives have to suffer a vision of life so bleak, so ugly, so terrible, that no wonder they sometimes kill themselves. Yet there are those among them who say that this vision is the real one, and we who do not share it are merely ignorant or frivolous. Just like the men who returned from the trenches, initiated into the extremes of suffering, to find civilians who understood nothing of what they had gone through.

It is not the flat grey plains of 'pessimism' or the equable perspectives of mild depression—for most writers work best in a low, cool, gently depressed condition—that are relevant to my thesis here. Lynda Coldstream, in *The Four-Gated City,* mad all her life—schizophrenic; Professor Watkins, in *A Briefing for a Descent into Hell,* who loses his memory for a while, has the opportunity to know himself better, but refuses it; *The Fifth Child; The Good Terrorist,* with its load of destructive people—these are what interest me here.

Into this gallery goes Kate Rawlings (another Kate), who is successfully married, with four children, a wonderful husband, and a comfortable life, but the substance of her belief in life leaks away and she ends up turning on the gas in a rented room in Paddington. 'To Room Nineteen' is a quite terrible story, not least because I don't understand it, or rather the region of myself it comes from. And quite recently I have written about a man, Stephen, in *Love, Again,* who feels as if life is slipping away between his fingers. When this kind of theme emerges again and again, one has to acknowledge—*I* have to acknowledge—that just under the surface there lies in wait for me, if I am not careful, something like those ant lions, the tiny insects that lie just hidden in the bottom of a little pit in the sand, waiting to drag a struggling ant into quicksand. Do I believe this will happen to me? No, because I write myself out of those potentials for disaster.

There is a pattern in my mind, there must be, where order breaks into disorder and extremity. It came from World War I and my parents' destruction by it. This pattern has to be in other people's minds, must be, for we are not sufficient to ourselves.

Long after the time I am writing about, the fifties, I had this experience: Sometimes it is useful to visualise a tale, a story, an incident, one that speaks to you. In this particular story, an old man, a woodcutter, has to walk away from his house, in the very early morning, following a Voice, which is calling to him. I had visualised the mountain, its wooded slopes and, low on these slopes, the little hut of the woodcutter. I could see the moonlight on the trees and on the ground, which was already fading because morning was nearly here. The old man walked across the rough ground into the trees, but then . . . he could not go on, because there was a chasm across his path. I flung a bridge across this chasm, and the old man walked over on it, but before he reached the other side the earth was sliding away, so I extended the bridge, and he scrambled to safety and was on the rounded slope of a foothill, which he knew every foot of, since he had lived here all his life, but now as he walked it crumbled away under him. To get that old man from the back door of his house to where he finally sat down, exhausted, a couple of miles away, waiting for the Voice, needed a patient construction and reconstruction of the whole route, making bridges and culverts, and all the time the earth was giving way in landslips and subsidence.

This must be a pattern in the stuff of my mind, for what else can it be? Sometimes a little thing—it could seem like a little thing—like an inability to perform the simple task of making an old man walk an imaginary path across the foothills of a mountain, can tell you so much about your ways of seeing life that your whole past is put in question.

If it were just one person, me, one small individual set for tears, then who could care?

For some months before I left Warwick Road, an old woman came to clean and tidy up and, most of all, put me in my place, for she was part of the aristocracy of Britain. She was Miss Ball, over seventy and still working, because she had worked all her life and did not approve of idleness. When she first came, to find out if I would suit her, I asked her to sit down. 'Thank you, but I know how things should be done,' said she, standing in the middle of the kitchen with its sky-blue floor, red wallpaper, white wood and ceiling, and on the table the blue-ringed white mugs that everyone had then. Miss Ball was tall, she was gaunt, she had big red bony hands, and she wore a grey Utility coat, a stained felt hat with a grey net cage around it, and on her feet once-elegant grey suede shoes, with a big hole in both to accommodate bunions. She said she had come from the West Country, aged seventeen, to work in a house in London. A good house, she said, examining my kitchen with contempt. She had worked for a duke in her time. She had worked in houses that had thirty staff. Once, she would not have looked at the work she had to do now. She told me this with a gentle good-servant's smile and coldly, malevolently observing eyes. How much she did hate me, how much she did hate all her employers now.

She came in two mornings a week, and I gave her top wages for the work, badly paid then as now, and she took the coins carefully and put them into a leather purse once solid black but now limp and silvery with age.

'Hello, dear,' she would greet me, smiling her poisonous smile, but the moment I was in a different room, or had even turned away, she began on a muttered litany: 'Filthy pigs, and I have to clean up after them, pigs too good for them, pigs don't leave dirty plates in the sink, slave, slave, slave all my life for pigs, I never thought when I was a girl . . .' And so forth. This low muttering went on all the time she swept and wiped and washed, but if I happened to go into a room where she was, up would come her head, and 'Oh, there you are, dear.' Miss Ball had acquired a genteel voice and vowels from her years in good service. And it was in this voice that the angry mutter continued. 'On their backs with their legs in the air, these fine ladies, I don't think, as bad as each other, every one of them, duchess and parlourmaid, cook and skivvy.' She had worked mostly in the kitchens, but she had also taken hot water in the mornings into cold bedrooms, made up the fires, tidied rooms before the families came down to breakfast. But the kitchen was best, she said, for she liked a bit of life. Good times, she said there were, down in the kitchens, and the best was the meals, with all the staff around a long table, with the cook and the butler at the top. Such good times, such good food and plenty of it, everyone knew their place then, not like now, all kinds of upstarts thinking themselves as good as their betters.

How, I asked Miss Ball, had she acquired that foot of hers? For she limped about, holding on to the back of a chair, or a table if she thought I was watching. She owed that foot to the death of King Edward Seventh, she said. She was cleaning out the grate in the kitchen, and the cook was scraping the vegetables, and the parlourmaid came running down the stairs, in a real state she was, all ready to burst with tears, and she screamed, 'Cookie, Cookie, the old cock's dead,' and Miss Ball was so shocked she dropped the grate on her foot and broke it.

And why had Miss Ball never married? I dared to ask at last. Men were filthy, she said, they're only good for one thing, if that's what you're interested in, but she had learned what's what at a dance in Tiverton, when she was sixteen. She had new shoes her cousin Betty lent her, they were white calf shoes and you had to clean them with milk. There was this young man who wouldn't let her alone, and he took her outside into the dark—a lovely evening it was—and he pulled her about and messed her up and then he ruined her shoes. And how did he do that? 'Can't you guess? Filthy pigs . . . The mess, all over my shoes . . . I had to pay for them, and it took me a year of saving my pocket money, and that was it, I didn't want anything to do with any man after that.'

Miss Ball's employers would ring each other up, at moments when we were brought low by that obscene muttering, and ask each other if we were doomed for ever to listen to it, but how could we possibly dismiss her; no, only her death would release us . . . but then I moved.

THE ZEITGEIST: HOW WE WERE THINKING

Women can't be comics; there never has been a female comic. The reason is that they have no sense of humour.

The capitalist press is always against the Labour Party and never reports any Labour Party rally, march, or issue fairly.

Full employment is taken for granted, and Kurt Vonnegut's novel Player Piano *(published in Britain, 1953), where work is so scarce it is given as a reward to favoured or particularly good workers, seems merely eccentric.*

There is a great deal of agitation for and against repealing the law that makes homosexuality a crime.

Colin Wilson is being portrayed by the press as some kind of latter-day Byron, moody and dangerous, an enemy of law and order. He has just announced that Shakespeare had no talent. One evening he appears in the Arts Club holding aloft a skull in one hand. He stands in the doorway with a charming, shy, and engaging smile, waiting for us to laugh.

An astonishing number of upper-class fathers are rushing about the country waving whips and bellowing that they are going to thrash young men who have slept with their daughters—just like John Osborne's Look Back in Anger.

You cannot pick up a newspaper without reading about an Angry Young Man.

To acquire a mortgage and start owning property was a capitulation to capitalism and meant you were in serious danger of losing your soul.

A strong anti-American feeling: the United States was the world's chief enemy, a fascist imperialist power, much worse than the Soviet Union. All Americans were rich. Clancy and other Americans used to insist that there was the most terrible poverty in the States, and I watched them being patronised and even laughed at by their British hosts: of course these communists had to say something like this.

Everything British was still best. Except for the food and coffee, for this excellence was permitted to other countries.

Sociology, that study of humankind by itself, not yet two decades old, if Mass Observation is taken as its start, is dismissed by—mostly—the Left, as 'discredited'.

Why don't we have a national theatre, like every other country in Europe? Why does our government consistently disparage and underfund the arts?

Vivien Leigh was acting Blanche Dubois in Streetcar Named Desire. *It was the first time the play had been done in Britain, and we were not used to rawly emotional American plays. A very big theatre—too large. It was half full. A matinee. There were some gangs of louts there because they had heard this was a dirty play. They were throwing rubbish on to the stage and shouting insults at Vivien and commenting loudly. There was so much noise in the audience it was hard to hear the play. Vivien Leigh's marriage with Laurence Olivier had just broken up, and she was ill, and her performance had a dimension of verisimilitude most painful for her sympathisers, but she was an unforgettable Blanche. I suppose this was like theatre-going in more unruly days here, when the audience jeered disapproval, and threw things at the actors.*

In Tiananmen Square a million people are listening to Mao Tse-tung. Ted Allan is there. Mao says the United States is planning to drop nuclear bombs on China to destroy the glorious new Communist Dawn, but 'we have plenty of people in China,' and even if America kills one-half the population and lays waste half of China, it doesn't matter: Communist China will fight back with the other half. Tumultuous applause, lasting for many minutes.

I sat in the audience for the musical South Pacific. *I was with friends my age. Slowly I became uneasy, then distressed, then outraged. Yes, we were all feeling the same. We had been brought up on books and plays protesting about the horrors of war. Here we were watching an insipid tale that had the Second World War as a background—the war in the Pacific, that terrible, murderous war, but here shown as something to be taken for granted, nothing very much compared to this paradise island, sexy American troops, a love affair, a mild message about race. No one else in the audience seemed to mind. It was one of the times when you realise that there has been, without your even knowing it, a change of moral values, and you have been left behind, stranded on some rather ridiculous outpost. I felt the same over* Hiroshima, Mon Amour, *with its images of death and tortured bodies mingled with bodies writhing in sex. A new sensibility, to my mind infinitely corrupted and sick.*

Nothing has changed more than attitudes towards love, sex, marriage—all that. Throughout the fifties there emanated from the United States an air of discouragement, sadness, dismay about what was going on between men and women. There was desperation, of a quiet patient kind. A film, whose name I have forgotten, was about a man and a woman both looking for love—real love, and that was the point. This was in New York. These two wandered through the city, which was cold and hostile to them, and while they were often in the same street, or bar, or restaurant, they never met. They were made for each other, born to fall into each other's arms— 'Here you are, at last'—but the great wilderness, the city, kept them apart. There has never been a more powerful vision of loneliness than that film. All that has changed: the sixties blew away those grey and sorrowful miasmas.

An adviser on food, one Dr. Gelfand, backed by government and medical experts, pronounced that the good diet must consist of protein and fat, and a minimum of carbohydrate. Meat, butter, milk and cheese and eggs, would see us all through to a healthy death. Men needed 3,500 to 4,000 calories a day, women 2,500 to 3,000. There were two kinds of protein: first-class protein, mostly meat, which is what the world's populations should aim at, and second-class protein, pulses, vegetable protein, which—if you came to think of it—were eaten only by second-class people. This dogma ruled for at least ten years.

American white men were insulting their own women, and white women generally, for being unsexy, hardly women at all: real women were black and knew how to move—particularly their butts.

Coffee bars, so recently born, the only refuge for young people, unless they wanted to use pubs, were thriving up and down the land but were often closed, and harassed, by the police, who had not understood the arrival of youth culture. They were all having such a good time: can't have that.

Walking up through Trafalgar Square, I passed a little knot of demonstrators outside the South African Embassy. A girl thrust some pamphlets at me. Believing I did not need information about South Africa, I shook my head. She shouted abuse at me, 'fascist' being the least of it.

A Commonwealth Exhibition of Art was ignored by all the critics. I was asked by West Indian friends to try and persuade them at least to go and have a look. I rang up newspaper after newspaper, wrote letters. The trouble was, these rooms filled with large colourful pictures, full of verve and vitality, were not what the critics then were admitting as art. Even the one or two critics who did go dismissed it. The uninstructed and uninformed public did not go at all.

In the sixties appeared a book about the fifties, called The Fifties, *and the references to me were inaccurate, so I supposed those to other people were too. The author had not bothered to interview any of us and was so inexperienced he seemed to imagine that the 'names' on the letterheads of organisations were the people who did the actual work. I wrote to complain, and his reply was, 'I see you don't like me very much,' not, 'I am sorry I wrote such a shoddy book.' I was shocked, not realising—well, none of us did— that this indifference to fact was shortly to become general in reporting.*

There was a community or commune in Kent, begun in the thirties by architects, all communists or part of the socialist fervours of the time. The idea was to create an exemplary way of living. The men worked in London, where they had toeholds, and commuted either every day or at weekends. By now everyone reading this will be able to supply what follows, but the effort foundered on something no one then expected. The men were happy, the children adored living in this extended family in the country, but the women were discontented. That was a surprise and a disappointment to everyone. I was told of it, with a humorous sadness, by one of the men, who said why was it that something that was a heaven for the men and the children could be such a martyrdom for the women?

Television and radio announcers still insisted on mispronouncing foreign names, presumably to show our independence. This was a source of embar-

rassment to some of us, who hated our country showing itself like a lout among the nations.

This country was still seen by visitors as so gentle and polite and civilised, compared with others.

Langham Street
W1

※

FOUR YEARS AFTER I HAD BEEN ASSURED IT WAS IMPOSSIBLE THE law could change, it was changed, and I was no longer a protected tenant. When I asked the lawyer how this could be, he said, Well, these things happen. At once a developer arrived to look at my flat. One very large room, two medium-sized rooms, two small ones, and a kitchen the right size to sit in, drinking coffee and talking, were to become twelve rooms: my big room alone would make four. Quite soon I would be gone and thinking of young Australians in their vagabond phase shut into these little boxes of rooms, for this whole area—Earls Court—would become Little Australia.

And so where was I to live? In 1958, nine years after I came to London, I found that if my earnings were evened out, they were the same as the average worker's wage—twenty pounds a week, I think it was. My unconcerned, it-will-all-come-right-in-the-end attitude towards money has always suited my way of life but proved a handicap at times when I needed to find a place to live. As everyone knows, writers' earnings are chancy and you never know what you will have coming in next year. I remember an income tax official coming to see me at Joan's house, to say, Why haven't you paid your tax? I told him that last year I had earned enough to pay tax, but not this year, with three hundred pounds. He was nice about it, found ways of seeing me through, but as with all regularisers and invigilators, my precarious life made him uneasy, and he thought I should be aiming at a steady income, perhaps as a secretary.

By now I was having opportunities to earn money in ways other than writing novels and stories: radio and television were beckoning. On the whole I resisted their blandishments. In those days we believed that to write for money was to sell your soul, dilute the precious honey, offend your Muse, who would punish you by making you incapable of seeing the difference between good and bad writing, so that you would end up as a hack. We were right, but such is the climate now that it is hard even to mention these dear old-fashioned ideas. And we still believed that a writer should be private, quiet, resist publicity.

My mother had left me a thousand pounds. She had also left a house in a suburb of Salisbury, which she had been renting out. I told my brother I didn't want my share of the house, he could have it. I knew that dividing up the house and furniture would lead to unpleasantness and difficulties. I also said I didn't want any of the photographs, the canteens of silver cutlery, the silver presentation trays. Now, that was a bad mistake, not least because my brother valued them so little that when I asked many years later where they were, he did not know, had forgotten how the big silver tray had stood on the writing desk (made of petrol boxes) in the old farmhouse, insisting on its Englishness, or how the photographs in their silver frames had stood about near the fluted silver vases for sweet peas, next to plough parts and bits of rock that might turn out to have gold in them.

I would be able to afford a modest rent or mortgage. I began one of those intensive day-after-day periods of home-hunting which have taken me to so many parts of London that I can hardly go down a street anywhere without thinking, Look, there's that house; I could have been living there all this while.

Two places stand out from that time. One was a house in Flood Street, Chelsea, where there were two floors of faded crumbling dingy dusty rooms. It was cheap, but although so many famous people had lived in Flood Street, the place depressed me. I would need yet again to spend weeks painting and mending and dyeing, and besides, there was that name, Flood—and the Thames was running at the bottom of the street. The other house was in Royal Crescent in Holland Park, very far from the fashionable place it is now. For one thing, it had been bombed, or looked as if it had. The house was clean, had been painted. But why was it so cheap? I was tempted, said I would go back, but as I reached the gate the woman from the next house beckoned me over and told me in a low voice—one eye on the estate agent, who was standing sulkily by—that if I bought the house it would be down about my ears in a year: the dry rot and wet rot had been festooning the walls and ceilings like rotten mushrooms, and the builders had simply scraped it off and painted everything white.

I was saved by my publisher. I already had two publishers, then not as common as it soon would be. Needing money, I had asked for an advance for a collection of short stories, *The Habit of Loving,* but Michael Joseph would not give it to me. This was stupid of them, for my previous collection, *This Was the Old Chief's Country,* had done well and was still selling. Tom Maschler, still at McGibbon and Kee, was waiting for just such an opportunity and gave me the money, though I expect Howard Samuels—the owner— was consulted. Howard Samuels was a millionaire, but no ordinary millionaire: for he was a socialist, a close friend of Aneurin Bevan, and he helped *Tribune,* the organ of the left wing of the Labour Party. He was self-made, and publishing was his real love, after politics. He owned Holbein Mansions in Langham Street, near the BBC. He offered me a flat in it, for five pounds a week. This was a very low rent, not only for that area—within walking distance of theatreland, Soho, Oxford Street, Mayfair, the river—but for anywhere in London then. The flat was tiny, six small rooms, and the building was hideous, with a grey bare cement staircase. On the fourth floor you opened the door to a narrow corridor, which bisected the flat. Opposite the door was a minute kitchen, then the bathroom, with its hissing and clattering gas geyser, and two other little rooms on that side. On the street side was my tiny bedroom, and a larger room, the living room. There was no way that flat could be made more than tolerable. Both Clancy and Tom Maschler helped me to move. There was far too much furniture from the Warwick Road flat, so I gave it away to anyone hard up enough to want it, and took with me a couple of beds, a table, and some chairs. And the bookcases. My bedroom was a box. Three walls were bright pink, with panels of whimsical birds on the fireplace wall. I painted the room white, a task for a morning, since it was small, but the fireplace was so hideous I could not stop looking at it, and I painted the fireplace wall dark plum colour, to try and make it disappear. To this day people say, Do you remember when you painted your bedroom black? I think the analogy must be when a painter puts a little patch of red on his canvas and, if you haven't looked too closely, you think: the picture with all that red in it. The only nice thing in the room was a big window, with beautiful dark-blue cotton curtains, and they made a good restful light. I ran up all the curtains on the ancient Singer sewing machine.

I thought the low rent and living in that area justified any ugliness, but Peter hated the place. He had hated Warwick Road, but at least there had been space. From the moment we got into this new flat, he was begging me to buy a house. He wanted security. A house meant security. The bank also was putting pressure on me to buy a house or a flat. Astonishing, for this doesn't happen in other parts of Europe. In Britain, if you have a mortgage, then you are a good citizen, and the banks smile. I was afraid of the regular commitment, and besides, I had to find money for school fees. Peter was now at boarding school. He was twelve when he went. I did not like doing it, remembering what I felt going to boarding school, but twelve years old is not seven. And in fact it was a good decision. Many children who are miserably unhappy sent to boarding school at six or seven like it when they are older.

There were two prostitutes living in that building, but I didn't notice until Clancy told me. Both conformed to pattern, but they were different patterns. One was, or had been, a little fluffy blonde, and her rooms were full of rosy corners, pink curtains, pink pouffes, pink eiderdowns, flirtatious dolls and fluffy toys. She used to wait for me in her doorway, so that she could waylay me and complain about Helen. Otherwise I did not see her, for it seemed she worked not in this area but in Soho. I put her into a story called 'Mrs. Fortescue'. Helen was dark-skinned, with black Gauguin hair and dark eyes full of the knowledgeable 'scepticism' so prized by Clancy and other Americans I knew. This 'scepticism' in a woman signalled that she knew the score, knew how to look after herself, and this meant damage limitation for both partners. I had only to mention to American visitors that two of the 'girls' were in the building for them to feel they were near the source of real experience. I liked Helen, and we would exchange friendly words. She had been, I was told, a good friend to Howard Samuels when he was a lonely and lost young man, and that was why she had the best flat in the building and why he would always look after her. Sometimes, down in the street outside the building, you would see a fluffy old whore, like a terrier with a bow around its neck, and a languid elegant dark worldly whore pass each other with cool disliking looks.

The streets around Langham Street invited curiosity and casual strolling. Here was the centre of the rag trade. You did see, looking down through railings, semi-underground rooms full of badly paid girls running up dresses and blouses on their machines, but most of this work had moved elsewhere. The shops were wholesale, designed to attract not shoppers but buyers, and if you glanced in, there were scenes of intense competitive bargaining. This business was mostly Jewish, and there was a restaurant to feed the trade. In Warwick Road the cheap good food was Indian, but here it was Jewish. In four years, when I would move again, the good cheap restaurants would be Greek. This restaurant was always full. I took a lot of people there, but the one I remember best is Mordecai Richler, who tried to persuade me to like stuffed chicken necks, but I said it must be that he was eating nostalgic memories of childhood. Clancy was there often. American visitors loved the place, because in those days people in show business and in publishing were often Jewish and had come from the Bronx, to the extent that when you heard 'I was brought up in the Bronx,' it was like the refrain of a song, or like one of those novels that have a large poor family struggling to live, but the clever children, all stuffed with literature and literary ambitions, are destined to escape and astonish the world. And the American visitors who were not Jewish said this homely restaurant with its family atmosphere, once common in New York was now disappearing, and so they felt they were visiting their own history.

The area was noisy and alive in the day but deserted at night, except for a couple of pubs and a restaurant that took advantage of the law which said that nudity was immoral if the naked ones were in movement, but moral if motionless. Patrons were supplied with pencils and paper and invited to exercise their artistic talents. A naked girl was wheeled in and held a pose for twenty minutes, and then she was removed while the eaters applauded and showed each other their sketches, and another girl arrived, as often as not goose-pimpled from cold. The eaters were encouraged to keep sketching, because if a policeman dropped in to check that a girl was not moving a muscle, then all those flying or dawdling pencils proved artistic intent. The police dropped in often. This restaurant was a great success with all Americans. It is a surprising thing that all the fifties and sixties Americans visiting London headed straight for Soho, prostitutes, and nude clubs. When you said, For heaven's sake, you have plenty of prostitutes in every one of your big cities, they said it was not the same. The Russians too. Each visiting delegation of Russians—this was the era of Delegations, each one chaperoned by a guide who was really the KGB—was at once taken to Soho to see capitalist degeneracy in action, in the same spirit as, in Moscow, *The Red Poppy* ballet included a long and sexy scene in a capitalist nightclub, to show how disgusting the West was. Communist Russia was forbidden these delights; prostitutes and sex shows were possible only under capitalism, so the flocks of the Russians to Soho were understandable.

Soho sex clubs had more attractions than one. The licensing law closed drinking places for a couple of hours in the afternoon, but in the clubs, alcohol was legal. Drinking men joined one of these clubs if unable to bear the deprivation. Reuben Ship took me to one, and I was the only woman in the audience. I sat and watched the show, but Reuben was at the bar, with his back to the platform. One girl remains in my mind: she was Irish, large and beautiful, and new to the work. She was supposed to writhe around and then shake her breasts so that the tassels on her nipples swung, but she was finding it all so funny that she could not resist making a joke of it, and ended by offering her large betasseled tits to the audience like puddings resting on her two hands, and they shook with her laughter at herself, and the men, and at the whole business. The men were not pleased: deadly dark concentration, full of latent hostility, was their mode, and she was breaking the atmosphere and making them ridiculous. The patron hauled her off and scolded her while she giggled. She lost the job, but then she became a barmaid in the local, where her sense of fun was an asset.

Another near restaurant was one I couldn't possibly have afforded then, but Howard Samuels took his authors there. It was the Spanish Club, and it was all dark-brown shiny panelling and red leather, very masculine, very heavy in style. There Howard Samuels and Aneurin Bevan, Howard Samuels and Jenny Lee,★ Howard Samuels and the Labour Party Left—but not the New Left—sat for hours over the solid Spanish food and then drank peach brandy. Howard liked being a host. He was a handsome, emotional, mercurial man, and such a man must have his Sancho Panza, and there he was, Reginald Davis-Poynter, who was his right-hand man in McGibbon and Kee. Reggie was calm, sensible, large, and kind, and he looked after Howard. And looked after me too, as his author, as long as I was, when Tom Maschler left.

And now I became for a short time that disgraceful thing a middle-aged woman buying half-bottles of whisky from the off-licence.

When I moved to Langham Street it was not at all like the move to Warwick Road, where I so foolishly believed I would be living with Jack. Clancy and I were breaking up—had been for months or, you could say, from the moment we began. For one thing, we had so little in common. And then he had never made any secret of his wanting to live by himself and have girls. But what my mind knew went on intelligently, on a level far from those depths where my emotions—no, this was deeper than emotions, or feelings—were. Again I was being dragged along like a fish on a line. With Clancy I hit the extremes in myself and had from the start, and this had nothing very much to do with Clancy the person. Partly it was because he was in 'breakdown'—that useful word which I am not going to define here. For one thing it is described (not defined) in *The Golden Notebook*. You cannot live with someone in breakdown, even if in a casual and undemanding way, without becoming involved, though it might be only in imagination. It

★The Minister for Arts, and Aneurin Bevan's wife.

was that old business of being dragged along, will-less. This was like the feeling I had when I got married for the first time, when the war drums were beating in 1939. I seemed to have no will; my intelligence watched what I did but was helpless. My surface behaviour accorded with: 'Oh no, Clancy and I are good friends; that's all it is now.' And we were good friends. But underneath I was all the betrayed woman, the abandoned one, I suffered and mourned and dragged myself about, with no more will than I needed to keep myself going and the fact that I despised myself made it all worse.

And there was Peter, who instead of dropping in and out, as he had when at school in London, or being there for long stretches, was now at boarding school, and there would be defined half-terms and holidays. But I felt as if this was the beginning of an end. Peter had been the one constant in my life, my ballast, what I held on to through thick and thin—which is of course why he had had to go away from me, because it was not good for him—but now he wasn't there.

I was working hard—it was *The Golden Notebook*—because there never has been a time when I wasn't, and I saw friends and acquaintances. But all the time I was being pulled along by something dark and out of sight.

And there was something else. Clancy had decided to trust a doctor who prescribed large doses of LSD. He did not treat his patients in hospital, but they arrived at his rooms in the mornings, were given a dose—and were thrown out again in the evening, about six. That is, when they were still high, crazy, out of control. I thought then it was criminal, and I think so now. This happened a couple of times a week, and I was in a frenzy of anxiety. Joan was worried too. We would ring each other up:

'Has Clancy arrived at your place?'

'No, I thought he was with you.'

He might turn up to say to either of us, 'I need to lie down.' Or we didn't know where he was. Well, he survived all that, so I suppose that doctor could say, 'What are you making such a fuss about? He was all right, wasn't he?' But he could easily have not been all right. I knew that this panic I felt, the anxiety, was because

I was reliving my father, drifting away into death but kept alive towards the end on injections of insulin and God knows what drugs. But what is the good of knowing something if that doesn't affect how you behave? I seem to have lived through far too many times when I was watching my behaviour, or feelings, with my intelligence—satirically, disapprovingly, anxiously—but was not able to stop.

I went to see Mrs. Sussman again, after three or four years' interval. She sat listening to me, her cheek resting on her palm. The connection between us had been cut, all right. She seemed a long way off. She said, 'I'm sorry I wasn't able to teach you any better sense.' Then she said, 'I am a very old woman. I am going to die soon. I am preparing myself for my death. Good morning.' It was salutary, learning that one would reach a stage when all these emotions became, simply, irrelevant.

This time my drinking was serious. I never counted the drinking that went on in my first marriage as serious. It was stupid, ill considered, and you'd think designed to do the maximum amount of damage—drinking for hours sometimes and not eating. But that was drinking because I was with people who drank, in a culture that not only permitted but admired hard drinking. And when I left that marriage I stopped. I had been in London for two years or more when it occurred to me, I've scarcely had a drink since I came. I had no money, and no one around me was drinking. Then I met the Canadians and drank again, but nothing like as much as in old Southern Rhodesia, with Frank Wisdom.

There is probably a recognised clinical condition: the middle-aged woman who slides into drinking, feeling abandoned, unloved, unwanted. This is what I had become. I would go into the off-licence, buy a half-bottle of whisky, and get through it before I slept. Not every night. And I did this particularly after I had been to visit Peter at his school. But this time it had become a craving, not social drinking. One morning I rolled out of bed and crawled on my hands and knees to the bathroom, to be sick. This shocked me into sobriety again. I thought, Now, this time I really am an alcoholic. Stop. And so I did. I no longer went to the off-licence for whisky. I did not get drunk by myself. Yet for that period, probably three or four months, that was what I was, an alcoholic.

Am I saying that men don't slide into alcoholism? Not, surely, in the same way. It is very common, seeing some woman whose marriage has broken up, or a love affair, or whose children have grown up and left, becoming a drinker, and the people watching think, Well, she'll get over it. And usually she does.

I know that writing, Doris Lessing crawled on her hands and knees to the lavatory to be sick, is asking for trouble. This is a problem for authors: certain ideas, words, phrases, that stand up out of the page, because we are sensitised to them. Sometimes the choice is between not mentioning something at all, because you know it will probably be exaggerated, and putting it in, in the interests of truth.

I mentioned this problem in *The Golden Notebook*. For instance, menstruation. Before that book I don't think menstruation had been in novels, and in *The Golden Notebook* it certainly got disproportionate attention from reviewers. But then menstruation lost its impact, and the word (and the idea) took its place in the print of a page and was not much noticed. Masturbation is another that has lost the power to shock. Almost. It depends on the context. Nabokov, in *Ada,* describes how his hero masturbates because he does not want to seduce a girl who is longing for him, and he is making himself safe. It shocks, because of the cruelty to the girl. Not because of the act. But not long ago, it would have been the act.

Drinking too much for three or four months seems now the least interesting of my memories of that time, because what is in my mind is something like the shimmer of sheet lightning, a glamour, for 1958 was the International Geophysical Year, and there hasn't been a year like it for excitement, for wonder. With every bit of news came new information, about space and space travel and, too, from the Antarctic, for me always an Ultima Thule, a beckoning place. That was the year the world decided to hold Antarctica in common, for all humankind, to co-operate in exploration and discovery everywhere, not only in Antarctica, to share knowledge. Sometimes I meet people and 1958 comes up. 'My God, what a year that was! There couldn't ever be anything as exciting.'

In Langham Street I was just a short walk from the New Left

and their purlieus, on the other side of Oxford Street, and sometimes they dropped in. I had become a sort of aunt figure, definitely a member of the Old Guard.

By now they had created the *New Left Review,* which I confess I found unreadable, though I was officially a supporter and at least on the board. There is a certain kind of academic polemical writing that is lifeless—an easy word to use and a hard one to define. The writing comes out of ratiocination, like a machine producing ideas fed by other ideas, and seldom has anything to do with what is actually going on 'in life itself'. But this fact is one that the polemicists seldom notice. What did all those yards, those acres, of analysis and argument and disputation actually do? Or change? Did they affect British socialism? Make a new Britain? Become part of the policies of political parties? It is taken for granted that when there is a 'new' wave, then it must have its journal, and the new young ones chop logic and write think pieces, but mostly it all goes on in a vacuum. The reply to that is usually: 'But it is creating a climate of opinion and indirectly changes thinking.' It certainly produced people who later wrote books whose ideas were not in the *New Left Review,* for they had moved on, and I suppose one could argue that the books were developments of those brave new articles. When a new wave has gone skipping or thundering past, and you ask the people who composed it, Well, what did you actually achieve? the reply nearly always is, 'But I learned such a lot.' And this is what I say when asked, about the communist group in Southern Rhodesia, What did that running around and making speeches and magazines and policies actually achieve? 'I learned a lot.' Now I believe the need to learn is the most powerful passion we have, and the deepest, and that young people, when they start magazines, or new waves, or communes, are really making situations where they can learn a lot in a short time. Nearly all these young ones ended up in universities and are now professors and write books and articles and are on television and the radio. They have nothing of the old passionate certainties left.

One person who came to my flat asking for money, a canvasser for the Cause, just as I had been fifteen years before, was Ralph Samuels. There he sat, intoxicated with his own persuasiveness, while facts and figures outlining dizzying possibilities whirled around our heads. He was an engaging youth, whose wild descriptions of the Britain my money would help create caused him suddenly, and in the very midst of his fantasies, to stop and then put his head back and laugh. At himself.* Well, I thought, our lot, at the height of self-intoxication, would have been incapable of that honest laugh. These youngsters were altogether more open-minded and less fanatic than we were, even if they did see Trotsky as no less a beacon for all humanity than once Stalin was. They were better balanced, they weren't crazy, as I now think we were. The reason was, they did not have the war going on, all killings and catastrophes and propaganda. For that is how I see our lot now—war crazed—even if we were hundreds or thousands of miles from the actual fighting.

Separately from the New Left crowd went on the activities that would lead to the Aldermaston Marches and then the Committee of a Hundred. I was invited to a meeting at Canon Collins's house, near St. Paul's Cathedral, where the Campaign for Nuclear Disarmament came into being. In that room that night were a lot of people, nearly all luminaries of the Left and well beyond the Left. I sat there thinking, Oh, Lord, not again, which is what I always felt in meetings then. No new organisation, no matter how well intentioned, no matter the standing of its founders, turns out as expected. It seemed to me surprising that this (to me basic) fact was not being recognised. And the older I get, the more surprising it becomes. I did not take part in the discussion; I was a listener and a supporter. As I left the room, Bertrand Russell was standing at the door, and he stopped me and said with an authoritarian nod, like a governess, 'Now I hope you are going home and to bed with your lover.' I had never met him before. I thought him impertinent and silly. I did not understand the incident. Later I did. He had been one of the Bloomsbury group, or on the fringes of it. These people were everything that was admirable and excellent, particularly in their loyalty to each other always, through their lives, but they had this silly streak. They reacted to the Victorians' hypocrisies and

*Ralph Samuels died in 1996.

silences about sex by using the word 'bugger' at every opportunity, to show their freedom from cant, and they galloped around drawing rooms chanting naughty words. All that was understandable in the context but left residual foolishness in unlikely places. I thought, Silly old philosopher.

Soon there was the first of the Aldermaston Marches, which went from London to Aldermaston, not the other way, as the later marches did.★ There had been marches and 'demos' almost every weekend for years, communist or labour, and I was in a permanent condition of neurotic guilt because I seldom went. But this was different, it was The Bomb, and I was not the only one to feel like this. Not many marchers left London that day, only a few hundred or so, like so many marches and demos—the core of the faithful, with their children. But there was something about this march, and people kept joining all along the route. At every underground station there were more, people jumped off buses to join in, and by the end of the second day there were thousands. News of the march reached the newspapers and the television news. And so the march grew and grew, and the organisers were taken by surprise. Right at the end, when we were marching into Aldermaston, the entire committee of the Communist Party was on either side of the route, watching. They had miscalculated: nuclear disarmament was not on their agenda, but here were these multitudes of citizens. There were many contemptuous remarks that day about the comrades, who, we said, were about to adjust the 'line' to events, thus finally proving their feebleness.

The first march attracted people from all over Britain; those in succeeding years, people from Europe and America. The marches united the whole spectrum of the Left and far beyond. If you stood for an hour watching the marchers, the banners were a map of socialist Britain. There were even Tory groups. Multiformity, that was the note of the marches. And many were there not primarily because of The Bomb but because of a general concern for the condition of Britain. With every year the marchers got younger, and by the end you would think this was another children's cru-

★The first Aldermaston March was in 1958.

sade. Going on the Aldermaston March became the equivalent of an initiation ritual: Only the other day I met a woman who said, 'My mother wouldn't let me go, and I'll *never* forgive her.' But the first few marches had of every age, size, sort, and colour, and it was a cheerful, optimistic, and often very funny crowd. Not to say irreverent. The Tom Lehrer songs were as much the anthem of the march as 'We Shall Overcome' and 'Down by the Riverside' and 'Jerusalem'. Christopher Logue made his personal banner 'Eat More *Food*', and that earned him satirical cheers. John Wain, who didn't approve of the march at all, stood on a bridge that crossed the route, looking down, and, while friends waved up to him, shouting, 'Come and join us,' tragically shook his head. Ken Tynan ambled along, attracting disciples, and at lunchtime, when we stopped for picnics, little crowds of theatre people gathered to overhear his witticisms. Often an older person would walk surrounded by young ones and give what amounted to a seminar on politics, civics, history, literature, film. I saw the marches as a peripatetic extension of a university or school course.

The most heartbreaking and delightful of all the banners was the little one fixed on top of a frail pushchair propelled by a pretty young woman, a brave amateur effort, low down among the great trade-union banners, Labour Party banners, Nuclear Disarmament banners: 'Clydeside Says NO' . . . 'Cornwall says NO' . . . 'Greenwich Says NO' . . . 'Ban the Bomb' . . . all in black on white, but hers said: 'Caroline Says NO'. If I were to choose one image that summed up the years of marches, it would be that one. Or perhaps Wayland Young and his wife, surrounded by their infants and children, in pushchairs and prams, on his back and in their arms.

On one march, Randolph Churchill greeted the marchers with a wind-up gramophone on which he was playing patriotic music, but the din was so great he was taken to be a supporter and then, when his furious gestures made his position clear, invited to join us and have his mind changed.

Journalists joined the marches for the purpose of getting quotes which would make the whole business ridiculous.

It was reckoned that when, after the first year, the marches ended in Trafalgar Square, there were half a million or so people there. Some weaker souls gave up in Hyde Park, which was a sea of picnics, but sometimes there were feasts in welcoming houses. Peter Piper's and Anne Piper's house on the river provided caldrons of soup and sandwiches to what seemed like dozens of people, some of whom had slept uncomfortably in schools and town halls along the route. Most of us older ones went home to sleep in our beds and took the train out to wherever the march had reached the night before. I wrote of the Aldermaston phenomenon in *The Four-Gated City*.

Meanwhile there had appeared the Committee of a Hundred, whose aim it was to convert this vast and incoherent movement into a weapon (their word) for directly assaulting, damaging, and in every way undermining nuclear installations, relevant embassies, and the police who tried to stop them. It was obvious that these hundreds of thousands of people, many of them only mildly political, would never commit themselves to 'direct action', and so it had to be equally obvious that this was a plan to split and disrupt the movement for nuclear disarmament. In other words, the heirs of Lenin were with us again. It is not necessary to have read Lenin or even to have heard of him to be his heir.

It was evident that very soon the Campaign for Nuclear Disarmament would find itself discredited by reports and rumours of violence, and there were plenty of journalists waiting for their opportunities.

There was a crucial first meeting of the Committee of a Hundred. Three kinds of people were there. First, a few people like me, who had been communists, were no longer, and wanted to find out if our worst suspicions were in fact correct. Then, people who might be disenchanted with communism but not yet with the idea of revolution and violence as a 'weapon'. And there were some innocents, tasting their first blood. I asked one of them recently—he was prominent in the Committee of a Hundred for years—what he now thought of all that sound and fury, what in his opinion had been achieved. His reply: We politicised a whole generation. In other words, he saw the long-term boon and benefit of the Committee of a Hundred as the creation of more people like himself.

It was a large room, crammed full, and the conspiratorial atmosphere was only too familiar. Here again was the potent and charismatic leader, this time Ralph Schoenman, a young American. It was he who spoke, in that style perfected by History itself, combining idealism with a cold, clipped precision, and full of contempt for opponents, who were by definition cowards, poltroons, and morally defective, for the people in this room had on their shoulders the responsibility for the future of all humankind.

The old guard sat and listened, and left early. It happened that I was with Michael Ayrton, the sculptor. I had not met him before, nor would I meet him again, but our rapport was that of cynical old soldiers. As we parted in the street, he said, 'I think we could say we've been here before. Well, it's a pity.'

The Committee of a Hundred, formed as a result of that meeting, promoted itself vigorously as the healthy, honest, and *good* part of the Campaign for Nuclear Disarmament, and its guiding star was—for the purposes of propaganda—Bertrand Russell.

A great deal of proselytising went on among the branches and groups, and attempts were made to get the support of people like myself, for an Old Guard is valuable to provide names to go on letterheads and—not least—money.

In a book called *The Protest Makers,* something like an official history of these movements, I am described as a platform speaker for CND and the Committee of a Hundred. I was not. I am described as an active demonstrator. I was not. Unless going on the Aldermaston Marches counts as actively demonstrating. Of course Ralph Schoenman claimed me as a supporter of the Committee of a Hundred.

Ralph dominated the Committee of a Hundred. He had no formal position, but then there were no officeholders, partly because this was considered 'old politics', partly so that the police would not know whom to arrest.

Ralph Schoenman came to see me. This sounds a simple event, but it was preceded by reports from people to whom he had applied for information on the best way to approach me. There we sat in that ugly little room, where the cries from the street market below and the din of the traffic made us shut the window so we could hear ourselves speak. Rather, Ralph, with a severe nod and a soldierly air, said, 'I think it would be advisable . . . ,' and smartly got up to shut the window. He sat down to lean forward and engage my eyes with a stern gaze that was reminding me of previous avatars of Lenin, liars on principle; but that gave rise to interesting questions, which I was debating with myself as I listened amiably to his polemics. Now, he knew that I knew exactly what was going on. Was he not running around London boasting that he not only signed Bertrand Russell's letters but often dictated them? 'He does what I tell him.' (There are plenty of people left who remember this.) Did we not know that if you said to Russell, 'Can I fetch you that file . . . get you a glass of water . . . answer that telephone?' he would reply, 'No, Ralph will do it for me.' Ralph had Russell in his pocket and boasted about it. And yet here sat Ralph in front of me, painting a lurid picture of Canon Collins, the chairman of the Campaign for Nuclear Disarmament, who he said was intriguing to undo Russell by means of dirty tricks and ruses that were in fact part of the armoury of communist tactics—Leninist tactics. Ralph knew that I must know that what he said was untrue, and yet he was radiating sincerity.

Which brings me—and brought me then—to the question: Does it count as lying when the liar knows perfectly well his listener knows he is lying? When both speaker and auditor are familiar with the Leninist 'style of work', which enjoins lying and every kind of dirty trick?

I sat listening, smiling, brooding inwardly about this and associated questions, while Ralph held forth.

Real lying, pure and perfect lying, seems to me to be embodied in the following tale: In the seventies, a certain successful woman television executive decides to marry, having reached the age when it is now or never, if she wants to have children. She meets—at last—the right man, a good man. She is so happy, she blossoms and blooms. She marvels, too, at achieving so easily what had seemed impossible. Suddenly she telephones, in shock, all tears. During all the period of courtship, some months, there had been an agreement she would not telephone him at his place of work or at his flat. He would telephone her. But there is a crisis, and, she rings his place of work, but they have never heard of him. She rings the block of flats where he lives; he is not known there. She confronts him. He is furious. 'We had an agreement you would never ring me.' *She* is in the wrong. It turns out that he does have a job, just as prestigious and well paid as he has told her, but in a different firm from the one he said employs him. He does live in a good flat, in a good part of London, but not where he said. His life, his achievements, are as he told her, but in parallel. She is frantic with incomprehension, with betrayal, with shock. 'Why, but *why?*'

'I don't want you knowing what I do and where I live,' says this shortly to be married man, presumably with plans for a shared life, and he actually threatens to sue her for breach of promise. This, surely, is as perfect an example of a pure lie as one is likely to find.

For months the anti Canon Collins campaign all bubbled and boiled, a nasty brew, and rumours proliferated and slanders flew about. The Committee of a Hundred was achieving the most satisfactory notoriety.

I went to a meeting at Canon Collins's house, to discuss the tactics of the Committee. I am not saying there was no one there who understood they were up against Stalinist tactics under a different name, for in any gathering of political people then there were bound to be those who had been in or near the Party, probably a majority. But I was struck by a kind of baffled and helpless innocence. And perhaps that was a fair enough reaction, for in fact there was not much they could do. Canon Collins's team were playing by nice democratic rules, fair play, honest reporting, and so forth, but the Committee of a Hundred were from a very different tradition and playing by different rules. The Old Guard were dismayed, because meanwhile the masses of the Campaign for Nuclear Disarmament were ignorant of what was going on, but that couldn't last for long

I was telephoned by Mervyn Jones, then working on *The Observer*. Ralph Schoenman had persuaded Bertrand Russell to sign a statement—drafted by him, Ralph—that would be in the *Observer* newspaper next Sunday, accusing Canon Collins of every sort of nastiness. Possibly Russell had never seen it. It was known that he was being kept in the dark about a great many things, and it was thought that Lady Russell was not being informed either. The other possibility was that Ralph Schoenman and Lady Russell together were keeping Russell in the dark, for she—amazingly—admired Ralph too.

Meanwhile Canon Collins and his supporters were framing a statement describing the activities of Bertrand Russell—rather, Ralph Schoenman—but in a much cooler style and based on fact.

Would I go up to North Wales and see Bertrand Russell and beg him not to issue this statement? Because the one thing that should be avoided was a public confrontation between the two stars of the movement, for—and this was the point—the people who cared passionately about nuclear disarmament, some of them very young, did not care at all about these stars, these personalities, these prima donnas. This was a democratic movement, and they would be disgusted at the news that the leaders were engaged in personal battles. At least some of them—or their parents—had just behind them the terrible personality struggles of communism and would be saying, 'Oh, not *again*,' as they drifted off, disillusioned. For what was the most wonderful thing about these new, mostly youthful, hundreds of thousands was that where there had been cynicism and disillusion was now a fresh bright interest and faith in themselves. It simply must not happen, this public brawl. But the difficulty was that the two combatants and their followers had long ago forgotten about the innocent hundreds of thousands, because this is what happens when you are immersed in day by day, indeed minute by minute, preoccupations with the misdeeds of your opponents.

In those days I was more easily flattered than I am now. And even now my disapproval of myself is tempered: I was genuinely and passionately concerned about all those youthful innocents—who, of course, are now all middle-aged and long ago lost their illusions about politics. But at the time it seemed important to preserve their innocence for as long as possible. I said I would go. I did not have a car—would not have my own car for four years yet. A young woman from Australia, Janet Hase, who was from the *New Left Review* crowd, said she would drive me up. That was not a pleasant journey. She had a small car, did not know the route, and it was raining all the way, that grey, steady, cold rain that England knows so well how to sadden you with. The windscreen wipers steadily pushed loads of dirty cold water back and forth across the windscreen, and we two colonials were in that mood when we could not imagine why we had ever come here. The big, fast roads had not been built. Janet was complaining all the way that the men of this new revolutionary movement treated the women as dogsbodies and she was sick of it. She had wanted to review *The Golden Notebook* for them, but they wouldn't let her. They were interested only in theories and academic ideas.

We kept getting lost. It was late when we reached North Wales and Plas Penrhyn—hours later than we had said. Bertrand Russell and Lady Russell met us with cold formality. Of course they had consulted with Schoenman and been told not to trust us. At once Russell began remarking spitefully about how he did that journey from London in a couple of hours and he was surprised we were so incompetent. We went to the drawing room. Lady Russell was watching us as if we might be assassins or poisoners. Russell was like a vigorous old gnome. In fact, this old warhorse from a thousand political battles recognised me as another, and at once a certain joky polemical style imposed itself. My job, after all, was a pretty impossible one. The one thing I could not say was: 'You are being made use of by an unscrupulous young politico who is telling everyone in London that you do as he tells you.' I could not say, 'You are not being told the truth about what goes on.' And I did not know where Lady Russell was in all this. I could not say, 'There are people who think that your wife (sitting over there with that angry smile) conspires with Schoenman to keep you in the dark, but others think she is being manipulated too. Some believe she is like many younger wives with old husbands, trying to protect them.' I tried to make a joke of it all, saying that all those ignorant young neophytes out there in the Unilateral Nuclear Disarmament branches scarcely knew about Canon Collins or himself, and they were full of foolish idealism, just as we were, too, when young and unused to politics, and it would not do them any good to hear about all these fights going on between the Committee of a Hundred and its parent organisation. I dared to say that both he and Canon Collins were misreading the mood, or tone, or style of the new movement, which did not care about who led the thing, did not care about leaders.

And now I reached the main point: If his—Bertrand Russell's—statement accusing Canon Collins did come out in next Sunday's *Observer*, it would do great damage, it would disillusion hundreds of thousands of CND supporters, most of them very young. I had driven up to beg him to withdraw it, to make sure it would not be in the *Observer*. At once Russell became very rude and said I was misinformed, there was no statement, he knew nothing of any statement. Lady Russell also said there was no statement planned or drafted but she believed that at some point Collins should be exposed for what he was.

While this was going on we were being served sandwiches and coffee. Russell said he saw no point in continuing the discussion and that he was sure we must be tired. He would not be seeing us in the morning, but he would instruct the housekeeper to give us breakfast. Lady Russell and he escorted us to the bedroom, and the atmosphere was such that we would not have been surprised to find we were locked in. It was nine o'clock.

Poor Janet Hase did not deserve this unpleasantness, for after all, she had offered to drive me up out of kindness of heart. She was, I am sure, pretty depressed by it all, and if the nasty little trip contributed to her decision to leave Britain as soon as she could, then I didn't blame her.

Back we crawled to London next day, and I reported to Mervyn Jones that my attempt had been a failure. By then I was angry with myself for doing it all, for in fact it achieved nothing.

Next Sunday the *Observer* was due to come out with the two statements, Bertrand Russell accusing Canon Collins, Collins accusing Russell. That, at least, was how they would be read by the innocent masses. But this did not happen. The statements got lost, disappeared. And so the innocents never knew of all this dirty work and the competing of their leaders. Such is the nastiness left in my mind that even now I feel nervous for fear of arousing ancient sleeping dogs when I say I think Canon Collins was very much more sinned against than sinning and the faults on his side were not double-dealing and dirty tricks but—quite simply—not understanding how little interested were the rank and file in leaders and leadership. I was sorry for him.

The Committee of a Hundred flourished, attracted to itself people with a liking for 'direct action' or, in other words, confrontations with the police, and the parent organisation, CND, was weakened. The Aldermaston Marches continued, grew, became unwieldy, and dwindled. But while it is easy to say that a great popular movement weakens and fades *because* of this and that, I don't think we really understand the dynamics or know why a mass movement grows, does well, then fades. If now you say to people who supported the Committee of a Hundred that you think its influences were bad, the reply often comes: 'But it gave birth to the anti-Vietnam riots and marches in America.' It is true that one influenced the other, but to suggest that the Americans were not capable of giving birth to their own anti-war movements seems to me absurd.

Sometimes I meet people from the Direct Action days and ask how they saw Ralph Schoenman. Some say they admired him, others that he made them feel uneasy. The admirers on the whole were those for whom he was their first experience of politics. Yet surely the man was crazy; or if he was not, then his behaviour was. An important distinction, one that has to be made in politics, with such inspirational characters.* The thing is, people who are indeed frothing mad, if they are in political or religious contexts are not seen as mad. Yet if the same people were in a different context, it would be seen at once. But some people who are crazy drift towards political or religious movements where their craziness will not be seen, and whether they do this consciously or not surely doesn't matter. Some people know exactly what they do—Hitler, Stalin. Others, I think, find deep inclinations and tendencies they are hardly aware of blossoming in sympathetic atmospheres and are

*There were hundreds of thousands—millions?—of these saints of politics in the world then, stern, ruthless, military in style, each accompanied by the ghost of Lenin, that Perfect Man—each acting leading roles of heroic martyrdom in dramas written by Revolution Itself and running in their heads day and night like tapes that could not be turned off. Sometimes I wonder how these characters see it all now. Are they saying, 'I don't know what got into me'?

even terrified: I am pretty sure that many of the youngsters who went into the Committee of a Hundred for idealistic reasons were later appalled by what they found—in themselves as well as in others. We have forgotten the poisonous airs and atmospheres of then—just as we have forgotten the powerful idealism. This happens to be a mild, fairly nonpartisan, comparatively sane interregnum in the human story. To judge the fevers and accusations that then proliferated in and around the Committee of a Hundred means trying to revive that time: impossible.

How can one account for the fact that Bertrand Russell, a man who had been engaged in politics all his life, beginning with his brave stand against the militarism of the First World War, an experienced man, one who had known a hundred different types of politico, failed to see through a Ralph Schoenman? And refused to see the truth even when people were warning him, telling him exactly what was happening and how he was being used? Russell simply would not listen, not for a long time, and by then it was too late. People all this time were asking, was Ralph Schoenman in the pay of the CIA? The KGB? This was because of the damage he was doing. Now this seems pretty mad, but it wasn't then. Almost anyone could be accused of being in the pay of the CIA or the KGB, and of course some pretty unlikely people were.

There are all kinds of hazards and dangers associated with old age, but the one I think may be the worst of all is hardly noticed. It is what happens when an old person is confronted with a simulacrum of a youthful self, a mocking shadow, an echo of lost possibilities—and loses all moral independence.

Tolstoy lost his pride and his balance to Chertkov, a second-rate person who called himself the old man's disciple and told him what to think, whom to keep in his life, and whom to exclude.

Maxim Gorky allowed Pyotr Krychkov to run his life for him for years. He was paid by the KGB and was probably involved in Gorky's death. It seems that Gorky did in the end have his suspicions, but the question is, why surrender to such a man at all?

Jean-Paul Sartre gave himself up to Pierre Victor (or Benny Levy) at the end of his life, a young man who caricatured all his qualities so that even the good ones became monstrous. Meanwhile the French were saying, Our great Sartre is going the way of Bertrand Russell with Ralph Schoenman; it must be prevented. It wasn't.

There is an exception to this sad rule, but perhaps it is because here are not two men, an old one and a young man, but an old woman and a young man. The actress Louise Brooks, at the end of her life, was visited by young Kenneth Tynan, and there followed the most charming of friendships, tender, self-consciously whimsical, full of nostalgia for impossible loves.

Old friends, old comrades—old people generally—must beware that moment when appears a young person all shining eyes and 'I've always so much admired you.' Almost certainly no good will come of it.

Bertrand Russell had a serious problem apart from Ralph Schoenman: he was canonized, seen as this dear sweet old man, full of years and wisdom. The appetite for saints of either sex, gurus, wise women and men, is unappeasable, and this means that the most unlikely material becomes sanctified. I myself have had to fight off attempts to turn me into a wise old woman. All that happens is that disillusioned fans and disciples attack unfairly where once they unwisely venerated. This is what happened to Russell.

I was four years in Langham Street and have lively memories of it, quite unlike Warwick Road, which I try not to think of at all. This was not only because my life had become easier, with more money, less worry, and the beginnings of emotional freedom, but because the general atmosphere had lightened. War-damaged and darkened Britain was in another age and could be recalled only with an effort. Ten years had done it, and already there was a generation who did not know what you meant when you said bomb sites, cracking facades, dreary unpainted buildings; when you talked of Utility clothes, the awful food, undrinkable coffee, and people going to bed by ten in the evening. The new coffee bars were full of young people remaking the world, there were the first good cheap restaurants, and the clothes were youthful and inventive. All kinds of small, pleasant things were happening, unthinkable ten years before. For instance, a band called the Happy Wanderers played traditional jazz up and down Oxford Street, which made it a pleasure to go shopping. Window boxes and hanging baskets and decorous little trees in tubs were appearing in new-painted streets. Now it is acknowledged that the recovery of shattered Europe after that war was an economic miracle, for it was not only Britain that had bounced back but all the countries in Europe, some of them laid flat by war. From ruins and hunger to affluence in fifteen years, less, but living through it, we took it for granted, hardly noticed it, and needed to have it pointed out to us. As by Eric Hobsbawn's *Age of Extremes,* which I read amazed, thinking, But why were we not more aware of how well we were doing?

Once again a new age was upon us, and its most dramatic sign was the Russian sputnik (in Russian, the word means 'travelling companion, satellite, comrade'), for it was the first of the new technical apparitions in the sky, and a lot of people stayed up all night to catch a glimpse of it bowling past overhead. I was on the roof, hoping clouds would not obstruct. I didn't see it, but what elation, what pleasure, and feelings of achievement: we really did feel that this was a step forward for all humankind. The blackbirds sang. For some reason blackbirds loved that area, and their song at once brings back the dawns and evenings of Langham Street.

The roof was reached by a tricky little ladder. I sunbathed up there, using the shadow from chimneys to temper the heat. The short story 'A Woman on a Roof' comes from that time. It was another world, because I was not the only one to use the roofs; there were plants and little gardens and deck chairs. Over near the BBC, building was going on, and the great yellow machines clambered and swung halfway up the sky, and the men operating the machines waved at us, shouting invitations and compliments.

The little market in the street was only a couple of stalls but people came from the BBC to get vegetables. The sounds from the market, cries where the meaning had eroded, so they were like shouts from the past, when the streets were full of hawkers and vendors, led to a story, a mere breath of a story, 'A Room', that came from lying on my bed in the daytime behind the dark-blue curtains of thick soft cotton. Touching them reminded me that now we could buy such material, so recently not in existence. Lying there in the half dark, with the street cries in my ears, I fell into a dream and visited, or thought I did, that room as it had been in the dreadful threadbare cold poverty of the 1914–1918 war.

I went to the theatre a lot, meeting people there, often walking back alone afterwards from Shaftesbury Avenue, St. Martin's Lane, the Haymarket, even the Old Vic. There were people in the streets, enough to make a street companionship, though it wasn't as it is now, the streets of Central London filled with young people enjoying themselves and looking for adventure till long after midnight. It still did not occur to me to be nervous, walking at night, stopping to have a bit of a chat. 'What are you doing out so late, dear?'

'I've been to see Laurence Olivier in . . .'

'Have you, now? That's nice, then. Enjoyed it, did you?'

That was the time when Joan Littlewood was making theatre in Stratford East. I saw there productions more original, more brilliant, than any I had seen till then: standards of production have risen, partly due to her. The theatre was always nearly empty, had a dozen or twenty people in it, all of us Lefties who had made the trip from Central London. Joan's idea had been to make a theatre for the working people of the area, but they did not come. Joan was in those days a vociferous communist, or rather made loud communist noises. I do not find it easy to see her actually in the Party. The Party did not do more than tolerate her.

For a couple of years, a handful of us knew we were seeing the most extraordinary theatre in Britain, and then Kenneth Tynan saw some productions, told the *Observer* readers, and thereafter the tube train to Stratford, in London's East End, a tedious journey, was crowded with smart Londoners, and it was hard to get a ticket.

Joan Littlewood has never been given the credit she deserves. This is partly because of her loathing for the middle classes, who were in fact her supporters. She could not stop insulting the bourgeoisie, the establishment, the BBC, and the West End theatre and West End theatre audiences. It was a necessity for her, her style, her trademark. When she was on television, she dropped a handkerchief over the back of her chair and turned to reach over and get it, so that her bum was offered as an insult to the camera. Childish. But she had to do this kind of thing. And she was a great director, a great force in the theatre. She and her team were really a continuation of the old tradition of strolling players, and she had made theatre in provincial towns with no money, no resources: political theatre, satirical political morality plays, improvised theatre.

I was visited by Nelson Algren. According to the newspapers and general report, he was bitter about having been put into *The Mandarins,* Simone de Beauvoir's novel about post-war Paris, as the evasive American lover—straight from life. Surely this could not have been true, because when he was brought to my flat by Clancy, who had the air of a successful marriage broker, Nelson's smile was all bashful sexual willingness, like a very young bridegroom. Yet I was a writer, female, and on the left—surely poison? But there is another ingredient in this puzzling brew. London was then glamorous for Americans in a way it has not been since the sixties ended. Sometimes when I was being presented by a male American to another as a good thing: 'She's a real mensch, you know'—for a woman could be as much of a mensch as a man—I felt as if I was being seen as a kind of trophy, a valuable piece of Englishness. The fact is, he didn't really fancy me, nor I him, but we did like each other and spent several agreeable days together, he telling me about the experiences that made *The Man with the Golden Arm* and *A Walk on the Wild Side.* He made it all sound picaresque, and glamorous. In London he was in search of romantic poverty, intending to write about it. Where are your slums? he demanded. He went down to the East End with Clancy, but the old working-class communities had gone. Back he came, discontented, to me. He wanted to find the slums of Dickens's London, just as to this day people come hoping to encounter a real fog, a pea-souper, a London Particular, and are sad when they are told of the Clean Air Act. I explained to him that all along the streets of this area were extremely poor people, living in poor flats, even houses, but poverty in London was often concealed; a well-off house could be next door to one crammed with poor people. All he had to do was walk around a bit. He did, could not understand what he saw, so I went with him. 'Look—see that house? See that little street there?' But gone were the days when people starved in Britain, or lived on tea, dripping, cheap jam, and bread, and children were without shoes. He was looking for the dramatic and evident squalor of certain slums in America. The goodwill we did feel for each other had to overcome a very basic difficulty. By now I had come to think that romanticising poverty as a style—for it is often that—was most irritating and puerile. It goes on all the time. The middle classes have always adored squalor—*La Bohème,* for instance. Nelson's novels were above all a celebration of the romanticism of poverty, the drug culture, prostitution. At that very time the slummy townships of South Africa, truly horrible poverty and destitution, were giving certain people a pleasant frisson: exciting to think that the inhabitants of a slum like Alexandra township were every one gold-hearted prostitutes, cheeky child thieves without a care in the world, gamin guttersnipes, singing and dancing vagabonds.

I had an inspiration and sent him off to Glasgow, a long way still from the attractive city it is today, where the Gorbals were everything he had been looking for. So he was appeased. These days, he would find the drug culture and at once be at home. He had the stunned, effaced, subdued quality that we then associated with a certain kind of American, the result, we thought, of trying too hard to conform to an over-rigid society, but in his case it was drugs.

I have a difficulty. In Warwick Road and even more in Langham Street, I was meeting quantities of people who were well known or on their way to being so. I could easily make a list of names. Rather, Names. This would be the equivalent of that experience when someone says to me, 'I've met a good friend of yours.'

'Oh, who?' But I've no recollection of him or her.

'But he says he knows you well.' This person met me at a party for five minutes or was brought to my house by someone when there were a lot of people, and now he—or she—goes about, 'Oh yes, I'm a good friend of hers.' You become their possession, they know all about you. 'She told me that . . .' (It is precisely these people who are so ready with reminiscences when biographers are on the prowl.)

The important point, I think, is that there was more mixing between different kinds of people than there is now. Social life was more fluid. This was partly because of the Aldermaston Marches, where the most unlikely people met and mingled. If I made a list of people met on those marches, it would make a kind of Progressive Social Register. Would there be an equivalent now? Probably not. There was still that post-war effervescence, the feeling that suppressed energies were exploding, the arrival of working-class or at least not middle-class talent into the arts, and, above all, the political optimism, which has so completely evaporated.

I think the Aldermaston Marches have not been given enough attention, as a unique social phenomenon. Just consider: for half a dozen years, every year, in springtime, hundreds of thousands of people from all over Britain, Europe, America, even distant parts of the world, converged on Aldermaston and for four days walked to London, spending nights in schools and halls, welcomed or not by the towns or villages they came through, exciting the world's press, mostly to hostile reporting, making friends, learning, enjoying themselves—people who could never have met otherwise. Scientists and artists, writers and journalists and teachers and gardeners, politicians, every kind of person, met, walked together, talked—and often remained friends afterwards. Apart from war, what other social process could possibly create such a mingling of apparently incompatible people? To this day I meet people whom I walked with long ago on one of the marches, or who say, 'I met such and such a professor from an American university, and that is how I got to spend four years there.' Or, 'I met my wife on the 1959 March.'

For a time I saw a good bit of Joshua Nkomo, now a leader of Zimbabwe. He was putting in that obligatory term in London, for future African leaders, of hand-to-mouth living and fearful thoughts for the future. In his case with good reason, for he was to spend ten years in Southern Rhodesia in an internment camp as bleak and as awful, without books and newspapers, as a prison sentence on the moon. But now he was bemused by a new status: he was being described as a sell-out. This was because at the time, the Moral Rearmament people were wooing Africans who might turn out to be leaders, and he had spent some days at their headquarters in Caux, Switzerland. He could not see what was wrong with them. 'But they are good people. They were good to me. They treated me well. And I am religious too.' I explained to him the niceties of the situation. He said he hated politics. What he wished was that he could have his own store in his village and be with his family. He was homesick and cold and lonely in London. Joshua was not the only African leader who has confided to me this ambition. He was a great orator. This was how he had come to be absorbed into politics. I had heard of him long before, enthralling crowds from a soapbox in Bulawayo.

I was certainly not the only woman giving Joshua advice and support. We would ring each other up and consult over knotty points, the chief one being that we felt Joshua had not been framed by nature to be political. There have been times in my life when I would have seen this as a criticism, but now, not.

For instance, Joshua was being pursued by our secret services. He came to me in a panic to say he had been at a meeting and a man had accosted him, taken him aside into a private room, showed him a suitcase full of paper money, and said all that money would be his if Joshua would tell him everything he knew about the Arabs—the Arabs make another entrance, as improbably this time as the last. But Joshua had never met any Arabs. I told him our secret services were obsessed with Arabs. I had been suspected of dealings with Arabs, and I had never met any either. The trouble was, Joshua was desperately poor. To show him all that money was cruel. I said flippantly that he should take it and then deny he had ever had it. This joke showed how distant I was from his harsh realities: he was terrified. This agent, whoever he was, MI6 probably, turned up more than once, with promises of money, and with threats too.

Having conferred on the telephone with other mentors, I wrote to a friend for enlightenment. Now here comes a little tale that is as good as a whole lecture on national moralities. The father of my friend—we will call him John—had been undone by the slump in the thirties, and as a result John had had a fairly precarious boyhood. But he had got to public school. The war began, and, apparently casually, he met a school chum, who enquired if he, John, felt like being really useful to his country—instead of *merely* going into one of the armed services was implied. Believe it or not, John was told to go to a certain gentlemen's club at lunchtime with a rolled-up copy of the *Times* in his hand. His interlocutor made no enquiries about his politics, which were on the extreme left, though whether this meant a Party card, I don't know. John served as a spy during the war, with distinction. But then many men with his background worked for the Security Services, and many were communists or fellow travellers. After the war John became a critic of the British Empire in all its manifestations and an expert on Africa. I had got to know him as a comrade-in-arms during campaigns about ending colonialism. I wanted to know why poor Joshua was being singled out like this. Was it right that some unfortunate black political exile should be persecuted by the secret services and his life made miserable by bribes of suitcases full of money? And what was all this about Arabs?

John went off to consult with his proper allegiances, the spymasters, and asked them what he should do, and the letter I got might have been framed by the senior head of department in the Ministry of Circumlocution. It said nothing at all, but nothing; it was a masterpiece of non-communication, and I kept it for years, reading it from time to time with awe for its skills. I lost it in one of my many moves. Its equivalent in a parallel area would go something like this:

'You say that the police have been harassing the family at X Street, but firstly, we cannot find X Street on the map, and secondly, what is your evidence? We have no information that supports your accusation, which is in any case improperly framed. As you know, it is our policy to treat all the citizens in this country equally, and as it is not possible for a black citizen to be singled out for this kind of treatment, your queries remain without validity.'

The Arab connection remains a mystery to this day.

Joshua was having lunch with me, and while we were discussing the ways of this great country of ours, he said, 'You are a good cook, girl. I want you to be my woman. And it is convenient not to have to explain African politics to you.'

'But I have a man already,' I said.

Joshua laughed. He was a very large, likeable man, with a good deep laugh which really did shake his whole body. 'Then give him the sack and take me instead,' he said.

This romantic offer was made to at least two of the other advisers—the ones I consulted with—in the same words and in the same circumstances, that is, over a good meal.

Soon I saw no more of Joshua, because he was swept up into the politics of exile. I did go and hear him speak, though. What an orator! What a magnifico! A spellbinder if there ever was one. And then came the years of exile, inside his own country, from everything good and kind and pleasant and decent, in the internment camp which was like being on the moon. This brutal treatment stands to the account of Ian Smith.

One visitor deserves special mention. He was a witch from Brighton, a town for some reason always a favourite haunt of witches. A white witch, he insisted; I really must understand that there were good and bad witches, and he was a male witch, not a warlock, for that was a very different thing. He had a serious problem. He needed to have sex with a virgin to further his spiritual development, but he could not find a girl who was a real virgin, immaculate, with a pristine hymen. He had looked everywhere in Britain for one. I enquired, 'But how do you go about this? Do you go about asking girls, Have you an intact hymen?'

'They're so ignorant about their bodies they wouldn't know what a hymen was. No, you don't understand. If you speak frankly and honestly to someone, they treat you the same way. I explain my situation and they listen and I ask some questions, but then I see that they aren't real virgins.' He was a lean, dun-coloured man with flattish colourless hair, and greenish eyes fixed not on the face of his interlocutor—me, several times, over a period of months— but off to one side as he frowned at the difficulties of his situation. This was a tormented man. He never smiled. God forbid that I should laugh or smile. Despairing of ever finding a real virgin in England, he went to Ireland, where he said the Irish girls were full of a fresh and natural attitude to sex long lost in this country. There he found a fourteen-year-old virgin, in County Clare. He intended to marry her and told her so, saying she must keep herself untouched for him, because legally they could not marry until she was fifteen. He said to her, 'Don't you go spoiling yourself down there. Keep your hands off. It's a tragedy: girls don't realise it, but you have a treasure; it is a pearl beyond price, and you treat it as if it's just a piece of flesh.' A long, long time to wait, he complained, on a visit—or two, or three—sitting there all fretful impatience, a knee jerking, fingers a-fiddle with a button or his tie, for he was always properly dressed and clean and respectable. The law was stupid. Girls should be allowed to marry on the onset of menstruation. In the old days they knew better. Girls married at twelve or thirteen, as nature intended.

He was very busy, being convener of his coven and adviser to them all on emotional and magical matters. He could not visit Ireland as often as he wanted. Kept in Brighton by witching pressures, he sent his best friend over to County Clare to tell the girl to hold on, time was passing, if slowly, and soon . . . Yes, the classic tale was told again, and he came to see me, all bitterness and betrayal. 'And he's not a witch, he's not one of us, it makes no difference to him if he has sex with a virgin. And it wasn't even serious, it was just an affair, and she's going to university next year.'

This was not his only obsession. He wanted to have sex with little girls: this was not part of his search for a virgin, since little girls were of no use for his road to spiritual development. 'Everyone can see what little girls want,' he said. 'Even a child of five or six, she'll stand there pointing her wee-wee at you, wriggling about, asking for it. Well, if that isn't what they are asking for, what, then?' he demanded, but never looking directly at me, always off somewhere, at a wall where perhaps his fantasies were projected, and meanwhile his aggrieved voice went on . . . and on: 'You can see what they want, but if you lay a finger on them, it's prison.'

I don't know what happened. I never saw his name in the newspapers. Sometimes I wonder, does this sad soul, now at least seventy years old, between nights of dancing naked on the downs under the moon, still pursue his dream up and down the British Isles and Ireland? 'Are you a virgin? Will you keep yourself for me?' . . . Don't you *see,* if you put something to someone fair and square, she always understands.

Now here is a real difficulty. There is a general agreement that sexual liberation began in the sixties. Philip Larkin the poet said it: Sex began in '63. He said it sarcastically, though when he is quoted, that seems to be forgotten. I meet people who say how repressed, how sex-frightened they were in the fifties, and if I tell my little tale about the white witch in search of a virgin, they are incredulous. But I don't remember any seasons of denial, people hovering timidly around beds fenced with prohibition. During the war, of course, sex flourished, because in wartime it always does, but it was romantic, because of imminent and possibly deadly partings. And in the fifties everyone seemed to be at it. 'Then that must have been your lot in London,' come the protests. 'Oh, if only I'd been the right age for the sixties. I spent all my time dreaming about girls.' Or men, as the case might be.

The novels of that time from the provinces—always an accurate picture of the times—don't record sexual dearth.

The whole thing is a mystery to me. Some things have to remain mysteries. I can only record that people seemed to be having a pretty good time: joy was unconfined—if joy is the right word, but of that later.

My most improbable visitor was Henry Kissinger. It was like this. Wayland Young,* still a long way from becoming Lord Kennet, had become a kind of liaison between the American Left and the British Left. This was probably because he had appeared in so many newspaper photographs on the Aldermaston Marches, for no one could resist this attractive family—handsome Wayland, his lovely wife, all the pretty children—so democratically marching with the multitudes. Henry Kissinger wanted to meet representative members of the Campaign for Nuclear Disarmament. Most of the Left were busy with an election. I had said finally and firmly, No, I will not canvass for the Labour Party, beg money for good causes, sell the *New Left Review,* make speeches ('Whither the Left?' or 'What Price Britain?'). My job in this world is to write, and if you don't like it you can lump it. I had fought that battle in Salisbury, South-

*Wayland Young was then a well-known journalist.

ern Rhodesia, against much tougher opponents than anything London could come up with. So I was free to see Kissinger. I was not an adequate representative of the New Left but was of the Campaign for Unilateral Nuclear Disarmament (these were not distinctions likely to impress an American, for whom then we were all communists anyway). And Henry Kissinger might be German—for it was a healthy young German who bounded up those hideous cement stairs and into the flat—but he was also a crew-cut prosperous American, who seemed too large and fresh and glistening for these unattractive surroundings. It is hard to convey the flavour of this encounter, because the atmosphere of that time is now so utterly gone. This is always the difficulty, trying to record the past. Facts are easy: this and that happened; but out of the context of an atmosphere, much behaviour—facts—social and personal, seems, simply, lunatic. While the Cold War had become muted in Britain—mostly because the new youth thought it silly, and anyway the Cold War had never been as deadly in Britain—in the States it was still at its height. Americans leaving their homeland for political reasons described what was happening, and the British young found it all incredible. The Communist Party in the States was always tiny, and its thoughts and feelings did not emanate far outside it, but in Europe 'everyone' had been a communist or been in a communist ambience. To have been a communist but not now to be one was normal and described most of the people one met. But the Americans have never understood this. Now, when you read accounts of Edgar Hoover of the FBI or Angleton of the CIA, it is evident that these gentlemen were fighting windmills, because they knew nothing of how ordinary communists thought and behaved. That is the most striking thing now about that time. Day and night, week in, week out, Hoover and his henchmen, Angleton and his, fought the enemy communism but would not have recognised a communist if they had met one. In Europe there were a thousand shades and degrees of opinion, of experience. In Europe, to say, But I ceased to be a Communist because of The Purges . . . the Stalin-Hitler Pact . . . the invasion of Finland . . . the Show Trials in Czechoslovakia . . . the suppression of the uprising in Berlin . . . in Hungary—all this was a Via Dolorosa well understood by everyone, but as far as the Americans were concerned, once a Red, always a Red.

Henry Kissinger reminded me of Eysenck of that Oxford lecture now so long ago. He had a thick German accent, he radiated energy and decision—and, too, wariness and disapproval. As far as the U.S. papers were concerned, the entire movement for nuclear disarmament was communist, and to say to him that only a tiny minority of members was communist was mere hair-splitting.

Our conversation soon crystallised around one word. He said that a nuclear weapon had been evolved which could be accurately targetted to kill a hundred thousand people. He called it a 'kitten bomb'. He kept using the phrase, kitten bomb. I was shocked and said that anyone who could use the word 'kitten' to describe such a weapon of war showed a lack of moral feeling and sensitivity and that just about summed everything which was wrong with American foreign policy. He said I was sentimental and unrealistic and understood nothing about *Realpolitik*. We were not quarrelling: to quarrel with someone, you have to have something in common. I experienced him as a harsh, abrasive, aggressive force, terrifying because of what he represented, and he experienced me as a sanctimonious wincing idiot who was using the language of humanism in the service of world communism. This encounter lasted about an hour and confirmed the worst prejudices we had about each other.

In fact, I admired the man for making the attempt. No other conservative American tried to understand the enemy—the Left. And it was brave. Kissinger had not yet achieved the summits of his success, but he had a lot to lose. I could just imagine the headlines in the States: 'Kissinger Under the Influence of the Kremlin.' 'Communism Corrupts Kissinger.' 'The Communist Trojan Horse and Kissinger.' No, I certainly do not exaggerate. How to convey now the lunacies of that time? The nearest to it is what we see when reports come from inside movements of the Muslim hardliners: a dark unreason, a murderous hate of the unknown. That is how Americans saw communism, whether in or out of the communist countries. And that is how large numbers of Europeans, whether left-wing or not, saw the States. A violent and terrifying unreason.

* * *

Another American sent to visit me by Wayland Young was William Phillips, he who had founded the *Partisan Review* in the thirties and edited it ever since. He had a wistful admiration for the British New Left, seeing them as a movement which might succeed in creating a socialist Britain. He became and has remained a good friend. The irony was that once I had been a Stalinist. He had been more of a Trotskyist, and in the States had fought the Stalinists, a battle which from the outside seemed like a spotlit bout between combatants inside a very small ring. Ancient differences seemed irrelevant now: ancient differences came so soon to seem irrelevant.

The *Partisan Review* began essentially as an organ of the anti-Stalinist Left and has always conducted the most passionate political polemics, but from the start it had another face. Some of the best and best-known American writers and poets were first published in the *Partisan Review,* and contributors from abroad too. That is why I read the *Partisan Review*—and still read it. And it was why many British people read it, those from the Left and people who were not at all socialist. I would glance through the polemics—feeling that I ought to be interested—to get to the literature.

William Phillips was a dry, well-read, ironic man, very American but fed as much from Europe. Long years later, when I confessed that I had never been really interested in the politics of the *Partisan Review,* I think he was disappointed. But the fact is, again and again in my lifetime, the vicious vituperations, the polemics, the dialectics, the sophistries, of politics have become vapour and mist, while what remains is the literature and the art, which at the time might have been merely tolerated by the politicos.

J. P. Donleavy was around and about in London in those days, the author of the scandalous *The Ginger Man,* yet another incarnation of the irreverent out-to-shock maverick, in the line of *Lucky Jim* and of *Hurry on Down,* but Donleavy, with a fine feeling for the unexpected, presented himself like a duke in exile, a grave, mournful, elegant man who with Murray Sayle enlivened our days with tales of improbable adventure. I remember him best for the tenderest little moment. It is early evening, the starlings are squealing around the roofs, and Donleavy drops in. He has been at the BBC, where he had felt an impulse to salute a muse, in my person. 'Oh, sit down, have a drink—my Muse is exhausted for today.' He indicated a carrier bag, which had in it four large bottles of milk stout. 'Good Lord, you haven't taken to tippling milk stout?'

'No, I'm on my way home, to take these to the wife. Any woman who has had to spend the day with the babbies needs her milk stout, and if there was such a thing as milk of ambrosia I'd buy it for her, every day, the poor, poor woman. And she'll be in need of some civilised conversation when the babes are in bed.'

Murray Sayle sometimes dropped in, for as with all natural entertainers, there were times when he had to have an audience. Once, he telephoned to say it was an urgent matter, and when he arrived it turned out that he had just turned thirty. We sat in a pub garden—at any rate, out-of-doors somewhere—for most of the day, while he explained to me that women had no idea of what a terrible thing it was for a man to be thirty. It was the end of youth. I am sure I was sympathetic, for his distress was real, even if he was being, as ever, very funny. Only afterwards did it occur to me that I had just become forty, and I had not thought to apply to him or anyone else for sympathy. I did not say, 'Damn it, Murray, what are your sorrows compared to mine?'

And so, too, with Kenneth Tynan, by whom I was summoned to mourn the passing of time. We sat in his flat most of the day, while his secretary brought this and that in the way of restoratives, and Ken said he was thirty but had already reached the summits of achievement, being a theatre critic for the *Observer*. At first I thought he was mocking himself, as he so often did, but no, he meant it. I did suggest that there surely were other summits he might aim for, while we exchanged words but not feelings, for there are times when the little horizons of the British simply stun observers into a sort of despair. He meant it; he meant every word: He saw himself as a brilliant projectile hurled against the philistinism of the British theatre but already falling back, having reached too high too soon.

Was I a particular friend of Ken's? I never thought so, but that was because his guard was so perfect, the glitter of wit, and you did not feel you had got any closer to him. I had to deduce that I must be in some special niche, perhaps as a kind of elder sister, for several times he called me over for what he probably thought of as a heart-to-heart.

Ken lived in Mayfair, in Mount Street, with Elaine Dundy, his then wife. The flat was decorated in what I thought was bathetic chic. The wallpaper was Bosch's *Garden of Earthly Delights,* and there was a chair covered in fake tiger skin. The flat was often full of the currently trendy. If you went to a party there, everybody was in the news or reflected some kind of fame. People who have to collect the well known are in fact suffering from insecurity, but I didn't see that then.

I always found Ken fragile, vulnerable, like an elegant grey silky moth, with his large prominent greeny eyes and his bony face. He was tall and much too thin. I wanted to put my arms around him and say, There, there. Hardly appropriate for a young king of the theatre. People were afraid of him, because he had such power. I enjoyed his wit but thought his judgements too often pulled out of good sense by dogma. He was archetypically that character who liked to shock by saying he was a communist or a Marxist, while he would rather die than actually join the Party. These people always have a kind of political innocence, or ignorance, because their thoughts are all in the air—are never brought down to earth. For instance, Athol Fugard, who is one of the original playwrights of our time, did not fit into Ken's political agenda. There were other mistakes too. But Ken's theatre writing was brilliant, it coruscated, and there has been nothing like it since.

When you met him at a party or somewhere, he would deliver himself of some witticisms, but with difficulty, because of his stutter and his hoarse breathing, while he watched your face for the reaction. He might explain he had been polishing them up that day, because 'you mustn't think that wits like me and Oscar Wilde don't have to work at it.'

Ken's marriage with Elaine Dundy was ending, in sound and fury, often conducted in restaurants, so you might see Ken at one table, white-faced and bitter but full of the energy of battle, hurling reproaches at Elaine at another table. She was more than able to hold her own.

He enjoyed the public show of himself, like an extension of theatre. He was a public man. Often when he telephoned me I knew I had had a good review or at least was in the newspapers. I was critical about it then, but now we take that kind of thing for granted, for we are more and more manipulated from outside. Fans may write, 'I loved that book,' or unfriends, 'I hated that book,' but usually it is, 'I saw that review.' The stimulus is the review, not the book.

Ken went off to New York, and for six weeks I was theatre critic for the *Observer*, to be succeeded by the next on the list of his friends whom he had designated to hold the fort until he came back. I enjoyed the experience, mostly because of seeing plays I normally wouldn't see. I had had no idea of the variety of plays on. And that was long before the fringe theatre, theatre in pubs, shows of all kinds in pubs. Some kinds of plays seem to have disappeared, a certain kind of farce, for instance, like the Whitehall farces, skilful, brilliant theatre. I suppose those audiences now would be satisfied with television. There were not nearly as many musicals. I came out of the experience with the conclusion that some critics did not review plays according to their class and kind, but patronised plays that were good of their sort though not for highbrow audiences. Surely it is not helpful to review something like *Carry on, Nurse* as if it were a failed attempt at *Hedda Gabler*.

Ken was heartbreaking. When he died so horribly, and so much too young, of emphysema, my feelings about his always ominous brilliance turned out to be justified, but that was hardly a consolation. There are people whose deaths leave an unfillable empty space.

John Osborne. He was as much involved with a disintegrating marriage as was Ken. I was at a restaurant dinner with John, Mary Ure, and . . . who? There was a fourth. John sniped steadily through the meal at beautiful Mary, who was in tears. Just like Jimmy Porter and Alison, whom Mary had recently been playing.

I knew three of John's wives, Penelope Gilliatt better than the others. At a certain dinner at the Gilliatt flat in Mayfair, there was John Osborne, his mistress Jocelyn Rickards, Ken Tynan, and one of his mistresses. Clancy was there too: though we had broken up, we were often asked together. Clancy, for a while, was part of fashionable London, whether he likes it or not. The Gilliatt marriage was breaking up, the Osborne marriage had broken up. Penelope was more than pretty, she was beautiful, your classic red-haired beauty: milky skin, green eyes, slinky figure. John was in love with her the way some men are in love, as if they are preparing for a session at the dentist. Doctor Gilliatt I liked very much and admired: he was a quiet man, watching his wife being charmed away from him but not showing what he felt.

It was at that meal that Penelope congratulated me on my enterprise in going 'to get material' for *In Pursuit of the English,* which had recently come out. I said I hadn't been getting material, it was necessity. I had had no money to speak of, a small child, and the only people prepared to take me in with a small child was that warm-hearted Mediterranean household. Penelope had always been rich. I was angry: the moment epitomised one of the reasons I sometimes felt uncomfortable in these circles and why I felt at home with, let's say, the new young people at the Royal Court: none of them would have needed to have it explained to them.

Later I knew Jill Bennett too. I thought then, and think now, that any woman allowing herself to be in love with John Osborne must be crazy. Yet all his women were remarkable, and all mourned him when he ditched them. My judgements are those of the noncombatant. With me he was never anything but courteous and kind. Affable, that is the word. Magnanimous in his judgements. Gentleman John, that was his real nature—and then something deep and spiteful forced him into venom.

I felt kin to John because of that pain of his, like an abscess deep within. I understood the throb of anguish, making you irritable. I went to dinner with John two or three times at Jocelyn Rickards's house. It was after Mary Ure but before Penelope Gilliatt. This leads me to the reflection that the reigns of mistresses are often more secure than those of wives. At least, Jocelyn was the only one of his women he was complimentary about after he had broken with her. Tony Richardson was there. This was the time of Woodfall Productions. They were working on their films and spent a lot of time together. The two men were irritable, affectionate, competitive, and in any gathering were the centre because of the electricity they engendered. In his memoirs John called it a *mariage blanc,* but I thought they were like brothers, and as with siblings, behind everything said or not said were suggestions of long, intense entwined experience. Yet they had not known each other long. How precarious, chancy, and brief those friendships were: looking back, what I see is how we were all being blown together into quick, intense, trustful comradeship, as if we were members of an extended family, and then a shift of the kaleidoscope, and for no reason at all—apparently—new arrangements of people. I used to meet John here and there, with Penelope, with Jill Bennett. He went in for ambiguous postcards: he sent me several, I think after Penelope but before Jill, or perhaps it was after Jill but before his final wife. They beckoned you forward but at the same time slapped you back. For instance, the picture of a grim seaside street with Bed-and-Breakfast houses that had 'Vacancies' on them, or 'To Let'. He wrote, 'I wish you were here.' A couple of kisses, but at first glance you might think they were crosses on graves. Unsigned. Or, 'J.' Then, 'Why haven't you rung?' Speech after long silence. I did nothing about it. I was very fond of John. But if there was ever a man who needed allowances made, attention paid, constant vigilance for fear you might say something he would find wounding, it was John, and I was so beset by burdens of all kinds then that it was all too much of a good thing. I have said that I was born with skins too few, but John seemed to have no defences at all. He reminded me of a young dog who has been badly treated. It bravely confronts the world, licks your hand, is grateful for a caress, but its hide is shivering and shrinking when a hand comes too close, away from a possible blow. I used to dream about John for years. Now, those were interesting dreams. Straightforward sexual dreams are not interesting; you wake and think, Oh, one of those. But there is a kind of dream about a man that is affectionate, friendly, and with a flicker of amorousness, like old lovers meeting, and there is regret and humour and charm. Charm—the main thing; landscapes that seem to smile; nothing to do with ordinary life.

Two stories came out of that time. 'Between Men', which later made a brilliant half-hour television play, very funny, and won a prize, and 'The Side Benefits of an Honourable Profession'.

I found all these fashionable Lefties irritating, no matter how much I liked them personally. There is such a thing as revolutionary snobbishness: What right have you to call yourself, etc. They had all put on Marxism like the latest jacket and enjoyed themselves shocking people. They knew nothing of the history of communism and would not listen to anyone who had actually been in the Party.

They were romantics, sentimental. Tears came into their eyes at any number of heartbreaking themes. There was a novel about poverty in southern Italy by Carlo Levi, called *Christ Stopped at Eboli*. It was always in a prominent position on Tony Richardson's desk. Ken Tynan was deeply moved by Dr. Schweitzer, as everyone was then. I did remark that people like Schweitzer had worked, were working, in hospitals up and down Africa without anyone noticing them, but we need a figurehead, an exemplar; a multiplicity of admirable people is too much for us. Some humble doctor, or a nun, or a missionary, working in a bare and ill-equipped hospital in the bush for years, unfunded, isolated—no excitement in that. We need Dr. Schweitzer to turn his back ostentatiously on European delights. All over India, so I am told, people work in intolerable conditions relieving poverty, but it takes Mother Teresa to make our eyes fill with tears.

An incident sums it all up for me. A group of theatre notables, all Lefties, were taken to Germany to meet and mingle with the Brecht Ensemble. The Wall was built by then. They were taken there by a woman who had left Germany as a child refugee. Her relatives were dead or had suffered under Hitler: her whole life had been wrenched off course by Hitler and then Stalin. There did come a moment when it occurred to them that this underling, this nonentity of a PR girl, was a full representative of the tragedies of

Europe. 'You haven't been back to Germany since you left as a refugee?'

'No, this is the first time. I haven't had the money,' said she. Their faces, she said, froze over. It was too much for them to take in, she said. They didn't know how to cope with the real thing, a real victim, a survivor. And that was that; they continued to treat her as they had been doing, a useful employee.

An odd thing happened with Lindsay Anderson. We hadn't met for some time, and he rang to say there was something urgent. He and David Storey had been working on the film script of *This Sporting Life* for a year, and they were stale. Would I read the novel and see what I thought? I read it overnight and in the morning telephoned to say I was excited by it. Lindsay came with three big folders—three scripts. He did not want me to do an original script; I was to read the three failed scripts and then cobble together a new one from them. I had a week to do this. I was angry: surely this was as unprofessional as one could get. If he had told me I would have to hash three botched scripts into one, I would have said no from the start. And I was disappointed, because by now the tale had taken hold of me. But no one was ever angry with Lindsay for long. Lovable, that is what he was, always, even when he got ill and old and unreasonable, for as with many of us, his failings were concentrated by age. Liking Lindsay was a spikey business. He was another who long ago had been deeply and irrevocably hurt. He said it was his public school, about which he was bitter. He jested about it, but jokes don't cure wounds.

On the rare occasions when we met, we argued. Of all the fashionable Lefties, I found him the most exasperating. Every second person mentioned was a 'sell-out'. Sell-out from what, to what? No one, and certainly not Lindsay, could ever say. This was a fashionable cant word for years. There are phrases that seem designed to stop thought, and 'sell-out' is one. Another one is 'committed', which was much in vogue. It meant someone who supports the same political aims or actions. Another was 'cause'. It has moralistic overtones, for a Cause is by definition good. 'Fascist' has only quite recently gone. Meaning anyone even vaguely right-wing.

There were dozens of cant words from the Soviet Union. For a time Edward Thompson, John Saville, and the rest of us were 'revisionists', meaning that we were deviants from the Party Line, were seen as having tried to change the Party Line, which had to be the correct one. Another of their words was 'correct'.

I liked the film★ *This Sporting Life* when it came out, but thought it did not make enough of the pride of body, physical pride, of young working-class men who see themselves at a peak of their lives and ahead of them nothing but a descent into grey ordinariness.

Reuben Ship was now married to Elaine Grand. She had been the 'glamour girl' of early Canadian television. She was like Lucille Ball and Lana Turner, with round tight bottom (or ass), tight pert protruding breasts, a friendly, sisterly sexiness. For a while Canadian and American young women coming over here looked like this, but then the sixties demanded new body shapes: combative, confrontational. Most of the Canadian community had changed partners. Reuben was an extraordinarily nice man ... do I mean 'good'? No. He had a dimension to him, a humanity. There are plenty of people you can say anything to when current tolerances allow a particular theme, but there is no echo back from their experience or their imaginative comprehension. With Reuben you could say anything and be understood. One reason I enjoyed visiting him was because he liked Peter and was kind to this boy so desperate for a father.

Reuben was unlucky in his timing. He wrote some film scripts, and they got made, one with Norman Wisdom, but his talent was for angry satire, as with *The Investigator,* and he was too early for the satire revolution of the sixties. He died of drinking too much, but I don't know if that was over disappointment about his work.

When Peter was away at school, then Reuben and Elaine were free to pursue their plans to get me married. I might find waiting apprehensively as I entered their place in Chelsea that male guest the spare or single woman finds so often—not as much now as

★This film was one of the new wave of British films of the time: Tony Richardson, Lindsay Anderson, Karel Reisz.

then. But unattached women make even close friends nervous. They tried to match me with visiting Canadians or Americans. At the first possible moment, I would whisper to him, 'It's all right—I don't want to get married.' Then we became like two children who have a secret from the grown-ups. 'What's the joke?' Meanwhile the two intended sat side by side, looking guilty, but pleased with themselves.

One of the men they inveigled me to meet is memorable for reasons that even at the time seemed alarming. He had been left a widower with a very small daughter, aged two or three. He would describe to me how they slept in the same bed, and he made sure she was familiar with his body and encouraged to examine his private parts and even play with them. 'She's never going to suffer from penis envy', he would say, proud of himself for defying obscurantism. I suggested that this practice might have unforeseen results, such as that later she might never be able to free herself from him to love someone else. He was disappointed at my lack of real insight. He was a large hairy sorrowful man, heavy in speech and thought, and imprisoned by Freud. We were spectacularly ill suited, and our private agreement not to be afraid of each other's matrimonial intentions had more than the usual force.

There was another young widower. His wife had died suddenly, and it was generally agreed that he should remarry as soon as possible. This was foolish, for he was pulverised by grief and in shock. I fell in love with him. Not too much, though. Enough to overthrow common sense. I actually moved down to stay with him in his house in Chelsea, a pretty bijou little place which had in it a beautiful red setter, badly missing its mistress, and cupboards full of the dead woman's clothes. Again I was being dragged along by an undertow, a continuation of the dragging will-lessness of after Clancy. Actually it was the end of something, the end of passivity.

He worked for the *Daily Express:* I was suddenly in a world so distant from mine that it was like walking into the pages of a novel. His friends went to the races, bet on horses, had favourite pubs, and were all right-wing. At the *Express* he was a promising young man, watched by superiors, and particularly the big boss himself. If Beaverbrook liked an article, he would send round a hundred pounds by messenger. This lordly behaviour amused me, but the aspirant apprentice loved it. He also worked, but I've forgotten why or how, for Bernstein, at Granada Television. He liked being in this position, the favourite son of powerful men. One night, at about three in the morning, the telephone rang. Bernstein. There was to be a strike next day at Granada, and Bernstein was outraged, but more incredulous. 'How can they do this to me?' he kept demanding. 'Don't they love me?' *Don't they love me*—ever the cry of the despot. I listened to my—temporary—love: 'Yes, of course they admire you, we all do.' This was not how Bernstein was being seen then, but women often have a worm's-eye view of history. Bernstein is another who has been unjustly forgotten. He set out to raise the level of television programmes, and he did. None of our present television moguls have it in them to be as adventurous and courageous as Granada Television was then.

There was a moment when my situation came home to me. There I was, in Chelsea, surrounded by shopping women, in the middle of the morning, taking the dog for a walk. What the hell did I think I was doing? *What was all this about?* I broke it off and went home. He was too armoured by real grief to be much hurt by this. As for me, I had come to the conclusion that I had become a falling-in-love junkie. What I had become addicted to was the condition of being in love—a high, a fix. That is, the mild intoxications, nothing to do with really being in love. How was it I hadn't seen this before? All I needed to do was to look at some things I had written, for instance, 'The Habit of Loving'. That was written because I had been trying to repeat the experience with Jack, but blindly fluttering about and blundering, and backing out again.

It was a shock to me—a real one—this experience. Truly the end of something. I wrote 'How I Finally Lost My Heart'. Then I went back to *The Golden Notebook,* assembling it from the material already more or less organised in my mind.

★　　　★　　　★

I wrote a good deal in that flat, mostly *The Golden Notebook* and *Landlocked*. Up I got in the morning. I dragged on trousers and shirt or sweater. I brushed my hair, cleaned my teeth, made tea. Cup after cup of tea all morning and all afternoon, interrupted by little sessions of restoring sleep. Sometimes I wrote off and on all day. Sometimes thousands of words, or perhaps all the day's work landed in the waste-paper basket. In the evenings, exhausted, a slump in front of the television, or I walked by myself through the streets. Week after week. Not very exciting, the life of a working writer. It went on for a year or so, but whenever Peter came home, with a friend, I took them off down to Cornwall. The flat was too small for the energies of teenage boys.

Sometime during this period were two experiences with doctors, not without relevance to the theme of passivity.

I am lying in bed in one of our most prestigious teaching hospitals, for a gynaecological check-up. I am always tired, and it is thought the condition of my womb may be the reason. There are twelve women on the beds, and we are waiting for the consultant. On the bed next to mine a woman lies rigid, miserably trying to repress sobs. A young nurse is keeping an eye on us. The great man enters, followed by a dozen or so very young men. He uses the cold sarcastic voice: to hear it is to shrivel. He starts at the bed next to mine. 'I've told you before, Mrs.—what's her name?—Mrs. Jones, there's nothing wrong with you. You've got to get your husband in to see me. He's the reason you don't conceive. Have you told him that?'

'He gets so angry,' weeps the woman.

'He gets angry, does he? Then why are you wasting my time? And public money? Do you know what you are costing the tax-payer? No? Then you should.' The cold drawling voice goes on. 'Don't come here again, Mrs. . . . . Tell him he's got to come.'

'But he won't come, Doctor,' she wails.

'That's your problem, isn't it, not mine.'

Meanwhile I am observing that the young nurse is embarrassed. And I am thinking, Surely I'm not going to be expected to open my legs in front of all these pimply youths? It had not occurred to me this could happen. Dedicated though I was to the repudiation of prudery, this was going too far. The young students are already self-conscious, grinning, sharing looks. I am the youngest woman in this ward. The nurse has in her hand a cloth or napkin about two feet square. What is she going to do with it? She twitches down the blanket covering my lower body as the doctor arrives at the foot of the bed. He is looking at his notes; then he glances up at me. 'Do you expect me to instruct my students while your legs are crossed?' The nurse hisses, 'Open your legs,' and holds up in front of my face the scanty cloth. 'Don't waste my time, Mrs. . . .,' says the doctor. I open my legs, though I know I should leap up, strike him, shout abuse at the ogling students. I do none of these things. 'Here we have an example of a perfect multiparia,' says the doctor. 'Three children . . .' He consults the notes. 'Yes, three. Pity we don't see more like this.' Then he stands square on his planted legs like Cecil Rhodes staring north at the continent of Africa from Cape Town, and raises his voice and says to the ward generally: 'You should have your children young. That's what nature wants. The reason you've got all these female troubles is because you don't have your babies young enough.' He strolls on, with his tumescent acolytes. I could have killed him, of course, but the pathetic railings and accusations of the cowardly victim always remain unvoiced. The nurse, ashamed and on my side, as scornful of the two-foot-square napkin as I am, says in a low voice, 'Better get yourself dressed. You're fine.' She goes quickly to the woman in the next bed, now weeping uncontrollably. 'Shhhhh . . . ,' she says. 'Go and get dressed. I'll bring you a cup of tea. His bark is worse than his bite.' We two trail off dismally to the cubicles. As I dress, I hear her collapse in an abandon of grief. I see through the curtain that she is lying on an examination bed, her arm across her face. Her noisy sobs are affecting everyone. I feel myself churning with angry emotions. How could I let myself be so bullied? *Why?* What was it about doctors that made me so helpless?

Before I left Salisbury for London, during that long bad time that seemed as if it could never end, I complained to a friend, a doctor, of feeling tired. You might have bilharzia, said he. He was an expert on bilharzia. One of the symptoms is lethargy and tiredness. Let us call him Matthew. When we first knew him, he was just a beginning doctor, but success and his patients had given him a slow, magisterial manner. We teased him about it. He tested me for bilharzia. Negative. Now, you can get bilharzia through the pores of your skin, the slightest contact with infested water can do it, and I had been in and out of water all my childhood. No, I had not swum in a stagnant pool full of the weed where the snails clung, but I might have put hands and feet into it, since in those days it was believed that bilharzia entered only through the urethra. It was the most likely thing in the world that I had bilharzia. A negative test did not mean I didn't have it, said Matthew. The treatment then was long and nasty: for at least a month, daily injections of antimony. Most of the black population had bilharzia, one of the endemic diseases in Africa. When the long and painful treatment was over, the sufferer was bound to get it again, if he or she lived in the country, as most did, because the rivers and pools where they all washed and drew water were full of bilharzia. These days a couple of pills do it—you're cured, just like that. I said I couldn't really face a month of injections, but Matthew said he had just evolved a new treatment, which consisted of giving the entire month's dose of antimony in three days. It was drastic, but it worked. Would I try? Besides, I would be contributing to science, because the treatment was still being tested. I put myself into a hospital staffed by angelic young nuns in sky-blue robes and veils. There were four injections a day. With each one your heart beat and pumped and shook as if it would explode, you lay gasping, thinking this was death, swearing you would not let them give you another dose, and then just when it was unbearable, the tumult in your body ceased. The young angels stood about, concerned but smiling, while four times a day I thought I would die. One day Matthew strolled in, grave, authoritative. 'Well, you're looking fine.'

'But, Matthew, I am feeling terrible. Are you sure?'

'Perfectly in order. The treatment of the future.'

I crawled out of hospital four days later, shaken, shaking, poisoned, sick. But presumably without bilharzia. I was no less tired, however. Then I had my third baby, wrote *The Grass Is Singing,* came to London.

Soon in London, too, was Matthew, attached to the Hospital for Tropical Diseases, and other specialist hospitals, a world expert on bilharzia. 'How are you?'

'I'm fine, apart from feeling tired all the time.'

'You might have bilharzia.'

'But you cured me of bilharzia.'

'Oh yes? Did you have the treatment?'

'You gave me three days' treatment. The blitz.'

'That's been discontinued. We killed quite a few people with that. Only natives, though. They don't have the stamina to stand up to it.'

I am afraid I have to report that I allowed myself to be tested again, was proved negative, and was assured that that didn't necessarily prove anything. It was almost as if I was anxious to agree to anything, anxious to please, unable to say the simple word No. Taking advantage of Peter being at school for a full half-term, I agreed to go into the Hospital for Tropical Diseases, under the famous doctor. I was there for a month. Free, of course. The treatment was now back to a dose a day, and while it was not pleasant, it wasn't painful or terrifying. I was glad of the rest. I lay in bed, read, thought about *The Golden Notebook,* and smoked. They assured me no one taking the antimony treatment smoked longer than a day or two. I smoked throughout the course. Matthew would arrive by my bed, tall, and slow, and magisterial, assure me I was doing fine, and then stroll over to the other woman in the room, who was fascinating all the doctors. She was a nun, English, who worked in Nigeria, where she had caught a mysterious disease which caused her legs intermittently to swell and flush pink, scarlet, or raspberry. It was the timings of these colourful visitations that intrigued the doctors. Clearly it was a worm of some kind, still unknown to science. Sister Lucy lay in bed reading women's magazines and the Bible, with a bell beside her which she was instructed to push the moment her legs began to swell and colour. Several times a day the corridor resounded with thundering feet, while doctors and nurses rushed towards us from all over the hospital. They stood around the blushing legs, took scrapings of skin, samples of blood, said, Fascinating ... Incredible ...

Amazing, and then reluctantly left, for often the legs had already subsided again. Sister Lucy was a woman of about fifty, who had been in Nigeria for decades, working in some remote place, teaching the heathen to love God but also to read and write. Like me, she was having a nice rest. Fellow nuns came to visit, bringing her magazines, novels about love, chocolates, pink-feathered mules, a pink bed jacket. Then she was taken to another, more serious ward for treatment, and instead came Mrs. Ada Dimitrios, a large, calm, plain Englishwoman with smooth pale hair and perfect shining pink nails: she had had her hair and nails done before coming into hospital. She sat up against the chaste white hospital pillows and the flowery cushions she had brought in and read the *Daily Mirror* and the *Daily Express* and large numbers of middlebrow novels. She couldn't get enough of them, she said; she was starved of reading matter.

This was her story: Two lively English girls had gone to Greece by themselves for a holiday. This was the early fifties, and it was unusual then, enterprising. She had been persuaded by her sister Maureen. 'She always did like foreigners. I never did, much.' In Athens they sat about at café tables, and they were observed by a Greek merchant, who had taken one look at this pink-and-white, fair-haired English girl and had fallen in love, just like that, *crash,* a nose-dive. He assaulted the girls with flowers and chocolates, and demanded that Ada should marry him at once. She said, 'Why don't you ask Maureen? She likes abroad.' But Ada married her Aristides. 'Call me Ari.' 'No, I'll call you Harry.' Off she went to Nigeria with him, to Kano in the north, a town whose name evokes camels, caravans, the muezzin, and markets full of spices and enticements. It is an ancient trading town, always has been, and its history is pure romance. Ada from Croydon found herself in a large old house with enormous airy rooms shaded from the heat by tall trees in an immense garden, and a flat roof, where she went most nights to sleep.

'First we make love,' said she. 'Then we go up onto the roof. Harry says, "Come on, we can make love on the roof, everyone does." I tell him no, I know the difference between right and wrong.'

'Do you love him?' I enquired, seeing no reason not to go to the point.

'People talk about love. I never know what they mean. I could never put up with any man but Harry, if that's love.'

It took her quite a time to see that he was very rich and successful. He was a trader. He worked hard. She did not see much of him in the day.

'Are you lonely?'

'Lonely? Don't understand that word either. I like my own company, I always did.'

Sometimes she went down to the markets, accompanied by a servant, because her Harry said she ought to get out of the house sometimes, but what she really liked was to sit by herself in the enormous room where she kept flowers banked on layered trestles by the windows, so that scents could waft around the room on breezes from the great ceiling fan, and read the *Daily Mirror,* sent by air from London. She did not have friends. She entertained her husband's business friends when he asked her to arrange dinners or lunches, but the servants did it all, she was just a nuisance to them when she asked them to cook this or that. She had nothing in common with the wives of her Harry's white colleagues, nor with the black women married to his black associates. There were doctors and missionaries and teachers, but 'Anyway, I can't stand do-gooders,' she says, buffing the perfect nails, inspecting her perfect pale skin, which has never seen so much as a ray of Nigerian sun.

She liked her life, but she had caught this bug and was having diarrhoea all the time, and she couldn't wait for the Hospital for Tropical Diseases to cure her, because she wanted to go home.

Letters from her Harry arrived by every mail. Passionate letters.

'He misses me,' she remarked, blushing as she read. 'He's over-sexed. That's what I tell him. "You've just got too much libido. It's not good for you, in this heat."

'But he wouldn't listen. He'd have it three times a day, if he could.' Sometimes he got home at lunchtime, but not to have lunch. He says, "I love you I love you I love you, come to bed." But the temperature is over a hundred. "Don't you love me?" he says. He begs me for it, and I give in because I don't like to see a man begging, like a dog. All that sweat, the sheets soaking wet, and then I have to change them quickly, because I don't like the servants knowing.'

She said this to him: 'Look, my dear, no, listen to me, get yourself a girl for sex; I don't mind.' He began to cry and said, 'You don't love me.' She said to him, 'A man like you should have two wives. It's not your fault. You've just got too much.'

'He was so upset,' she said, her tranquil blue eyes clouded for once. 'I could see I should never say that again. But what is wrong with it, I want to know? A girl for sex and me for everything else. Because I do like him, you know; I couldn't ever be married to anyone else.'

'Would you mind if he had a Nigerian girl?'

'A black girl? I'd rather she was white, but I don't mind. I like the blacks there. I like the food. The only thing I don't like is all the noise. They're a noisy lot. But it's their country.'

'What do you spend all your money on?'

'I've got lovely clothes. I wear them in the evenings for him. He loves that. I've even got a Dior dress. But there's nothing to spend the money on. He gives most of it to his family in Greece. I like people who look after their families. I can't have children. I was expecting children, but nothing happened, and I asked him, Don't you mind? And he said no, all he wanted in this world was me, and if we had children I wouldn't have time for him.' She sits applying cold cream to her pretty skin, lifting her mauve satin nightdress to pat cream into her neck and upper breasts. 'You have to take the rough with the smooth,' she says gravely, sighing.

Quite a few people visited me in hospital, and Ada lay reading, and listening to our talk.

'I like conversations,' she says. 'You have interesting friends. You're a real boheem. Did you know that?'

'So I've been told,' I say, 'but only in Africa. And how would you define a boheem?'

She considers this, seriously. 'Well, I'm not one. Harry isn't one. His family aren't. My family aren't. But you are. Your friends are. You just like being different,' she pronounces. She turns over. 'And now I'm going to get a bit of sleep. Don't let the nurses wake me. I never get to have my sleep out at home, because Harry won't let me. Do you know what? I wake up sometimes and there he is, mooning over me and crying. He says I am so beautiful he has to cry. I say to him, "If you say it often enough, I'll begin to believe it."'

Did I ever have bilharzia? There is no way of ever knowing.

These little medical reminiscences are a record of quite pathological passivity under pressure from Authority. I did not write 'female passivity', because when it comes to doctors I don't think there is much difference between the genders. We have all been taught to do as we are told. The first thing a baby, an infant, then a small child, hears is: 'Here is the doctor . . . the doctor says . . . take your medicine, the doctor says so . . . the doctor says you must stay in bed.' He, and nowadays she, is the supreme authority in the family right from the start, and in the era of home visits a child would observe how a whole household waits for the doctor to arrive and tell them what to do. But now that the era of home visits is gone, perhaps this will change.

What is astonishing to me now is that although my mother used to tell doctors what to do, or what to prescribe, she nevertheless needed this authority between herself and her patient—my father, my brother, me. This was because of the ferocious discipline nurses were taught then, for they were never allowed to do anything at all unless the doctor had ordered it. On the farm, when my father was very ill because of his diabetes or the illnesses resulting from it, she would put him in the old car and get in beside him to watch his face for signs of coma or collapse, and I drove the car into Salisbury. What is seventy miles? Nothing. But the road was corrugated all the way, big slow waves in the gritty and sandy surface, which you had to drive over fast, causing the car and its occupants to rattle and vibrate, or so slowly you slid down from the top of one ridge and up to the next. It had to be slow, because my father was so ill. The trip might take five or six hours, with stops for him to rest. When the roads were faster because of the strips—instead of tarmac covering the whole road, there were strips for the wheels—it was still a slow business, because the edges of the strips were jagged little cliffs and if you were not careful you could slide off and skid into a drift of sand. My father sat there pale and sweating, one hand gripping the side of the car, the other my mother. And then at the hospital he was admitted for a morning, or a day, for tests that my mother had already done on the farm, and the doctor told my mother what she already knew, because it was what she had told him. My father was put to bed for the night in a hotel, and then the terrible slow drive back to the farm next day. All this to get the stamp of authority from the doctor. Crazy. Yet so it was. So it had to be then.

The Golden Notebook is generally considered my best novel. Perhaps it is, but I have my own ideas. Authors are thought not to be good judges of their own work. Nearly forty years after it was written, it is still selling steadily and is often reprinted, and not only in European countries. Its history illustrates the vicissitudes a novel may experience.

People are always asking, Why did you write this novel, that novel, that story, how did it come about? But the answer is never simple. You may think about a novel for years, because you cannot find the way to do it, and then the solution may be sudden, perhaps in a dream or a series of dreams; at any rate, what has been impossible has become easy. This happened to *The Marriages Between Zones Three, Four, and Five*. The format, 'Canopus in Argos: Archives', for some reason put an end to the ten years of inability. *Marriages* is the second of the series and very much the odd one out. As so often, the solution was a simple one: I used the ancient voice of the storyteller, and everything fell into place. A novel may arrive in one's mind suddenly, like *The Good Terrorist*. The genesis of *The Golden Notebook* was not lengthy, but it was complex, not only because of what went into it but because of my state at the time. I really was at a crossroads, a turning point; I was in the melting pot and ready to be remade. I knew I was—nothing unconscious about it. For one thing, I was determined my emotional life would from now on be different. For another, there was politics, the collapse of communism as a moral force. All around me, people's hearts were breaking, they were having breakdowns, they were suffering religious conversions or—very common, this—

formerly hard-line communists were discovering a talent for business and making money, because an obsession with the processes of capitalism was the best of preparations for a career in commerce. The point was, I was seeing people who had put all their eggs in one basket come to grief. What had been shut out of their thinking was rushing in, sometimes in the form of madness. I had been brought up in a society that compartmentalised—white, black—and the results were already evident in the news out of Southern Africa: rigidities were breaking down into violence and war. And further back still came the voices of my parents: my father's—at least when he was still well, still himself—was nonjudgemental, humane, human, tolerant; my mother's was always ready to categorise, condemn, judge. I knew that a remarkable time in the world's affairs was ending. I knew that quite soon it would seem mad. I had learned that atmospheres and climates of opinion which seem at the time eternal may disappear overnight. My most extreme experience of this was the onset of the Cold War just after the end of World War II, when friendships were destroyed overnight and allies became enemies. For some years I had been thinking that novels I would like to read about the nineteenth century had never been written. There were books of history in plenty, but few novels. Where were the novels about the intellectual debates, the arguments, and the passions and hatreds that are so often the real story behind formal history? Where the life as it was lived in socialist circles?

I wanted to write a novel which people could read later to find out how people saw themselves, those who were communists and dreaming of a golden age—which, I must remind you, we actually believed for a short time was just ahead. How could we have believed anything so stupid? At least these lunacies should be chronicled.

I needed a framework, a form, which would express extreme compartmentalisation and then its breaking down—the experience I had lived through, was living through now. The ideologies were not only strictly political but about the way women saw themselves. It is now a conviction that the women's movement began in the sixties. Like sex. The fact is, there were many group discussions, meetings, conversations, about women in the 1940s and 1950s, in and near the communist parties, and the socialist parties too. Women were on the agenda. Women have always sat around talking about men, and those voices came out of my earliest childhood too. My memory was full of conversations about men, women, the differences between them, love, sex, marriage. New was the idea that these ancient balances had to change.

For instance, the talk in Joan Rodker's kitchen, which I mined for Molly and Anna. Joan was Molly, much altered, of course, and I, Ella. It ought not to be necessary to say that this was not a strict use of what happened, or of what was said; but such is the hunger of readers for the autobiographical that one has to repeat: no, it did not happen just like that.

Extraordinary, this need for the autobiographical. 'No, Molly was a composite of several women I've known. Ella's situation in *The Golden Notebook* was mine, but not her character, not really.' At once—disappointment. A need for the literal, facts, the exact. Virginia Woolf truly said that of a hundred readers of a novel, only one will really care about the imaginative work a writer has put in: they want to know if the writer has 'put herself in', and is that a portrait of Freddy or Jane?

How we do learn to treasure that hundredth reader!

But why do they always want to make characters in a novel into autobiography? How often have I seen a face fall into disappointment when I say no, such and such a character was imagined, or composed from half a dozen similar people, or transposed from another setting into this one. What we are seeing is a reluctance of the imagination. What is wanted is the real, the actual, what 'really' happened. If I say, Yes, all those things did happen to me, then oh, the relief, the smile, the pleasure. Why is this? Once, all our storytelling was imaginative, was myth and legend and parable and fable, for that is how we told stories to and about each other. But that capacity has atrophied under the pressure from the realistic novel, at least to the extent that all the imaginative or fanciful aspects of storytelling have been shuffled off into their definite categories. There are magical realism, space fiction, science fiction, fantasy, folklore, fairy stories, horror stories, for we have compartmentalised literature as we do everything. On one side realism—the truth. On the other, in another box, imagination—fantasy. But most readers now want to think, as they read: This is *really* what happened to the author. And the author who has tried so hard to take the story out of the strictly personal, to generalise personal and private experience, sometimes feels he or she need not have bothered, might as well have set down a strict and accurate record of what happened—autobiography, in fact.

When in the realistic novel that other dimension forces its way in, because it has to come in somewhere, then often it is admitted in the shape of madness. When the voice of the first Mrs. Rochester is heard by Jane Eyre, what is evoked is much more than the sounds made by a poor crazy woman: it is all the grotesque and irrational worlds lit wildly by the fires of hell and heaven which we exclude from daytime life. At our peril. Madness in realistic literature has too much weight given to it, and that is because madness is permitted. Dreams are overimportant, because dreams are 'realistic'. We all dream, after all. It would be easy to make a long list of 'realistic' novels where the irrational appears, or is even pivotal, but is in accepted guises, such as dreams, or madness.

The Golden Notebook was written at high pressure—pressure from within, which brings me to another murky area. Sometimes the emotional pressures that fuel a novel are very far from its subject matter. All writers understand this, but I think few readers. *The Fifth Child* was fuelled by sheer frustration and anger because it was impossible to get newspapers to write the truth about what was happening when the Soviet Union invaded Afghanistan: a whole generation of editors and journalists (people who had once been on the extreme fringes of opinion but, as so often happens, had become mainline opinion) still cherished a sentimental loyalty to the Soviet Union, which made it first impossible, then hard, to say one word of criticism of their beloved. *The Fifth Child* had that head of steam behind it, but that is not to say that it is 'about' the Soviet invasion of Afghanistan. *The Golden Notebook*'s fuel was feelings of loss, change: that I had been dragged to my emotional limits by Jack and then Clancy—rather, I had been dragged by *my* emotional needs, which really had nothing to do with them as individuals. I had understood my need for the wounded hero, the suffering man, and knew all that must stop. Peter, the third and last child, was growing up. Loss, departures, the ending of dramas begun long ago, the need for drawing lines—*finis*. All this dynamic energy went into *The Golden Notebook: emotional* energy, which is so much stronger than we think . . . and this besides having to acknowledge that what is so often called 'intellectual' is in fact emotional. What is more violently emotional and passionate—and poisonous—than a room full of intellectuals in ideological debate? . . . But I slide past this dangerous area, holding my breath.

That novel had a framework made by thinking. The thought was that to divide off and compartmentalise living was dangerous and led to nothing but trouble. Old, young; black, white; men, women; capitalism, socialism: these great dichotomies undo us, force us into unreal categorisation, make us look for what separates us rather than what we have in common. That was the thought, which made the shape or pattern of *The Golden Notebook*. But the emotions were stronger than the thought. This is why I have always seen *The Golden Notebook* as a failure: a failure in my terms, of what I had meant. For has this book changed by an iota our tendency to think like computers set to sort everything—people, ideas, history—into boxes? No, it has not. Yet why should I have had such a hubristic thought? But I was in the grip of discovery, of revelation. I had only just seen this Truth: I was watching my own mind working like a sorting machine, and I was appalled.

The Golden Notebook did not at once become the 'Bible of the Women's Movement', for that is how it was described in country after country. The reviews in both Britain and the States, by women as well as men, were sour, grudging, hostile. A researcher came to see me and said she was astonished by how bad the reviews for *The Golden Notebook* had been: did I realise that? Oddly enough, yes. I was shocked and upset by those reviews, in a way which I have never allowed to happen since. First, I had been lucky till then: what I had written had on the whole been appreciated, or I had been justified by events. My first writing, about conditions in Southern Africa, had been criticised as being 'unfair' to the whites, but that time had passed. There was a note in these reviews of *The Golden Notebook* that showed some nerve had been touched. When you see or hear it, you know that the reviewer is writing not about the book but about herself or himself. When a reviewer writes with a certain kind of sour spite, it is not 'This novel upsets me because it made me think of my mother, my husband, my child,' but 'This is a dreadful novel.' To understand this you have to be more experienced than I was then. And the level of the reviewing was shocking. I did not know then that in any field there are always only a few good people, and the rest are second-rate and ignorant. Not one of the reviews even noticed that *The Golden Notebook* had an interesting shape, and this at a time when critics were complaining about the conventionality of the English novel. They were so disturbed by the sex-war aspects of the novel, they did not see anything else. What has to be understood about reviewers is that they are—mostly—a very emotional lot. Their function is—surely?—to weigh, balance, think, consider, but often they merely emote.

It happened again, though less obviously, with *Love, Again.* Just as the supposed subject of *The Golden Notebook,* women and men, was all the reviewers could see, so the immediate subject of *Love, Again,* love in old age, was surprising and shocking, and the fact that the novel has a rather complicated structure was hardly noticed.

One criticism then the loudest, has since become less. It was that the men characters were so unpleasant. I could not see this. (Behind this one hears, 'Women writers cannot write about men,' that old last-ditch defence.) Then, it was that *all* the characters are so unpleasant. At once one has to wonder: what extraordinarily wonderful people the critic must know, unlike any human being one has ever known oneself. And how flatteringly he or she must see himself, herself, not at all as others see them. Proust made a sly and funny comment on this very point. He imagines an urbane and flattering account, rather like a society editor's column but based on the Goncourt brothers' journals, of the Verdurins and their circle, which he has portrayed from the worm's-eye view. As if *Hello* magazine had decided to write *Les Liaisons Dangereuses.*

Like this, perhaps:

I was strolling down Church Street past Molly Jacobs's house, and there in the window seat on the first floor was Anna Wulf, the lovely author of *Frontiers of War*. She was looking into the room. Then she laughed, so she must be in conversation, probably with Molly herself. I could not help feeling a wee bit envious of these two, one a well-regarded new author and Molly Jacobs, whose career as an actress has just taken off again with *The Wings of Cupid*, which is expected to run for ever. Then the milkman arrived from a side street, and Molly heard him and came to stand beside Anna Wulf in the window. The milkman looked up and greeted the two girls. They were making a charming picture. Molly saw me and waved. I mimed a plea, and she said something to Anna Wulf, who gave me a quick inspection, recognised me— we had only met that one time briefly in the theatre foyer—and in a moment a key wrapped in a silk scarf arrived beside me on the pavement. Charming bohemian ways ... I went up the stairs— noticing that the harp still stood on the landing—and heard as I entered the living room, from Molly, 'Yes, but I'm not a theoretical type; I'm simply worried about Tommy.' Clearly, I had interrupted a discussion about the lad's future, and I said, 'I've just dropped in to pay my respects.' Molly said, 'The milkman's son has won a scholarship, and he was up here yesterday, telling me about it.' I could not prevent myself saying, 'Molly, you should be more careful; you shouldn't let just anybody into your house.' It occurred to me as I spoke that I had been taking this line with her since she was a tiny girl on my knee. Now she simply grimaced and shrugged. She is not an actress for nothing, and I felt as put down as if I'd done something gauche. Then from the street came the cry, 'Fresh country strawberries.' Both women waved down at him to stop, and Molly ran down the stairs. I stood near Anna, watching the scene and watching Anna, who was smiling down at what she saw. Molly loudly invited the strawberry seller up to eat some of his strawberries with them, was refused, and came running up the stairs with a great bowl of strawberries, which certainly did look first class. Molly seemed put out. She said she had recently returned from Italy and it was a culture shock, having to adjust to the English class system. Anna said to Molly that she had hurt the man's feelings. And certainly Molly has never had any idea of how her uninhibited ways can shock.

I said I wouldn't have any strawberries; I was leaving.

'Oh, did I ask you to have some strawberries?' said Molly laughing. Naughty puss!

'You'll have to leave anyway,' she said, 'because Richard is coming. We're in for a ding-dong about Tommy's future. But do sit down until he comes.'

I sat and watched a scene right out of Bonnard, two pretty women with their white bowls of red strawberries and cream, the sun gleaming on the yellow wine, both frankly and greedily enjoying their little treat.

I was thinking that whatever other worries Molly Jacobs might have, money could not be one of them. Richard is not only Skies Unlimited, which is a household word all over the world, but a dozen other international enterprises too. The sky certainly does seem to be his limit. And he and Molly, I am glad to say, are good friends, in the civilised modern way.

The doorbell rang, and Molly threw down the scarf-wrapped key. She exchanged a smile with Anna I did not know how to read—and I have always prided myself on my psychological acumen—until she said, 'He has always hated me doing that. He's such a pompous man.' But she spoke affectionately, I am sure.

I stood up to go, saying, 'I hope you aren't going to say I'm a pompous ass the moment my back is turned.'

But Richard had arrived. His greeting to me was perfunctory, and I could see he had eyes only for the two women. I was envying him that he could discuss his problems with two such sympathetic friends. He was dressed sportily, and Molly teased him. 'Are you off for a day in the country?'

I left. I must confess I didn't want to. It was such an attractive scene—that special friendship that is possible only between a man and a woman when they have been intimate, and pretty little Anna Wulf, of whom so much is expected by the literary world, and that Sunday morning scene, lazy, slow, charming.

341

I went off down Church Street, thinking that next Sunday I would walk by again and permit myself the claims of a very old friendship.

From *The Journals of Philip Maxbury Westbourne,*
Theatre critic, man of letters, columnist

Women at first certainly did not rush in to approve the book. On the contrary, some distanced themselves from it, including personal friends, on the lines of: why give away our secrets? But that women were critical then of men was surely hardly a secret. It was men who at first approved the book: Nicholas Tomalin, Edwin Muir, who sent me a message about it, and in the States, Irving Howe and then, a bit later, Hugh Leonard, and later still Robert Gottlieb, who became my editor first at Simon & Schuster, then at Knopf.

One immediate problem was that the upheavals in Michael Joseph coincided with the publication of the book: that is when the firm was sold over the heads of the people working there, though they had been promised they could refuse or agree to any sale, and half the editors resigned. My own editor did not like *The Golden Notebook;* he never said so, but I was told by others in the firm.

Then feminists discovered the book, in Britain, in the States, in Scandinavia, and it became the 'Bible of the Women's Movement'. A book that had been planned so coolly was read, I thought, hysterically. The extremest example of this was when, in Sweden, an actress came up to me: 'I never read anything but the Blue Notebook—oh no, it belongs to me; it has nothing to do with you.'

In Germany and France the novel was not published for ten years, considered too inflammatory. When they did pluck up courage, it was a success at once and taken up by the feminists. In France it won the Prix Medici for translated novels. My editor in the French firm Albin Michel was an American, Peter Israel, and he told me that when he first read *The Golden Notebook* he was so enraged he threw it across the room, nearly hitting his then girl-friend. But he came to like it, and it was he who was responsible for its doing so well in France.

It was not only women who saw the novel as on one theme.

While women were claiming me as their own, seeing nothing in the book but their own agendas, I was getting letters from men and from women, about the politics, so rapidly receding into history, and about madness. The sixties were on us, and the romanticising of lunacy. The theme of people 'breaking down' into greater understanding of themselves and their times was very much to the taste of the sixties. Just ahead were Ronnie Laing and his associates. They were supposed to have introduced the theme, discovered it, been its originators. But I wonder. In the fifties was a book by one Haimi Kaplan called *The Inner World of Mental Illness*. It is a wonderful book—humane, decent, balanced—using examples of mad people from earlier centuries as well as this one. I believe that a lot of people found this book, were inspired by it—but did not acknowledge it. Very often do we see this: people acknowledging every source of their inspiration but the most important one. I think the reason for this is not a reluctance to give acknowledgements where they are due, as much as that the originating impression is so strong it becomes a part of the inspired one, and it is hard to say, 'That was the impulse, but now this is where I start.'

I also got letters from men about the sex war, appreciative ones. I have always had letters from men about *The Golden Notebook*. Regularly, year in, year out, I get this one: 'I found *The Golden Notebook*. I have given it to my wife/girlfriend/daughter.' Recently, a letter from Mexico: 'I have just read *The Golden Notebook*. I did not know women ever talked about anything but men and babies. I have given it to my wife.'

This letter to Edward Thompson, in reply to one of his criticising *The Golden Notebook* from a left-wing point of view, speaks for itself:

Dear Edward,

Many thanks for your letter—it was sweet of you to telephone and sweet of you to write.

Let's assume it is dangerous, given our temperaments, to have this kind of argument, particularly by letter:

1. I do not understand how anyone could describe the G.N. as

subjective—subjective attitudes are objectivised and related to society—or that is what I tried to do.

2. About past history with New Left Review, no, Edward, that is not an accurate description of what happened, but let's leave it.

3. I think to say that I am something that wandered out of the bush dazzled by bright lights is perhaps an easy way out of thinking about the kind of outsider's view someone with my kind of upbringing is bound to have about Europe.

4. No my dear Edward, I did not copy bits out of the Soviet newspapers for my imaginary reviews. Strange as it may seem, I made them up.

In fact, if I were to write an obituary about me and The Golden Notebook it would consist of me saying very tartly indeed, like a rather brisk governess, the words written in a balloon over my head: 'Strange as it may seem, I made it up . . .'

Or, to put the same idea more *theoretically*—because the novel is dying, because we are all avid for *information,* believing erroneously that salvation is going to come from more knowledge about varying aspects of our fragmented world, no one, but no one, not even the literati, the people who are supposed to be interested in novels as novels, reads a book as it should be: people read The Golden Notebook as they might have done an autobiography. Marvellous. This is truly a time of journalism.

My dear Edward, that was a highly *constructed* book, the point of which was the relation of its parts to each other. It was a novel about the kind of intellectual and emotional attitudes produced now, that people have now, and their relation to each other.

Call that subjectivism and you confess you didn't read the book . . .

My love to you both, let's be friends, do come and see me.

I liked meeting your friend Tom. He was nice.

Love,
Doris

It leads the strangest life, *The Golden Notebook.*

I meet women who say, 'I read *The Golden Notebook* in the sixties. It changed my life. My daughter read it and now my granddaughter.'

This business of a book changing one's life. That can only mean that one is ready to change and the book tips up a balance.

In Rio once, I was sitting outside my hotel on the pavement, as one may do in southern climes. Girls from the *favelas* come to sit there, sometimes all day over a single coffee or a fruit drink, because for the price of a decent dress they are out of squalor and poverty for a while—a week or so. The waiters tolerate them, turn a blind eye if—not very often—they find a customer. Too many girls, not enough customers. Two of the girls were at a near table, and one called across, 'My friend wants to tell you something. She doesn't speak English. She loves you.' But no, what she wanted to tell me was that she loved *The Golden Notebook*. How did the book find its way into one of the worst slums in the world? I was infinitely touched, grateful.

In China the book has been printed twice, in editions of eighty thousand, small for them, with their vast population, huge for us. Both times it sold out in a couple of days, to women, for there, too, it is a woman's book. The lives of women are so hard I am glad the book is of use to them, never mind about what the book is 'really' about.

But that is China. I do object when the feminists claim my books as their property in the States, or Britain, because another letter I get quite often says, 'At university I didn't read you because the feminists said Keep Out. But then I read one of your books and saw that they aren't just for women.'

And so now, forty years on, this controversial book which so upset publishers and reviewers has become a kind of classic, taken for granted. The other day I was greeted by sixteen-year-olds from a London school, saying their teacher had said they must read *The Golden Notebook*. 'We love it,' they said.

And another young woman, from Eastern Europe, when I had finished lecturing about something or other, said she and her friends were reading *The Golden Notebook,* and 'It's fascinating, reading about all those old times.'

Sometimes I hear the book has been prescribed in history or political courses, and this pleases me, for after all, that is where I began, wanting to write a chronicle of the times. And that is where, if the book lasts at all, its value will be found. For I do think, whatever I failed at, or succeeded in, it is an honest and truthful and reliable account of how we all were at that time. It could not be written now, because a novel has to come out of some matrix of atmosphere, or feeling, or thought, and now that all seems so remote. It is hard to believe they happened, 'all those old times'.

Now the most bizarre of *The Golden Notebook*'s many lives. It became a text for deconstructionists. This book, born directly out of so much blood, sweat, and particularly tears, a little intellectual game? You have to laugh; there's nothing else to be done.

Writing *The Golden Notebook* changed me. Writing any book changes you: this has to be so, if you think about it. On the lowest level, if you are thinking hard about a subject, information and insights on that subject seem to come in from everywhere: books arrive in your life, you hear it on the radio, in conversations, and on television. This is a fact, it is true, you can rely on it—and there is no 'scientific' explanation for it. Yet. But I am not talking about this kind of rapid information-getting. Writing that novel changed the way I thought and more fundamentally than thinking. When I began it, while I had thrown out communism, all of the mind-sets of communism remained. Now, that set of mind not only defined communists and ex-communists but had become the property of people who had never been communist or even socialist. Before the fifties had ended, I was reading leading articles in the 'capitalist press', impeccably conservative articles but using communist jargon: concrete steps, contradictions, demos, the interpenetration of opposites, the class war, and all the rest. We were observing that continually repeating process, the ways of thinking of an excluded or even ostracised minority spreading gently up and down and around and about until they have become part of the 'climate of opinion'.

For some decades now there has been something I call the 'package', the accepted, fashionable package which every young person emerging from our western education has been taught to accept as the only possible one. This is less true than it was, for the ideas of later-excluded minorities are permeating it. First of all,

Marxism, one of the fifty-seven varieties of Marxism, and this even when it is not recognised as Marxism. Then, the belief that human society is destined to become even better in every way, and particularly materially: more and more material prosperity is everybody's future—there will be ever more cars, refrigerators, comfort, security, an upwardly moving escalator on which everyone in the world is standing. (But this one has become less persuasive.) This is materialism, a chicken in every pot—the United States' hard-times political slogan, displacing 'pie in the sky'. A chicken in *every* pot, everywhere—but that is as out of reach as ever. Then, the largest item in the package, philosophical materialism, the God-is-dead, Science-is-king materialism.

Anyone who does not subscribe to this last one—for it is as strong as ever—is patronised as feeble-minded and a coward. There is a sneer, implicit or overt, when someone says, 'I do not understand people who believe in God.' They may even say, 'Uneducated people, yes.' God to them becomes a kind of insurance policy against the terrors of eternity for those who cannot face extinction. Yet those who puff themselves up by this kind of contempt never seem to reflect that many of the people who believe in God believe in hellfire and all kinds of painful damnation, as well as in paradise. The Muslims, for instance, and certain extreme Christian sects. Surely this should be seen as courage, not cowardice? It is a stage people go through, despising the believers in God. I did. I remember my smugness and my feeling I was saying something original that had cost thought.

Necessary subclauses to this agenda were that South Africa was a wicked tyranny—true—which could only end in a bloodbath, 'a night of the long knives': untrue. Southern Rhodesia was in the process of coming to be seen in the same light. The United States was the world's chief enemy, a tyranny much worse than the Soviet Union, which still, despite all the revelations, occupied a haloed spot in many people's minds. A contempt for our own country, Britain, so deeply felt it had not, then, been examined at all, showed itself in a steady nagging denigration of everything British. This was the other side of 'British is best'. Taken for granted was that *real* politics went on somewhere else, because *real* politics mean unrest, violence, riots, and revolution, and Britain—then—did not go in for that kind of thing: we were peaceful, non-violent, believed in settling matters by the vote—contemptible; and, then, did not go in for extremes of opinion. At the slightest hint of revolution, or even unrest somewhere else, as many British 'activists' as could afford it were off to Poland, Hungary, Czechoslovakia, or moments of excitement in Paris.

By the time I had finished *The Golden Notebook* I had written my way out of the package, but it was not that I came to the last sentence and shouted, 'Eureka, I have got it at last!' I began by noticing that when I was with certain comrades and ex-comrades and even ordinarily middle-of-the-road political friends, they radiated complacency, not to say conceit, because of this 'package'. To believe in continual upward progress, the materialist escalator, was proof of good intentions and concern for the human race; to have thrown God out of the window and to stand alone in the face of the cold universe was to be brave and indomitable. To believe in revolution meant you were courageous, particularly if, in your secret fantasies, you defied torturers and survived concentration camps.

I am sure there was not, anywhere in the world, a communist who did not prepare, in fantasy, for interrogation, torture, imprisonments, the camps, and this in countries where revolution was nowhere on the agenda. 'There is just one thing, Comrade Investigator'—a sarcastic drawl. 'We all know about the interrogator who is kind and friendly, to be replaced by a sadistic swine. You forget, we live in countries where there is freedom of information. Yes, of course I shall confess to everything. Everyone knows that no one stands up to torture. But what you don't seem to realise is that no one outside this country will believe a word of it. Everyone in the world knows how you [the Soviet Union, China, and so forth] torture people into confession. Really, you oughtn't to be so naive, so ignorant.' If this kind of fantasy was in millions (many millions) of minds, what kind of effect did it have on general thinking?

It is a strange business, changing your mind about what you think—rather, having your mind changed for you. You wake up one morning and think, Goodness, I used to think like that, didn't I?—but you hardly know how it happened. It is a process that goes on all the time, whether you have put yourself in the way of ideas and beliefs or not.

The package had come to seem thin, gimcrack, superficial, and above all blown together most arbitrarily, shreds from the French Revolution and the Enlightenment, orts and fragments from Cromwell's time or the industrial revolution, articles of faith from Marx or from Lenin. I knew exactly the moment when I had shed religion and God: it was when my mother, upset that her child had a crush on the Virgin Mary—that is what it amounted to—recited a list of the misdeeds of the Roman Catholics, all of which could be matched by the Protestants; and with what relief I heaved the whole itchy and uncomfortable burden off my shoulders for the brave stoicism of atheism. I knew that I had accepted the Marxist package for no deeper reason than that the communists I met in Southern Rhodesia had actually read the books I had, were in love with literature, and because they were the only people I knew who took it for granted that the white regime was doomed. But if I had been born in another place, at another time, I would with equal ease have accepted whatever 'package' was the correct one there and then.

And there was another thing. I had experiences writing the book which did not fit in with tenets of the package. I hate the word 'inspiration', distrust all claims to elevated experiences, but had written things not in my personal experience, which were coming true. I don't want to list them, because people's hunger for strangeness is so strong that the most modest claims become exaggerated into whole cosmologies.

Many writers have the experience of describing events or thoughts which they have invented but which later come true. To put me well beyond the possibility of being taken seriously by people who still regard the package as the only possible way of looking at the world, I think that enveloping our level of thinking, apart from it but sometimes penetrating it, is a stratum of thought or being, a wavelength, and that writers often ride along on it, perhaps only for moments. This is the explanation, I believe, of that common phenomenon when several writers come up at the same time with the same theme or title or idea, believing they are unique and original and no one else can possibly have thought of it. This has happened to me more than once. Somewhere close to us is a sea of ideas, a finer level of vibration, and this makes itself felt, no matter how much this is denied by conceited materialists.

It seems to me that when I wrote *The Golden Notebook* I had so thoroughly reached the end of a whole spectrum of ideas, thoughts, and feelings that the world I had excluded as 'impossible', as 'reactionary', was surrounding me, pressing in, making its claim.

I began a systematic search for something different. I did not know where to look or how. Because that excluded world is represented in our culture by dubious practices and beliefs, like séances, horoscopes, fortune-telling, and so forth, I was again and again put off, but persevered, and followed up every lead I could—a reference in a book, something overheard, a remark on the radio. For instance, Yeats led me to the Golden Dawn, but Madame Blavatsky and Aleister Crowley led me out again. That, I knew, was not what I was looking for—magic and mystery and bizarre behaviour. All this went on for months, and parallel to my ordinary life; there was no one I could discuss it with, for everyone I knew clutched tight to the package, whether on the left or, even, the right. I described this search in the person of Martha in *The Four-Gated City,* but shortened it, neatened it, simplified it—you simply cannot put the untidiness of life into a novel if you don't want people to yawn and throw it aside. I was again in the situation I had been in as a girl: I had to keep quiet about what I was thinking.

I was at once struck by one basic, overriding fact—that here was a world of ideas and belief that I had scarcely even heard of, let alone been seriously introduced to. Though I had not had anything like a good education, I had read widely, been part of the intellectual ferments of the time, met a wide range of people, but nowhere had there been even a hint of what I was discovering now—that is, if I wanted to exclude the sickly 'spiritualism' of the last days of the communist group in Southern Rhodesia.

Nowhere in our education, our culture, was there so much as a whisper about the great religions, the great spiritual traditions, of the East. In our own culture, at its heart, is the inner spiritual tradition of Christianity, writers like St. John of the Cross, or Mother Julian of Norwich, with books like *The Cloud of the Unknowing,* but these were surely unusual individuals, with a particular temperamental endowment, shared, I think, by very few, and it is mostly religious people who know about them.

I think that this lacuna at the heart of our education—absolute then, but things have changed a little—was the reason young people brought up on the jaunty, cocky, conceited, shallow intellectualism of the West had no defences when they encountered an Eastern tradition and even the most deteriorated form of it. In the sixties, just dawning, again and again we saw highly educated youngsters suddenly succumbing to charlatanism and gurus and cults of all sorts, to the astonishment and despair of their parents, but it was because whole areas of their minds had been left uncultivated, ready to give root room to any old weed. As I said in my story *The Temptation of Jack Orkney*.

I read first of all the various traditions of Buddhism. Very soon Buddhism was to become attractive to large numbers of people, and it still is. (At the time, we had scarcely heard of it. It is really hard to convey the absolute general ignorance and the sterility of our ideas just before the sixties.) Buddhism is attractive to the violent and warlike West. Then, various aspects of Hinduism, to me appealing because of its polytheism, its heteromorphism, just like Roman Catholicism, absorbing gods and saints into itself according to the culture it finds itself in. But I am not an Indian. I know that this is no barrier to the numbers of souls putting on lungis, saris, red forehead spots, and so forth, in ashrams in India and elsewhere. But I was reading all the great Eastern classics—the Vedas, the Bhagavad Gita, the various Zen scriptures; I was reading for information, and with enjoyment and pleasure, and above all for guidance, but for ever came out by the same door I went in. There was, however, one fact that emerged from all this, a basic one, and it was that one needs a teacher. No teacher, no guide, and you may be sure of trouble. At that time, it was merely the one solid thing I was clutching on to in a sea of differing voices and paths, but since then it has become far from theoretical, because for years I was to watch rash people exploring these dangerous regions without a guide and coming to every kind of grief, going mad temporarily or permanently being the most common.

If there is one thing we pride ourselves on in the West, it is our independence. This was not something I was even aware of, until I challenged myself over it. It comes hard, surrendering precious self-reliance, particularly when your life has been that—fighting for it, defending it, struggling to regain it when it is lost, temporarily, as when you become a communist. If you are a woman it is particularly hard, because the pressures on you are so strong, particularly internal ones, emotional ones, more insidious than the external pressures.

The 'gurus' offering themselves in the late fifties and early sixties were not persuasive reasons to surrender. I did in fact sample one, partly from curiosity, and found myself sitting opposite his local representative, who offered me what amounted to psychotherapy, on such a low level that I retrospectively admired Mrs. Sussman. Psychotherapy then was very 'far out', 'way out'—phrases just coming in—very distant from our present conditions, where every second person you meet is a counsellor, and particularly those (it is hard to refrain from pointing out) whose own emotional lives have been particularly disastrous.

I decided to keep my eyes and ears open, and continue my search. Meanwhile an unpleasant truth about myself—the first of very many—was knocking at the door. It was that these Paths, or Ways, I was investigating were sometimes called Disciplines. And I had no self-discipline—yes, I was exaggerating, in those days when the enormity of what I was confronting overcame me—apart from one: I did have the self-discipline to set myself to work every day, and I knew that some people found that hard. I had been able to adapt my life, my work patterns, to accommodate my son: I could say that at the centre of my life had always been his needs, his patterns of school, holidays, comings and goings. But what else? Well, nothing, when I looked at myself coolly.

Food preoccupied me, whether I was going to eat it or not eat it. That is hardly unusual in our lavish times, but I was becoming increasingly aware of just how much time I spent thinking about it. And besides, you may be on a diet yourself, but if you are a good cook, and enjoy making feasts for others, that is still thinking about food.

I was not drinking as I had for that short time, but wine was part of my life, and I could hardly say I denied myself.

I smoked fifty or sixty cigarettes a day and could not have believed that one day soon I would simply stop.

(All the Paths I had investigated till then assumed the necessity of asceticism.)

I was physically out of shape. It wasn't very much, I knew that, but I decided that at the very least I would exercise every morning, and I have done so ever since. I certainly was aware of the bathos of it, doing physical jerks and hoping this might be a step on the road to higher things.

The thought was beginning to nag at me—only just beginning—that my behaviour since I had left childhood, my 'life-style', was one that at any other time in history would have been described as corrupt, decadent, even degenerate. Yet it was this behaviour that I had taken my stand on, fought painful battles to gain and keep, actually felt defined me. (And all my generation too.) But the trouble was that if the balance swung too far the other way (as can always be seen going on, the swings from one extreme to the other), then the danger must be a reversion to the most bigoted and barren puritanism. And if so many of us had gone so far in the direction of sexual and every other kind of freedom, then the point of balance was surely already far into the regions of indulgence. . . . These thoughts and others like them were so difficult—and as usual not to be shared with anybody—that I simply postponed them all.

Now I find it painful, embarrassing, how I thought about the 'Search', the 'Path', and yet I know that for a child of our culture, nothing much better could have been expected, that I was one of many.

We in the West, and in cultures permeated by Western values, expect everything. We have been promised everything, implicitly or loudly and openly. We believe we deserve everything good. Our reaction to being told that there is something there, a desirable thing—a great hidden treasure—is that we must have it. As a right. When I knew that there was this other world, the spiritual one—though using that word comes hard, for it is so debased—I had two strong reactions. First was scorn for my own culture, because it had so ignored this other world—but scorn came easily to me, and I was a long way off recognising that. The other reaction was a powerful grasping need, a secret exultation. It was greed, but I didn't know it, thought it was laudable, that secret 'Gimme, gimme' that I was hugging to myself. Worse even than 'Gimme' was 'I *will* do this, achieve this. *I* will.'

It is a common experience of people following a 'Path' that they look back at their first steps with shame, and regret that they can have been so very wrong.

And now I have a real, a serious difficulty. From now onwards—that is, from the end of the fifties—there was a main current in my life, deeper than any other, my real preoccupation. A few people will understand, because they have lived through something similar, but most I think will be indifferent or bored. And so I shall simply state it: this was my real life.

There is a tiny story from the Sufis and from a book called *The Sufis,* by Idries Shah. But I had not encountered Sufis yet.

A certain man is a prisoner on an island, but he does not know he is a prisoner and that there is more to life than prison life. A rescuer offers him an escape, on a ship, but he says, 'Oh thank you, thank you, I'll come, but I must bring my ton of cabbage with me.'

When I first read it, I thought, *I* could never be so stupid as to want to take a ton of cabbage—but alas, that ton of cabbage is hard to rid oneself of. In those early days I was saying far too often, 'Of course *I* would never be so stupid as to . . . ,' whatever it was. And that brings me to another difficulty. If you are good at one thing, you unconsciously assume you are good at others too; if you have succeeded in one area, then you assume that that success 'counts' as good marks in another.

Again, this little tale of the prisoner will mean a great deal to a few people but nothing at all to others. And so, enough of that. People who are interested can pursue for themselves what it was I was studying. It was the Sufi teacher Idries Shah★ with whom I was to discover—as I saw it then—*my* search rewarded. The books are available.

★He died on 23 November 1996.

'Surrendering' independence was seen wrongly by me, because of ignorance and conceit, as I soon found out, but there was a real embarrassment, and annoyance. When I began to look around for some 'Path' or discipline, I kept quiet about it because the atmosphere of the time was so strongly against it, but the cult-crazy sixties was in fact easy to predict, particularly if I had remembered how our rigid atheistical dogmatic communist group ended in ghost tales and séances.

There was an incident at a party, in 1963. The room was crowded. Everyone had been in the Communist Party or near it. Somebody picked up a book and asked me, scandalised, 'What's this you're reading?'

'It is a book on Hatha Yoga,' says I. Hatha Yoga is the physical discipline of Yoga. Exchanged looks, raised eyebrows, tactful changings of the subject. Within five years every one of these people would think nothing of saying, 'No, I can't on Wednesday; it's my Yoga class.'

The real embarrassment, the continuing one, needs some quick and of course unsatisfactory generalisations. If you are a practising Christian, or have read books like *The Cloud of the Unknowing* for their literary qualities, then the word 'mysticism' does mean something serious. But this is not a culture, unlike some Eastern cultures, where it is unremarkable for people to look for a Guide, a Teacher, a Way, a Path—a discipline. Here in the West, most people if they hear you are interested in mysticism will at once start talking about ghosts, poltergeists, reincarnation, fortune-telling, the *I Ching,* UFOs, horoscopes. They think mysticism means exciting experiences of one kind or another. Yet there is no serious spiritual discipline anywhere in any culture that does not instruct its students to ignore all attractive sideshows, like ESP, and, if they do in fact experience 'supra-normal' phenomena, to regard them as distractions, as irrelevances.

I have not enjoyed being thought so silly-minded.

And again—enough of that.

I am going to put in here two poems, because poems can say in a few lines what you need pages of prose to say. Both come from the early sixties, but they belong here. As poems they are not particularly good, or bad. Old-fashioned, of course. Informative, though.

HERE

Here where I stand,
Here they have stood,
All with our flowering branches.

Behind us five locked doors.
Behind them snarl the beasts
That licked our hands before.

Dark it is, and dark.
Lord, how strange to bring me to this close.

They too have stood asking:
Who shut the doors?
Who taught our beasts to snarl?

Who, what brought me here?

If I stand here then
Where the dark came close
Then here must close the dark,
Yes, here the dark must close.

THE ISLANDS

The legendary islands are all very well,
But too strong a blast from there can set you wondering
If it's angels or devils that hold them.
Small sniffs at a time, yes, that's the way,
While the saving hands tutor a child
Or set new plants to grow.

When life beats too strong,
Promising more than this mind guesses at,

An underdrag of lethargy succeeds,
Filling where light was opening
With sleep like dirty water.
Then my doctoring, my knowledgeable hands,
Smooth white sheets or draw a cover up.

Once I thought the daily adding of small act to act
Food for the dulling of the heart,
Griefs and violence being the proper diet of liveliness,
Now, held back in every breath from folly of extremity
By what must be done, the here,
As frontiers are held by patience after war,
The quiet friend enters as my time-taught hands
Mix bread and set a damaged house to rights.

These verses should not be seen as anything more than a stage or step. The trouble is, people who are not on a Path, or Way, may be interested in those who are, but often take some temporary stage, even one seen by the travellers themselves as mistaken, or unfortunate, as a final accomplishment or summit. The parallel in the literary field is when some reader or critic thrusts a page under your nose and says, 'Look, you wrote this in 1953, you said it yourself, how can you deny it?'

I say I don't like parties, don't go to them, but there were a lot of parties. Many were in the Pipers' house on the river, full of pretty children, and now it seems as if I was part of some idyll. No, life is not like that, but there are places and people so endowed with charm you don't see anything but that. And, too—ironically—this fugitive from family life felt as if she was standing, forever excluded, on the edge of some magic land where all the unpleasant aspects of the family had been banished by a magic wand.

A scene: Peter and Anne are lying in bed, with their arms around each other, and I am sitting on the foot of the bed, and we are chatting about this and that. The door flies open, a daughter appears, and shrieks, hands dramatically raised, 'What are you *doing?*'

'We are having a cuddle,' says Anne.

'But . . .' What the daughter is wanting to say is, But why am I excluded? 'You're disgusting,' she announces.

'We parents have our rights,' remarks Peter peaceably.

'I'm coming in too,' says the daughter.

'Then you'll have to call all the others,' says Anne. 'Otherwise its favouritism.'

The girl emits a moaning shriek and runs off. 'I *hate* you.'

Histrionic shrieks of laughter from here and there over the house. 'Oh, they are so *awful!*'

In that family the unpleasant aspects of adolescence seemed to have been effortlessly transformed into attractive and certainly self-conscious theatricals.

Sometimes I sit and think about the especially good and nice people I have known, which is a way of making myself feel better in bad times, and David Piper—Peter—is always there. He was quiet and ironical and an observer, so he was not immediately remarkable. He died much too young, probably because he had been in a Japanese prison camp for some years, never a recipe for a long and healthy life. At the time I knew him, he was running the National Portrait Gallery.

Writing these memoirs, I have learned a good deal about memory's little tricks, most of all how it simplifies, tidies up, makes sharp contrasts of light and shade. It simply cannot be true that the four years of Warwick Road were as bad as I remembered them, nor that Langham Street was all movement and pleasurable meetings. But the slow living through the fifties really was like crawling up out of a pit.

I look back on scenes in my flat, my small ugly flat, but crammed with people. I cooked extravagantly, because I enjoyed it. The faces are in my mind, but alas, not all the names. And what a mix of people, and of all ages too, for there were Peter's friends and the children of friends. I have always asked everyone I know or whom I have even casually met to my parties, and it has always worked. There have been violent arguments sometimes, and then: How *can* you know that fascist/communist/neurotic/psychopath/idiot? But not often.

At one party—but now we are jumping ahead to the house in Charrington Street and a large gathering, about thirty, for a lunch— two women, together, came across the room to say, 'Do you realise how extraordinary it is for us to see a woman doing this?'

'Doing what? I don't understand.' One woman from New York, one from Moscow, and they had been conferring.

'In New York, if you are a single woman you don't have parties, you wait to be invited by married friends. You go into a kind of purdah until you find a man.'

'And with us, no woman without a man would dare to have a party like this.'

I had not seen myself as out of the ordinary and had to take their word for it. But I was having two thoughts, one of them far from new: if you just do something, people accept it, whether it is socially customary or not. The other thought was that New York was being seen by us all as the acme of social sophistication, and surely Moscow should be free of all such middle-class taboos? Very soon would arrive the feminist revolution, and then it would be taken for granted—surely?—that a single woman could throw a party and invite anyone she wanted to.

A scene: Late-ish one evening, Lindsay Anderson came to my flat with a group of actors from the Royal Court, one being Robert Shaw, who would shortly marry Mary Ure, just being dumped by John Osborne. I had never met Robert Shaw, but he at once, as if carrying on some conversation we had been having, told me that he was sleeping with So-and-so, and this much improved sex with his wife, and wives should never object to their husbands' sleeping around, for it was as good as an aphrodisiac. Women simply didn't know what was good for them. He was full of the restless glitter actors bring with them off the stage. As for me, he had always adored me, he was meeting me at last, and so he went on for some minutes, while Lindsay listened, with a schoolmasterly air, and said from time to time, 'Enough of that, Robert, now stop it.' And then off they all went into the night, Lindsay shepherding them. 'Now come on . . . enough . . . time for bed.' Lindsay knew he was absurd, playing the role of fussy governess, knew he was infuriating, impossible. Yet he always was loveable, but why that should be so I have no idea. And that was the last I saw of Robert Shaw until they put on *The Changeling* at the Royal Court, Robert playing opposite Mary Ure, and everyone in the theatre knew that he was madly in love with her. 'I love that woman!' was delivered with such passion that life itself overthrew the play, and everyone applauded.

Edward Thompson came to see me. What about? It had to be about something. He wouldn't have just dropped in for a cup of tea. Afterwards he stands in the street outside my flat. It is an ugly flat, in an ugly building, and the street is not inspiring. Edward raises his right fist and declaims to the sky: 'Babylon! What am I doing in Babylon? I must leave.' And shaking the dust of London from his feet, he departs for the healthful north.

Edward Thompson is in the middle of that process, being frozen into the past, as the Marxist historian of working-class Britain. But his contemporaries remember him as several times larger than most people, romantic, always in passionate debate, and with that kind of imagination that lights every scene he is part of or describes with generous hopes for humankind. I wish I believed that there were young Edward Thompsons growing up in Britain to take his place, but alas, we live in a grudging, cold, cautious time.*

Just before I left Langham Street, *Play with a Tiger* was at last put on, and I spent a good bit of time at the rehearsals, partly because I had become a good friend of Ted Kotcheff's. While I liked Siobhan McKenna, it was not possible to be friends with her, because after the play she went off with seriously drinking friends to all-night parties, wild drunk-ups, erratic and defiant behaviour of all kinds, for she had to be the wild child, a broth of a woman. I simply did not have the stamina for it. This was what Ireland had made of her, the role she had been given, and she played it to the hilt, her long wonderful dark-red hair more often than not uncombed, her rich voice and vocabulary heard all over the theatre or wherever she was. At the risk of all kinds of accusations, I am going to say that to be an Irish artist is to carry an extra load. You are in

*Edward died in 1993.

Spain, you are at a dinner party, and there is the archetypical Irishman, with his wild poetic talk, his charm, and he is drunk, he says he is on a spree, he hasn't been home for three days, and what will his poor wife say? His poor wife will have no alternative to doing what she has so often done—she must forgive him when he comes guiltily back. 'Oh, how could you?' But he can, he has, and will, again and again, because that is in the script, or perhaps is some sort of curse: if you are Irish and a poet, then here is written what you have to do.

I was in Dublin and visiting the poet John Montague. He was married to a French aristocratic woman, who could not have found life easy in that small flat, and he sat with a bottle of Irish whisky in his hands, and we listened and laughed, while his wife vacuumed the floor, he moving his legs this way and that to avoid the machine, and he said, 'French aristocrats, they are peasants really, isn't that the truth, my darling?' and she said, 'Just as well for you I am, and if any more of your drunken friends arrive at the door I will not let them in.' So he swung down those long thin legs of his to the floor and said, 'Come on, we'll go and see Behan.' A couple of streets away lived Brendan Behan, the playwright. It was about ten in the morning. Brendan was sober when we arrived. We sat talking about—what else?—the Royal Court Theatre, and Joan Littlewood's theatre, and the conversation was all good sense and theatre expertise. But a journalist was expected, from London. He was to come at twelve. We watched Brendan work himself into the part of a drunken Irishman. I saw that Brendan was watching Brendan adjusting his performance, creating this character who was currently so often in the newspapers, sometimes on the front pages. Brendan would take a mouthful of whisky from the bottle in his hand, say a few sentences, permitting them to show drunkenness, then another mouthful of whisky, and by the time the London man came, and we left them together, Brendan was at the height of his performance, the wild Irish poet. If the journalist had not been coming, I think we would have spent a pleasant, sober enough day, fit for conversation and very far from smashing things up and wild poetic ravings. But the script says a poetic Irish playwright has to drink, and the media confirm it. The media never wasted an opportunity to describe Brendan as wild and drunk, and so in the end the drink killed him, it did him in—now that was a big loss to the theatre and to the rest of us.

The person from the cast of *Play with a Tiger* whom I did see a bit was Maureen Prior, the one who was ill in bed when the script arrived but dragged herself up on a freezing day to audition, and got the part. Maureen Prior was warm, impulsive, with the gift of instant friendship, and her husband was judicious, cool, intellectual. I thought, Well, here we go again. What would happen if Nature actually liked it when two compatible people married—for instance, two warm, open, bubbly people, for surely joy would be unconfined—but then if two cool, detached, inhibited people married, I suppose they would never be able to get their arms around each other.

For a while I was with theatre people a good deal, and not only because of having a play on. A wildly idealistic plan was being hatched, to take the starch, as we saw it, out of the London theatre. There were bright—very bright—spots: the Royal Court, Bernard Miles at the Mermaid Theatre in the city, the Arts Theatre, Oscar Lowenstein. But most theatres were being run by very conventional commercial managements. The scene was different from today's, with so many small innovative and adventurous theatres, plays being put on in pubs, and above all the National Theatre and the South Bank. Now we take it for granted that a theatre can be a social centre, with all kinds of activities going on—lectures, study groups, seminars, music, restaurants, bookshops. But there was nothing like that then.

The idea was to get hold of a warehouse in Covent Garden and create a structure which would accommodate every kind of experimental theatre, new playwrights, workshops, and plays from other countries. For then few foreign plays reached Britain.

Who were we, these hopeful dreamers? The idea was Gareth Wigan's. He was then an agent (he is now helping to run Warner Brothers in Hollywood), and it was in his Belgravia house that we met. Ted Kotcheff, Ted Allan, Sean Connery, Mordecai Richler,

Shelagh Delaney, the theatre designer Sean Kenny, who died too young, Clive Exton. Over a period of some weeks in 1960 we met a dozen or so times, and our plans became as solid as an architect's blueprint. There was a lot of experience in that room, of theatre, film, television, radio. We had no doubt we could raise money. Conversations with monied people showed how much support there would be. I still think that money would have been the least of our problems. As for us, we would all work for nothing, or for nominal pay, for we intended to be a living reproach to commercial theatre. We found a warehouse. It was in poor condition, but that did not matter, for it would be easier to adapt for our purposes. We called a meeting in the warehouse one Sunday morning. Word of mouth and a small advertisement attracted a couple of hundred people—actors, playwrights, designers, directors. Many of them were in work; it was not just a question of people who were feeling rejected. The atmosphere was as encouraging as we had hoped. It was a political atmosphere in that the enemy was the West End theatre managements, despised thoroughly and instinctively by us, like Joan Littlewood anathematising them as rotten, if not evil. This was partly the set of mind which took it for granted that anything commercially successful had to be bad, and is still with us: I think it is a displacement of the aristocratic contempt for trade, come to rest improbably as a part of left-wing thinking. Partly it was a hangover from communism. Most of the people in the arts then had been communists of some kind, and this new theatre was being seen as a stand not only against the West End but against all tyranny in the theatre, the Communist Party Line in particular. It is now forgotten that many, perhaps most, of the actors of that time had worked in Unity Theatre—the communist theatre—at some time or other, and everyone had seen a theatre famous for its lively iconoclasm destroyed by the heavy hand of King Street. And then the theatre union, Equity, was run by communists, using all the tricks of the trade, and most actors thoroughly disliked them. That morning in Covent Garden there was much excitement, optimism, agreement: everything was in place, we were set to go. At the meeting after that Sunday we all knew we had reached the point of having to decide who was to run it. None of us wanted to; we had our work to do. We would contribute in every way we could, but we could not run it. So whom would we ask? No one seemed exactly right. If this were happening now it would be easy, for there are many lively, flexible people of the kind we needed, in a wonderfully gifted generation.

Well, then, all right, who? A good many readers will recognise this situation. It is the same as when writers decide they can do better than publishers, get together to make a publishing house, may actually set one up—and then go back to their real work, writing, having hired someone to do the job. But in what way is this new creation different from any publishing house? I've seen this more than once, and it doesn't work. At the heart of such an enterprise must be, not a hireling, but that passionate, inspired, dedicated lunatic who knows how to move mountains.

So there we were, with our grandiose and romantic schemes in place, being besieged by letters and telephone calls from people wanting to be part of it all, but there was a vacuum at the heart of the thing.

And now enter Arnold Wesker. I ran into him somewhere, said I was involved with a scheme that might interest him—he was himself engaged in similar enterprises, all of them in the early stages. He came in late to a meeting when we were all mellow and relaxed, full of confidence, because our scheme had gone so well, with everything organised but the one essential. Arnold sat unsmiling and then announced, 'There is only one person who can run this thing, and I am the person.' Ted Allan joked that Stalin had spoken. And that was the end—the end, that is, of the scheme as we envisaged it. Off went Arnold to start Centre 42, expecting opposition from us. But every one of us had had more than enough of confrontational politics, and we simply left Arnold to get on with it. What we felt was something like, 'Oh well, he'll grow out of it.' I am sure we did not see how absurd this parental stance was when we had so recently grown out of it ourselves. It is only fair to record that he saw us all as a lot of clapped-out old Marxists.

So that was how Centre 42 really started. Like Joan Littlewood before him, Arnold found the working class less than enthusiastic about his efforts. But always, when this point is reached in a debate which after all recurs, and recurs, I remember the miners in Armsthorpe, with tears in their eyes, talking about Sybil Thorndike and others going to the mining village to play Shakespeare for them. And only a couple of years later I was to see a couple of idealistic young teachers giving some working-class fifteen-year-olds a holiday before they began work and their adult lives, and this consisted not only of all kinds of trips into the Oxford countryside but of three visits to the theatre at Stratford. And these children, whose parents had never been near a theatre, loved the theatre, loved Shakespeare. Probably the organised trade-union movement was the wrong mechanism to use: the name Centre 42 derived from a resolution passed at the 1960 TUC that there should be an enquiry into the state of the arts.

And now, as I look back, what seems so extraordinary is how important we thought it all was, our plans for creating a 'new' style of theatre, which in the end evolved quite happily without us.

There is a sad joke. The Round House,★ where Arnold centred his efforts but then had to give up, became rather what our original scheme had hoped for. A great many people were involved with it, and there were workshops and lectures and a bookshop and restaurants, and many productions from other countries. The Round House was a most agreeable place to spend an evening. It would be flourishing to this day, but the dead hand of ideology struck again. The Camden Town Council decided this was the place for a black artistic centre. Why, when the black communities were mostly in another part of London, were nowhere near the Round House? But one cannot argue with ideologies. They never got their black centre going, but they had destroyed what there was, and the Round House stood empty, for years, and is still empty. Sometimes when I drive past I wonder what those brave left-wing councillors feel about what they did: probably a small secret feeling of satisfaction, for I am sure that in their hearts is a fear of art. They probably

★The Round House in north London, an enormous building, has had many incarnations and was the place where Customs and Excise kept liquors and wines, before it became a theatre.

hated the anarchic lively flourishing youthful atmosphere of the Round House.

The Committee of a Hundred organised a big 'demo' in Trafalgar Square for Sunday, 18 September 1960. At once the police banned it. This was not an intelligent thing to do. For one thing, it was to behave exactly as their worst enemies said they did. For another, Trafalgar Square had seen big popular demonstrations for a century or more, and to ban one was deliberately to insult all that history. Then there was the practical aspect. So many streets run into Trafalgar Square that to keep people out must need hundreds of police. And there was one little thing that the police overlooked: the National Gallery is in Trafalgar Square, but probably this wasn't on their mental map of the place.

I am told by those people who know the top levels of the police that they are the most intelligent, charming, admirable people in the world, but most of us meet the police on somewhat lower levels, and my experience has been that on the whole they aren't very bright. I am white, middle class, and after about ten years in London became middle-aged, and so am not the kind of person to attract the famous police brutality, though I have friends of various colours, ages, and kinds who have. But I have a whole repertoire of incidents involving the police where they figure not as callous but as inept.

There is one small happening that is as revealing as any. I was witness to a traffic accident; a policeman came to interview me and remarked that he was leaving the force, not long after joining, because he didn't like what he had to do. 'For instance?'

'Having to tell so many lies,' said he.

But the police have been reformed more than once since then.

'How could the police possibly be so stupid?' enjoyably scandalised voices resounded up and down the ranks during the week or so before the confrontation. For a confrontation everybody knew it was going to be. A lot of people looked forward to it. A clash. A fight. So many people enjoy this kind of thing.

Before that Sunday I had two visits. One was from Shelagh Delaney, who said she hated demos and riots and even large numbers of people massed together, but she supposed we had to do it? My sentiments, exactly. The other was from Vanessa Redgrave, in a high fever of excitement, like a beautiful young Joan of Arc, or Boadicea, going on about the brutality of the police. It was getting late, and I indicated that I wanted to go to bed. She got herself to her elegant height and demanded, 'How *can* you even *think* of going to sleep on a night like this?' It is a cliché that the stage you have just grown out of is intolerable when you see it in someone else; and I was thinking, Oh my God, that was me not so long ago, and how did people put up with me?

On Sunday at midday, before they closed the square, hundreds of us made our way to the National Gallery, and there I met with John Osborne and we whiled away the time pleasurably enough. At the right time, we all grouped ourselves, and I took John's arm, to support him, for he hated doing this: he was miserable. We walked down the steps of the National Gallery, a large crowd of us, and went into the square and sat down. The police massed themselves around the perimeters. Many of the sitters-down steadily insulted and taunted the police, as usual, and some of us, as usual, found this childish and useless. It all went on and on. Everyone knew that the moment the press and television left, the police would pile into the square and start arresting us. I was sitting near John. Oscar Beuselink, his lawyer, with whom he later quarrelled, was there. Oscar said to me, 'Why is it that there are all these hundreds of people, but John is being treated as if he is an invalid or a rookie going into battle for the first time?' True, but people get treated in the way they demand or need to be. The fact is, John was feeling ill. Most people thoroughly enjoyed themselves. There sat Bertrand Russell, like a little terrier with his acolytes. There was Lindsay Anderson, stern, martial, disapproving of everyone as usual. Nearly everybody I knew seemed to be there. I was unhappy for various reasons, one being that Peter was hovering about just beyond the ranks of police, very anxious, though I had promised him I would not permit myself to be beaten up. And he was not the only child there, afraid for parents or older siblings. And then I was beginning to question the value of 'demos', of 'sitting-downs', of clashes with the police, simply because some people did enjoy it all so much.

Was it in fact that their first impulse was the enjoyment, the excitement, the thrills, or the socialising, and secondly came the politics? Now I believe this to be so. The cameras were rolling away, the journalists moved up on their bottoms to be close to their interviewees, the taunts at the police grew louder and louder, you could see how the police eyed certain people they were targeting, and then off went the press, the cameras—the witnesses—and in swooped the police. They lifted up the people sitting down who would not get up, took them to the vans, but ignored people like myself, who stood up and walked. I heard the mayor of one of the London boroughs shouting at the police, who in fact had not touched her, 'Filthy beasts,' just like Miss Ball. I was with Oscar Beuselink, who was observing in his professional capacity how the vans went off with their loads. The police were careful not to handle famous people roughly, but they were knocking about those who had been taunting them. In one of the vans, a youth nearly died: he had been flung in with his jacket pulled up over his head in such a way he could not breathe. Others in the van, realising he had not moved or spoken, got the jacket off him and found him blue and unconscious. They told the police, 'You nearly killed him,' but they replied, 'Lucky you were there, then, wasn't it?'

I had difficulty then and have difficulty now about what I think about these 'demos'. Did that one change government policy? Change anybody's mind when they saw it on national television? Was I saying, am I saying, that the fact there are people who adore fighting with the police means their efforts have no value? I know one thing, though: during subsequent Committee of a Hundred demonstrations, shortly to begin, when there was a real battle outside the American Embassy and confrontations outside nuclear installations, a hard core of people was there because of the thrill of it all.

As for that sit-down, it at once took its place on the roll call of great fights between citizens and authority in Trafalgar Square.

Shortly after that I was an observer of another political confrontation. It was decided to 'sit down' outside No. 10 Downing Street to protest about the Bomb. I was standing on the pavement, watching. Ernest Rodker was sitting down, among a mass of people. He had been until then unpolitical, probably in reaction to his political mother. When the police came in to rout the sitters, Ernest performed his first political act. He tipped forward a policeman's helmet, not the cleverest thing to do. At once he was set on by six policemen, who kicked and punched him as he lay between their legs, trying to cover his head. Next morning I was in Bow Street when the judge sentencing him said, 'You are obviously a young man with an inveterate propensity for violence.' So started Ernest's career as a political activist. He was a prominent member of the Committee of a Hundred for years.

Somewhere in this area belong thoughts of 'the Bomb'. That is how the nuclear threat was perceived: as a single final conclusive dead-end explosion which would at a stroke kill everyone in the world and lay it waste probably for centuries. There were two initiatory exemplars, Hiroshima and Nagasaki. Two bombs. Yet it was 'the Bomb' that dominated our minds, our songs, the speeches, the manifestos. The idiot thumb presses down, the Bomb falls, and that is the end of everything. In the very distant future a few mutated survivors will creep about on poisoned soil, and life will begin again.

But where did that pattern come from—the pattern in our minds—because it had to be that, a pattern common to everyone marching, demonstrating, writing. The Apocalypse, Armageddon, the fire next time.

I got a letter from some young scientists—but that was in the seventies—asking why I was helping to perpetuate a false way of looking at the threat, which was not a single final doom, or apocalypse, but rather a multiplicity of dangers, such as, for instance, the fact that large areas of the Soviet Union had been devastated, poisoned, made uninhabitable by explosions and accidents which had never been reported officially. This kind of thing was much more of a danger than a single Bomb. (Still ahead, of course, was Chernobyl.) If I wanted to be useful, was the suggestion, I should not be adding to the talk about the Bomb but rather pointing out that there were many different dangers.

When I wrote *Shikasta,* the first volume of 'Canopus in Argos:

Archives', and I had the Bomb falling, it was the Northern Hemisphere that was devastated and uninhabitable—but this was not what people 'took in' when they read, because readers talked as if I had described the ruination of the whole world. It is not the story, the plot, that interests me now, but the fact that it was taken absolutely for granted that if a Bomb fell, then it had to be totally destructive. *The* Bomb—and *the* end.

Is this pattern still in the collective mind, and if so, where is it operating? What did it—does it—contribute to what actually has happened? It certainly set me thinking about South Africa: for decades everyone thought there was going to be the 'night of the long knives', the 'bloodbath'—no two ways about it.

Hushabye baby on the treetop,
When the wind blows the cradle will rock,
When the wind blows the cradle will fall,
And down will fall baby and cradle and all.

Somewhere towards the end of the sixties, I found that I was laughing, unexpectedly, helplessly: first, a disbelieving and incredulous yelp, and then a real laugh, ha ha, oh my God, but it's so funny . . .

What was? Sex, that's what. This laugh is out of its proper place only chronologically, because it was not merely the sixties I was looking at but the fifties too: as I have already hinted, sex did not begin in the sixties.

What distinguished the fifties, and then the sixties, was that there were no rules. Surely this must have been the first time in history—in any history that we remember—that there were no commonly accepted conventions and at the same time there was access to birth control. Anything went. And there were to be no rules until the advent of AIDS, which restored morality at a stroke.

I would say that in the fifties, in the way of love, or sex, the most obvious thing—obvious later—is that people were going to bed because it was expected of them. (The Zeitgeist demanded.) Some people were coupling like hypnotised fish bumping into each other. Curiosity? Perhaps, a little. Sexual fever, not at all. These embraces had nothing to do with love, and not much to do with sex either. I mean, real sexual attraction. There was a passivity about it all.

No one knew how to behave, neither men nor women. And this is why there was so much unhappiness, so much incomprehension. Do I exaggerate? Yes, I do, because I am leaving out of this account the enjoyable and happy encounters.

We are all now well equipped with handbooks explaining the basic differences between men and women, but the sixties coincided with a stage in the feminist movement which denied all differences between men and women. Or, as D. H. Lawrence put it, women were just as good as men, only better.

No ideological rages are likely to be aroused now at the news that men and women are biologically programmed to want different things—at the root of their natures, never mind how civilisation or culture or current morality decides to tame us. There is no man who has not dreamed of that brief encounter where emotion does not enter for even one moment, that quick fuck without any strings or obligations, and not with a prostitute either. A fantasy of some golden age hovers here, I think. And there is no woman whose first emotion is not 'Is this the man I'm looking for?' and this even when she has resolved to set this aside, having decided to be more like men, enjoying the fun of it all, for a night or two. I am prepared to bet that there is no woman who has not been left after the most enjoyable night imaginable, and even if neither knows the other's name, or wants to, without, as he leaves—full of love, admiration, and gratitude for her aplomb—a suddenly dull and empty feeling, for she has gone against her real deep nature and she must pay for it, even if only for half an hour.

How often have women who have with the most honest, open-hearted intentions spent a night with a man not found themselves swearing, raging: 'You bloody heel. Surely you could at least ring up? Can't you even send some flowers?' For the flowers would be ample, would be enough, a psychological balance would be redressed. And meanwhile the man, full of affection and pleasure, is thinking, Now, at last, a woman who understands how to enjoy life and who doesn't say, 'Do you really love me?'

The Victorians knew what they were about, with their prescribed tributes of flowers from man to woman. I am tempted to say they knew what they were doing in laying down so many rules and restrictions. Romance is the child of prohibition. But let's leave romance out, for there are some parts of the world where it seems to have become obsolete, And already in the fifties there was the beginning of the feeling that sex was on an agenda, something that ought to be done, and blame would accrue if it was not performed.

I am walking down Church Street, Kensington, with Donald Ogden Stewart, and we are going to have dinner, his suggestion. He must be sixty or so, a lean, balding, freckly, sandy man, and I am thirty-something. He says to me, 'I ought to tell you that these days I am more interested in food than in sex.' I was absolutely, coldly furious. That it was so graceless—well, what did one expect? meaning, specifically, from Americans; but there had never been, not for one second, any suggestion of a physical attraction, and anyway he was old. Now I see this as a quite sensible (if graceless) way of dealing with the situation. After all, he had come from Hollywood, and from the Left in America, and probably had had affairs by the dozen. To his contemporaries he must have seemed an attractive man. None of us find it easy to know that we are not as attractive as we once were. He had thought, I'm not going to sit through the whole dinner while she is wondering if I'm going to make a pass.

Again I have been out to dinner with a high executive in Granada Television, for I am going to write for them. He drinks heavily all evening. But everyone drank a lot then; these days if you invite people to dinner or a party, the amount of alcohol drunk is a tenth of what it was then. He drives me home and says, 'I'm sorry, I can't make it, I'm too drunk.' Yet there had not been a flicker of sexual interest between us. I am furious. The oaf. The idiot. The conceited fool. The story 'One Off the Short List' is apropos.

I look back and see myself, a forthright, frank young woman, often tactless out of a genuine outrage at what I still saw as dishonesty. I despised all female ruses, as insults to real friendship, to humanity, and to humanism itself. I would have scorned to play hard to get, to coquette, play hot and cold. I would say this is generally true of the Western female, but I was also a colonial and even more liberated from the hypocritical shackles of the past—as I saw it. A comradely equality, that was my style, easy friendliness, even intimacy.

To see the difference between liberated Western girls and, let's say, Indians, one only has to spend an hour in a mixed group and watch the languishing eyes, deep glances, sighs, little fluttering withdrawals, coquettish veils and scarves always at their work. It is not that such operators do not exist in the West, and when she appears then the liberated ones have to stand back helpless and watch men fall before her, for the traditional dishonesties are based on the soundest knowledge of male and female nature. A woman playing hot and cold is at the oldest and most successful game in the world—the rules are admirably set forth in Stendhal's *Love*. But how can one enjoy that ideal, perfect, *honest,* loving friendship with a man on whom you are playing such tricks? And yet for some women these aren't tricks, they're doing what comes naturally . . . and so we go around and around.

With Western women, particularly the English, men don't know where they are: except those men with an instinctive understanding of women, with whom one immediately sets up a current of happy complicity.

To put an end to this flounder in marshy waters: the comradely and helpful equality meant that (means that) a man may think a woman is in love with him—simply because he has been admitted into an easy intimacy—and may rejoice or run a mile. But equally, since she is still a woman and full of a certain residual shyness underneath all that friendliness, she may be madly in love with him and he never suspects it.

I look back on tangles of misunderstanding. Men whom I liked, with whom I intended friendship, imagined I was in love and were confused when refused, became huffy, were hurt: *Why did she lead me on?* Men who I hoped would see I fancied them did not know it, since the signs were so well camouflaged by general mateyness. The free-and-easy, anything goes of the fifties, and then the sixties, obscured genuine emotions, attractions, repulsions. If there is a convention that easy sex is a sign of general liberation, civilisation, and equality, then what happens to all the subtle to-and-fro, the natural affinities and antipathies—real sex, in short?

To add to the confusion, I enjoyed flirting, but then I don't see that as any more than a pleasant game, an agreeable convention. Well, it is in some parts of the world. Recently I met a couple of young Mexican women who had gone to Canada and the United States for a holiday. Used to the flattering attention of men and to the pleasures of flirting, they soon wondered what was wrong with them: had they lost all their looks and their charm? Enquiring of a sympathetic male friend, they were told, 'You don't understand: men can't show they find women attractive any longer; they may find themselves in prison.'

My most bizarre sexual encounter was with Ken Tynan. I had gone with him to the theatre and then to some party of actors winding down after a performance. Ken was the star, shedding witticisms and benevolent advice and criticism. Then it was very late, and he suggested I stay the night in Mount Street. The young of every generation have to imagine they have invented casual ways, but the innocent sharing of beds did not begin in the sixties. Not once, nor twice, have I spent a friendly night with some man because we haven't finished our conversation or because he missed the last train. Never, not for the slice of a second, had there been sexual attraction between Ken and me. I cannot imagine two human beings less likely to make each other's pulses flutter. I had often been in the Tynan bedroom, because it was where we left coats during parties. I came back from the bathroom to get into bed beside companionable Ken, and suddenly the bedroom walls had been grotesquely transformed, for on them were arranged every sort of whip, as if in a whip museum. Now, you'd think, wouldn't you, that Ken would say, 'Are you wondering what all those whips are doing there?' Or I would say, 'Now, about those whips, Ken?' Not at all; there we lay, side by side, conversing agreeably about a hundred things, but certainly politics, because that was our favourite subject. I used to tell him he was romantic, not to say sentimental, and ignorant, and he complained I was cynical and lacking faith in humanity. I remember an occasion when he summoned me to a meeting to discuss how to protest about something, I forget what, with several prominent people. I said I found this business of celebrities 'sitting down' in public to fast as a protest absurd and laughable, because everyone knew that the moment the 'fast' was over we would all be off to a five-star restaurant. Ken thought I was lacking in any instinct for publicity, and he was afraid I often showed reactionary tendencies.

And so we fell asleep and were woken by a female menial bringing breakfast on two trays. (Ken refused to cook, and so did Elaine Dundy. Neither knew how to boil an egg, they proudly claimed, and they always ate in restaurants. Even breakfast was brought in.) Then she tidied away the whips.

The same sort of thing happened to me with other well-known men—whose names I am withholding—but Ken not only made no secret of his tastes but flaunted them. He took to extremes the didact's need to believe that everyone must be the same as himself, describing his somewhat perverse musical *Oh, Calcutta* as 'after-dinner entertainment for civilised people'.

A scene: A party in Mount Street. Ken is confronting a young actress, newly arrived in London. He is trying to persuade her that her refusal to accept whips and associated delights was because she had been taught prejudice.

'You have been conditioned,' says Ken, his stammer reinforcing his pedagogical self. He towers over her while she smiles delightfully up at him.

'But, Ken,' she murmurs, 'I don't enjoy it.'

He is checked, but the force of his need to instruct carries him on. 'You have been taught to think that there is only one way of having sex.'

'I wouldn't exactly say only one. . . .' She smiles, earning applause from the listening party-goers.

'Only one kind,' says Ken, and is probably on the point of launching into informational anecdotes from Greece and Rome and the Lord knows where else, but she again says firmly, 'Ken, I don't enjoy it.'

And now one may observe the switch in him from the teacher to the wit. 'I must protest that you have unfairly silenced me,' says

Ken. 'I have no more to say. How, logically, could I have? How could you not have my blessing? Enjoy, then, my darling.'

It is a disconcerting thing for a more or less normal woman, after having enjoyed dinner and chat about literature, the theatre, politics, to find one's host suggesting a little diversion with whips, as if saying, 'A drop of port, perhaps? Or I have some nice dessert wine.' Or even producing the whips—once it was a sjambok, always irresistible to sadomasochists—and reacting to a refusal as if it were you, not he, who was a little strange.

The following little tale is here because of the talk about black men's superiority in bed. White women lusting after black penises is one of the myths furnishing the colonial mind, and I was listening to variations on the myth as I grew up. And then this particular incident happened at a time when the prowess of black studs was much vaunted, because for some reason the superiority of black people's sexuality (men and women both) had become part of 'progressive' thinking.

A certain exiled black writer was putting in his time in London. He pursued me for months, full of ardour; he loved me, he could not sleep for thinking of me. Sighs and suffering, the language of romantic despair—the lot. Now, I had never been to bed with a black man. This was because I did not really fancy them. You could say it was my early conditioning, if it were not that the same conditioning has produced people, but I think mostly men, who yearn for black flesh. It was because of pity for his state that I eventually gave in, expecting to assuage a painful passion. The actual sexual contact lasted perhaps three minutes, and then he fell asleep. His snores were such as I had never heard before nor have since. I removed myself to another bed and slept peacefully till morning. When I took him in a cup of tea he was uxorious and complacent. Then he saw I had not slept beside him and demanded to know why. The inhibitions of a proper upbringing—'You must *never* hurt people's feelings'—intervened, and I murmured, 'You were snoring.' He seemed surprised. Having drunk his tea, he dressed and said that he was so happy. He then resumed his romantic pursuit—telephone calls, passionate letters, encounters in the street, where he had been lying in wait. I cannot help feeling that all this romantic passion of his had derived from literature. I have some-times caught a certain ironical look on the faces of black women friends when told of the amorous fame of their partners. But perhaps I was unlucky.

Another occasion I remember with shame. This was a black man too, and he was from Jamaica. Madly in love, he was, and his pursuit was lengthy and exhaustive. Remembering my previous experience, I kept saying no, and then at last I thought, as women may do, Oh, for God's sake, what am I making such a fuss about, if it means so much to him? I took off all my clothes—and then I put them on again, for by now I was thinking, Why the hell should I, when I don't want to? This was a terrible thing to do. Cruel. As my mother might have said, though in a somewhat different context, There are things a decent woman doesn't do.

There was a theatre director who was as queer as they come, and famously so, with whom I shared the easy friendship women do with some homosexuals. A rumbunctious sexual romp of a play was running, *Lock Up Your Daughters,* and in it was the line, 'When is the ravishing going to start?' I am descending a staircase, glass in one hand and a cigarette in the other, and this suitor stops me by gripping both my arms while he stands in front of me, demanding, 'And *when* is the ravishing going to start?' A joke, you'd think, but no, for a time whenever we met he'd accost me, by now full of accusation, saying, 'It is your duty to initiate me into the joys of this heterosexual sex we hear so much about.'

And now an embattled subject, American men. Things may very well have changed, for they always do, but in those days a lot of comparisons were being made, invidious or not. A woman cannot have as bed partners first a man from the centre of Europe and then one from America, both womanisers on principle, without brooding about differences. I say 'womanisers' and not 'lovers of women' here, because no one could accuse—then—Americans of that willing if sometimes whimsical subjection to the magics and manias of love that we call romance. All the Americans I knew had a certain attitude to sex—let's not call it love—and they all played a role. Mensch. Tough guys. Where did it come from? I think, like jazz and a lot else in American culture, from black culture. A real man loves them and leaves them—no, fucks them and leaves them. There was something willed about it and something joyless. A practical lot, they are, down to earth. Or were. Now, the essence—surely—of this masculine woman-haver- and -subduer is something active, dominant, is one who sets the pace and draws the boundaries. But as we all know, extremes meet, and extremes turn into their opposites.

Imagine a room and in it several women, all European, and it is the mid-sixties. We are talking about American men. We have all had American lovers—no, bedfellows—and two of us have actually had, or been had by, the same man. It is not common, this kind of conversation between women—or it wasn't then—and it all happened by chance. There we were, ten or so of us . . . the talk led from one thing to another. The conclusions I am offering are too comprehensive to be the result of only one woman's researches.

Would we all agree that American men loved with their heads and not their hearts? Absolutely; their hearts were not involved. Would we agree that in those heads was a blueprint for behaviour with women, in bed and out of it, and they performed—or fucked—not from some deep instinct or (perish the thought) the need to express love, but from a need to affirm to themselves that they were indeed mensches? Here D. H. Lawrence was quoted: 'warm-hearted fucking', for instance. It is interesting how often this writer is quoted in conversations of this sort. For if he knew very little about sex, he did know a lot about love. But in parenthesis, perhaps we should remember that the expertise in sex we all pride ourselves on is after all recent: nothing unusual then about Lawrence's ignorance; it was general.

It was as if—we agreed—in the solar plexus of this performer was a cold place, an icy promontory, an extension from some continent all tundra. There was the intelligent head, there were the hot prick and balls, but in between, a cold defensive place.

The talk strayed off to the legacy of the troubadours and trouvères in France, in lovely France, for could we perhaps make a case that loving of a certain poetic and even fanciful kind had never reached Germany, whose culture had so extensively influenced America, and particularly its universities . . . ? Well, that was the kind of talk, and its culminating moment was when one television woman offered a little tale of a certain American film-maker, an exemplar of cock-and-balls, poised over her like an arched bow, but motionless, scolding her, 'Use it, use it, damn you.' Was not that the extreme of passivity, male as fucking machine, for the pleasure of the female, to be used by her (but was the word 'pleasure', with its frivolous associations, permissible here?)? Here was the absolute embodiment of a mensch but, at the moment of truth, passivity and instructions how to make use of him. Was this not a case of an extreme turning into an opposite? Well, yes, that was about it—at least for that time, for if you read novels and other witnesses of American culture, it was not always thus. No, a certain time produced the fucking machine, which, as everything has to do, disappeared. Or has it? Has feminism restored the warm heart, the male solar plexus radiating hot need like a little sun?

Probably the most interesting thing about this long-ago scene is its tone, so far from vindictiveness of the Cruel Sisters. For years—decades—perhaps centuries—women have been complaining about men's lack of sensitivity, their unkindness, but no sooner have women acquired power than they permit, even sanctify, some of the nastiest manifestations of human nature.

A television programme: In front of several million viewers, a liberated woman says, 'My husband is a bit of a wimp really.'

Turn it around: 'My wife is a very frightened soul, I am afraid, no courage.' Oh, the *callous* swine.

A dinner party: The wife, casually: 'My two husbands—' The husband: 'But surely you've had three, darling?' 'Oh, I wasn't counting you; I haven't had a child by you.'

'My wife's a disappointment to me. She's barren.' The *pig*.

Another party: 'My husband often can't get it up. He's semi-impotent.' This, loudly laughing.

Monsieur Sorel in *The Red and the Black,* the archetype of the thick insensitive boorish husband, with a sneer: 'Woman's delicate machinery . . .'

Only last week I got a letter from an American woman: 'Do you ever think about the female monsters you unleashed with *The Golden Notebook?* They hate men and hate women who love men.'

A scene: A famous American feminist is visiting London, and I go to see her with a man who has consistently taken a feminist position, and long before it was fashionable. As we walk through the hotel she deliberately slams one door after another in his face.

A scene: A building in London that houses a feminist publishing house has in it other offices, one of which is regularly visited by a friend of mine from the Middle East, as it happens an exemplary husband and father. It took him a long time, he said, to understand why it was that every time he passed the door of the publishing house, one of the females came out and deliberately stamped on his feet, as hard as she could. He was a Muslim and by definition enslaved women.

Not least depressing is that this kind of thing was thought of by the Cruel Sisters as *political* action.

The other day a group of women on one television channel were complaining about men's rudeness to them, and on another a woman was saying that all men are slimebags.

Could we have foreseen this efflorescence of crude stupidity? Yes, because every mass political movement unleashes the worst in human behaviour and admires it. For a time at least.

It certainly hasn't been easy to be a feminist these last thirty years.

Now Englishmen, if possible an even more embattled subject than American men: Englishwomen perennially sit around complaining about Englishmen. They don't really like women, they don't really like sex. Englishwomen go searching for true love among their compatriots but then often find it with men not English. It is not unknown for Englishwomen to take themselves abroad to find lovers, 'just to remind myself that I am still a woman.' Which hints at the real trouble, which is really a lack not of the thump thump of sex but the approaches to it. But surely these unromantic Englishmen are only the counterpart of the sisterly, comradely, straightforward women who, if they knew how to use female wiles, would despise them?

They are homosexuals, comes the plaint; it is because of those all-male schools they go to. But I think Englishmen are the most romantic men in the world, and this is precisely because of their incarceration in boys' schools, aged seven, to sob their hearts out for mummy night after night, with their heads beneath the bed-clothes. There is nothing like early-childhood deprivation for creating people (men and women) who fall drastically and repeatedly for out-of-reach loves. Some spend their lives with their romantic imaginations inhabited by unobtainable loves. Yet when they are at last matched, they are the best lovers, the most intelligent, and—most important—the funniest. What is wrong with Englishmen is not that they hate women, or even do not like them, but that their impressionable years were spent entirely with males. Life in a male public school is harsh. 'If you have been in English public school, then prison life, or being a hostage, is a mere bagatelle'—we have heard this again recently. And if public schools are less brutal and bullying than they were, these places are still, above all, hierarchies and structured like armies. After years of growing up in a narrow slot of humanity, at first desperately homesick and then learning emotional coldness; of finding some kind of warmth in sex with other boys or in intense emotional friendships . . . they escape to romantic love with women, powered by memories of the destitutions of their childhood and adolescence. And they grow older, marry or not, and there is always something missing, and it is the companionship of men. Women married to Englishmen don't have to fear losing them to another woman nearly so much as to the club or the companionableness of the office or any place where men are in groups. This is because no romantic or sentimental or domestic love can ever come up to the intensity of those years at school, like the companionship of soldiers. By now we all know that painful and unpleasant experience impresses itself; that we are taught masochism in a thousand ways. It is a horrid fact that soldiers may adore cruel commanding officers: 'I'd follow the brute to hell and back.' What they are adoring is the intensity of the experience. 'The best years of my life,' old soldiers will say, looking back at the horrors of war, but they were fiercely alive and, above all, in the close and undangerous companionship of men.

But you are talking about public school boys, surely a minority, readers may complain. True. But it is not only the upper classes; far from it. The most revealing clue to the dark depths of the English male psyche, a little fragment of evidence, is that perennial British comedy situation: an impervious, or unnoticing, or—and here is the essence of it—*serious* male is being pursued by a woman or a girl, and she is in love with him or fancies him. This can be good-humoured, or it can be cruel, but she is a figure of fun, she is ridiculous. It is a ritual humiliation, and it recurs again and again, and again and again; you can scarcely have a British comedy without it. Or there is this upright Englishman, and he finds himself in a harem or a group of sexy women, but he is sturdily indifferent to their absurd wiles. And surely it is not an accident that 'Not tonight, Josephine,' is a favourite and perennial joke. Only in Britain—or perhaps I should say England . . . And yet, now, I must say that there were two men I could have married or lived with happily ever after, and they were English.

There is a complaint by women, I think a new one, a concomitant of the sexual equality, and it goes like this: Here I am, an attractive woman, I cook like an angel, I am good in bed, I am self-sufficient—surely I am a pretty good bet for any man. But while they fall for me in droves, they go off and shack up with some green girl.

When that hopeless and helpless laughter overtook me, the best of it was because of this; and it was a long-overdue seeing of an absurdity. As one of our most famous poets puts it, with a wondering awe at the plentitudes of Nature, 'Every year they come tumbling out of their schools, these lovely girls, as certain as flowers in spring, and I always wonder, what have we done to deserve them?'

A sad little tale apropos: A certain friend, in her late forties, attractive, clever, competent, well-read, knowledgeable about politics, and financially independent, thought it unfair that a woman like herself was not valued above some nymphet. After too many unhappy experiences, she announced to her friends that she had seen the light. What she wanted was a middle-aged man, intelligent, well-read, interested in politics, not to live with or marry, but to share walks, meals, theatre, and bed 'when it comes over us. And I don't want ever again to wake with a man in my bed and then have to make breakfast for him. And I promise you this: I've been a port in the storm to my very last hopeful novelist or musician or poet.'

At the same time, a handsome, well-read, covetable man of middle age was saying he was sick to death with these girls he kept marrying and then having to divorce, and he wanted a mature, self-sufficient, well-read woman, who didn't want him to move in. What he valued now was his independence.

And now a group of us went to work, and with what tact, care, and deviousness. Neither of the protagonists was allowed even a hint of what was going on. We planned a party, a casual affair, of enough people for nothing to be obvious. This is what happened: Betty—we will call her—came in at the same time as—we will call him—Jeffrey. They at once noticed each other and began to exchange sharp witticisms. We, the observers, were pleased, since antagonism so often leads to happy endings. But alas . . . rather later there arrived an uninvited daughter of one of the conspirators, an apologetic girl of twenty or so, who was drawn to her fate like a little boat going over a waterfall, and she and Jeffrey left together to embark on yet another misfortune, while Betty went off with a neophyte actor from the Midlands, just arrived in London. He was hungry, he said loudly: 'For God's sake, won't some good woman take me home and feed me?'

There were two men then in London who had both removed themselves long before from the dangers of being chosen as a husband or a 'partner', who were unlike each other in every way, and yet on each passport, under 'Occupation' could have been written *Sex*.

One was South African, and behind him was a classically bad childhood, brutal father, beatings, coldness, and an early escape into the underworld of a big city. He had created for himself a house like a temple, not to love—certainly not—but to sex. How had this poor boy done it?—for it was a fine house. Much better not ask. It was a violent and sentimental house: here again the link between sentimentality—the tears in the eyes, as if an invisible observer were counting the tears, each one evidence of superior sensibility—and pain, but not necessarily physical, for this was as much psychological domination. The girls—of all ages—were adored, were worshipped, and subjugated. This kind of sex is not every woman's cup of tea.

The other man was from South America, part Japanese, part Spanish. He had a vast flat, and every item in it could have starred in a museum. He was very rich. He had been studying—and still was—sexual practices of the subtle and esoteric sort from many cultures. Unlike the man on the other side of London, he did not collect women, for he aimed to find at last that woman who would be his sole companion in the ways of love, because, he claimed, for real achievement in love, two bodies and hearts and—he would insist—souls, as well, should be perfectly in tune with each other, and this could take months, even years. He despised, could not take seriously, people with several or many sex partners, or even more than one. Mere amateurs: they understood nothing. His wife had been his colleague, his ideal, but she had insisted on having children, and so with regret they parted. She lived in a flat nearby, and he was a good father to the children, but as he said, children do not go well with the erotic life. With her he had sex of a utilitarian sort. I am of course tempted here to invent a chronicle of amorous adventure, a diary of arcane delights, but I had to earn my living, and there was a child to consider. My interesting friend understood the problem well: the pursuit of real love needed a reliable private income and childlessness, he said often. We met occasionally, before he left London for Spain, for a meal and a chat, and I heard all about his present researches, and occasionally did sigh a little, for surely there are few more delightful ways of passing the time—but even to use that phrase explains why I could never have been a suitable candidate. Besides, I must confess, perhaps slightly ashamed, like someone who has failed a high examination, that *long-term I would get bored*. Truly he was right when he said that one had to put one's whole heart into the thing, like searching for a Holy Grail or for a key to a mysterious hidden realm—the growing point, in fact—or otherwise expect the ravages of futility, a soured desert.

Four years after I arrived in Langham Street, Howard Samuels died. I was summoned to the office of Basil Samuels, Howard's brother, and found your classic hard-headed businessman and proud of it. 'I don't see why artists should be subsidised. I never agreed with my brother; he was always giving handouts to you people. Do you realise I could get ten times the rent for your flat than you are paying?' Clearly, what I was seeing was just another episode in a long-running disagreement or even antagonism between the brothers, and it was easy to understand it, looking at this tight-mouthed angry tycoon and thinking of easy-going, charming, witty—and left-wing—Howard Samuels. I asked if I could have three months' notice, because I had had every reason to think I could stay there indefinitely and I needed time to find a place. At last he agreed. It was not gracious, but I was grateful to him.

And now I had to find a house: partly because Peter wanted one so badly, needed that famous roof over his head, his roof, our roof, secure and for ever; and partly because, as always in Britain, the pressure was so strong for me to own something. When I needed an overdraft, it was always, Why don't you get a house? And everyone said, Why throw away your money paying rent? Put it into a mortgage. For in this country using your money to pay rent to keep yourself housed is not good enough: if you lack the ambition to actually own your roof, it betrays unserious, even bohemian, tendencies.

This time I was looking for houses in only one area, Camden Town. I found a place in a street shortly to house many famous people in the theatre and the arts, but the estate agent said, 'I wouldn't let my mother or my sister live in such a street.' Camden Town had yet to become fashionable, but meanwhile it was seeming to a lot of canny people a convenient place to live. Tom Maschler had difficulty getting money to buy a cheap house in Chalcot Square, shortly to be the last word in chic. A friend could not find a bank to lend her money for a vast house in Regent's Park Road, but borrowed, bought it for £6,000, and sold it twenty-five years later for over a million. Again and again the experts get it wrong. Who gets it right? Impractical and airy-fairy artists who do not care about being fashionable, care only about finding somewhere cheap and convenient.

Not only the estate agent but my bank would not hear of my buying a house in seedy Camden Town, and I was frantic with worry. Then appeared a certain gentleman I will call Len. Ten years earlier he would have been an evident fixer, or spiv, a crook, always on the lookout for a good thing—you can't put anything past *me*—but this was 1962, the beginning of the matey classless sixties, and looking back, I can pick out from a pretty variegated cast of characters quite a few who were not crooks but merely in tune with the times, and if this had been the eighties, then they would have been the darlings of the nation. Len was uneasy middle class, he wore a duffel coat, he had a smart haircut, and he dropped the names of actors and TV personalities. He took me to Charrington Street, in Somers Town, now famous for riots and crime, but once it took in refugees from France, the Huguenots.

Mary Wollstonecraft lived in Somers Town, with William Godwin, and their names are on the tombstones in the little graveyard round the corner. Shelley must have visited. It is a short street, and on one side the houses have been pulled down to make room for a big new school. The whole street was shabby and unpainted. No. 60, which was being sold because the old woman who owned it could no longer look after herself, was £4,000 cheaper than anything I had seen. It cost £4,500. Cheap with reason. It had not been painted for decades, probably not since it had been built, and its facade was cracked like the bed of a river in drought, and covered with dark-brown flakes, like stale chocolate. Nothing had been done inside since it was built, in 1890.

My bank said no, absolutely not, not that area, had they not said so already? But Len said he could get me fixed up with a mortgage, no trouble at all, and I could take his word for it the place was structurally sound, for in those days they built to last. No, don't bother with a survey; he had already had it surveyed. And so I became a customer of the National Westminster Bank. My father had worked in his youth for the Westminster Bank. So much had things changed that when I told the manager that my father's great nightmare was always that he might be in debt, or rather fall into worse debt than he was in, the man was quite shocked and said that the whole point of banking was to lend money. And so I had a mortgage and a loan to do the place up. This was far from doubtful and dubious finance; on the contrary; but what was dubious was

Len's vagueness about the status of No. 60. There was a possibility, said he, that it could be scheduled for redevelopment, but I had to realise the Greater London Council often had houses scheduled for years. Besides, they would have to compensate me. I have always taken chances, and that is what I did now. I never regretted it, for I could not otherwise have afforded a house in an area where I wanted to live, and I did take that step away from freebooting free-wheeling unloanworthy bohemianism, which is what suited me, to being a property owner and deserving of respect and of overdrafts, even if every penny was borrowed. But I could not begin to live in that house until it had been done up, and Len knew a builder, let us call him Doug, another like himself, free and easy, you can trust me, and he would see the house done up as it deserved.

I took Peter and one of his friends to stand outside the house. 'There's the house. I've bought it.' The two boys were silent, looking at the dark-brown flaking exterior in the shabby street. 'Look,' I pleaded, 'it will be very nice, you'll see.'

That house could have been kept as a museum, a time capsule. The first thing that had to strike the outsider was its extreme dis-comfort. It was on three floors, two rooms to a floor, over a vast basement. There was no proper heating, only tiny fireplaces. In such a house, I kept reminding myself, Mary Wollstonecraft and William Godwin lived, wrote their high-minded thoughts, and they must have been cold all the time. Over every ill-fitting win-dow hung dirty rags of cretonne. The four rooms on the two top floors had been bedrooms and recently let out to lodgers, for in each were coin meters for electricity. On the two landings were gas jets, the flame four inches away from the wallpaper, and they were still in use. The electricity was dangerous; wires trailed, the holders were cracked. There was one ceiling light in each room. One lava-tory for the whole house, a cement bowl in the basement, with a cracked porcelain cistern and a chain pull. The basement was once the kitchen, with the coal-burning kitchen range still functioning, and the old copper for boiling clothes, a great cone-shaped copper basin sunk in cement, with a place for the fire under it. The mangle was there, and the ironing table, and its steam irons. There was a bath—unused—vast, stained brown, and cracked. The great enamel jugs that had once been carried up the rickety stairs with hot water still stood, stained and chipped, on the range. Up those stairs had been carried meals to the little dining room, which overlooked a neglected back garden, with a view on to the roof of Unity Theatre. I never went to Unity Theatre in all the time I lived in that house, because it had fallen into its dogmatic, strictly party-line time.

The first thing to be done was a damp course in the basement. Then a cork floor went in, and soon it became a warm and pleasant low-ceilinged room, the nicest in the house. The front ground-floor room was a kitchen, with the big dining table we all seemed to have in the sixties. The ground floor back, once the dining room, became a bathroom, large, luxurious by then British standards. The first floor was the living room. The dividing doors came out, but later I was to regret getting rid of those folding doors, painted red and gold, and the wood shutters, which were thief-proof, and, later still, the fireplaces. For as we were all doing then, the fireplaces were plastered over and the mantelpieces abolished.

I had to fight radiator by radiator with the central-heating people.

'You don't want a radiator in the bedroom, love. It's unhealthy.' This was how they thought then, and some people still do.

'I want two radiators, because here in your specifications it says to achieve such and such a level of heat there must be two.'

'You'll regret it.'

And in the bathroom: 'You don't need a radiator in the bathroom. The steam will heat it.'

'Yes I do, and a heated towel rail too. Please put them in.'

'Well, you're paying for it, but I don't like to see you waste your money like this.'

And why was I doing this fighting? Why was not a surveyor doing it for me?

I was saving money, for Doug had said there was no need for an architect or a surveyor, trust me.

Doug was a small firm. He employed two workmen on a regular basis and electricians and carpenters as he needed them. He had done the basics: damp course, the cork basement floor, making most of the floors good, some of the rewiring, and the windows. Then he went bankrupt. He came to tell me, looking not at all unhappy about it. 'I have bad luck,' he said. And then off he went to the Mediterranean on a holiday with his girlfriend. He had gone bankrupt several times before. I was enough out of tune with my times to be shocked by this.

There I was with a half-done house, no builder, no one to fight in my corner, but then everything came right. The two workmen employed by Doug—he had left owing them two weeks' wages— said they would finish the house for me, I could employ them myself. Everyone I knew, friends and experts of all kinds, said I would be mad to do it, I'd live to regret it: they would cheat me. In fact, the men were wonderful, and everything was easy. I paid them top-level union wages, once a week, and a good bit over, because they were saving me the profits of a builder, and they brought me bills for the materials they used. They called themselves the Two Pirates, they were Jack and John, and they had worked together since they left school, twenty years before. Jack was a large slow fair man, with calm blue eyes he fixed on your face while he told you about his mum, who looked after him, for he had never married, and who cooked all his favourites, so why did he need a wife? John had been married. He was spry and full of energy and apparently the boss in this partnership, but when they had to make decisions they stood looking at each other and then came to a silent agreement, and John turned to me and said, 'No, you don't want a shelf there, love; look, you wouldn't be able to put your hand to it comfortable; better there.' Or they would show me why a floor needed to be not relaid but only to be patched, and why an electric-light socket should be just there.

When it was time for a carpenter, they brought in a mate, Jimmy, whom I think of to this day with affection. He was a tall, much too thin grey man, and he was sad, for his wife had run off, and his two children had grown, and he was alone. He had a bad cough and that shadowy look that says, This one won't be around for long. The three men had often worked together. They would sit drinking tea around the trestles they had set up in the kitchen to stand on to paint the ceiling. They asked me to sit with them, and we gossiped about this and that. Jack and John both told me, separately, that Jimmy was the salt of the earth, and their manner to him was protective, considerate, tender. Jimmy did all the carpentering up and down the house, often putting me right when I made suggestions he knew were a mistake. And then there was another man, the electrician, Bill Connolly. I knew Bill until he died twenty years later, and at intervals he would recall how the three of them were in the kitchen, and suddenly my two feet appeared through the ceiling, for the floorboards had been taken up and there was only plasterboard. They were good for a laugh, my feet, for years.

And in fact we all had many good laughs, and my knowing friends, dropping in to find out how I did, would discover us all sitting around in the kitchen, and they might want to sit down too, but the men said, 'Time to go back to work,' and went. They knew I had been warned against them.

Jack, the fat pirate, was heartbreaking for reasons he never suspected. He loved to draw and paint, and wanted to put friezes of Bambis and Donald Ducks in every room. He was disappointed when I said no, and told me about the houses he had decorated with flowers and rabbits and robins. He made me presents of cards with cartoon animals. As soon as we sat down, a pencil and paper would appear, and he would start. He was an artist, he said, but when he used the word, he meant only what he knew, for he had never been introduced to real pictures, real art. He had never been to an art gallery. When I said they were free and anyone could go, he looked guilty, but reproachful too. I showed him reproductions, and he was full of admiration, but not as if they could have anything to do with him. Yet even his Mickey Mice and his Bambis had something original about them. If there was ever a case of a village Hampden, he was it.

But I wasn't spending all my time in Charrington Street, for I needed money and had to earn it. I had not written for money before—that is, not from an inner need or pattern but from an outside demand. And yes, it does weaken your real strengths. For your real work, which is an invisible-to-others growth curve—the growing point—is one thing, the real thing, and the rest is hack-work, no matter how skilled it is, how well it turns out. Apart from a couple of sketches written for *The New Yorker,* I had not written for money. . . . No, the truth compels me to state: twice an impecunious friend and I had attempted frankly commercial film scripts, but you cannot write successfully for money with your tongue in your cheek, and these dishonest ventures had come to nothing. Serves me right, I had thought. Now I was secretly seeing myself as a fallen soul, yet there was nothing wrong with what I wrote for television. On the contrary. Quite soon I was to be one of three writers doing the Granada series of Maupassant stories, with Hugh Leonard, the Irish writer, and the Granada executive Dennis Mackay. We sat around a big table and dealt the stories around like playing cards. 'I want "Boule de Suif"!'

'No, I'm having "Boule de Suif."'

'Then I'm having "The Diamond Necklace."'

'I want "La Maison Tellier."' We all knew enough French but used English translations as well.

It was a wonderful series. Granada Television at that time was taking the kind of risks no television company would take now. They did series of Saki stories, A. E. Coppard, Somerset Maugham, Maupassant, and others, each of thirteen hours, with three one-hour plays and the rest of two or three tales each. Top-level directors, actors, writers, designers. So little did television value itself that it wiped them all. And yet these series were among the very best things ever done by television. ITV could be brave in those days too. Stella Richman did wonderful things for them, using all the best talent available. *Half-Hour Story* and *Blackmail* are still remembered. Again, ITV destroyed them all.

Sometimes you want to put your head in your hands and weep, or howl with incredulity, because of this our great country, Britain. If television films of this quality had been made in any other country in Europe, they would be cherished, honoured, preserved, seen as national treasures. There would be festivals for them, as we now have festivals for classic black-and-white films. At the least, there would be archives of the work of the best directors, actors, designers, and writers of the time. But no, this is Britain—so into the wastebin with them all.

I reckon that to live in London costs a good third of one's resources—that is, the actual money. Then there is the time spent looking for a place to live, and once you have one, then the continual repairs, plumbing, roof, windows, and so on—the real cost of owning a house. Is it worth it? A thousand times, yes. London is a cornucopia of delights.

Time was running out, I had to leave Langham Street, and still the house was not decorated. While the pirates worked on serious things, like floors and walls, a group of us, friends and Peter and I, stood on chairs and trestles and ripped layers of wallpaper off, seven, eight, nine, ten, and even more, and the layers at the bottom were Victorian, beautiful, on heavy thick paper. If you held a wad of the paper, then in your hands was seventy years of social history, of information, but into the bonfire at the back went all the coils and shreds and tatters of wallpaper, and the cracked and decaying linoleum that once had been shiny and good, and the worm-eaten wood from the floors, and old shelves and the rags of curtains. But the substance of the walls was solid, and when you looked under the plaster the lathes were new and clean, and the bricks bright and new. That was a solid serious house, built to last.

Not a quarter of a mile away, streets of these houses were being pulled down. It was the beginning of the sixties and the heyday of official vandalism. When I said to the Pirates it was a tragedy that these good houses were disappearing in clouds of dust and debris, they thought and said yes, when you think of it, they are just like the houses in Chelsea; we were working down there on our last job, weren't we, Jack? weren't we, John? Yes, we were, that's right, John, that's right, Jack. You can't buy those Chelsea houses now, not unless you've got more money than you or I are going to see in our lives, isn't that right, Jack? isn't that right, John? That's right, John, you're in the right of it there, Jack.

I used to walk up and watch those houses come down, and my heart ached. I saw crash into dust the house the Sommerfields had made into a little paradise. Where it stood now stand coldly hideous grey council flats, hundreds of yards of them.

I was in the newly fitted kitchen when an official from Camden came in, a left-wing councillor, and said, contemptuously waving her hand at the little knot of streets we stood in, 'The sooner we clear all these people out into the new council flats the better.' And I said, 'But this is an old working-class community. They've been living here together for decades.'

'We'll clear them all out,' she said. 'We'll get all this cleaned up.'

What the people in the area wanted, if any official had cared what they thought, was for their houses to be done up, bathrooms and proper lavatories put in, and the dangerous wiring replaced. They were saying, 'But we've all been living here for years. My mother was born here. My kids were born here.' This was a plea to me, for I was middle class and therefore by definition knew the score and the ropes and probably had influence. But the tide of history was against them. Up and down this happy land, people whose hearts beat day and night with love and concern for the working classes were saying, 'We'll clear them all out, we'll clean it all up,' and that is what they did, and presumably they noted with concern how their charges, finding themselves in some cold grey tower, far from their old neighbours, kept dying and having strokes and heart attacks. 'They just want to get rid of us all, dear, that's all it is,' said Mrs. Pearce, from No. 58. 'It saves them trouble. What they like is to see another funeral.'

The day I decided to buy No. 60, I knocked on the door of No. 58. During my visits to the street and the house, I was being observed from windows up and down Charrington Street. At No. 58, a large pale woman with pale ridged hair rested her arms and bosom on the window sill and commanded the street with her presence. By now a thousand surveys have instructed us in the role of working-class matriarchs, dominating their families and the community, and here she was, Mrs. Pearce, who would be my neighbour. It was not easy to knock at that door, because I believed such a close community would not welcome newcomers and particularly not one like me. The word 'gentrification' had yet to come into common use. I announced myself, said I was to be her new neighbour, and I hoped to be a good one. This was in the spirit of the times, the matey sixties, but policy too. And I meant it. Mrs.

Pearce sat in the window, her back to it for once, and said, 'Sit down, dear. We're pleased you're going to do right by that house. It's been going to rack and ruin for years. Isn't that so?' A tiny man, a chip of a man, but as muscular, lean, and bow-legged as a jockey, agreed: 'Rack and ruin,' and grinned welcome to me, and an immensely ancient crone, all in black, without teeth and smelling bad, bobbed about, screeching, 'Rack and ruin, rack and ruin.' There was a dog, a cheerful mongrel, keeping out of the way of all the feet, the cleanest, prettiest thing in the room.

'Tea,' commanded Lil Pearce, and the little man at once put the kettle on.

'He's my husband,' said Lil Pearce, 'though he wasn't always. And this is my friend Mrs. Rockingham.' I think that was the name. 'I took her in off the street, I took her out of the gutter. She was in the gutter, wasn't you?' she screeched at the crone. 'She's deaf. She's deaf and almost blind. But I'm good to her.' She leaned forward, hands on her thighs, and screamed, 'I'm good to you, aren't I?'

'Yes, yes,' the crone yelled back, 'you're very good to me.' She was arranging fancy biscuits on a plate and flicking biscuit crumbs at the dog, who snapped at them like flies.

'Don't you mind her,' said Lil. 'She's a bit touched. You are a bit wrong in the head,' she yelled at the old woman, who yelled back, 'That's right, dear.'

'And now you ask me everything you need to know, and I'll tell you,' she said. And she did. She had lived next door to No. 60 since the end of the war. The old woman from whom I had bought No. 60 had been her good friend. Lil knew every detail of every happening in that house—who had been born, who had died, who had scarpered without paying rent, all the dogs and cats that had lived there.

Mrs. Pearce had her house off the GLC, but was in complicated relation to the Camden Council too, and she rented out the two top rooms. The condition of No. 58 was the same as No. 60 when I first got it—gas light, dangerous wiring, no bathroom, a single nasty lavatory, and of course no heating. A fire burned permanently in the ground floor front, where the three of them in fact lived.

Lil Pearce would have talked till the following morning, if I had had the time, and certainly I had seldom been as fascinated as by this Dickensian chronicle. When I left she said she was glad there was going to be a bit of life next door, and instructed the crone, 'Tell her we're pleased she's come,' and obediently the old woman shouted, 'That's right, dear, you make yourself right at 'ome.'

As for Len Pearce, he is one of the people I think of when I need to cheer myself up about the state of the world and the people in it. He is right at the top of my private list of candidates for heaven. He was a good, kind, generous, sweet man, and he was treated like a dog by his wife: Do this, get that, fetch me the other thing. He never complained. He had worked as a market porter most of his life, but now he was too old, and he did little jobs for the local council. He was illiterate. He was so small and thin and bow-legged because he was the product of the dreadful poverty England provided for its working people between the two world wars. Many a day, he would tell me, he and his brothers and sisters had nothing to eat but a piece of bread and margarine with sugar on it, and he went to school without shoes on his feet. Married to Lil, he had found security and enough to eat and space at last, but now he had to share this space with Mrs. Rockingham, who was incontinent, foul-mouthed, and generally disgusting, yet he waited on her, too, when Lil commanded. If I was observed trying to lift something she thought too heavy for me, let's say in the garden, Lil Pearce, who always knew what I was doing, would shout at Len Pearce, and he would be beside me, grinning. 'Let me do that,' and he did it, as if I were doing him a favour. He shone, that little man, he shone like a lamp in a dark place. Like the carpenter Jimmy. I often think of them both, grateful that I knew them.

Only once, years later, when old age had made of Lil a real raging tyrant, did he ever refer to his situation. He said sadly to me, 'If you'd known Lil when she was young, then you'd not think bad of her now. I always think of her the way she was then. She was lovely. She was a lovely young woman. I saw her the first time when she was cleaning the floors in Woolworth's, to keep her kids fed, and she had no stockings on her legs and they were red and sore. She let me buy her some stockings, and then a pair of shoes for her feet. That was my happiest day. She had all those kids then, and she let me help her.'

Lil Pearce expected to be kept informed. If I had left too long, let's say three days, before dropping in, she summoned me from her window sill with a peremptory forefinger. 'What are you paying for that cooker? . . . It's too much. I know where you can get one ten pounds cheaper.' She had the pirates in, together and separately, and instructed them in how to treat me well. She had to be told how much I was paying them and informed them I was doing well by them. She told me they were doing right by me and I could trust them. She sent cups of tea to the pirates and to Jimmy when he was there, with a bottle of cough mixture for him, or some cake to take home with him, since he didn't look after himself. 'He's not long for this world,' she shouted at the crone, 'just like you.'

'That's right, dear,' the crone shrieked back.

I knew Lil Pearce until she died, twenty-odd years later. I never, ever, not once, went into that house, or, later, into the council flat they took her to, without being greeted by histories of calamity. It began on my second visit. 'It's my breast,' she announced. 'I've this abscess. It's the size of an orange. They're going to cut it out.' And she pulled out from her dress, under the cretonne apron, a long white fat bag of a breast. 'Look at that, see that lump there?' As well, the meter would have been broken into and three months' electricity money stolen, the cat had worms, the dog had a torn ear, she herself had fallen through the floorboards in the second floor back, because they were rotten and the council wouldn't mend them, and then she had reached for a pan over the stove and the heavy saucepan had fallen on her hand—see that bruise? There was no way you could visit Lil Pearce without hearing a tale of disaster, to her, or Mrs. Rockingham, or one of her children, who were always ill or a worry to her. I used to tell my friends, at first nervously—for it was hard to adjust to this level of ill luck—and hearing her name, they would enquire, 'Well, what this time?' It was not possible that a single human being could support such accumulations of misfortune, but Lil Pearce could, and did, year after year. It had all started because she was illegitimate, she was a love child, and that was why her mum had hated her and would not feed her right, but her gran loved her, and so she had not died of being treated bad. 'That's why I'm good to Mrs. Rockingham, see? It's because I want to make it up to my Gran.'

I used to sit there through my visits, keeping a good grip on myself, because I could feel the laughter welling up until it threatened my face. She had fallen out of bed and sprained her wrist. Her thighs were black and blue because her veins bruised easy. The dog had knocked a tray of boiling tea onto her lap and she had blistered you-know-where. Her knees had bad bones, and the doctor said they were past hoping for; she had lost her purse, with all her rent money in it; she had been mugged at the grocer's, but luckily she had had only a quid; she had just heard that her son had to have a terrible operation. Believe me, I learned from Lil Pearce how tight the roots of comedy and tragedy are intertwined, for I would watch the helpless hysterical laughter rising in me as each lugubrious bit of news emerged from that dramatic fate-wracked face, until I had to excuse myself and run next door, where I put my head down on my arms on the kitchen table and laughed and laughed. She never invented, made it up; it was all true. There are people who step onto some escalator marked Disaster and cannot get off again, or perhaps plug into an unlucky wavelength, and so it was with her.

'And there I was with the three kids, it was the Blitz, the bomb got the street corner near where we were, and the kids had the blast all over them, and I got my eyes full of plaster, but the hospital said they had much worse to cope with that night and gave me some aspirin. But the bomb shelter was full of water and so we had to get under the bed, me and the kids, while the bombs fell on us, and then the roof fell on the bed and . . .' But we are in the exponential swell of catastrophe that is the distinguishing mark of such favourite victims of ill fate, and the tale has to go on: '. . . and a bedspring cut my face and the blood got onto us and we didn't have no more clothes to put on, only the bloody ones, and in the morning the air raid warden saw us and said, Quick, Lil, into hospital, but I said, Too late, Ron, it's too late for hospital, and the hospital didn't have time for us when we needed it last night, aspirin, that's what they gave me, and now what we could all do with is a good cup of hot tea, but the gas main's cut and I've got nothing to give my kids and I can't get to my stove because there's a cupboard fallen down over it, and my wrist's bent backwards with the blast and I couldn't push the cupboard back for myself. And Ron said to me, he said, Lil, you're a real heroine, I always said so, but now you've got to get out from under that house, because it's going to fall around your ears. And I said, Then where are we to go? And he said, I'd say the church, you'll get some soup and sandwiches, but the church took the best of the blast, so you'd better get yourself onto that bus and down to the main Shelter, but I said to him, I haven't got a penny in the world, Ron, because my purse was blown out of my hand by the bomb. . . .'

I used to start on one of these sagas and watch my friends' faces for that moment when a look of anguished guilt showed that they were wondering just how it was they had turned into such monsters of callousness they could laugh at this tale.

No amount of trouble could stop Lil from keeping a helpful eye on her neighbours. She would send John, or Jack, to tell me that she had heard I planned yellow wallpaper for the second floor back, and I should know the sun fell into that room for hours on a sunny day, and I'd better be sure the wallpaper would stand it; or she would shout at me as I went by in the street that she saw the plumbers were digging out that new drain just where the dogs were buried, six dogs were buried in that place, and I'd better take care the bones didn't find their way into the dustbins, or the police would be asking questions. And she would haul herself along the street and up my steps, on her two sticks, because of her bad legs, to knock on the door, because she had heard from the man who had the vegetable shop on the corner that he was making a special trip to Covent Garden next day and he would get those fancy fruits for me I had asked him for. 'Was it garlickt? Just run along, darling, and tell him what you want; he'll do it for me.'

With the date set for the move only a few days ahead, I got German measles. For some reason, German measles makes people laugh. Is it the word 'German' in this context? What long-forgotten travelling epidemic does this word commemorate? Suppose we said Peruvian measles? There's a smile lurking there too. (Italian measles? Russian measles?) Measles is all right, commiseration is in order, but German measles is funny. This was the second time I had it, both times badly, with a sullen rash all over, a high temperature, a headache. I got into bed in a darkened room and waited, having rung the pirates to tell them to just get on with it. I was deep under that queasy dark ocean which is illness when the doorbell rang. Cursing, I staggered to the door, and there stood a young woman with a sullen face, angry eyes, and a baby in a pushchair, which she had had to hoist up all those flights of stairs. I said I had German measles and was certainly a danger: she was pregnant. She disregarded this. The obligatory laugh was transmuted by her rage into a sneer. She said, 'I've come for money. You're rich and successful, and I need it.' I said, truthfully, that I was very short of money at the moment. She said, 'Don't give me that.' I have seldom disliked anyone more. 'I've got to have it for my children.' She wanted five hundred pounds. Or I think that was it. The trouble is, the value of money has shifted. I know it was so much that I had to increase my overdraft. Only a few weeks later I paid ten pounds for a picture to give a friend and was in a panic because I couldn't really afford it. Perhaps it was fifty pounds, or a hundred. Later I wrote to this young woman's extremely rich and famous uncle and asked if he mightn't consider refunding the money, but he said he didn't see why he should.

All this is not as simple as it may seem.

In the dark, with watering eyes, and very sick, I considered certain facts. I was what is known as an easy touch. There were good reasons for this. First, my parents, who even at their poorest gave ten percent, as enjoined by the Bible, to charity. I remember exchanges about this ten percent.

My father, testily, laughing: 'But we don't have any income. When the money for the crops comes, it goes straight to Land Bank to reduce our debt.'

My mother: 'Well, I suppose we could say we never do have any income, but that means we'd never give anything.'

Should my father's war pension be included when they reckoned that ten percent? What about the money she made selling chickens and eggs to the store at Banket?

They gave money every year to the League for Distressed Gentlewomen, a charity for indigent seamen, and another for the dependents of World War I soldiers. I was told I should give ten percent of my pocket money, of the money I earned for the guinea fowl I took to the store, and of the money I earned writing advertisements. I felt permanently guilty because I didn't do this: but had I not decided against the existence of God?

Ever since I had left respectable middle-class ways, when I left Frank Wisdom, and thrown in my lot with the comrades, I had been with generous people: in my experience, the communists were always that. And, too, my early days in London coincided with a general contempt for money, probably because none of us had any. Since I had earned any money at all I was being asked for 'loans'. A lot were for young men. Poor young men are often helped by older women, as is right and proper, for it is a psychological need of both parties, and this doesn't have to have much, or anything, to do with sex. I could by now make a good list of 'debtors' if I wanted to. I did not regret any of this but was furious with myself for giving that unpleasant young woman anything at all. But I had had to give it to her, and that is why now I was lying in the dark, sick and hot and cross, contemplating my character. Now, it is easy to write insightful thoughts about one's youthful character decades later, but I was even then glimpsing something basic about myself. Several times in my life I've done this: had a glimmering of understanding about myself long before I properly understood. I determined then and there that if I had this weakness in my nature, then at least it would be under control. I would, when settled in the house, actually choose someone for whom I would be responsible: it would be my choice, my decision, taking control:—acting instead of reacting. The house was going to be too big—so I thought then. Peter, in mid-teens, was already behaving as the young did all through the sixties: he was sometimes an honorary child in other families, just as his friends were with me rather than with their own parents. Soon that house would be full of adolescents.

That incident of the unlikeable young woman presaged more than I could know. For one thing, her manner, a generalised snarl of contempt. She embodied a rancorous envy, and this was already beginning to interest me—it interests me even more now. She clearly felt she had been promised something she hadn't been given. Whole generations of young people have had this as a primal drive. '*They* have cheated me out of my due.' This one, with her load of unfathered children, was a victim, only that; her situation had nothing to do with any fault of hers, and she was entitled to loathe the world. Her very existence was an indictment, and yes, I had just begun to understand how much of what I said and, particularly, thought was that: The Indictment. *J'accuse.* I accuse the world.

And there was the way she spat out, 'You are rich and successful.' Choosing me because my name had been in the newspapers. There it was, our national vice, envy, the tall poppy syndrome.

I moved. It was no big deal. As in my youth—that is, when I lived with Frank Wisdom and then Gottfried Lessing, and we moved all the time, thinking nothing of it—I took books, a couple of beds, a table, bedding, the curtains, kitchen things. I left all the ugly furniture behind.

So. That was the fifties, as I experienced the decade, which slopped over at both ends—1949 to 1962—as decades tend to do. I moved into the new house in the autumn of 1962. Just ahead was the famous winter of '62–'63, when there was a nationwide freeze for seven weeks. There was one bad fog too; not as bad as the terrible dark fogs of the bad old days, which had been outwitted by the Clean Air Act, but my dazzling white walls lost their innocence. This was not because the new window frames had been badly made but because I cannot endure shut windows. All the pipes froze, up and down the street, and in all the other streets in Somers Town, but not mine, so I was supplying water to No. 58 when the standpipe the Water Board put at the corner of the street froze too. I wrote about this freeze in my little book *Particularly Cats*.

I gave a great noisy housewarming party and asked all the people who had worked on the house. At its height, the man from three doors down came into the street and shouted abuse at me. Thinking, Well, I'm living in a working-class street, do as the

Romans do, I went out onto the steps, put my hands on my hips, and shouted at him to shut up, stop being a spoil-sport, why didn't he come and join the fun?

Peter and his friend, witnesses of this unladylike behaviour, were upset.

'Quite right, dear,' says Lil Pearce, out of her window. 'You don't want to take any nonsense from that nasty old thing. And you don't want him in your house either.'

A few months later I got a Notice of Compulsory Purchase from the council. That is, you have to sell your house to whichever authority demands it. I managed to spin it all out until almost the end of the sixties, but there came a day when I was standing with a representative of the council in an empty room, to deliver the keys. My mother's daughter could not have handed over the house in a less than sparkling condition, and it had been scrubbed from top to bottom. The man, full of official bonhomie, congratulated me on the clean house.

No sooner had we left than the council workmen fixing the house in the next street came in and stripped my house of all the radiators, the pipes, the boilers. Lil Pearce rang me and then the council. The council then set a watchman on the front of the house, from six every evening until six in the morning, but left the back of the house open, so that the workmen continued to drop in to help themselves to anything they might have overlooked. This went on for weeks. When Lil Pearce told the council that the unguarded back of the house was admitting thieves, who were their own workmen, the reply was that they would look into the matter.

The house was left empty for eight years, while the council debated what to do with the area, continually changing their minds. I could have taken them to court, but what sensible person can be bothered with that sort of thing? I have lived under Camden Council now for thirty-odd years, watching dazzling levels of incompetence and corruption. I was writing down what I observed—an Indictment—beginning with the treatment of the people in Somers Town being 'rehoused' against their will. Then I had to ask myself, What is this obsession? And I understood that this was a famous socialist borough, and they were loudly proud of themselves, just like the communist countries, boastful and swaggering; but as with the drunken braggart dressed up in smart clothes, you saw he had forgotten to button himself up, and there was the truth of the matter, a hairy red warty smelly arse. Why was I expecting any better? Because of the word 'socialist', of course. Would I be keeping this bitter record if it were a Tory council? Certainly not; that would be: *'But what can you expect?'* So—*basta.* Enough. Stop it. People my age are always finding themselves in this situation: A young person is looking at you, trying not to show incredulity. The tactful, embarrassed query: 'But, Doris, tell me— you say you expect a socialist borough to be better than a Tory one? I don't think I understand.' What he or she understands is that here is just another old bat with bees in her bonnet. And you are understanding that yet again, decades—a couple of centuries?—of idealism, of optimism, have disappeared as if they had never been.

We were all still on the escalator Progress, the whole world ascending towards prosperity. Did anyone challenge this happy optimism? I don't remember it. At the end of a century of grand revolutionary romanticism; frightful sacrifices for the sake of paradises and heavens on earth and the withering away of the state; passionate dreams of utopias and wonderlands and perfect cities; attempts at communes and commonwealths, at co-operatives and kibbutzes and kolkhozes—after all this, would any of us have believed that most people in the world would settle gratefully for a little honesty, a little competence in government?

For about six years in the sixties I proved my rapport with the times by becoming a housemother—now, that is a sixties' word— for adolescents or young adults who either lived at 60 Charrington Street or came and went. All of them were in some kind of trouble: were 'disturbed', were being seduced by drugs, were alcoholic, were having serious breakdowns, were known to the police. This was, for that particular time, my growing point, what I was doing, though I was writing hard too, notably *The Four-Gated City.*

The sixties are seen glamorously; seen, sometimes wrongly, I think, as the starting point for all kinds of behaviour that in fact began in the fifties—or before. But there is one thing that did start in the sixties: drugs. Drugs arrived from the East, available to everyone, and this had never before happened in our culture. I believe that the long view, the perspectives given by enough time, will reveal that this was the important fact about the sixties. 'They are quite harmless really,' people are still saying. A friend from Central Asia was saying then, 'You people in the West have never seen these drugs. It's all new to you. You are like a child trying to pet a snake: Look at the pretty snake. If you had lived in a culture where drugs have been endemic for centuries, you'd know that it is only the failures, the losers, the hopelessly poor, who use drugs.'

My view of the sixties is jaundiced by what I was living through. And we are living in its aftermath. So many people landed in mental hospitals and prisons, and there are sudden silences in talk when someone who committed suicide is being remembered, and every week comes news of a far too early death.

But that is the dark view, from the shaded side of the street, for only this week I heard a man now middle-aged say, 'That was the time when everything was possible, we were going to move mountains, we were going to change the world. And what people forget is that there was this great upwelling of vitality from the working class and the lower middle class—it was the grammar schools that did it. Everywhere you looked, there were grammar school boys, like me, often in the arts. It was the first time this has happened in this country.'

But usually, when I hear someone talking nostalgically about the sixties—'If you remember it, you weren't there'—what comes into my mind is a line from a poem I wrote when I was very young, not more than a girl: 'When I look back I seem to remember singing.' Well, yes, that seems to be about it.

About the Author

Doris Lessing was born of British parents in Persia in 1919 and moved with her family to Southern Rhodesia when she was five years old. She went to England in 1949 and has lived there ever since. She is the author of more than thirty books—novels, stories, reportage, poems, and plays. Her most recent works include *Love, Again* and *Under My Skin,* the first volume of her autobiography. Doris Lessing lives in London.